For all Darwinians,
especially *Susan*

Darwinism Defended
A Guide to the Evolution Controversies

LEGENDS

Frontispiece — Charles Robert Darwin. (Reproduced by permission of the Royal College of Surgeons.)

Darwinism Defended

A Guide to the Evolution Controversies

Michael Ruse
University of Guelph
Guelph, Ontario, Canada

Foreword by
Ernst Mayr
Harvard University
Cambridge, Massachusetts

1982

ADDISON-WESLEY PUBLISHING COMPANY
Advanced Book Program/World Science Division
Reading, Massachusetts

London • Amsterdam • Don Mills, Ontario • Sydney • Tokyo

FRONT COVER: A pair of "Darwin's finches" illustrated in the official zoology of the *Beagle* voyage. Variation among the Galapagos finches provided Darwin with one of his arguments for the theory of evolution. The species of finch pictured here has evolved a blunt beak suitable for eating large seeds; other species evolved differently shaped beaks for eating insects or small seeds.

BACK COVER: This fruit-eating bird, *Tanagra darwini,* was named in honor of Darwin by the zoologist who classified Darwin's South American bird specimens.

Plates for both the front cover and the back cover were taken from:

Gould, John. *Zoology of the Voyage of the HMS Beagle.* Vol. 3: *Birds,* 1841: Courtesy of the Trustees of the Boston Public Library.

Library of Congress Cataloging in Publication Data

Ruse, Michael.
  Darwinism defended.

  Bibliography: p.
  1. Evolution.   2. Evolution and religion.   I. Title.
QH371.R76   575.01'62   81-19131
ISBN 0-201-06273-9   AACR2

- 4 OCT 1983

Printed in the United States of America

ABCDEFGHIJ-HA-898765432

Contents

313 - Dinosaurs
Diagram

Foreword

To a convinced Darwinian like myself it may seem puzzling that in this day and age Darwinism should still be in need of defense. Yet, that this is the case is obvious to any reader of the current literature. The attacks come not only from fundamentalists, but surprisingly also from humanists, philosophers, and even from certain biologists who accept evolution but reject the Darwinian explanation. We must be grateful to Michael Ruse for having undertaken to scrutinize the validity of the anti-Darwinian arguments.

Having just published a splendid study of the Darwinian Revolution, in fact the best Darwin book of the contemporary literature, and having occupied himself for years with Darwin's conceptual world, Ruse is qualified for his task like few others. And it is a formidable task since most opposition to Darwin is based on committed ideologies and on some rather basic misconceptions. It requires a superior understanding not only of the facts of biology but also of the conceptual framework of Darwinism and its opponents to be able to forge an effective defense.

What is usually overlooked is that the Darwinian Revolution was not simply an overturning of certain biological theories, but rather an intellectual revolution of the first order, indeed the greatest ever. That the concept of a constant world of short duration was replaced by one of an evolving world of thousands of million years duration is only one of the major revisions of almost universally accepted thought. Philosophy in Darwin's day, and virtually to the present, was dominated by essentialism, that is a belief in a world of discontinuities, and of constant, underlying essences, sharply separated from all others. Darwin, by contrast, introduced population thinking, a conceptualization in which the uniqueness of every individual plays a major role. Populations grade into each other in the time dimension and in the geographical dimensions. Hence gradualism is a dominant component in Darwin's evolutionism.

The real core of Darwinism, however, is the theory of natural selection. This theory is so important for the Darwinian because it permits the explanation of adaptation, the "design" of the natural theologian, by natural means, instead of by divine intervention. Furthermore, natural selection permits an escape from the dilemma of the alternative "chance or necessity" that had bedeviled philosophers from the Greeks on. Natural selection is a two step process: The production of gametes and zygotes is preceded by a whole series of chance events, but survival and successful reproduction are largely determined by anti-chance properties of genotypes. By accepting natural selection one no longer must make the unpalatable choice between chance **or** necessity. They are both represented in the process of natural selection.

The belief in a design of the world and all of its creatures by a wise and omnipotent creator necessitated also a belief in a perfect world, or at least, as Leibniz phrased it, "the best of all *possible* worlds". When Darwin shifted from design to selection, he credited natural selection with the same capacity to produce perfection as a designing creator. The modern evolutionary biologist is more modest in his claims on behalf of selection. He knows of many structures and other adaptations that are less than perfect and ascribes this to the chance component during the variation-producing first step. The selecting forces during the second step of natural selection can make use only of such variation as was made available during the first step. Perfection can not be attained if the right variants are not available.

Like all revolutionaries, Darwin did not succeed in bringing all components of his complex theory to their current state of maturity. Variation, its nature and causation, puzzled him all his life, and he even accepted a certain amount of inheritance of acquired characters. Also, even though he vigorously promoted geographic speciation, he thought that on continents various other kinds of speciation were operating about which we are now rather dubious.

Yet, it is altogether inadmissible to speak of a refutation of Darwinism when some minor component of the theory is modified or some neglected portions are now being filled in. This point is rightly and vigorously made by the author of this volume; which provides a lively and well-informed guide through the history of Darwinism, its present state, and the challenges it will have to meet in the future. Most importantly it shows what the problems are that Darwinism has raised for the understanding of Man and for the questions posed by a philosophy of Man. Finally, Ruse deals with the relation between Darwinism, ethics, and religion. The question whether there is any validity to a science of creationism is answered with a resounding No.

There has perhaps been no other period since the immediate post-Darwinian decades when there has been such a widespread and lively interest in evolutionary questions as today. Michael Ruse's *Darwinism Defended* provides a secure guide through the currently so active evolution controversies.

ERNST MAYR

Preface

Charles Robert Darwin, the fifth child and second son of Dr. Robert Darwin of Shrewsbury in England, was born on February 12, 1809. Although plagued by ill-health for nearly all of his adult life, Charles Darwin lived to the age of seventy-three, finally dying on the afternoon of Wednesday, April 19, 1882. His family had hoped to bury him in the parish churchyard of the village of Downe in Kent, where he and his wife Emma had set up house some forty years before. But it was not to be. Responding to a petition by twenty Members of Parliament, arrangements were made that he should be buried in Westminster Abbey. And so a week later, on April 26, Darwin was taken to his final resting place. Carried by past, present, and future presidents of the Royal Society, two dukes, an earl, the American Minister, and others, he was interred just a few feet from that other great English scientist, Isaac Newton.

For all of his crippling physical problems, Darwin left behind a formidable body of scientific achievements in geology, invertebrate taxonomy, botany, and in other areas, not to mention one of the most attractive and deservedly popular travel books of the Victorian era. But the work beyond all others for which he was famous, then and now, was that published in 1859: *On the Origin of Species by Means of Natural Selection, or the Preservation of Favoured Races in the Struggle for Life.* In this single volume Darwin argued, with more authority and success than anyone before, that the fauna and flora of the Earth had not appeared full-blown, the instantaneous miraculous creation of an all-powerful God, but were rather the end result of a slow, natural, "evolutionary" process. Moreover, he proposed a major mechanism for this process: "natural selection," or, to use a phrase which became popular later, the "survival of the fittest."

As every schoolchild knows, the publication of the *Origin* caused one of the greatest controversies of the nineteenth century. Darwin's ideas were condemned and ridiculed from the pulpit, from the podium, in parliament, and in print. Just as vigorously Darwin's supporters fought back, arguing that his ideas were one of the brightest beams that ever shone into the gloomy shades of religion and superstition. And yet one senses that by the time of Darwin's death, little more than two decades after the *Origin* first appeared, already much of the fire had gone from the dispute. Opponents, even religious opponents, were starting to realize that it was possible to live in a world fashioned by evolution. The forces of atheism and immorality do not rush in, destroying all before them. Supporters, feeling more confident of their position, were turning from polemics to the arduous task of building on the foundations that Darwin had laid. Symptomatic of the mood of conciliation is the fact that, not only was Darwin buried in a House of God, but one of his pallbearers was a clergyman, Canon Frederic Farrar.

A century later, on the anniversary of Darwin's death, one might think that all would be past history. However, the spirit of Darwin still cannot rest. As we enter the penultimate decade of the twentieth century, we find that there is more controversy about Darwin and his achievements than at any point since the decade immediately following the *Origin*. Historians, amateur and professional, differ drastically and sometimes bitterly about Darwin, the man. In the eyes of some he could do no wrong, intellectually or morally. Hence they produce portraits of a bearded patriarch seen dimly through a thick goo of unctuous sentimentality. In the eyes of others, Darwin was a bucolic bungler, who stumbled on something that far outreached his grasp. Puzzled as to why such an incompetent should have produced as much as he did, critics are not beyond accusing Darwin of plagiarism, suggesting that main credit for the *Origin* should go elsewhere. Either way, by sycophants and detractors, the memory of Darwin is ill-served.

An even more dismal tale can be told of Darwin's scientific claims, both in their original form and in the way that they have come down to us through the years, modified and clarified by the discoveries of a century. "Darwinism," as I shall refer to Darwin-inspired evolutionary thought, is threatened from almost every quarter. On the one hand, in North America particularly, we have an articulate and ever more powerful movement calling for a return to a literal, Biblically inspired perspective on organic origins. Not only do the "Scientific Creationists" argue that the truth is to be found in the early chapters of Genesis, but they insist that this "truth" be given at least equal billing with evolutionary teachings in school biology classes. And those in charge of education, ever a craven group, have started to yield in the face of such demands. That the incumbent President of the United States of America — Ronald Reagan — supports the Creationist call for equal time does not suggest that the course of Darwinism is shortly to be made any easier.

On the other hand, even among committed evolutionists we find that Darwinism per se is under attack. A growing number of biologists, particularly although not exclusively biologists drawn from the paleontological end of the spectrum and biologists with Marxist sympathies, argues that any evolutionary theory based on Darwinian principles — particularly any theory that sees natural selection as *the* key to evolutionary change — is misleadingly incomplete. Hence, it is claimed that a total rethinking of the causes of organic origins and change must be undertaken. Paralleling this claim we find a number of other thinkers, many of whom are professional philosophers, agreeing as to the inadequacy of Darwinism. These fellow travelers find serious internal conceptual flaws with anything stemming from Darwin's work, and they conclude that it is little wonder that Darwinism has never really measured up to the standards of the best kind of science, namely physics. We are told that evolution (whatever that might mean) is just a theory (whatever that might mean) not a fact (whatever that might mean).

This essay is the case for the defense. I can think of no better way of celebrating Darwin's life and achievements than by trying to rescue them from the morass into which so many seem determined to drag them. This is not a biography of Darwin; but I hope to show, albeit briefly, why he should still command the respect of disinterested observers. More importantly — and I feel sure that this is the emphasis that Darwin himself would have wanted — I hope to show why Darwin's ideas have lasting importance to us today, as scientists, as humanists, as people.

What I am not trying to do is to pretend that everything that Darwin said was right. It was not. Nor am I trying to pretend that every fruitful move made in evolutionary studies since Darwin was really "contained" in his thought. It was not. And I am certainly not going to pretend that today we have the absolute truth. Most certainly we do not. Rather, I am going to try to show that Darwin produced good, respectable, tough science; that this was a basis on which others could build fruitfully; and that the version of Darwinism that has come down to us today is a scientific theory or discipline that can stand proudly next to the other great theories of science, or to the other great human achievements in the arts or philosophy for that matter.

In Part 1, "Darwinism Yesterday," I look briefly at Charles Darwin, the man, trying to see him in the context of his time as a thoroughly professional scientist. Also, I look at the arguments of the *Origin of Species,* showing the reactions of Darwin's contemporaries and trying to assess their lasting value. Part 2, "Darwinism Today," continues the story by looking at the coming of genetics and its synthesis with Darwinian principles. The mechanism of natural selection is considered, and I argue that not only is it not flawed in principle but that there is strong scientific evidence underlining its powerful, empirical nature.

Part 3, "Darwinism Tomorrow?" takes up four topics, distinguished both in having a particular historical interest and in being areas in which much activity is presently centered. I survey recent advances and consider prospects for future exciting moves in these areas, which in turn concern the origins of life and the early evolution of organisms; the coming into the evolutionary synthesis of the hitherto independent population ecology; the nature and evolution of animal social behavior, the study of which today goes under the name of "sociobiology"; and recent developments in and challenges to Darwinism from paleontology, particularly those centering on the hypothesis of "punctuated equilibria."

Part 4, "Darwinism and Humankind," considers a topic that has plagued and inspired evolutionists from before Darwin, namely the status of our own species, *Homo sapiens.* Did we evolve just like any other animal, or are we in some sense special? I look at Darwin's own work and thoughts on this topic; I survey recent discoveries and theories about human evolution; and I examine recent highly controversial speculations about the possible evolutionary basis of much social behavior among humans today. Does Darwinism tell us anything about our sex, our aggression, our social status, and the like?

Then, I cast my net somewhat more widely, going beyond the narrower confines of science. From the beginning, there have been attempts to use Darwinism as a guide to proper behavior — in respects, deliberate efforts to make Darwinism a substitute for religion. I assess these attempts, having very critical things to say about some of them, but also pointing towards proper extensions and applications of Darwinism.

Finally, in Part 5, I look at the great threats posed to all evolutionary studies by the rise and success of "Scientific Creationism." The tenets of this doctrine are considered in close detail, and an extended refutation is given of every one of the Creationists' claims. Additionally, I raise the question of whether Creationism should be taught in the schools, and I conclude that it should not. Free speech is one thing; teaching lunatic ideas to children is quite another.

Lest there be any confusion, let me make two final points about this book. First, realize one thing that I am *not* trying to do, namely to write a textbook on contemporary evolutionary thought. To make general points and to show historical continuities, yet keeping the essay within sensible limits, deliberately I have selected and discussed from only a part of the full spectrum of evolutionary studies. Also, where possible and appropriate, I have tried to draw on work that has stood the test of time, as well as the most recent speculations. I found that I had to curb a tendency to suggest that all the important findings have been reported in the past five years! However, for the benefit of those readers who want to follow up on my discussions, at the end of the book I have appended a short survey of useful background and supplementary reading.

Second, I hope it will be obvious that I draw a very strict line between the scientific evolutionists that I criticize and the Creationists. I do not underestimate the political skills of Creationists, but regard their doctrines with contempt. However, although I think the scientific evolutionary opponents of Darwinism are wrong, I have failed if I have not given a sense of the real respect that I have for them as thinkers. Charles Darwin's greatest merit was to break with orthodoxy and to think the unthinkable, and for this reason I hope that those evolutionists who today stand most opposed to Darwin's mechanisms will nevertheless feel that they are included in my dedication. Possibly the scientist of whom I write most critically is Stephen Jay Gould, and yet I can truly say that there is no evolutionist today who writes more thoughtfully and engagingly.

No man is an island, especially not one engaged in such a task as this. Let me therefore, conclude this preface by giving full credit to the following people, who have over the years given advice, information, moral support, criticism, and everything else that a scholar needs to bring his work to fruition: Francisco J. Ayala, A. J. Cain, Beverly Halstead, Jonathan Hodge, David Hull, Ernst Mayr, and Edward O. Wilson.

Two younger scholars, who I am sure are destined to have their marks on Darwin studies, have read and criticized the whole manuscript: John Beatty and Paul Thompson. One thing I do know already is that not everyone will agree with everything I have said!

MICHAEL RUSE

One hundred years without Darwin is enough.
HERMANN J. MULLER

Satan himself is the originator of the concept of evolution.
HENRY M. MORRIS

Part I
Darwinism Yesterday

Chapter 1
Charles Darwin Becomes an Evolutionist

On June 18 1858, Charles Darwin sat down after breakfast in his study to go through his mail. One package came from the Far East; it was sent by a young naturalist and collector, Alfred Russel Wallace. Wallace and Darwin had never met but for a year or two now they had been corresponding, exchanging views and queries about the biological world. Wallace had written a short paper, mailing it to Darwin and hoping that the older man might think it worthy of publication.

As Darwin started to read, his heart started to sink. For twenty years, he, Darwin, had been sitting on a secret: a theory and a mechanism that would explain in a scientific way the organisms we find around us and in the fossil record: a theory of *evolution*. His friends had long urged that he publish, lest someone else forestall him. Now the worst had happened, for Wallace had hit on the same ideas, and the paper he had just sent to Darwin was as if Darwin himself had written it. Even the language was the same!

Depressed, Darwin turned to his close friends, Charles Lyell, the geologist, and Joseph Hooker, the botanist, for advice. Honorably and fairly, they saw no reason why Darwin should be deprived of his share of the credit. So, at the next meeting of the Linnean Society in July 1858, Wallace's paper was read, together with extracts from unpublished evolutionary writings by Darwin (Darwin and Wallace, 1958). Then Darwin set to work with a vengeance, in fifteen months producing a 450-page essay that explained and elaborated on his ideas. Thus, towards the end of 1859, the world was given Charles Darwin's *On the Origin of Species,* containing his theory of evolution through natural selection. The publisher issued 1250 copies, and booksellers snapped up every one on the first day.

What was the problem that Darwin tried to solve? What sort of man was he who tried to solve it? What was his solution? How was it received, and how has it stood the test of time? Let us look at these questions in turn. (Here, as throughout the book the reader should consult the bibliography for general references.)

The organic origins problem and the Lamarckian solution

end of Biblical theory

* The Bible has a full answer to questions about where we all come from. God created the whole universe in some six days, filling out the earth with plants and animals: on land, in the sea, and in the air. Then, just before God finished work, He created His masterpiece: man. It is true that there is a slight ambiguity about the arrival of woman. In one version of the Creation, woman is produced alongside man. In another version, she is something of an after-thought — a playmate to keep man occupied and happy. But no matter. Either way, God did His work quickly and altogether outside of the normal course of nature. There was no normal course of nature until God set to work! *

For most people up to the second quarter of the nineteenth century, in-deed, for many people even today, this story of creation was an entirely satis-fying and complete answer. But, 150 years ago, increasingly, thinkers in and around science were feeling dissatisfied with the story of Genesis. This dissatisfaction was chiefly a function of the rapidly developing science of geology, which was driving people to the ineluctable conclusion that the earth on which we live is far older than the 6000 years that scholars traditionally ac-corded it, an estimate that was based on the genealogies to be found in the Old Testament. The complex rocks, bearing testimony to an earth-history molded by fire and water, just did not seem to be the kinds of things that could have been produced in an instant. If God just made them out of nothing a short time ago, why were they not smooth and homogenous, rather than the ap-parently tortured products of cataclysmic processes?

And then there were the fossils. Beginning at the beginning, it had first to be accepted that fossils are indeed the remains and records of dead organisms! At the same time of the Renaissance, this connection was far from obvious. To Platonists, seeing this world as a shadow image of the eternal Forms, the natural interpretation of fossils was that they reflect Forms in the inorganic world as living organisms reflect Forms in the organic world. There was therefore no direct connection between fossils and organisms. For Aristotelians, conversely, fossils were the natural growths from the sperm of living animals that fell by the wayside onto rocks and the like, just as living organisms were the natural growths from sperm that fell onto or into living matter. Again, the connection between living and dead was tenuous, to say the least.

Gradually, in the seventeenth century, the true connection between fossils and organisms came to be realized and accepted. As can be imagined, this caused all sorts of tensions between science and religion, although interesting-ly, at first, many welcomed the fossil/organism connection, because marine fossils high on mountain ranges were taken to be indubitable evidence of Noah's flood! However, as the years went by, fossils started to cause more and more problems for Believers. Fossil after fossil was unearthed for which no liv-ing counterparts were found. Could this mean that God created organisms and then just let them go extinct? Surely not! Apart from anything else, given that the earth was expressly created for man, how could there have been organisms that lived and died before Adam?

This problem of extinction was a festering sore for Believers, right through the eighteenth century. One could, of course, deny that it had ever occurred — that somewhere, living counterparts of all fossils still happily exist and reproduce. But as the world was explored in ever-greater detail, this ad hoc strategem seemed less and less plausible.

Moreover, if all the problems with fossils were not enough, thanks to the enthusiastic reports and collections of world explorers, the devout Believer had increasing troubles explaining contemporary organisms in such a way that would save God from looking like a capricious bungler. For instance, why should God have created quite different organisms for similar terrains and climates, when so often He made the same organism struggle over wide ranges, encompassing vastly different conditions? Why should God have made such apparently useless features as male nipples? And why should God have made such grotesque parodies of humankind as orang-utans and gorillas? Are we really to the angels no more than these apes are to us? Perish the thought! (See Fig. 1.1.)

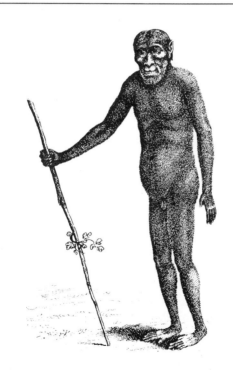

Fig. 1.1
This is a picture of a young chimpanzee which appeared in a volume on apes, published in 1766. Notice how human it is made to seem.

Thus, as the Victorian age approached, there grew a pressing need to explain what, in my own terminology, I call "the organic origins problem or question": the question of the origin or origins of the world's organisms, past and present, including our own species, *Homo sapiens*. It cannot be denied, although there were many who wished that it could have been denied, that there was one well-known, or rather notorious, non-Biblical answer to the question. At the beginning of the nineteenth century, the French biologist Jean Baptiste de Lamarck (Fig. 1.2) had produced and argued for a theory of evolution. That is to say, Lamarck argued that, over the course of generations, we

Fig. 1.2
Jean Baptiste de Lamarck (1744-1829)

have one form of organism (say, codfish) changing to another kind (say, frog) and then to another kind (say, pig) and so on, until finally we reach the orangutan and, with one last burst of energy, man. (See Figs. 1.3 and 1.4.)

Lamarck saw this transmuting chain as being an ongoing process, with the lowest forms of life continuously being formed out of mud and dirt by electrical action, and, following this "spontaneous generation," one then has an inevitable progression up through the various forms. At least, it is an almost inevitable progression. Lamarck believed that normally there is a fixed upward path, triggered by the various needs organisms experience in the course of their lives. Thus, for instance, one could expect a species like tigers to be formed again and again, from predecessors that had been formed again and again.

Nevertheless, Lamarck believed also that sometimes one will get side branching, brought about by the inheritance of acquired characteristics. An organism will develop some feature due to work or stress or the like, and then this will be passed straight on to the offspring. Conversely, a characteristic might be lost forever through disuse. Paradoxically this idea was not new to Lamarck — although indeed it was he who gave it evolutionary significance —

and it was not really that great a part of his theory. But the mechanism did get peculiarly associated with him, and it is to this inheritance of acquired characteristics alone that we refer today when we use the term "Lamarckism."

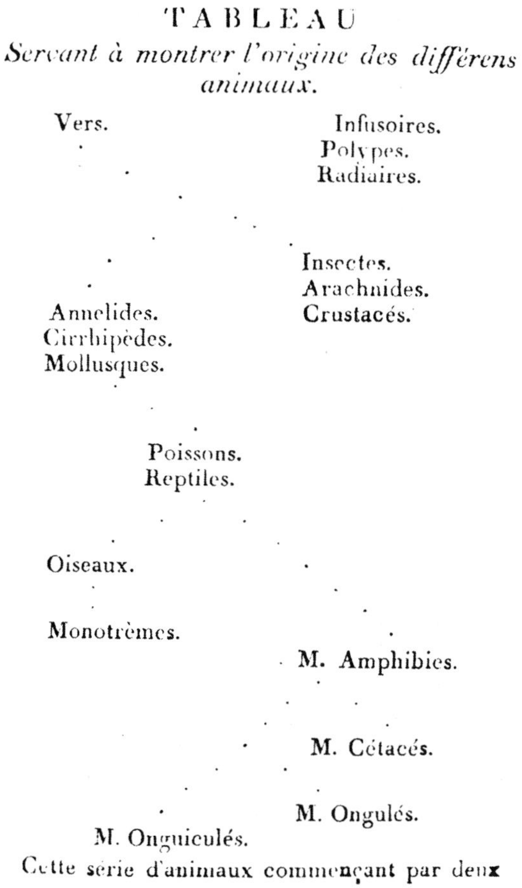

TABLEAU

Servant à montrer l'origine des différens animaux.

Vers.   Infusoires.
                                         Polypes.
                                         Radiaires.

                                         Insectes.
                                         Arachnides.
Annelides.   Crustacés.
Cirrhipèdes.
Mollusques.

            Poissons.
            Reptiles.

Oiseaux.

Monotrèmes.

                        M. Amphibies.

                        M. Cétacés.

                        M. Ongulés.
        M. Onguiculés.
Cette série d'animaux commençant par deux

Fig. 1.3

Lamarck's picture of evolution (from his *Philosophie Zoologique,* 1809). Compare with Fig. 1.4, and do not confuse Lamarck's diagram with Darwin's superficially similar diagram (Fig. 2.4).

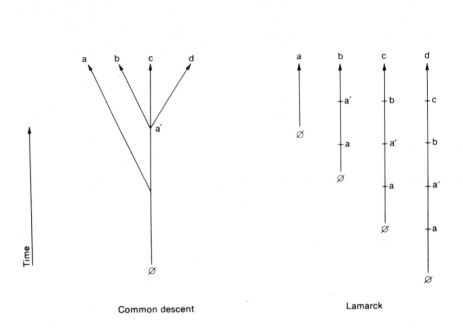

Fig. 1.4
The difference between a theory like Lamarck's and one of common descent. Life is supposed to begin at ∅, and *a, b, c, d,* are kinds of organisms extant today.

Lamarck's evolutionism was totally unacceptable to almost all of his fellow scientists. Undoubtedly the main underlying objection was religious. Even those who could no longer take the Bible absolutely literally found evolutionary speculations religiously offensive on at least two scores. First, there was the question of design. Natural theologians of all kinds harped incessantly on the fact that the living world shows abundant pressing evidence of God's forethought, care, and intelligence — adaptively integrated, functioning phenomena, like hands and eyes and wings and feathers, were thought to show beyond doubt the existence of a Creator. Just as a telescope demands a telescope maker, so the eye demands an eyemaker (or Eyemaker).

Consequently, Lamarck's evolutionism, explaining all in terms of unbroken rules of nature, was seen as running counter both to the facts and to God. If Lamarck was providing a natural explanation of organisms, and as an evolutionist this seemed to be what he was doing, then he was explaining organic origins through blind, unguided law. But, blind law leads to randomness and chance: the dice could fall on any face; the sand gets scattered and mixed. There is no place here for the making of the hand or the eye — nor is there place for the Handmaker or the Eyemaker.

Second, in even stronger religious objection to Lamarck than that founded on design, there was the question of man. Virtually no one was prepared to see *Homo sapiens* as just another organism. All saw the world as created for man and saw man as something special in God's plan — however liberally they were prepared to interpret the Old Testament. Protestations notwithstanding, Lamarck was taken as denying this. If all is blind law, what place is there for immortal souls — or for intelligence or a moral sense, for that matter? By his very own admission, Lamarck degraded us all to the status of hairless ape.

Religion stood squarely against Lamarck. But do not think that people simply paraded their religion and left matters at that. No indeed! Lamarck claimed to be scientific, so people were very happy to tackle him on this score. Furthermore, general opinion was that there was plenty of good scientific grist for the critical mill against his "absurd" doctrines. With reason, spontaneous generation was thought to be a ridiculous notion. There was no evidence of any kind that worms and slugs and other low life forms can be created from dirt. Indeed, although Pasteur's work was fifty years in the future, general opinion in France was that massive experimental evidence was piling up showing that inorganic sludge stays as just that, no matter how much one may heat it, cool it, fry it, electrocute it, pickle it, or whatever.

And against evolution proper, it was thought that there are many decisive empirical facts. For instance, as writer after writer pointed out, the changes that animal and plant breeders can effect are all transitory, as is shown clearly by the fact that when domestic organisms go wild, they revert to original form. Why then should nature be any different in the first place? Also, if evolution occurs, why are the mummified animals and humans brought back to Europe from Egypt by Napoleon's conquering forces no different from types living and breathing today? Ancient Egyptian cats are the same as modern French cats. And, ancient Egyptian humans are the same as modern French humans.

Then, most devastatingly against Lamarckian evolution, there was the fossil record. This might strike you as a little odd. I am sure that today, if you asked people why they believed in evolution, nine times out of ten they would reply: "Because of the fossils!" They would point to the broadly "progressive" nature of the record — that one begins in the oldest and lowest rocks with primitive invertebrate forms, and then one works up to ever more sophisticated and complex forms in younger and higher rocks, until one comes to forms very much like those today, including man. This, they would argue, is the record of evolution, as though it had been writing a diary for posterity.

But, Lamarck's contemporaries did not quite see matters this way. In fact, Lamarck himself was relatively indifferent to the fossils and certainly did not tie in the progressiveness within his own theory with the progressiveness of the record. Paradoxically it was Lamarck's great fellow French scientist

Georges Cuvier who really uncovered the record, emphasizing its progressiveness: fish, reptiles, mammals. But, Cuvier was at the same time an archantievolutionist! He thought that the gaps one sees in the record — one always has sharp breaks between forms and never sees one sliding into another — speak definitively against evolution. And virtually everyone agreed with him! Thus it was concluded that religion and science harmoniously and jointly refute evolutionism.

Unfortunately, as we all know, it is far easier and more satisfying to cast out motes from the eyes of others, than to remove the beams from our own eyes. If Lamarck is wrong, what then is the truth? As we shall learn, Darwin started to become a self-aware scientist around 1830. So, to conclude our background preparation for him and his work, let us see what the position on organic origins would have been around that time in England — the position, that is, of someone who had moved beyond a crude literal belief in the Old Testament and yet who, for religious and scientific reasons, found the evolutionary option quite unacceptable. There were, I believe, two basic theses, neither of which was entirely satisfactory.

The uniformitarians and catastrophists

First, we have the *uniformitarians,* headed by Charles Lyell (1797–1875). (See Fig. 1.5.) They saw the earth as being in an ongoing steady state, rather like a perpetual motion machine. Rain, wind, frost, and snow wear away at mountains; rivers, streams, and the sea carry away silt, eating at the land, depositing it elsewhere; earthquakes and volcanoes break up and raise ground.

Fig. 1.5
Charles Lyell (1797– 1875).

Thus we get a constant churning and altering of land masses, of lakes, of mountains, and of the sea. But, essentially, all goes on indefinitely, bounded by limits of intensity and effect: "no trace of a beginning, no prospect of an end." Methodologically, uniformitarians urged geologists always to explain past events in terms of causes of a kind and intensity we see around us today. (See Fig. 1.6.)

Fig. 1.6
The frontispiece of the first volume of Lyell's *Principles,* intended to illustrate a Lyellian steady-state earth. See how the columns are in perfect condition up to about eight feet, at which point erosion begins. This shows that, since they were built, the land had first sunk (putting the columns under water), and then risen again to its original level.

Within their self-contained world, uniformitarians saw organisms as coming and then going (extinct) on a regular basis. Organisms appear, they struggle for life for a while, but then like the dodo, the struggle proves too much for them and they go forever, perhaps leaving a trace in the fossil record. (See Fig. 1.7.) Organic progression, Lyell dismissed as a chimera, simply an artifact of our ignorance of the total record.

Fig. 1.7
The dodo.

As to the most important question of all — "How do organisms first appear?" — Lyell and his followers were somewhat fuzzy. They were like a student answering an exam question to which he does not really know the answer: lots of confident assertions, plenty of sneering remarks about opponents, rhetorical questions galore, and a direct response to the main question conspicuously absent. Somehow the uniformitarians thought that organisms are created naturally, that is, according to regular unbroken law, but exactly how these laws operate was never made clear. A number of obvious questions were neither asked nor answered. Does one, for instance, get one kind of organism created from another kind, or from inorganic matter, or simply out of thin air? Search as one may in the uniformitarian writings, these queries are missing.

This one can say about the Lyellian position: supposing that laws are indeed responsible for organic origins, these laws would be rather odd, because they would have to make room for God's designing powers. Lyell and his followers, like everyone else, wanted plenty of room for forces capable of making the hand and the eye. Lyell in fact was so far imbued with traditional natural theology that he made the remarkably British suggestion that the dog was designed expressly for man and the man for dog! But, more seriously, Lyell had no doubt that man is a special case, calling for individual miraculous intervention by the Lord of Hosts: "We are not, however, contending that a real departure from the antecedent course of physical events cannot be traced in the introduction of man" (Lyell 1830–1833, 1, 162).

Clearly much was wrong with the uniformitarian position, considered in its own terms and time. It was all very well to criticize Lamarck for spontaneous generation and evolution. Were the uniformitarians themselves offering anything better? Surely the solution to organic origins that puts least strain on the uniformitarian position involved the supposition that organisms came from other organisms. But, was this not in itself to edge awfully close to evolution? Subscribers to the alternative view, which came to be called *catastrophism*, were able to pride themselves that they stood in no such danger of slipping into evolutionism, whatever else they may have slipped into. They argued flatly that new species of organism, including God's final creation, man, were produced miraculously by God. God wants no nonsense about unbroken laws coming between Him and His handiwork. He intervenes personally. Thus, there is plenty of room for design, and the special status of *Homo sapiens* is preserved and emphasized.

But, the catastrophists were far from Biblical literalists. They saw the world as having a definite direction, from an original incandescent state, cooling down to today's habitable form. Hence, although they were not prepared to invoke the indefinite time-spans of the uniformitarians, the catastrophists obviously thereby committed themselves to a relatively aged earth. To get this time, while remaining true to the Bible in some sense, catastrophists supposed either that the "days" of creation are very long spans of time, or they supposed that a long, unmentioned time block exists between the initial creation and the six days of special effort by God, described in detail at the beginning of the Bible.

In addition to direction, catastrophists believed that every now and then in Earth history there were massive upheavals — earthquakes, conflagrations, floods, and the like — and then following these catastrophes, the last of which was Noah's flood, there are periods of comparative calm. The catastrophes wipe out all or virtually all living beings (hence the gaps in the fossil record), and then God begins again. (See Fig. 1.8.) Thus the catastrophists were delighted to emphasize the progressiveness of the fossil record, tying it in with their view of Earth history. Organisms flourished when, and only when, the Earth was right for them. A primitive Earth called for primitive organisms. A complex Earth calls for complex organisms. Man could not have come before he did, because the world was just not yet ready for him.

Of course, a disinterested outsider might be forgiven for thinking the catastrophists' cure worse than the uniformitarian illness. Catastrophists may have avoided the major difficulties of the uniformitarians — "How can one simultaneously have law and yet have direction by God?" — but the catastrophists were saved only because they took the whole question of organic origins right out of science itself! In short, one might be inclined to say: "A plague on both your houses!" Certainly this seems to have been the feeling of one bright young entrant into the scientific community of that time, as we shall learn.

Fig. 1.8
One of the illustrations given by the catastrophist geologist William Buckland (in his *Reliquiae Diluvianae*) purporting to prove the existence of a universal flash flood. Skeleton G is of a rhinoceros, washed down into a cave and enclosed in diluvial rubble (E). That there were bones to reconstruct only one rhinoceros proved, Buckland claimed, the extreme rapidity of the flood.

Charles Darwin: English gentleman

Charles Darwin was born with a silver spoon in his mouth. At least, he was born with a bone china bowl out of which to eat his pablum, for his maternal grandfather was Josiah Wedgewood, responsible above all others for the introduction of stunningly successful innovations into the British pottery trade. His paternal grandfather, Erasmus Darwin, was also a figure of some

Fig. 1.9
Erasmus Darwin
(1731–1802).

note on the late eighteenth-century scene. Like his son Robert, Charles's father, Erasmus Darwin was a successful doctor. Additionally, he was a leading intellectual light of the Midlands, friend of industrialists, and writer of unbelievably bad verse on evolutionary topics. (See Fig. 1.9.)

ORGANIC LIFE beneath the shoreless waves
Was born and nursed in Ocean's pearly caves;
First forms minute, unseen by spheric glass,
Move on the mud, or pierce the watery mass;
These, as successive generations bloom,
New powers acquire, and larger limbs assume;
Whence countless groups of vegetation spring,
And breathing realms of fin, and feet, and wing.

Thus the tall Oak, the giant of the wood,
Which bears Britannia's thunders on the flood;
The Whale, unmeasured monster of the main,
The lordly Lion, monarch of the plain,
The Eagle soaring in the realms of air,
Whose eye undazzled drinks the solar glare,
Imperious Man, who rules the bestial crowd,
Of language, reason, and reflection proud,
With brow erect who scorns this earthy sod,
And styles himself the image of his God;
Arose from rudiments of form and sense,
An embryon point, or microscopic ens! (Darwin, 1803, pp. 26-28)

It is with some relief that we can turn to Erasmus's grandson.

Charles Darwin's mother died when he was only eight; as a consequence, he was brought up by an older sister. Nevertheless, his childhood seems to have been a happy one. He was a lively, curious lad; although apparently not much of a scholar in his early years. Schooldays were at Shrewsbury, one of England's great public schools, and then Darwin was packed off to Edinburgh to study medicine. One senses that this move was directed more by family tradition and expectation, than by burning desire. Indeed, two years later, bored by the lectures and revolted by the operations, Darwin had had enough. In despair, therefore, his father did the only sensible thing one could do with an idle, undirected son: at the beginning of 1828, Robert Darwin sent young Charles to Cambridge, intending that he should become a clergyman. One should add that this decision was as cynical as it was sensible: the mantle of religious belief lay very lightly on Dr. Darwin.

Three comfortable years later — "my time was wasted, as far as the academical studies were concerned, as completely as at Edinburgh and at school" (Darwin, 1969, p. 58) — through connections he had made at Cambridge, Charles Darwin was offered the chance of joining an Admirality-sponsored charting expedition around South America, on board *HMS Beagle,* under the leadership of Captain Robert Fitzroy. Essentially his status was to be that of gentleman companion to the captain, who otherwise would be isolated in his lonely post of command. But, by this time, Robert Darwin had had enough. The point had come when Charles should stop idling and turn seriously towards his chosen profession. The trip was barred.

Fortunately, or unfortunately according to one's perspective, Robert left the loophole that if Charles could find any man of sense who approved of the plan, he could join Fitzroy. Of all people, Josiah Wedgewood, the son of the potter, Robert's brother-in-law and a man whose advice and common sense he valued, strongly endorsed Charles's project. (See Fig. 1.10.) Wedgewood thought it would be just the touch of experience that Charles needed to settle him (and how very right Wedgewood proved), and that it would be the ideal training for a man of God (and how very wrong Wedgewood proved). Thus, on December 27, 1831, we find Charles Darwin setting sail from Plymouth on *HMS Beagle,* becoming dreadfully seasick once the ship got out into the English channel.

The *Beagle* voyage dragged out until 1836. Much time was spent around the coast of South America. Then the ship went on to South Africa, back once again to South America, and finally home to England. (See Fig. 1.11.) Charles spent many long hours cooped up with the mercurial Fitzroy — a man whose great generosity and charm was matched by his obsessive religious beliefs, his vile temper, and his deeply suicidal moods (eventually, like his uncle, Castlereagh, Fitzroy killed himself). However, since he was not an official member of the ship's crew, Darwin was able to make long trips into the hinterland of the South American continent, during which increasingly he made massive biological and geological collections, which he arranged to ship home.

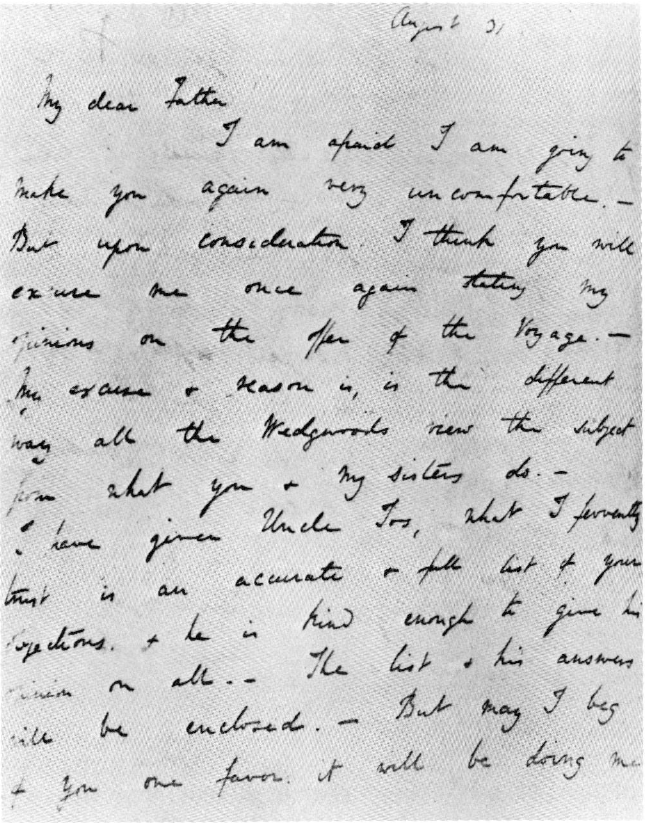

August 31

My dear Father

I am afraid I am going to
make you again very uncomfortable.—
But upon consideration I think you will
excuse me once again stating my
opinions on the offer of the Voyage.—
My excuse & reason is, is the different
way all the Wedgwoods view the subject
from what you & my sisters do.—
I have given Uncle Jos, what I fervently
trust is an accurate & full list of your
objections. & he is kind enough to give his
opinion on all.— The list & his answers
will be enclosed.— But may I beg
of you one favor. it will be doing me

Fig. 1.10
Letter from Darwin to his father, 31 August 1831, asking him to reconsider his refusal to let his son sail with the *Beagle.* (Reproduced by permission of the Royal College of Surgeons).

Returning to England, all thoughts of a clerical life had vanished, and Darwin turned to the analyzing and cataloguing of his collections, together with the writing up of his travel diaries into what became one of the most popular travel books of the Victorian era: *Journal of Researches into the Geology and Natural History of the Various Countries Visited by HMS Beagle, etc.* (later reissued with the more manageable title, the *Voyage of the*

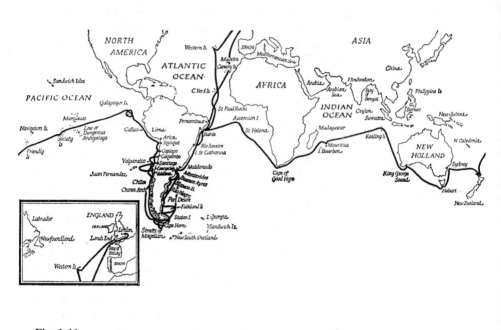

Fig. 1.11
Voyage of *H.M.S. Beagle,* 1831–36.

Beagle). One senses that Dr. Darwin did not altogether regret the loss of the possibility of a clerical son. There was quite enough family money for Charles to live on, without paid employment: medicine, then as now, paid good dividends, and the pottery works of the old Josiah Wedgewood meant that none of his immediate relatives would live in want. What concerned Robert was that Charles have some direction in his life, and with the various effects of the global trip such direction seemed now to have been found.

At first, in the years after the *Beagle,* Charles led an active social life, mixing much at Cambridge and in London with leading intellectual lights of the day. For instance, for a while he became close to Thomas Carlyle, an intimate friend of Charles's older brother, Erasmus. But then two things occurred which quite changed the course of his personal life. He became engaged to, and early in 1839 married, his first cousin Emma Wedgewood, daughter of the Josiah Wedgewood who had made possible Darwin's time on the *Beagle.* And second, Charles Darwin fell ill with an ailment which reduced him from a vibrant, carefree young man, into a being prematurely middle-aged, destined to be racked for the rest of his life with headaches, stomach upsets, and a general physical and mental sense of unease.

The true cause of Darwin's illness is one of those Great Victorian Mysteries, along with the identity of Jack the Ripper and the possible marriage of Queen Victoria to her gillie John Brown. One suspects that, like these other mysteries, it is something that is great fun to discuss, but not really that important to solve. Certainly, discussions on the subject destroy any faith one might have in medical objectivity.

If one is a pathologist, one identifies the illness's cause in poison. A recent suggestion is that, in ignorance, Darwin overdosed himself with arsenic, something contained in so many nineteenth-century patent medicines. If one is an epidemiologist, then disease of some sort is one's choice. There is evidence that Darwin may have caught Chagas' disease in South America. And, if one is a psychiatrist, then, expectedly, Darwin's problems started in his mind. Not only does one have the suggestive fact that Darwin became an evolutionist at a time when such views were anathematized (what hidden tensions this must have caused!), but one has the potential effects of the dead mother and of Dr. Robert Darwin, a huge overbearing man. Even worse, instead of hating his father, Charles professed to love him!

Pay your money and take your choice. Just be thankful that no sexologist has yet written on Darwin's illness. If I am to confess to any feelings on the matter, I suppose it must be to a slight distaste for the psychological option. This may be primarily a function of the fact that mental problems are "unclean" in a way that physical problems are not, but it is also because the young Charles seems so normal that I cannot see in his character the seeds of forty years of nervous prostration. No doubt, experts will tell me that "normal" people are precisely those who crack most thoroughly!

Be this as it may, by 1840 we find Darwin newly married and a complete physical wreck. He and his wife bought a large house in the village of Downe in Kent (near Orpington), and having remodeled it, they settled into the conceiving, bearing, and rearing of a typically large Victorian family. Isolated from the world, they turned in on themselves and their very happy relationship, and became semi-recluses, at least with respect to social intercourse. Friends had to visit them, and the main breaks in country life were trips to spas and other health resorts, as Darwin sought relief from his ailments. In the course of his life, he became a veritable guinea pig for the medical profession.

As far as the physical details of life for Darwin after the move to Kent are concerned, the most appropriate word that springs to mind is "monotonous." When he was not too sick to rise, Darwin would breakfast, read the mail, read and write, walk, lunch, rest, read and write, supper, and then play innumerable games of backgammon with Emma. This would go on day after day, Saturdays and Sundays included. Outside work, the joy was in the changing of the seasons, occasional visits from friends, letters, and the growing family, in which both Charles and Emma took the greatest interest and pride. The burdens were in the ill health and, most of all, in the death in 1851 of their second and most-loved child, Annie. Domestic changes aside, it seems fair to say that the personal life of Charles Darwin after 1840 was uneventful as his life was action-packed and varied before 1840. Happily, in the last decade of his life, Darwin's illness eased somewhat, and thus he was able to enjoy a comparatively peaceful and comfortable old age. (See Fig. 1.12.)

Fig. 1.12
Charles Darwin in old age.

What sort of man was Darwin? It is hard to say exactly, because most of our reports come down through Darwin's own pen or those of friends and relatives. But, even accounting for bias, it does seem fairly certain that he was blessed with looks and with personality, as in a corresponding way he had been blessed with financial ease and social status. Darwin was tall and, from his portraits, apparently good looking; although photographs tell the tale of the immediate toll on his frame that his illness took. From all accounts, as a young man he was vigorous and brave, and anyone who was able to live with Fitzroy on the closest of terms for five years in reasonable harmony must have had the tact and good-nature of a saint.

Not only was Darwin a strong family man, he was loyal to friends. When his chief supporter, Thomas Henry Huxley, collapsed into a nervous breakdown, Darwin organized and led a subscription to ease Huxley's financial worries. However, towards enemies Darwin could be a good hater. One who incurred Darwin's enmity particularly was the Catholic anatomist St. George Jackson Mivart, who was believed to have impuned the integrity of one of Darwin's sons. Overall, one can say this: Darwin was the paradigmatic English gentleman of breeding, taste, and reserve. He believed strongly in the liberal traditions of his family; and, always, one senses that inborn feeling of self-worth, which is so indicative of he who is brought up and treated as one of nature's fortunates.

Charles Darwin: professional scientist

By this state, one may be starting to wonder. How could such a man as this, aimless in his youth, sick and secluded in his prime, have become the author of the greatest theory in biological science, one of the archetypal heroes in the history of Western intellectual thought? All this talk of upper-class English country gentlemen summons up visions of characters in novels by Anthony Trollope or Evelyn Waugh: their only knowledge of the organic world is as provider of things to shoot, hunt, or eat.

In fact, I confess that I have been cheating somewhat in my portrait of Darwin. There was another as-yet-unmentioned side to him: the side of the totally dedicated, utterly professional man of science. As we start to reveal this, there ceases to be any mystery in the fact that Darwin of the *Beagle* (as early Victorians knew him) should later become Darwin of the *Origin* (as later Victorians knew him). No better candidate for the father of evolutionary theory could be found.

Let me start with the negative side, pointing out that Darwin hardly impressed as a thinker in his early years simply because he did not have to, and furthermore was not given the chance to do so. Even as the younger son of a family with the Darwin-Wedgewood riches, there was no need for Charles Darwin to exert himself — which he obviously did not! Nor did anyone expect it very much. Cambridge was, to all intents and purposes, a time for a young man to make connections and to sow wild oats. For the average youth, it was certainly not a time for serious study. Furthermore (and this is important), for someone with a potential interest in the biological sciences, there was no formal place at either school or university to encourage and train it. One did not have science courses and degrees in those days: just the classics, mathematics, and a certain amount of scripture. That was all! Darwin simply had no opportunity to shine in the way that one might expect of a modern genius, even if Darwin had wanted to.

However, the Darwinian story also has a positive side, which leads to respect for Darwin as a scientist. In the eighteenth and early nineteenth centuries, British science lagged desperately behind continental science and science organization. But, by about 1830, the time that Darwin was at Cambridge, things were starting to change. Some of the professors were at last taking a positive interest in science, and this interest and their knowledge could infect and inform undergraduates. Typical was the Reverend Adam Sedgwick, Woodwardian Professor of Geology. In 1818, when Sedgwick had campaigned for the post, the attractions were the status and the emoluments, and his geological knowledge was none. He succeeded simply because he had more friends than his rival. However, when elected, Sedgwick set about turning himself into a first-class geologist, doing striking work uncovering the Cambrian strata.

Hence, by the time Darwin came up to Cambridge, Sedgwick, like other science professors, had much to offer. Moreover, almost from the first, Darwin took advantage of this opportunity, even though it had to be done outside the formal bounds of the degree program. Perhaps because they were such a pioneering minority, science professors and interested undergraduates had few social constraints between them, and we find that young Darwin mixed and conversed with his seniors on a regular basis. For three years he attended lectures given by the professor of botany, John Stevens Henslow. And just before the *Beagle* voyage occurred, Darwin was taken on a geologizing trip to Wales by Sedgwick, an ardent catastrophist. (See Figs. 1.13 and 1.14.)

Fig. 1.13
John Stevens Henslow
(1796–1861).

I do not want to exaggerate. While at Cambridge, Darwin was far more interested in having a good time than in pursuing science in a serious systematic way. At this point in his life, science was just a hobby, which dovetailed nicely with another hobby that Darwin had taken up, one eminently suitable for a future clergyman: beetle-collecting. But the seeds were sown, and showed the future path that he was to take. From his undergraduate days on, Darwin mixed with good scientists, learned from them, and copied them. On the *Beagle,* Darwin's thought channeled more and more towards science, particularly geology, and we find that his collecting reflected this: from the dilettante interests of a gentleman naturalist, we find that his constant reading of the reference books he had taken with him turned Darwin into a single-minded observer, concerned to find that which would confirm or refute the hypotheses he found in his books.

Fig. 1.14
Adam Sedgwick (1785–1873).

Returning from the *Beagle,* there was never any question in Darwin's mind — or that of anyone else for that matter — that henceforth his full attentions and energies, however low they may sink, would be given to science. Taking up and expanding from the group he had known at Cambridge, Darwin talked science, thought science, and wrote science. He became intimate with many of Britain's leading men of science, most particularly forming what was to be a lifelong friendship with Lyell. It is true that Darwin had no science post, ever: he did not need one! Indeed, he was at an advantage compared to his fellows, for he had no distractions like students and college administrative meetings! But, this must not conceal the fact that Darwin was a full-time scientist, thinking of himself as one and being respected by his fellow scientists as one. After the move to Downe, virtually all of Darwin's correspondence was with fellow scientists, those few personal connections he kept up or was able to make were with scientists, and from his pen poured forth a stream of books and articles on matters scientific. Apart from his evolutionary work, as we saw in the Preface, one had writings on geology and on topics drawn from right across the biological spectrum.

I shall not labor my point. Darwin's work itself will be the best evidence. For the rest of this book, keep asking yourself whether a bumbling amateur really could have done what Darwin did. Let me end my introduction, trying to underline my claims about Darwin's status, by noting that as a true "professional," by his own admission, he wrote, not for the general public, but for his fellow scientists. And it was their praise that counted: "[T]hough I cared in the highest degree for the approbation of such men as Lyell and Hooker, who were my friends, I did not care much about the general public" (Darwin, 1969, p. 82).

What more revealing comment could there be than this?

Darwin's route to discovery

So, what made Charles Darwin an evolutionist? Thanks to grandfather Erasmus's poetic forays, Darwin knew of evolution at an early age. But, there seems little reason to doubt his later claim that, even when he left university, he believed more or less literally in all of the Bible. At Cambridge, his professorial seniors must have filled Darwin's head full of the virtues of catastrophism, particularly since Sedgwick was one of its most ardent advocates. But, while some aspects of the catastrophists' directionalism may have influenced him, it seems clear that it was not from this quarter that Darwin's main inspiration was to be drawn. Much more important was the rival world-view. Just as Darwin was completing his degree, Charles Lyell started to publish the definitive statement on uniformitarianism: his immensely attractive *Principles of Geology* (1830–1833). On Henslow's advice, who urged him to read it but not believe it, Darwin took the first volume with him on the *Beagle* (the other volumes were sent out as they appeared), and thus Darwin was presented with about as clear a statement of the uniformitarian position on organic origins that anyone was prepared to give.

In fact, Darwin was much attracted to the overall uniformitarian approach to geology, and all of his early scientific work was aimed at filling in details of the Lyellian picture. But, with respect to organisms and their origins, Darwin could sense the obvious difficulties that Lyell faced. If one appeals to law to explain the origins of organisms, what kind of law could this be? If one is at all forthright and consistent, then, if the laws involved are to be real laws, one edges very, very close to evolutionism.

Cutting a long story short and, to be honest, glossing over some points of detail about which we are still not completely sure, it seems that, around the end of the *Beagle* voyage, the tensions in the uniformitarian position became too much for Darwin, and he became a (secret) evolutionist. Probably the facts that tipped the scales right over were the tortoises and finches of the Galapagos Archipelago, a group of Pacific islands on the equator off South America, that the *Beagle* had visited. Within the finches and the tortoises one finds many very similar but distinctly different forms from island to island. How else could one explain these similarities and differences, except as the product of evolution? Darwin certainly could find no other answer. (See Fig. 1.15.)

Being an evolutionist is not enough. At least, in a way, being an evolutionist is the start of one's difficulties, not the end. One has to have also some

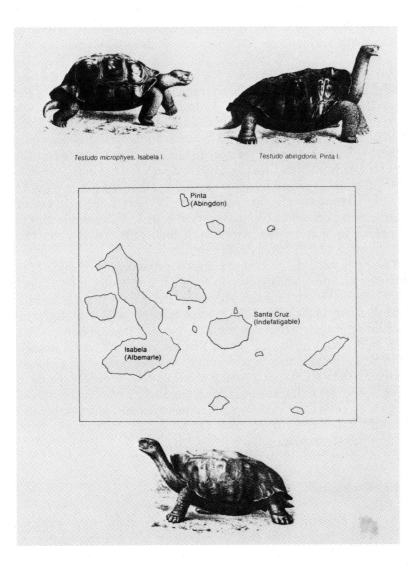

Testudo microphyes, Isabela I.

Testudo abingdonii, Pinta I.

Fig. 1.15
Three different tortoises from three different islands of the Galapagos. (Adapted with permission from Theodosius Dobzhansky *et al,* (1977). *Evolution,* San Francisco: W. H. Freeman.)

causal mechanism to explain evolutionary change. Darwin soon became convinced that the secret behind change lay in the methods used by animals and plant breeders to improve their stock: *selection*. Breeders choose their best and most-prized cows, sheep, fruit trees, vegetables, or what have you, and breed from them alone. Thus one gets dramatic change, as the meatiness, the woolliness, the tastiness, the fleshiness gets channeled and built up in a few generations.

But, how could this selection work in the wild? Darwin looked in vain for a reason, until, in September 1838, he read the *Essay on a Principle of Population* (1826) by the Reverend Thomas Robert Malthus. This is no work in biology; rather, it urges an extremely conservative thesis in political economy. Appalled at what he took to be naive hopes for universal human progress, Malthus argued that state welfare systems aimed at improving the lot of the indigent are totally pointless. He suggested that such systems only compound the problem they are supposed to solve, because however much help one gives the poor, there will always be that many more of them in the next generation. Population pressure works on a geometrical scale and always outstrips potential increases in food supplies, which work on an arithmetical scale. There is, therefore, an inevitable "struggle for existence."

Darwin ignored the economic message, paradoxically one that change is impossible, and drew analogically to forge his own biological message: that change is inevitable and ongoing! He recognized that the struggle for existence holds universally in the wild and that it can and does, as it were, fuel a natural equivalent to artificial selection. Not all organisms that are born survive and (more importantly) reproduce. Those that are successful in the struggle will tend to be so, because they have features not possessed by the unsuccessful. Thus there will be a constant selecting or winnowing, with only the successful passing on features to future generations. Supposing a continual supply of new variations and that these variations are in fact heritable, given sufficient time, one will get full-blown change: what Darwin called "descent with modification" and we call "evolution."

Darwin and religion

At once, a question intrudes. Given that religion provided such a barrier to evolutionism for everyone else, why should it have been no barrier to Darwin? Remember, this was a young man who ten years previously had intended to be a parson, no less. My own feeling is that the question is slightly misleading, even though Darwin scholars have wrestled with it for the past hundred years. At least, I think the question is misleading unless one supposes, as both catastrophist and uniformitarian supposed, that religion and evolution pose a mutually exclusive either/or: if one believes in evolution, one cannot believe in religion. There was no barrier posed by religion for Darwin, because ultimately Darwin did not see religion and evolution in conflict! Rather, at the time of becoming an evolutionist and indeed right through the period until after the writing of the *Origin,* Darwin was quite happy to hold simultaneously to his scientific beliefs and to some rather lukewarm kind of belief in a creator.

Darwin was obviously no traditional Christian, believing in an immanent God who intervenes constantly in His creation. Most accurately, perhaps, Darwin is characterized as one who held to some kind of "deistic" belief in a God who works at a distance through unbroken law: having set the world in motion, God now sits back and does nothing. Unlike Lyell however, for Darwin all of God's laws are of the same logical type: there are no special directed laws.

This is not to say that Darwin was insensitive to the religious objections to evolutionism, urged by his contemporaries. In fact, in his search for an adequate evolutionary mechanism, he had constantly before him the need to find a natural cause for the design-like appearance of the organic world. After all, he was a student of the catastrophists and a follower of Lyell. Moreover, there is no doubt that in natural selection Darwin thought that he had such a design-creating mechanism: something that could explain organic "adaptations" like the hand and the eye.

Whether or not God was ultimately at the back of everything, blind law could indeed cause integrated functioning, simply because those with certain advantageous characteristics were those that survived and reproduced. Instead of a God consciously planning and making an eye along the lines of a telescope maker, one gets a gradual growth of the eye, because those naturally occurring variations that work best, which are in fact those variations most along an eye-like path, are those and only those that are kept in living circulation and existence. Design-like phenomena therefore come into being, although clearly for Darwin adaptation was not some objective phenomenon, but simply that one that worked.

One point that is worth making now because its clear statement will prove so useful later is that for Darwin the variations on which selection was to work — the "raw stuff" of evolution — are always "random," in the sense that they are not specially directed toward the most useful form for their possessor. Variations come each and every way, and evolution is a function of selection picking out just those variations that so happen to work best. For Darwin, to think in terms of directed variation was simply to plunge right back into the morass in which Lyell was trapped. Darwin always thought that the key variations would normally be small, perhaps virtually imperceptible. For a while, after hitting on the concept of natural selection, he toyed with the idea that large variations, "saltations," might also be involved sometimes, but he soon dropped the idea. Saltations typically involve things like dwarfism, and Darwin could not see how a large variation could ever lead to integrated functioning at one jump. Darwin saw saltations as deleterious, not useful.

Even more than design, we know that the status of man was seen as a bar to evolutionism. Here, also, Darwin broke with his fellows in seeing no insurmountable objections. In fact, Darwin's first musings on selection as an evolutionary mechanism involve man! Probably there were many reasons for Darwin's feelings, or, as his contemporaries would have said, lack of feelings. Looking close to home we find suggestive hints. Robert Darwin was not the only member of the Darwin family to feel little enthusiasm for full-blooded religious belief. Charles's brother Erasmus had no time whatsoever for orthodox Christianity, and one suspects that some of this rubbed off on Darwin. One suspects also that the quasi-religious ideas of Erasmus's friend Carlyle may have had their effect on Darwin. At the time Darwin knew him, Carlyle was preaching his doctrine of natural supernaturalism, which sees everything as miraculous, including the workings of unbroken law.

Then again, influencing his position on man, Darwin had had first-hand experience of the most primitive and wretched of all human societies: the pathetic savages living at the tip of South America, the Tierra del Fuegans. (See Fig. 1.16.) They undoubtedly made Darwin somewhat cautious, not to

Fig. 1.16
A Tierra del Fuegan, drawn by the artist on *H.M.S. Beagle.*

say cynical, about suggestions that humans are so very different from the monkeys. And most importantly, considering his attitude towards his own species, one suspects that Darwin was just one of those people who really does not care too much about religion. Darwin had little taste for theological speculation; he just wanted to get on with his science.

Dare one even suggest that five years of being cooped up on board *HMS Beagle* with Robert Fitzroy, a Bible-thumping religious fanatic if ever there was one, would have been enough to turn anyone away from the Christian God?

Darwin waits

Be all this as it may, Darwin knew full well that his fellow scientists took religion very seriously indeed. By the early 1840s, he had written up a detailed treatment of his position on evolutionism (Darwin and Wallace, 1958). But, thanks to his geology, Darwin was now really starting to make his mark in the scientific community. He had neither the desire nor the confidence to face the scorn from those whom he admired that would inevitably be directed towards any evolutionary speculator. Therefore, instead of publishing, Darwin let himself get sidetracked — if that is the appropriate metaphor for something that took ten years and produced four volumes — into a detailed study of barnacles (Darwin, 1851a,b; 1854a,b). Only when this was completed did he return to evolutionary work, starting to prepare a massive volume and putting together all aspects of his theory in great detail. It was this project that was disturbed by the arrival of Wallace's manuscript, and, as we saw, it was shelved as Darwin turned to write a brief "sketch" (!) of his position, that which appeared in late 1859 as the *Origin of Species*.

What did Darwin produce after all those long years of brooding? Let us see.

Chapter 2
"On the Origin of Species"

Opinions on the merits of the *Origin* differed when it first appeared, and to today we still find conflicting views on its value, its structure, and even its readability. My own opinion is on the side of the angels, although perhaps under the circumstances I should say, "on the side of the apes." Even though in many places time has passed Darwin by, I believe the *Origin,* yesterday and today, stands as a skillfully constructed work of genius.

But, I am sure that the reader is even less interested than I am in my singing the praises of Darwin and his work, so let me get right on with the task of exposition and analysis. In this chapter, my primary concern is with analyzing Darwin's theory in its own terms and its own period. I want to dig beneath the surface and see what it was that Darwin was trying to do in the *Origin,* and how far he was judged successful by his contemporaries — most particularly, how far he was judged successful by those whose approbation Darwin valued, his fellow scientists. Before completing the chapter, however, I shall try to judge Darwin's achievements from the perspective of our own day and age.

Artificial selection

The *Origin* begins by introducing the reader to the world of the animal and plant breeder — the world that had played so crucial a role in Darwin's discovery twenty years previously. Now asking publicly the question that hitherto he had asked privately, Darwin inquired how it could be that the breeder might effect such great changes in his charges in so short a time: pigeons are altered out of all recognition, food stuffs like cabbages are transformed, sheep and cattle are made far more profitable from everyone's perspective? (See Fig. 2.1.) The answer comes through loud and clear: the secret to change in the farm yard, in the market garden, in the world of the pigeon fancier, is selective breeding. The best and most desirable are those chosen to parent the next crop. There is no magic involved — just systematic principles applied to agriculture and other domains where animals and plants are involved. "The key is man's power of accumulative selection: nature gives successive variations; man adds them up in certain directions useful to him. In this sense he may be said to make for himself useful breeds" (Darwin, 1859, p. 30).

But can we hope for anything analogous in nature? Only if we have abundant evidence that in nature, as on the farm or in the breeder's coop, we have a ready supply of variation. Selection requires plenty of differences between

Fig. 2.1
Bald head and pouter pigeons: clear evidence of the power of artificial selection.

organisms: there can be no choice without alternatives. Darwin however was happy to be able to note that all the evidence we have points to the unmistakable conclusion that whenever we have a group of organisms in the wild, as in captivity, there are lots of differences between individual members — just what a natural equivalent to artificial selection would require.

Natural selection

Darwin was now ready to present the crucial arguments for his major mechanism of evolutionary change. First he introduced and argued for a universal struggle for existence.

A struggle for existence inevitably follows from the high rate at which all organic beings tend to increase. Every being, which during its natural lifetime produces several eggs or seeds, must suffer destruction ... otherwise, on the principle of geometrical increase, its numbers would quickly become so inordinately great that no country could support the product. Hence, as more individuals are produced than can possibly survive, there must in every case be a struggle for existence .... It is the doctrine of Malthus applied with manifold force to the whole animal and vegetable kingdoms .... Although some species may be now increasing, more or less rapidly, in numbers, all cannot do so, for the world would not hold them (Darwin, 1859, pp. 63–64).

Next, taking this struggle, and the existence of natural variation, he moved straight on to natural selection.

How will the struggle for existence ... act in regard to variation? ... Let it be borne in mind in what an endless number of strange peculiarities our domestic productions, and, in a lesser degree, those under nature, vary; and how strong the hereditary tendency is. ... Can it, then, be thought improbable, seeing that variations useful to man have undoubtedly occurred, that other variations useful in some way to each being in the great and complex battle of life, should sometimes occur in the course of thousands of generations? If such do occur, can we doubt (remembering that many more individuals are born than can possibly survive) that individuals having any advantage, however slight, over others, would have the best chance of surviving and of procreating their kind? On the other hand, we may feel sure that any variation in the least degree injurious would be rigidly destroyed. This preservation of favourable variations and the rejection of injurious variations, I call Natural Selection (Darwin, 1859, pp. 80–81).

Although Darwin always regarded natural selection as his primary mechanism of evolutionary change, it was never his sole mechanism. He was ever a Lamarckian in the sense of believing in the inheritance of acquired characteristics. Also, Darwin posited that there is a second kind of selection. Natural selection involves a straight struggle for existence and reproduction: the lion kills the antelope, the weed chokes out the flower. However, Darwin believed that sometimes within the same breeding group, the same "species," one gets a struggle for mates between members of the same sex.

Darwin identified two forms of this selection, which he called "sexual selection." The first form is triggered when the males of a group fight for the females ("male combat"), and the second occurs when females choose the most attractive males ("female choice"). Thus, we get the evolution of the weapons of intraspecific combat, like those of the male salmon, and the evolution of such fantastical features of mate attraction, as the gorgeous tail of the peacock. (See Fig. 2.2.) It seems highly probable that it was Darwin's analogy from artificial selection that led him to sexual selection. As Darwin himself noted, when breeders select for pleasure, they want either fighting attributes (as in the cock or the bulldog) or beautiful attributes (as in the pigeon or peacock). These two wants are reflected right into the two kinds of sexual selection.

With his main mechanism of evolutionary change introduced and argued for, Darwin gave some examples to show how natural selection would in fact work. He invited the reader to consider the case of a wolf, always pursuing a fleet prey, like a deer for instance. Supposing that food supplies at certain times of the year would be low, "I can under such circumstances see no reason to doubt that the swiftest and slimmest wolves would have the best chance of surviving, and so be preserved or selected" (Darwin, 1859, p. 90). Moreover, Darwin suggested how new groups might be formed: "the wolves inhabiting a mountainous district, and those frequenting the lowlands, would naturally be forced to hunt different prey; and from the continued preservation of the individuals best fitted for the two sites, two varieties might slowly be formed" (Darwin, 1859, p. 91).

Fig. 2.2
Effect of sexual selection. (This picture is taken from Darwin's *Descent of Man.*)

The most fundamental group in nature is the aforementioned "species," examples of which are the common house sparrow *(Passer domesticus)*, the even more common house fly *(Musca domestica),* and, of course, we humans *(Homo sapiens).* The mark of a species is that its members can breed with each other, but with no other organism: there are "reproductive barriers" between species. A horse can breed with a horse but not with a cow. (See Fig. 2.3.) Now, in the formation of a new species, "speciation," the question of the building up of reproductive barriers might not arise. If one species simply evolves into another species ("phyletic evolution") no new barriers are needed. More troublesome is a case like the wolf example, where one gets new species when an old one splits into two. Here one does get barriers. In such a case of speciation as this, could it occur if the two new populations were not separated geographically, or does there always have to be such spatial isolation? In today's terminology, could one have "sympatric" speciation, or does it always have to be "allopatric?"

The Linnaean System

All organisms are classified according to a system inaugurated by the eighteenth-century Swedish taxonomist, Carolus Linnaeus. The key to the system is a series of nested sets ("taxa"), coming at different levels ("categories"), with any particular organism being successively included in a more-comprehensive taxon at an ever-higher category level. There are many different category levels, but by convention all organisms must at a minimum belong to taxa at seven specified levels:

```
Kingdom
        Phylum
                Class
                    Order
                        Family
                            Genus
                                Species
```

This sequence, from top to bottom, indicates the decreasing scope of the various levels. Thus, for instance, your individual pet wolf, Rex, would be classified as follows:

Kingdom	Animalia
Phylum	Chordata
Class	Mammalia
Order	Carnivora
Family	Canidae
Genus	*Canis*
Species	*Canis lupus*

Note that the specific name includes the generic name, which names are italicized. Thus, one says that Rex belongs to *Canis lupus*. Similarly, you and I are members of *Homo sapiens*.

Other categories fit between the seven specified levels, and are used for more precise classification. The one common category below the species is the subspecies, and it is customary to add a subspecific name onto the generic and specific names. The South American fruit-fly *Drosophila willistoni,* for instance, is divided into two subspecies, *Drosophila willistoni willistoni* and *D. w. quechua* (after the first mention, where there is no ambiguity, one uses just initials).

Fig. 2.3
The Linnaean System.

To be honest, Darwin wrestled somewhat with this whole question. After some hesitation, he decided that perhaps one could sometimes have sympatric speciation, although his stand was not really that far from someone believing that speciation is always allopatric. Even in those cases where one may not have spatial isolation, Darwin did rather suppose ecological isolation: "haunting different stations" or "breeding at slightly different seasons" (Darwin, 1859, p. 103).

Also, in the context of his direct discussion of natural selection, Darwin introduced what was to become a famous metaphor, likening the course of evolutionary history to a "tree of life." (See Fig. 2.4.) Why should one get all the divergence and splitting that one sees in evolution? Darwin invoked what

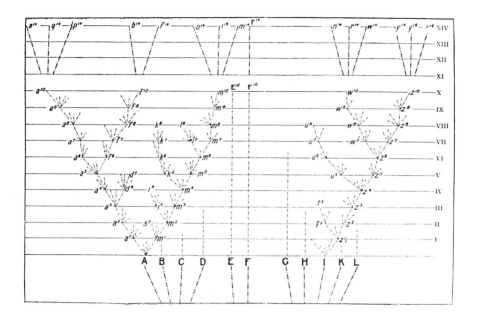

Fig. 2.4
Darwin's diagram of descent (time moves upward). From the *Origin of Species*.

he called his "principle of divergence": "the more diversified the descendants from any one species become in structure, constitution, and habits, by so much will they be better enabled to seize on many and widely diversified places in the polity of nature, and so be enabled to increase in numbers" (Darwin, 1859, p. 112). In short, given the varied nature of the world — in large part a function of the organisms that already exist — there can be strong selective pressure towards the production of features enabling one to exploit conditions that are barred to other organisms. Hence we get divergence.

But all of this discussion of selection rested on some unproven assumptions. Darwin really needed to show that the variations on which selection works are heritable, and that one can confidently expect that new supplies will be inexhaustible. If these facts are not true, evolution will grind to a rapid halt, if indeed it can start at all. However, although Darwin was able to give circumstantial evidence supporting the facts, essentially his case was not strong. As he himself admitted, on this subject "our ignorance . . . is profound" (Darwin, 1859, p. 167). We shall learn that Darwin was not the only one who recognized that at this point there was a major gap in his theory.

Difficulties and applications

Gap or not, there was still much work to be done. After his rather sparse remarks about heredity came a discussion of *Difficulties on Theory*. One problem that Darwin tackled here was that of the natural theologian's paradigm: the eye. Could such an intricate organ really have come about through a law-bound process of evolution? Was it even possible that we might start with a rudimentary eye and then work up to the complex eyes we find today in higher organisms? Darwin met this challenge head-on. Obviously he could not go back in time and show the eye evolving, but he could and did defuse the thrust of the criticism by showing that today among living organisms, among the Articulata specifically, there exists a scale going all the way from rudimentary to complex eyes. This is not an evolutionary scale, but it does show that such an evolutionary scale is organically possible. In any case, pointing to the improbability that the eye is a special creation of God: "The correction for the aberration of light is said, on high authority, not to be perfect" (Darwin, 1859, p. 202).

Already, in this discussion, Darwin had moved from direct concern with his evolutionary mechanism, to the attempt to show how evolution in general and selection in particular could be applied to many diverse areas of the biological world, explaining and illuminating. Continuing with this effort, we find Darwin looking next at problems to do with *Instinct*. Could it be that animals like the bee, which show such fine-honed instinctive behaviors when they build their nests and the like, are simply the product of natural selection working on undirected variation? Pointing out that behavioral characteristics seem no different in type from any other characteristics, Darwin argued that the evolutionary development of sophisticated instincts is indeed possible. We find variation and the scope for selection in behavior, no less than we do in other organic characteristics.

Darwin also looked at the problem of the evolution of sterile castes of insects, trying to show that selection could have formed these. Could sterility really benefit an organism in the struggle for existence? I shall have more to say in later chapters about instinct and behavior and about Darwin's hypotheses on the subjects. One point that Darwin noted is worth repeating: if Lamarckism is the only effective evolutionary mechanism, it is difficult to see how sterile castes might evolve. An organism that has developed the inability to reproduce has trouble passing on such a characteristic to its offspring.

A discussion of *Hybridism* followed, as Darwin considered the types and degrees of sterility that we find existing between organisms in nature. One thing that I shall pass over without comment here, for it will receive discussion later, is the fact that Darwin thought such sterility to be a by-product of natural selection, brought about by other characteristics that selection formed and perfected. Natural selection does not work on sterility directly. "I hope, however, to be able to show that sterility is not a specially acquired or endowed quality, but is incidental on other acquired differences" (Darwin, 1859, p. 264).

Geology was the next area that Darwin tackled, trying to bring it beneath the evolutionary umbrella. First there was the question of time. For evolution, particularly for an evolution through the relatively slow process of natural selection, Darwin needed an earth-span of great size. Here, Darwin got into some rather Lyellian arguments about the supposed rate in which the sea might be expected to wear down cliffs, trying to work toward absolute estimates of how old the earth really is. To be perfectly frank, to a certain extent, Darwin's calculations remind us of the popular engineer's way of finding a solution: one thinks of a number, doubles it, and then takes half to get the answer. At least, Darwin produced some comfortably large figures for time-spans, although one is not that sure how firm the backing for them really is! He estimated that at least 300 million years have elapsed since the mammals became common. (As we shall learn, today it is believed the "Age of Mammals" began only about 60 million years ago; although mammals themselves go back 200 million years.)

This task out of the way, Darwin moved on to direct analysis of the fossil record itself. Lamarck's evolutionary theory (i.e., the real theory) supposes that there is a full-blooded progression, right up from the most primitive forms to man. However, as we know, Lamarck failed to make the connection between this progression and the fossil record. Darwin certainly did not suppose such an absolute progression as Lamarck supposed — anything but. Natural selection is opportunistic, taking advantage of the situation, with no "ultimate" goal. Nevertheless, Darwin allowed that one might expect to see some vague progress overall, in the fossil record specifically, as many organic forms get more sophisticated in the organic struggle for life. After all, when the simple options are exhausted, and this will happen first, one necessarily needs more complex organic "technology."

And, Darwin was happy to point out that such an expectation of a progress-like rise is apparently not entirely without foundation: "The inhabitants of each successive period in the world's history have beaten their predecessors in the race for life, and are, in so far, higher in the scale of nature; and this may account for that vague yet ill-defined sentiment, felt by many paleontologists, that organisation on the whole has progressed" (Darwin, 1859, p. 345; see Fig. 2.5).

Over and above the general pattern, there were other fossil facts that Darwin thought fit in rather nicely with his theory. For instance, the further down the strata a fossil is, the more it tends to combine features of widely different extant forms. One needs no special abilities to see the evolutionary import of this. Again, in support of his position, Darwin noted that we tend to get similar fossils in succeeding strata, but not in very much separated strata. This all clearly fits in with a key point in Darwinian evolutionism, namely that once an organism has gone extinct, it can never return. There is no possibility of a second chance, given so undirected a phenomenon as natural selection. As we saw, for Lamarck, it is only a matter of time before the dodo returns.

Nevertheless, two facts in the fossil record really gave Darwin trouble. There are many, many gaps between succeeding forms, which supposedly evolved from one to the other. And, at the beginning of the Silurian, part of

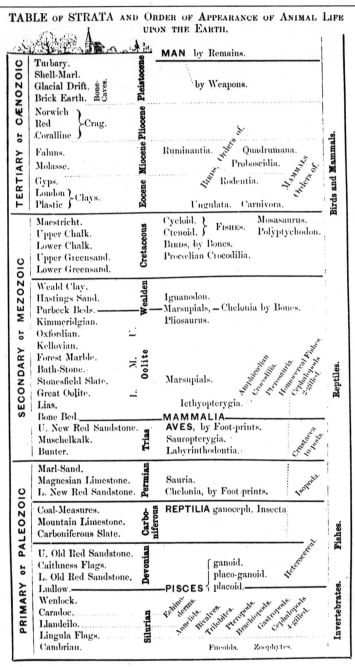

Fig. 2.5

The animal fossil record, as known at the time of the *Origin*. As explained in the text, by this time all serious scientists, including non-evolutionists, realized that the history of life was not a single progressive rise, but involved much branching. Table from Richard Owen's, *Paleontology,* 1861.

what we now would call the Cambrian, life appeared full-blown — the earliest fossils included very sophisticated forms. Why were there gaps? Why did life appear suddenly? All that Darwin could do was to appeal to imperfections in the fossil record. The difficulties in fossilization are so great that the wonder is that we do have what we do have, not that we do not have what we do not have! In any case, pre-Silurian organisms might well have flourished where oceans now are and perhaps are today metamorphized by the great weight of water above them. Candidly, however, Darwin conceded that: "The case at present must remain inexplicable; and may be truly urged as a valid argument against the views here entertained" (Darwin, 1859, p. 314).

Most interesting and revealing were Darwin's views on the relationship between the fossil record, embryology, and evolution. They are a lot more subtle than many have thought, and they show more clearly than anything, I think, the extent to which Darwin was abreast of the modern science of his day. Darwin thought that fossil organisms frequently resemble the embryos of extant (i.e., living) organisms, even though the forms of the adult extant organisms are widely different. Given that Darwin believed in some sort of vague fossil progression, one might be forgiven therefore for thinking that Darwin subscribed to some form of the "biogenetic law." This law, or "law," was later to be made very popular by the German evolutionist Ernst Haeckel, under the slogan "ontogeny recapitulates phylogeny": the belief that in the development of an individual one sees the embryo go through all the forms of the ancestors. Thus, both in the fossil record and in embryological development one sees the sequence: fish, frog, mammal, man.

Since this "law" is generally discredited today, Darwin seems mistaken. In fact, however, Darwin, like other knowledgeable scientists in the mid-nineteenth century, followed the great German embryologist Ernst von Baer in his views about individual development. Hence, Darwin did not lock himself into accepting some proto-version of the biogenetic law. von Baer argued that, in development, organisms diverge from the same basic pattern or ground plan. This is why one cannot distinguish the embryos of dog and man. In von Baer's scheme there is however no fixed pattern of development, with man first going through the earlier doggy forms. Once embryos of different species develop beyond the ground plan, any parallelism of development is coincidental on the restraints of growth, not necessary.

Darwin's position, reflecting and conforming with von Baer's views on embryology, was simply that ancestral forms probably developed less than modern forms do. Hence ancestral adults are like ancestral embryos, which — coming from the same ground plan — tend in turn to be the same as today's embryos. In other words, Darwin thought the true identity was between ancestral embryos and extant embryos, not, as the recapitulationist thought, between ancestral adults and extant embryos. Shortly it was to be explained precisely why Darwin believed that von Baer's views are true, and why ancestral forms might have less development than modern forms.

More applications

After some of the trials of geology, especially those caused by the age of the Earth and the troublesome fossil record, Darwin turned with some relief to the *Geographical Distribution* of organisms, what today is often referred to as "biogeography." This subject was a really strong card that Darwin had to play. He dwelt at length — at loving length — on all those facts that seem so anomalous if one turns one's back on evolution. For instance, given an all-wise God, just why is it that different forms appear in similar climates, whereas the same forms appear in different climates? It is all pointless without evolution. Additionally, Darwin looked in detail at natural methods of transportation around the globe — sea currents, rivers, winds, and the like — and he was happy to be able to conclude that such phenomena are all one needs for a Darwin-style theory!

And, as one might have expected, given what it was that turned Darwin himself into an evolutionist, he made much of the organisms on archipelagos: "We can clearly see why all the inhabitants of an archipelago, though specifically distinct on the several islets, should be closely related to each other, and likewise be related, but less closely, to those of the nearest continent or other source whence immigrants were probably derived" (Darwin, 1859, p. 409).

Moving along briskly, Darwin gathered more and more subjects into the evolutionary fold. One such subject is *Classification.*

All the foregoing rules and aids and difficulties in classification are explained, if I do not greatly deceive myself, on the view that the natural system is founded on descent with modification; that the characters which naturalists consider as showing true affinity between any two or more species, are those which have been inherited from a common parent, and, in so far, all true classification is genealogical; that community of descent is the hidden bond which naturalists have been unconsciously seeking, and not some unknown plan of creation, or the enunciation of general propositions, and the mere putting together and separating objects more or less alike (Darwin, 1859, p. 420).

Darwin was happy to note that even the staunchest critics of evolution use the very classificatory principles that are inexplicable without an evolutionary interpretation. For instance, all competent systematists ignore superficial similarities between whales and fish, concentrating rather on features that have little or no adaptive value. The reason why this makes sense is that the hidden features represent descent (or, in the whale/fish case, nondescent) from common ancestors, whereas the superficial similarities represent similar ways that natural selection has fitted the otherwise unrelated fish and whale for a watery existence. There are no real bonds — only similarities — between them. Likewise, given his views on embryology and the fossil record, Darwin was happy to note that embryos are considered more crucial in classification than adults are.

Another area tackled by Darwin is *Morphology*. It had become more and more obvious by the mid century that the isomorphisms between different organisms, what we now call "homologies," are incredibly pervasive, and have no direct adaptive advantage. For instance, why should the bones of man, bat, porpoise, and mole have the same nature and order? (See Fig. 2.6.) Such similarities help no one. Supporters of the argument from design were,

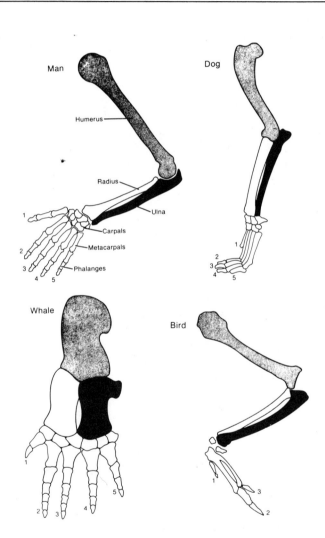

Fig. 2.6
Homology between the forelimbs of several vertebrates. Numbers refer to digits. (Adapted with permission from Dobzhansky *et al*, (1977).)

therefore, compelled to fall back on suppositions that God had all sorts of subsidiary creative intentions, like the achievement of symmetry and order and harmony. Expectedly, such ad hoc suggestions convinced virtually no one. However, for an evolutionist of Darwin's ilk, the existence of homologies is expected and forms a bright thread in the evolutionary fabric. Adaptively valueless isomorphisms point to the fact that widely different organisms are descended from common ancestors. Natural selection has taken the ancestral form, molding it to different ends.

Entering the home stretch, we encounter Darwin's direct treatment of *Embryology*. Why should man and dog have similar embryos? (See Fig. 2.7.)

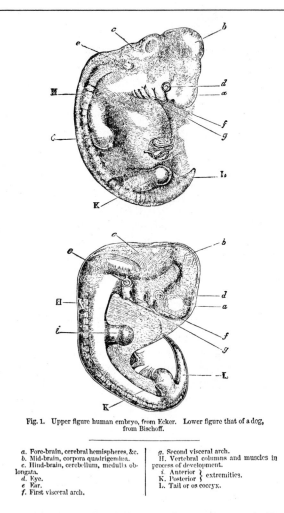

Fig. 1.   Upper figure human embryo, from Ecker.   Lower figure that of a dog, from Bischoff.

a. Fore-brain, cerebral hemispheres, &c.	*g*. Second visceral arch.
b. Mid-brain, corpora quadrigemina.	H. Vertebral columns and muscles in
c. Hind-brain, cerebellum, medulla ob-	process of development.
longata.	*i*. Anterior } extremities.
d. Eye.	K. Posterior } extremities.
e Ear.	L. Tail or os coccyx.
f. First visceral arch.	

Fig. 2.7

Comparison of human and canine embryos. Why are they so similar if man and dog have not descended from a joint ancestor? (This picture is taken from Darwin's *Descent of Man*.)

The answer lies obviously in common ancestry, but why the similarity? Darwin argued that the causal reason lies in the fact that, originally in our ancestors, embryo and adult were more or less the same. (Remember the paleontological discussion.) Then, over the course of time, given all of the competing descendents, selective pressures tore the adult forms apart. But, protected in the womb, the selective pressures on embryos of all kinds are the same. Since presumably the embryo is well adapted to its situation, there has been no reason for an evolutionary divergence of what, in the adult, becomes widely different. In other words, through selection working at different times and in different ways on an organism's development, we get connections between embryos of different species, connections between embryos and ancestors, but differences in extant adults.

Worth noting is the fact that here, as throughout the *Origin*, Darwin relied heavily for illustration and support on the analogy from the domestic world. When, as is usual, breeders select only on the basis of adult forms, one expects and finds that there are strong similarities between the juveniles, even though the adults are widely different. Varieties of horses, dogs, and pigeons, which have very different adult forms, typically have very similar juvenile forms.

The last topic to be considered and explained was that of *Rudimentary Organs.* Why should male mammals have nipples? Why should snakes have rudimentary limbs? Why should flightless insects have wings? Darwin turned scornfully on usual explanations — that such organs exist for "the sake of symmetry" — pointing out that they would get short shrift in the physical sciences. "Would it be thought sufficient to say that because planets revolve in elliptic courses round the sun, satellites follow the same course round the planets, for the sake of symmetry, and to complete the scheme of nature?" (Darwin, 1859, p. 453).

Darwin himself had no doubt as to the real status of such organs: they are the flotsam and jetsam of evolution. They are traces of the evolutionary process, probably representing things once needed but now without value, or things that were somehow brought in as a factor of other, more important, changes. Interestingly, although Darwin thought that selection might have reduced rudimentary organs to their present pathetic size, he inclined to the view that a Lamarckian disuse probably was the most important factor in bringing them to the low state that they are now in.

Bringing the *Origin* to a close, Darwin had but one final thing to do. Obviously the question of man's status was going to be that which would, most dramatically, lift the theory of evolution through natural selection from the relative quiet of the laboratory and the scientific colloquium right into the glare of the public arena. But, cautious as always, Darwin himself had no desire to rush head-long into the bright lights of controversy. He wanted his general views on evolution to get as full a hearing as possible at first. There would be time enough later to turn to *Homo sapiens.* Consequently, throughout the *Origin,* Darwin was careful not to inflame matters by discussing our own species. Nevertheless, as we do know, Darwin believed that man was produced by evolution, by natural selection even, and he had no wish dishonorably to conceal his opinion. Hence, in what must be a classic understatement of all time, Darwin simply concluded his book by saying that in the future, "light will be thrown on the origin of man and his history" (Darwin, 1859, p. 488), and then he left matters at that.

Later we shall see how true Darwin's prediction has become. Let us turn now to critical evaluation of the theory of the *Origin*.

Darwin's theory examined: Methodological background

We want to look at Darwin's theory. Obviously we cannot just plunge in naked, as it were. We have to have some sort of aid to act as our thread of Ariadne, guiding us through his arguments. Let us take our clue from Darwin's professionalism — from the fact that Darwin knew the best scientists of his day, and that he wanted very much himself to produce good quality science. Although Darwin's theory of evolution through natural selection would undoubtedly offend, its author wanted to make very sure that, judged as science, the theory would be — and would be seen to be — as good as possible. This means that, in analyzing Darwin's theory, we should see what the leading authorities of the period were saying about the true nature of science. What was it that his elders would tell a bright young novice, about the proper form of science?

In fact, answering this question almost swamps us in an embarrassment of riches. In the 1830s, in Britain — at the very time that Darwin was coming to scientific consciousness and realizing that the organic origins problem was there to be solved — there was much detailed and animated discussion about the true nature of science. Although it never concerned Darwin himself directly, a major reason for such inquiry was an intense controversy about the nature of light: if light does indeed go in waves, what kind of evidence would count as definitive in support of this fact?

Speaking generally, everyone agreed that good science had to be "Newtonian," that is to say, good science had in some sense to conform and perform along the lines prescribed and exemplified by the greatest of all English scientists, Isaac Newton. There was however disagreement about the true essence of Newtonianism. It was agreed that Newton's great gravitational theory was, what we today call, "axiomatic": that is to say, Newtonian theory started with certain universal laws of nature as basic assumptions or axioms, and thence showed how other laws followed deductively. In particular, Newton's theory started with the inverse square law of attraction and the laws of motion, and then from these as premises such laws as those of Galileo and Kepler could be deductively inferred.

But, given this general framework, there was still room for dispute over the nature of "cause." Newton's theory was obviously causal. In other words, it showed not merely what things happened, but why these things happened: planets go in ellipses and cannon balls go in parabolas, because of the force of gravitational attraction. But, what was the true nature of this force, in the sense that one knew one had a cause? More generally, what was the mark in a scientific theory that one had actually grasped on to such a cause?

One school of thought, the leading exponent of which was the great astronomer John F. W. Herschel, argued that one knew that one had such a cause (a "true cause" or "*vera causa*") when one could either see a causal force in action or, failing that, could argue analogically from such seen causes to unknown causes: "If the analogy of two phenomena be very close and striking, while, at the same time, the cause of one is very obvious, it becomes scarcely possible to refuse to admit the action of an analogous cause in the other, though not so obvious in itself" (Herschel, 1831, p. 149). This position is like that of a detective attempting to explain a murder who refuses to arrest a suspect unless he has an eyewitness report of the crime, or at least until he has an eyewitness report of the suspect committing a similar crime.

Fig. 2.8
John F. W. Herschel
(1792–1871).

Other commentators on science, most particularly the historian, philosopher, and general man of science William Whewell, argued that one knows one has a true cause when and only when all the indirect evidence points to the cause, and conversely when the cause manages to unite within one theory many varied pieces of information drawn from different areas. In the Newtonian case we know we have a true cause because gravity unites motions here on earth, the movements of the moon and planets, the tides, and much, much more (Whewell, 1837, 1840).

This insistence on what Whewell called a "consilience of inductions," reminds us of the detective who is prepared to make an arrest on grounds of circumstantial evidence. Who killed Lord Rake? His Lordship was stabbed with an oriental knife and it turns out that the butler spent many years in the Far East. His Lordship was killed efficiently by a left-handed man. The butler was in the commandos and is left-handed. His Lordship was a noted philanderer, and the butler's daughter was one of his conquests. And so forth. One has no direct, eyewitness evidence, but, by presuming the butler's guilt, one can explain a wide range of disparate pieces of information. Without such a presumption, nothing connects. (See Figs. 2.8 and 2.9.)

Fig. 2.9
William Whewell
(1794–1866).

Now, keeping these various claims about the true nature of science firmly in mind, we are ready to begin our analysis. Guided by comments that Darwin himself made about the structure of his theory, it would seem that in the *Origin* we can properly locate three main elements: the artificial selection analogy; the derivation of natural selection; and the application of the mechanism to the various sub-areas of biology. Let us take these elements in turn. (See Fig. 2.10.)

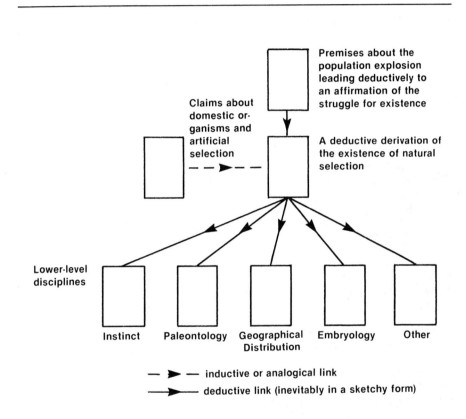

Fig. 2.10
The three key structural elements of Darwin's theory: (1) Herschel's *vera causa,* from artificial selection; (2) the deductive core, leading to natural selection; (3) Whewell's *vera causa,* unifying the lower-level disciplines beneath natural selection. The diagram simplifies Darwin's theory: for instance, all the subsidiary mechanisms are ignored, as are some subsidiary disciplines. Also the exact links between the core and the rest of the theory were to be questioned.

Darwin's theory examined: The analogy

I have already hinted at one of the most interesting features of the artificial selection analogy. Darwin excepted, everyone who referred to the
domestic world before the *Origin* did so to *disprove* evolution! When Lyell
argued against Lamarck, as he did at length in his Principles, he invoked the
world of the farm yard to show that evolution could not occur: one gets
limited change and it is not permanent. Even more paradoxically, when
Wallace wrote up his evolutionary ideas (in the paper he sent to Darwin), one
of the things he argued most strenuously was that one should see no analogy
between domestication and nature, and thus the results of breeders have no
relevance to evolution!

Why did Darwin turn things on their head? Possibly he did as he did
because the artificial selection analogy was that which led him to natural selection, and consequently for heuristic reasons Darwin wanted to share with the
reader his own path of discovery. Another reason for Darwin's move is
perhaps that he, unlike Lyell and Wallace and all the other scientists, knew a
great deal about the realities of animal and plant breeding. The Darwin family,
including Charles, were pigeon fanciers; and had themselves actually bred
birds for show. Darwin grew up in the heart of rural England, where
agricultural innovations were at their peak; and his uncle and father-in-law
Josiah Wedgewood (Junior) was a leading sheep breeder. Darwin therefore
was aware of the extent and permanence possible in the domestic world
(Meteyard, 1871).

But I am sure that there is more to the story than this. In the *Origin* the
analogy between the domestic world and the wild world, between artificial
selection and natural selection, is not introduced hesitantly as something that
might in fact be legitimate but that would certainly be controversial. It is
flaunted! Why? I am convinced that the major reason for its prominence lies
in Darwin's reading of the above-mentioned popular scientific methodologies
of the day: what the leading theoreticians of science were saying that good
science *should* be like. Most particularly, we know from Darwin's own
Autobiography that, at Cambridge, the reading of Herschel's major work on
the nature of science in 1831 was a key inspiration and factor in Darwin's am-
bition to take up a life of science. Pertinent to our inquiry, my suggestion is
that against such an overall Herschellian methodological background, Darwin's enthusiasm for the world of the breeder and his touting of it in the *Origin*
becomes obvious.

Quite simply, in artificial selection Darwin had an *analogy* for his main
causal force of natural selection: just what theorists like Herschel demanded!
In order to convince the reader that the main putative mechanism of evolution
really existed and was effective — that it was a true cause, a *vera causa* — Darwin looked for eyewitness evidence, direct or analogical, and in the work of
animal and plant breeders he found what he was seeking. Therefore, in the
Origin artificial selection played a very important role. Darwin gambled that
he could convince the reader that artificial selection is much more powerful

than hitherto suspected, and that therefore natural selection ought to be regarded as a true cause. Darwinism is to biology, what Newtonianism is to physics!

Did the gamble come off? I think we have to say, "not entirely." Undoubtedly Darwin persuaded his fellows that the work and successes of breeders are far more significant than most had suspected previously. No longer was it felt that the domestic world provides the definitive counter to any kind of evolutionism. And, one suspects indeed that many were brought much closer to evolutionism by the analogy. On the other hand, many readers saw the analogy as of limited effectiveness only, and they certainly were not (as Darwin rather hoped) converted right away to natural selection as the major evolutionary mechanism. In the opinion of the critics, it is one thing to make bigger and better sheep from smaller and worse sheep. It is quite another thing to turn a sheep into a cow, or as Darwin obviously believed, a fish into a mammal.

Of all people, Thomas Henry Huxley (1825-1895), a man who became Darwin's close friend and most vocal supporter, always had doubts about the overall effectiveness of natural selection, simply because he saw artificial selection as being of but limited effectiveness: even though we may change forms through artificial selection, we do not set up sterility barriers between groups. "[Darwin] *has* shown that selective breeding is a *vera causa* for morphological species; but he has not yet shewn it a *vera causa* for physiological species" (unpublished letter from Huxley to Charles Kingsley). Consequently, in part because of this failure, although Huxley became an ardent evolutionist, he always drew back from natural selection. (See Figs. 2.11 and 2.12.)

Fig. 2.11
Thomas Henry Huxley (1825-1895). Important in his own right as an anatomist, Huxley became one of the chief spokesmen for evolution.

Fig. 2.12
Joseph Dalton Hooker (1817–1911). England's leading botanist in the latter part of the nineteenth century, Hooker was a close personal friend of Darwin, doing much to spread his ideas.

And, this was very much the position of others. Indeed, one suspects that as the years went by, Darwin himself felt rather less enthusiasm for the analogy. He certainly never agreed with Huxley about selection; but, the importance of the domestic world declined somewhat in Darwin's opinion.

Darwin's theory examined: Natural selection

We move now to the second major element in the *Origin:* Darwin's presentation of his chief causal force, natural selection. We have seen that Darwin did not just simply present it cold, as it were. He argued first to the struggle for existence, and then, with this established, he drew on the existence of naturally occurring organic variation to go on to natural selection — the differential success of organisms in the struggle for existence and reproduction, as a function of their distinctively peculiar characteristics.

Again, I think the methodological background throws light on what Darwin did. Although, certainly, nothing is presented with the rigor that would satisfy a formal logician, as the passages quoted earlier make very clear, Darwin obviously intended his arguments to be taken in at least a quasi-formal fashion. He presented universal laws — "Animals have a tendency to reproduce geometrically" and "Food and space supplies are inevitably limited" — and these were supposed in a fairly definitive way to entail that there will be a universal, never-ceasing, struggle for existence. We are told that the struggle "inevitably follows." Similarly, in the derivation of natural selection we get universal premises and something approximating deduction. In other words, in this part of the *Origin* we again have Darwin's idea of the biological equivalent to what goes on in Newtonian physics: he was trying to be axiomatic.

Indeed, one suspects that it was this Newtonian ideal and the search for its manifestation that so excited Darwin on reading Malthus. Many people mentioned the struggle for existence in the 1830s — this was the decade of *Oliver Twist* and of poor law reform, as monstrous new workhouses were built to threaten the poor with the consequences of unrestrained sexual congress. In fact, Lyell mentions and discusses the struggle by name in his *Principles*! However, just encountering isolated references never triggered anything for Darwin. But, going back to the original, Malthus, showed Darwin how the struggle fitted into a formal (or, at least, semiformal) framework, for Malthus presented his ideas in the quasi-rigorous way that Darwin was to follow. Human numbers have a potential to increase at a geometrical rate; human food supplies have a potential to increase (at most) at an arithmetical rate; therefore, since geometric growth outstrips arithmetic growth, there will necessarily be a struggle for existence. In short, Malthus showed Darwin how to be a good Newtonian — at least Malthus showed Darwin what Darwin took to be the path to good Newtonianism.

As with the artificial selection analogy, Darwin had rather mixed success with his readers. Just about everyone agreed with Darwin about the widespread existence of the struggle for existence, and most were quite prepared to go on to accept that natural selection exists and operates. But, it is one thing to accept selection per se, and it is quite another to agree that selection can do everything that Darwin claimed for it. There was much drawing back from selection as an all-powerful evolutionary mechanism, even by those who were turned into evolutionists by the *Origin*. The general feeling was that evolution had to be powered primarily by something else.

Many readers felt that selection working on blind, small variations simply could not be the cause of the wonderful adaptations like the hand or the eye. Therefore, not a few of Darwin's contemporaries, primarily for religious reasons, supposed that the main cause of evolutionary change are instantaneous, God-designed "jumps" from one form to another — as from the fox to the dog. That is, they believed in an evolution powered by "saltations." Paradoxically, Huxley was also in favor of saltations for major evolutionary changes, although the reason why he argued as he did was not because he could not see a way to create design through blind law, but because his insensitivity to religion made him rather unfeeling about the design-like quality of the world in the first place! He saw no tight adaptation; therefore, he saw no need for a mechanism like selection.

Of course, a saltationary "solution" like this, especially one supposing directed variations, was quite unacceptable to Darwin. It was virtually to go back to that from which he was trying to escape. One had therefore an unresolved impass between Darwin and those who agreed with him on selection, and his critics. At the very least, one had to wait until religion started to loosen its grip on the popular imagination. At the scientific level, natural selection was a mechanism that would demand years of patient checking and testing in order to assess its full potential. Whether it could indeed do all that Darwin hoped was certainly not known in Darwin's lifetime; although, interestingly, within a year or two of the publication of the *Origin,* we find biologists using selection as a tool by which to analyze the organic world. (See Fig 2.13.)

ILLUSTRATIONS OF MIMICRY BETWEEN BUTTERFLIES.
(*Reproduced from Plate 55, Trans. Linn. Soc. XXIII. Pt. 3*)
by kind permission of the Linnean Society

1.—*Leptalis Theonoë.*   2.—*Leptalis Theonoë,* var. *Melanoë.*   3.—*Leptalis Theonoë,* var. *Lysinoë.*

1a.—*Ithomia Flora.*   2a.—*Ithomia Onega.*   3a.—*Stalachtis Phædusa.*

Fig. 2.13
Batesian Mimicry: In 1862, Henry Walter Bates made brilliant use of the Darwinian *mechanism* of natural selection. Asking why it is that some species of butterfly (in his illustration, the top row insects) very closely mimic species of butterfly, essentially quite different (the bottom row insects), Bates proved beyond doubt that the answer lies in adaptive advantage brought about by selection. The mimicked insects are highly distasteful to birds; the mimicking insects are not, but are avoided by birds who think that they belong to the distasteful species. Bates showed experimentally that birds learn to avoid distasteful insects, and that the closer the mimic, the less chance there is that the insect will be eaten.

Darwin's theory examined: The application

We come now to the third, final, and by far the largest part of the *Origin:* the application of selection to the various subareas like instinct, geology, and biogeography. It will come as no surprise to the reader to learn that I believe that here, as before, contemporary methodological dictates guided Darwin. Indeed, I expect the reader can guess what I am going to say! I have argued that Darwin adopted a Herschelian strategy when he invoked and developed the artificial selection analogy. I believe that, just as deliberately, he invoked a Whewellian strategy in the final part of the *Origin*! In other words, Darwin covered his options, just as the detective does when, having already obtained eyewitness testimony, he looks nevertheless for a wide range of clues that point indirectly and independently to his suspect.

As everyone who has read the *Origin* remarks, and as even the brief synopsis given in this chapter surely proves, perhaps the most distinctive feature of Darwin's theory is the way in which one is moved from one topic to another, as its author applies evolution in general and selection in particular to the widest range of topics. Outside of Newtonian mechanics, it is hard to think of a better example of the consilience of inductions being manifested. Darwin wanted the reader to see how his causal ideas could throw light right across biology, and conversely how these ideas were supported at the focus through their wide explanatory success.

And, let there be no mistake about the deliberateness of Darwin's intentions. Time and again he told people what he was up to, urged that no theory with so wide a scope could be false, and if anything grew to rely even more on his consilience, as his Herschelian analogy fell under attack. "I must freely confess, the difficulties and objections are terrific; but I cannot believe that a false theory would explain, as it seems to me it does explain, so many classes of facts" (F. Darwin, 1887, I, 455). Moreover, most interestingly, Darwin invoked analogy with the wave theory of light, suggesting that it had the same status as his theory.

Once again turning to Darwin's contemporaries, let us ask how they responded to his line of argumentation. The answer may surprise you a little. Today we all know what controversy the *Origin* caused in religion-impregnated Victorian Britain. Bishops thundered against it on every occasion, book after book was directed against it, and, ever ready with the funny remark, the future Prime Minister, Benjamin Disraeli, declared that he was on the side of the angels, not the apes! (See Fig. 2.14.) *But, in the active scientific community — toward which the "Origin" was directed — virtually overnight, in Britain, nearly everyone became an evolutionist of some kind!*

As early as 1862, that is, within three years of the publication of the *Origin,* active scientists in Britain — particularly those with any interest in biology — had crossed the divide to some form of evolutionism. Taken individually Darwin's claims were impressive. Taken together they were definitive. It simply did not make sense to deny evolution, given homologies, given embryological similarities, given the growing knowledge of the fossil

Fig. 2.14
Cartoon from *Punch,*
10 December, 1864.

record, given vestigial features (rudimentary organs), given the fact and rules of classification, and above all given the nature of organic geographical distribution. Scientist after scientist conceded that an intelligent, sincere God just would not have miraculously created different finches for different islands of the Galapagos. (See Fig. 5.2.)

But, this all said, it must be admitted candidly that this part of the *Origin* did no more to convince most people of the importance of selection than did the earlier parts. People could accept evolution as a cause of the organic world; they could not accept selection as a cause of evolution. And, expectedly, many of the old, anti-Lamarckian, religiously based fears surfaced. People were simply not convinced that natural selection could cause design features, and frankly people did not particularly want to be convinced. Moreover, there was that dreadful question of man. Could he be no more than the result of random variation?

Nevertheless, religion aside, there were also scientific arguments against selection. The fossil record was one of the chief stumbling blocks to whole-hearted acceptance of natural selection. Generally speaking, most people now felt able to endorse an evolutionary interpretation of the record. Note that Darwinian progression, inasmuch as it exists, could never be a single-line progress, from primitive to complex. At most it could be a vague phenomenon, superimposed on a constantly branching tree of life. In 1838, when Darwin first thought of his mechanism of selection, I rather suspect that few paleontologists would have granted Darwin this diffuse pattern. By 1859, professionals realized how complex the record really was, and most accepted just such a picture as that proposed by Darwin. However, the sudden appearance of organisms in the Cambrian, the gaps in the fossil record, and like phenomena made many leery of all of natural selection's pretensions.

And, many other arguments were raised against natural selection, as it supposedly existed and performed in the areas discussed in the third part of the *Origin*. Very troublesome to Darwin, and indeed to all the Darwinians, was a series of arguments about time, spearheaded by the physicists of all people. Fairly obviously, a rather leisurely process like natural selection requires a great deal of time: the Earth must be very old by human if not by cosmological standards. We know that Darwin himself was sensitive to these matters and indeed gave arguments suggesting that the absolute age of the Earth is great. Not surprisingly, given the quality of the arguments, they soon came under heavy fire — people had little difficulty choosing their own numbers, doubling, and halving! — and Darwin quickly retreated into vague, unspecified claims about vast Earth histories.

At this point, William Thomson (later Lord Kelvin) stepped into the fray. Treating the Earth as a cooling body, having taken into account such factors as the incoming heat from the sun, Thomson (1862) was able to show that the Earth really is not that old, relatively speaking. He put its absolute age at somewhere betweeen 25 and 400 million years old, with the most probable figure being 98 million years. This was not necessarily taken as being a definitive argument against evolution. In fact Thomson's chief supporter and popularizer, the Scottish engineer Fleeming Jenkin (1867), fully accepted evolution. It was however taken to be a strong argument against the all-sufficiency of natural selection. And rightly so! Remember, Darwin had calculated that there were at least 300 million years since the mammals became plentiful!

In response to the physicists, there was not a great deal that Darwin and his supporters could do. They had to fight a rearguard action. Huxley (1869), who never really cared that much for natural selection anyway, sloughed the whole problem off, blaming geology! Wallace (1870a) argued that ice ages no doubt intensify the struggle for existence, and hence selection. Perhaps, therefore, less time is needed for evolution than Darwin supposed. Darwin himself relied a little more on his Lamarckism to speed up processes generally, and then rather gloomily he stuck to his guns hoping, rather like Mr. Micawber, that something would turn up.

Matters were not much helped by the fact that, in the intimate world of
Victorian science, Thomson's brightest young research assistant was none
other than one George Darwin, Charles Darwin's son! "I have no doubt
however that if my father had had to write down the period he assigned at that
time [of writing the *Origin*], he would have written a 1 at the beginning of the
line and filled the rest up with 0's. — Now I believe that he cannot quite bring
himself down to [the] period assigned by you but does not pretend to say how
long may be required" (unpublished letter from George Darwin to William
Thomson).

As is well known, something did in fact come up. At the beginning of this
century, the physicists were proven wrong — gloriously wrong. The discovery
of radioactive materials and the heat that they cause when they decay led to an
immediate, drastic lengthening of estimates for Earth history. By today's
calculations, the Earth is believed to be over four and one-half billion years
old, and although even today Darwin's own huge estimates have to be trim-
med, it is allowed that there was over half a billion years since the beginning of
the Cambrian. In short, time is no longer seen to be such a threat to natural
selection.

But, of course, these revisions and the foundations behind them were all
unknown to Darwin and his contemporaries. In the eyes of most people, the
argument of Thomson and his supporters was yet one more support for their
general conclusions: accept organic evolution, but reject natural selection as
the main cause behind it. And this was the position into which people felt
driven by what was probably the greatest of all of Darwin's problems: his
almost total ignorance about the causes and nature of new variation and about
the way or ways in which organic characteristics are transmitted from one
generation to the next.

Jenkin, particularly, centered in on heredity, using Darwin's ignorance to
subject natural selection to withering fire. He argued that common-sense
assumptions about heredity show that selection can never really be that effective. Inviting the reader to consider the hypothetical case of a white man ship-
wrecked among black savages, Jenkin suggested that although the white man
would obviously be a great selective advantage (!) and thus have lots of offspring, no one could suppose that the race would turn white.

In the first generation there will be some dozens of intelligent young mulattoes, much
superior in average intelligence to the negroes. We might expect the throne for some
generations to be occupied by a more or less yellow king; but can any one believe that
the whole island will gradually acquire a white, or even a yellow population, or that the
islanders would acquire the energy, courage, ingenuity, patience, self-control, endurance, in virtue of which qualities our hero killed so many of their ancestors, and
begot so many children; those qualities, in fact, which the struggle for existence would
select, if it could select anything? (Jenkin, 1867, p. 156)

More generally, Jenkin concluded that, however advantageous a new
characteristic might be, in the course of a generation or two the effects of

breeding would dilute it out of existence. There would never really be time for selection to take hold.

Darwin's main response was to step up the Lamarckian element in his theory. This would give him lots more heritable variations in each generation, and thus the swamping effect of breeding might be countered. Not just one man, but a whole shipload would arrive among our savages. However, in large part his defence was ad hoc and not very convincing. The afore-mentioned St. George Jackson Mivart, for one, was happy to point to the implausibility of Lamarckism: if it works so well, why do the Jews have to keep circumcising their newborn male children?

As might be expected, argument and counterargument flew back and forth; but, essentially, in the problems of heredity, one had one more source for people's feeling of unease about natural selection. All in all, there were just too many problems around it. The *Origin* took people a lot farther than they had gone hitherto; it did not take people as far as Darwin had hoped.

Retrospect

So what can be said in retrospect and conclusion, looking back? I hope now that the reader will accept my assessment of Darwin and his work. Notwithstanding some of the criticisms we have just seen aired, Darwin was a very good professional scientist. He knew his problems, he knew how to argue for his solutions, and altogether he constructed an impressive case in the *Origin,* as he proposed his theory of evolution through natural selection. For me, this view of Darwin makes him far more interesting and praiseworthy, not to say plausibly human, than a portrait of a semi-God who single-handedly formulated the only significant ideas in the whole of human history. Darwin is as ill-served by such friends, as he is by biased and threatened critics.

What about the strengths of Darwin's theorizing? Were his contemporaries right when they accepted his evolutionism but rejected his cause, natural selection? Standing in the last quarter of the twentieth century, I have no hesitation in saying that Darwin's case for evolution is definitive. What I mean is that Darwin's contemporaries were justified in being turned to evolution by the *Origin.* Moreover, although we today have even more knowledge of the truth of evolution, restricting ourselves solely to what Darwin has to say, it would not be reasonable for us to reject evolution.

If one subscribes in any honest way to the principles of empirical science, then the *Origin* should convince one that organisms are the end-product of a gradual process of law-bound change, however caused. Homologies, embryological similarities, fossils, and rudimentary organs all attest to evolution. How, otherwise, can one explain the ridiculously useless isomorphisms that exist between the forelimbs of man, the horse, the bat, the porpoise, and the mole when each and every one of these limbs is used for a different purpose? And perhaps above all, the nature of the geographical distribution of organisms should make one an evolutionist. The finches and tortoises of the Galapagos just do not make sense without evolution.

As noted in the Preface, one often sees it said that "evolution is not a fact, but a theory." Is this the essence of my claim? Not really! Indeed, I suggest that this wise-sounding statement is confused to the point of falsity: it almost certainly is if, without regard for cause, one means no more by "evolution" than the claim that all organisms developed naturally from primitive beginnings. Evolution is a fact, *fact, FACT!*

I do not want to appear dogmatic or to overstate the case here! We have to argue to evolution; we do not see it directly. Commonly, we use the term "theorize" meaning no more than "argue" or "infer." I have no fault to find with talk of Darwin's "theorizing to evolution," meaning that he argued for it! Indeed, if, somewhat idiosyncratically, one decides to use the term "theory" simply for something not observed directly, then I suppose one must indeed allow that evolution in the sense just specified is a theory. But I would point out at once that obviously this sense of theory is no bar to something's being a fact also! Indeed, such a "theory" can be a "fact" so well established that no one in their right mind would deny its status. The evidence that I have a heart is all indirect, neither I nor anyone else has ever seen it, but does anyone really believe that it is not a fact that I have a heart? Of course it is a fact, and in like manner I suggest that Darwin proved to us that evolution is a fact. The evidence he gives is overwhelming.

The trouble here is that we often use "theory" in other senses. Sometimes we mean a body of general scientific claims, as in "Einstein's theory of relativity." Now clearly when we start talking about natural selection we are moving towards this sense of "theory." I certainly have no objection to this use, although it hardly seems an appropriate term to apply to evolution per se, which is less a body of general claims and more a unique event — on this Earth at least. What really worries me is that there is yet another sense of "theory," which is used to refer to something speculative, as in "I have my own theory about Kennedy's assassination." I believe a lot of people, deliberately or through ignorance, conclude that evolution is a theory in this last sense – which obviously is opposed to fact — when their arguments prove only that evolution is a theory in the first sense — which is not opposed to fact. All I can say is that if the reader still believes this last sense of theory applies to evolution, I have failed in my task. Please read Darwin himself!

So much for the topic of Darwin and evolution. Please note that I am talking only of the actual fact of evolution. I am not talking now about putative paths of evolution, "phylogenies," for instance, whether or not birds evolved from dinosaurs. In the *Origin,* Darwin says virtually nothing about these at a particular level, noting only general patterns. (Refer back to Fig. 2.5 to see the general animal outline, as known at the time of the *Origin.*) But, what about something Darwin does say much about, namely his proposed major mechanism of natural selection? To be honest, I find it very difficult to answer questions about whether Darwin's contemporaries were right in withholding full support from selection, and I find it even more difficult to say whether, in the light of what we now know, we ourselves should or should not be convinced of the adequacy of selection on the basis of the *Origin.* Probably these are the kinds of questions like those about Darwin's illness: fun to ask and argue over, but really having no proper answer!

If one insists, as most of Darwin's contemporaries did not and would not insist, that absolutely no divine causes may be brought into science, one must surely agree that Darwin was right in following the natural theologians in highlighting the facts of organic adaptation, in insisting that an adequate evolutionary theory must explain them in a natural way, and in feeling pleased that he himself had an answer to them. Furthermore, the argument for natural selection looks even stronger when one takes into account such things as Darwin's explanation of embryological similarities. Darwin's argument for his mechanism is certainly not without its points, and it is strongly supported by Bates's brilliant work on butterflies.

However, on the other side, what one must also say in looking back is that there were gaps in Darwin's case for natural selection. Within the context of his own time, Darwin and contemporaries were undoubtedly right to be concerned about the age of the Earth, although this is obviously not something that we would want to consider now in assessing the *Origin*. I say this from the perspective of the orthodox scientist, ignoring until later arguments by today's Creationists that the Earth is very much younger than most people suppose.

Again, considering lacunae in Darwin's position, the analogy with artificial selection, as given in the *Origin,* certainly did not do all that one might have hoped. Whether the analogy can be strengthened is another matter to be discussed later. Additionally, listing problems, Darwin's actual examples of selection in action left something to be desired. But, most important of all in assessing the weakness of Darwin's case for causes, one surely has to agree that his ignorance about the nature of heredity badly undercut his case for natural selection.

Summing up, probably the best one can say is that, had one been a contemporary of Darwin, almost certainly one would have been somewhat hesitant about accepting natural selection as totally adequate; and this holds even today, judging purely on the case made by Darwin himself. But, had one been a scientist needing an actual mechanism, no doubt one should have pushed ahead using natural selection as one's tool of analysis. In speculating thus, I am on fairly safe ground, for what I am suggesting one ought to have done is more or less what everyone in fact did do!

This one can say: the *Origin* left open problems for future research. Perhaps three questions stand out. There was the matter of the age of the Earth. This was the physicists' problem, and as we know, the physicists solved it. No more need be said. (See Fig. 2.15.) Then there was the matter of showing selection as a fruitful tool of inquiry: can it explain natural and experimental phenomena, and is it conversely supported by them? People like Bates started the work in this direction, and such work has been going on ever since. Some of the results will be discussed shortly. But above all other questions raised by the *Origin,* there were those centering on the need for an adequate theory of heredity. It is in this area more than any that evolutionary theorizing has moved on since Darwin, and it is to the ground that such movement has covered that we turn next.

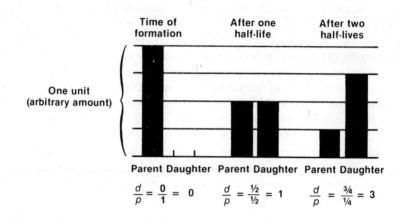

$$\frac{d}{p} = \frac{0}{1} = 0 \qquad \frac{d}{p} = \frac{\frac{1}{2}}{\frac{1}{2}} = 1 \qquad \frac{d}{p} = \frac{\frac{3}{4}}{\frac{1}{4}} = 3$$

Fig. 2.15
Dating rocks through radioactive decay: Certain "radioactive" elements break down or "decay" spontaneously into other elements (producing heat in the process, and thus slowing the cooling of the earth). Rates of decay are constant, and are measured in terms of the time needed for half of the original ("parent") element to turn into the new ("daughter") element. Given the "half-lives" of particular parent elements, by comparing the parent/daughter ratios in rocks, one can thus calculate the age of the rocks. (See the diagram above.) Obviously various special techniques must be used to compensate for disruptive factors, such as possible modification of the rocks after initial formation. One way is to cross-check different elements in the same rock and see if they yield the same result. (Does one have a consilience?!) Different elements decay at different rates. Rubidium decays to strontium very slowly, whereas potassium decays to argon relatively quickly. Thus, one can date both old and young rocks quite precisely. (See Fig. 6.9 for some major findings.)

Part II
Darwinism Today

Chapter 3
The Coming of Mendelian Genetics.

History has certainly taught us one thing. The evolutionist needs a theory describing and explaining the principles of heredity — a theory of *genetics*, to use the modern term. In fact, previous discussion suggests that for a totally adequate understanding of the evolutionary process, one needs answers at two levels. On the one hand, one wants to know precisely what goes on at the physical, empirical level. Do black guinea pigs always give birth to black guinea pigs, and if there are exceptions, what are they and how frequent are they? Let us call this the "phenomenal" level. On the other hand, one wants to know why. What lies behind the phenomena? Why do black guinea pigs give birth to black guinea pigs, and why would there ever be exceptions? Let us call this the "causal" level. Obviously the phenomenal/causal distinction is somewhat artificial. I doubt one would ever think seriously about the phenomena without speculating on causes, but it is useful nevertheless to recognize the two levels.

Already we have glimpsed some of Darwin's phenomenal-level assumptions about heredity. His response to Jenkin shows clearly that essentially he saw heredity as a "blending" phenomenon. That is to say, as the norm, Darwin saw the physical characteristics of the parents melding in the offspring, diluted from their strongest form forever. This was the thrust of Jenkin's criticism about the superior qualities of the white man being swamped and lost among the savages. Had Darwin not agreed with Jenkin that characteristics do blend through breeding, he could have ignored the criticism entirely.

What about Darwin's thoughts on causes? In the *Origin,* Darwin never really introduced any causal speculations, but elsewhere in fact he did develop and present a causal theory of heredity: "pangenesis" (Darwin, 1868; Geison, 1969). Darwin supposed that there are little particles being given off from all over the body, these "gemmules" circulate and collect in the sex organs, and then they are transmitted and mingle in the offspring, with the gemmules of the other parent. Thus we get an explanation of Lamarckism, environmental factors can effect the gemmules; with a little inventiveness, we get an explanation of new variations, chance factors impinging on the body alter the gemmules; and we get an explanation of blending at the phenomenal level, the mingled gemmules in the offspring cause more or less blended physical features.

It hardly needs saying that this last assumption, about the mingling of the causes of heredity, totally finished any chances that Darwin may have had of escaping from the Jenkin criticism. Although in a sense Darwin was not arguing for total blending of the causes — the particles still remain separate — one does get a strong element of causal blending. New useful variations would be diluted right down in a generation or two and would be irretrievably lost. But this consequence apart, there are many problems with Darwin's theory. The theory is dreadfully ad hoc, with all kinds of conceptual gaps. For instance, why are features sometimes transmitted in a nonblended way (let us speak of this as "particulate transmission")? Why does a child always have a whole penis or none at all? Why do sexual organs fail to blend, whereas something like skin color does blend? Again, why do we sometimes get features skipping a generation? Presumably the answer is that the gemmules can lie latent, but why? Darwin had no answers to these questions, nor did he have answers to obvious questions concerning the exact physical nature of the gemmules, and precisely how these particles end up in the sex organs. As can be imagined, none of Darwin's contemporaries was very much enthralled by pangenesis, and critics like Mivart (1871) really went to town. Today pangenesis is on the scientific trash heap, along with phlogiston theory and Ptolemaic epicycles.

We ourselves need spend no more space on Darwin's troubles. Paradoxically, just at the time of the *Origin,* the successful quest for the true principles of heredity was beginning. This is one of the greatest ironies in the history of science, for no one knew of this fact! In his monastery garden in Brno (today part of Czechoslovakia), an obscure Moravian monk, Gregor Mendel, was growing plants and speculating about the principles of heredity, at both the phenomenal and the causal level. (See Fig. 3.1.) Taking a far more fruitful approach than did Darwin, Mendel saw particulate phenomenal inheritance as the norm, and he based his causal theorizing on this insight. Cultivating pea plants, Mendel looked at the different contrasting features — tall/short, green-pod/yellow-pod, and so forth — and he formulated rules which presupposed that the causes behind the features could go on from generation to generation, undiluted. Any phenomenal blending is a transitory phenomenon which can be undone in future generations.

If only Darwin had known that the way was being opened to defuse the Jenkin criticism entirely! But, although Mendel sent papers incorporating his ideas to prominent scientists, his work was totally ignored. Despondent, he turned from science and died a few years later, quite ignorant of the fact that the twentieth century would look upon him as one of the seminal figures of nineteenth-century biology. It was not until the Victorian age was at its close that Mendel's work was rediscovered, and the fact that three people did so independently in the space of a few months, surely shows that then, and only then, was the scientific climate ripe for Mendelism.

Fig. 3.1
Gregor Mendel (1822–1884).

What was it that made people ready for a fresh approach to heredity? A major cause was the rise and success of the science of cytology, the study of the ultimate parts of the living body, the "cells." This science had undercut many of the foundations of a theory of heredity like Darwinian pangenesis. It was shown that the sex cells are formed and passed on without input from the rest of the body; there simply is no physiological basis to the inheritance of acquired characteristics. Hence, quite apart from its internal difficulties, there was no longer even the urge to produce a theory like pangenesis; the "facts" it was trying to explain were no longer seen as facts!

Cutting short a fascinating story, with the rediscovery of Mendel's approach it was not long before general biological opinion swung to the belief that the causes involved in heredity remain nonblended, particulate, from generation to generation. Blending at the phenomenal level does not reflect underlying reality. Cytology and this new perspective on heredity were fused, and thus we find that within a few years, most particularly thanks to the work of T. H. Morgan and his associates at Columbia University, a whole body of theory was developed and articulated.

Let us now look briefly at this "Mendelian genetics" (perhaps more accurately, neo-Mendelian genetics). Because my interests are guided entirely by the value of Mendelism for Darwinian studies, I shall ignore subtleties, deal only with what is normally true for relatively complex organisms, and shall take a somewhat ahistorical approach. Indeed, so cavalier an attitude shall I take toward the past that, having presented the biological Mendelian theory, I shall at once link it up to its modern successor, molecular genetics!

Mendelian genetics

The first cell of an organism, that from which life begins, is known as the "zygote." All the cells of the physical body, the "somatic cells," trace back to this beginning, linked through a chain of replicating cells by a process called "mitosis." Every somatic cell has a center, the "nucleus," containing a set of long thread-like objects, the "chromosomes." It is postulated that the ultimate biological causes of physical characteristics are minute, indivisible units carried on the chromosomes. These causes, the "genes," are therefore by definition the units of biological *function*. Since the genes are not themselves directly observable, knowable only through their effects, Mendelian theory specifies that if two genes have identical effects, by definition they are identical genes. Strictly speaking one should say that the totality of the physical features of an organism (collectively known as its "phenotype") is the product of the totality of the genes (collectively known as the "genotype"), modified and fashioned by the interacting effects of the environment on the growing, developing organism.

The chromosomes come in pairs. Every gene therefore has a mate. The place of a gene on its chromosome (and obviously the place of its mate) is known as its "locus." Within a population of organisms, most particularly within a species, one has individuals with a (more or less) similar set of chromosomes. Therefore one has a (more or less) similar set of loci. The different genes occurring at the corresponding loci across the group are known as "alleles." At any given locus, therefore, an organism has two alleles, either the same or different. If the former is the case, the organism is known as a "homozygote"; if the latter, "heterozygote." Given some particular heterozygote (using obvious notation, a_1a_2, where a_1 and a_2 are the alleles at issue), the phenotype might be a blend of the homozygote phenotypes (a_1a_1 and a_2a_2), it might be something quite new, or possibly it resembles the homozygote of one of the alleles (say a_1a_1). When the heterozygote resembles one of the homozygotes, the "stronger" allele is said to be "dominant" over the masked allele, which is said to be "recessive." Dominance and recessiveness are not absolute properties: a_1 might be dominant over a_2, which is in turn dominant over a_3.

So far, we have just been considering the gene considered as a unit of function. But, within Mendelian theory, the gene is also the unit of *heredity*. It is that which is passed on from generation to generation, ensuring that guinea pigs give birth to guinea pigs and not to humans, and more specifically ensuring that the distinctive characteristics possessed by a population of organisms are transmitted in the particular way that they are. The transmission of the genes in sexual organisms is governed by two rules known, in belated honor of genetics' obscure pioneer, as "Mendel's laws."

To present these laws, it is necessary to introduce the sex cells, those products of the body which carry the genetic information from parent to child. These cells are not produced in the way that somatic cells are produced (i.e., through mitosis). Rather, through a process known as "meiosis," one has a production of cells containing just a half set of chromosomes (a "haploid" set), derived by dividing an original cell with a full chromosome complement (a "diploid" cell). Although haploid cells have only half the chromosomes of diploid cells, they have one chromosome of each kind. In reproduction, two haploid cells, one from each parent (a sperm and an ovum), unite to form a new diploid cell, the zygote, which then starts multiplying as a new individual. Each parent thus provides half the genetic material of each offspring; moreover, each parent has contributed one of the allele pairs at each locus in the new being. (See Fig. 3.2.)

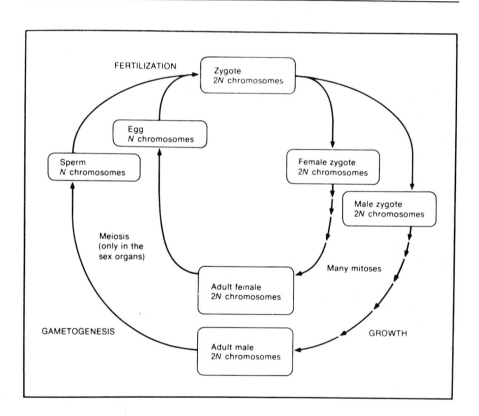

Fig. 3.2
Growth and reproduction: As explained in the text, (most) organisms start as zygotes with two sets of chromosomes. Through continued mitosis, the zygote multiplies and develops into an adult, either a male or a female. Then, through meiosis, haploid sex cells ("gametes") are produced, which then combine in fertilization to form new zygotes. (Adapted with permission from F. J. Ayala and J. W. Valentine, (1979). *Evolving,* Menlo Park, Calif.: Benjamin/Cummings.)

Mendel's first law (the "law of segregation") states that it is totally a matter of chance which of the paired alleles that a parent has at any given locus is in fact the one copied and passed on to the offspring. In other words, any parental allele has a 50 percent chance of being transmitted to any offspring. Although, obviously, if a parent is a homozygote at some locus, then the offspring must get a copy of the only allele that the parent has at this locus. (See Fig. 3.3.) Mendel's second law (the "law of independent assortment") states

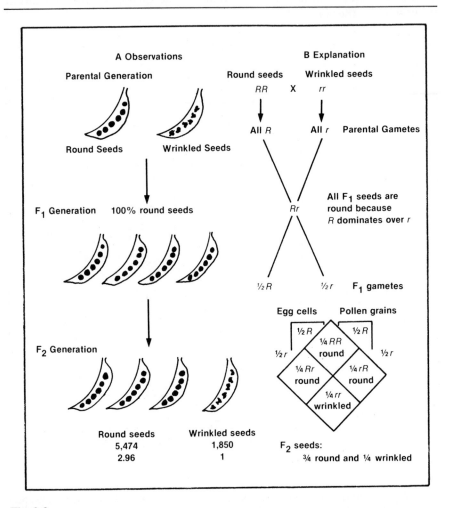

Fig. 3.3
Mendel's first law: Mendel crossed pea plants with round seeds and pea plants with wrinkled seeds. In the first generation all of the peas were round; but in the second generation, when plants from these peas were crossed with each other, approximately a 3:1 ratio of round to wrinkled peas were obtained. The explanation is given on the right. (Adapted with permission from Ayala and Valentine, (1979).)

that if we consider genes at different loci, then the fact that one allele at one locus was transmitted is quite independent of which of the alleles at the other locus was transmitted. (See Fig. 3.4.) Actually, early in the development of

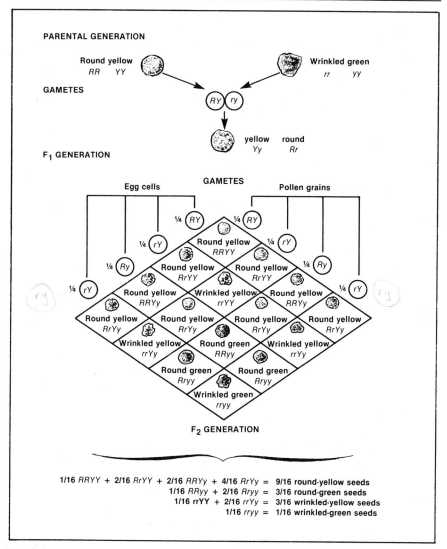

Fig. 3.4

Mendel's second law: Plants with round-yellow peas are crossed with plants with wrinkled-green peas. All of the offspring produce round-yellow peas; but, after cross fertilization, their offspring produce peas which are round-yellow, round-green, wrinkled-yellow, and wrinkled-green, in roughly a 9:3:3:1 ratio. The explanation follows because the transmission of the genes at one locus (those controlling shape) is independent of the transmission of the genes at the other locus (those controlling color). (Adapted with permission from Ayala and Valentine, (1979).)

Mendelian theory, it was recognized that a major qualification has to be added to this second law. It holds exactly only for genes on different chromosomes. Somewhat naturally, genes on the same chromosome tend to be transmitted together — they are "linked."

One final, crucial item to this picture of the gene needs to be added. Sometimes it is found that an organism shows new characteristics, not explicable through normal processes of transmission. Since the gene is known only through its effects and identical genes imply identical effects, it is therefore supposed that sometimes a gene changes from one form to another spontaneously, as it were. It "mutates," and the gene thus is the unit of *mutation*. This change is a random phenomenon, in that the appearance of a new mutant is not a function of the needs of the organism (i.e., no Lamarckism). Mutation is also random in the sense that one cannot predict that any particular gene will mutate. It is nevertheless true that, on average, changes happen with sufficient regularity for quantification over groups. No causes for mutation are specified within traditional Mendelian theory. But obviously no holder of the theory has ever believed that there are no ultimate causes. It is just that the theory says nothing about the causes. (As well as mutation involving change in genes, one also gets mutation involving changes in the chromosomes: duplication, and so forth.)

We have now before us the major elements to the Mendelian picture: the gene as unit of function, of heredity, and of mutation. But before going on with the story, it would be disingenuous not to make a few comments about the very considerable progress made in genetics, since the basic details of this theory were first articulated and confirmed. A fact that I am sure is well known to every reader is that *the* major biological advance in this century has been the coming of the physical sciences to genetics. Since the pioneering work of James Watson and Francis Crick in 1953, it is now known that the ultimate biological unit of heredity, the Mendelian gene, can be identified with the macromolecules of deoxyribonucleic acid (DNA). And, building on this identification, an immense amount has been learned about the nature of heredity, considered at the physicochemical level. Most particularly, it is known how the DNA molecule replicates itself, how the molecule serves to make the essential ingredients of the cell, and how it can change; the DNA as unit of heredity, function, and mutation. Causes inexplicable under traditional Mendelian thought are now identified and analyzed in detail. Moreover it is possible to distinguish different DNA molecules, "molecular genes," even when the differences have no effect on the overall phenotype. (See Figs. 3.5, 3.6, and 3.7.)

The point of importance and relevance to us is that the general relationship between the new molecular genetics and the older Mendelian genetics is one of harmony rather than conflict (Ruse, 1981; but see Hull, 1972, 1976). By this I mean that molecular biology does not, except perhaps in some rather unimportant details, refute the theory of the gene just presented in this section. Rather, it provides a much deeper insight into processes hitherto understood dimly or incompletely. Because of this fact, my feeling is that, with respect to evolutionary theorizing at the conceptual level, molecular biology has not had that great an impact!

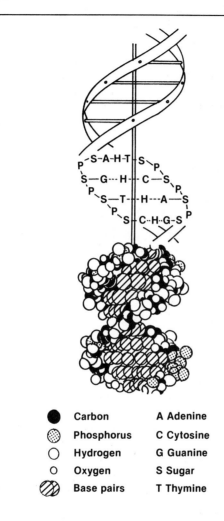

	Carbon	A Adenine
	Phosphorus	C Cytosine
	Hydrogen	G Guanine
	Oxygen	S Sugar
	Base pairs	T Thymine

Fig. 3.5

Three different representations of the DNA molecule (the "molecular gene"): DNA is a long chain-like molecule, which coils around a mate, in a double helix. The outer backbone of the DNA consists of chemically linked alternating molecules of sugars and phosphates. Nitrogen bases connected to the sugars point inward, and, through hydrogen bonds, connect with bases on the complementary molecule. (A base, together with sugar and phosphate, is called a "nucleotide.") There are four bases: adenine (A), cytosine (C), guanine (G), and thymine (T). A always pairs with T, and C with G. The order of the bases yields the "information" necessary to build organisms. When a cell divides, new DNA molecules are "copied off" the old ones, and thus, the information is passed on. Mutation is essentially a "mistake" in this process of duplication.

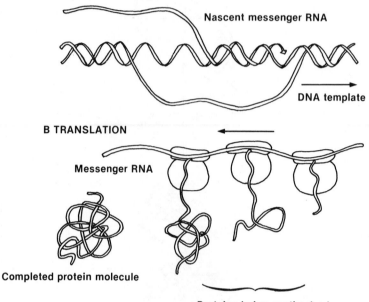

Fig. 3.6

The processes of transcription and translation: The chief constituents of cells are "proteins", long chains of smaller molecules known as "amino acids." There are twenty amino acids crucial for organisms, and the orderings of the acids make the proteins what they are, which make the cells what they are, which make the organisms what they are. The information to make the proteins resides in the DNA. First, through "transcription", the DNA molecule is copied onto another macromolecule RNA (ribonucleic acid). Second, through "translation", this "messenger" RNA serves as the site of protein synthesis. Other segments of RNA pick up free amino acids within the cell, bring them over to the messenger RNA (which becomes attached to certain bodies known as "ribosomes"), and then the transcribed information on the RNA is translated into an ordering of the amino acids into a new protein. (Adapted with permission from Ayala and Valentine, (1979).)

SECOND LETTER

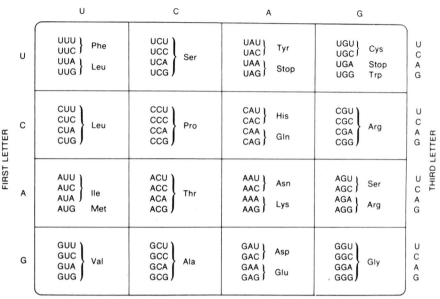

Fig. 3.7

The genetic code: There are only four bases on DNA and in RNA (which differs from DNA in having uracil, U, instead of thymine). There are, however, twenty amino acids. Obviously, therefore, a single base cannot correspond to a single amino acid. One needs a specific ordered sequence of bases for any particular amino acid, and indeed in nature it is found that an ordered sequence of three bases (a "codon") does translate into one amino acid. The correspondence between codons and amino acids is given in this figure. The twenty amino acids making up proteins are as follows: alanine (Ala), arginine (Arg), asparagine (Asn), aspartic acid (Asp), cysteine (Cys), glycine (Gly), glutamic acid (Glu), glutamine (Gln), histidine (His), isoleucine (Ile), leucine (Leu), lysine (Lys), methionine (Met), phenylalanine (Phe), proline (Pro), serine (Ser), threonine (Thr), tyrosine (Tyr), tryptophane (Trp), and valine (Val). Note that there is a great deal of redundancy, because there are 64 possible codons and only twenty amino acids (together with an additional unit of information required to stop the synthesis of the protein). This means one can have a considerable amount of change occurring on the DNA molecule, which will simply not get reflected in the proteins. As we shall learn (chapter 5), there is much debate about whether one gets "non-Darwinian molecular evolution": an evolution lying below the level at which natural selection could act.

Please do not misunderstand me. The last thing I want to claim is that "Darwinism today" is indifferent to or unaffected by the molecular revolution. There is nary a modern textbook in evolutionary thought that does not start with the double helix! My point rather is that what Darwinian evolutionism needed conceptually was an adequate theory of heredity, and that the essential insights were already there in the biological genetics. As we shall see, the really exciting place for molecular biology in evolutionary studies is in solving problems intractable under traditional approaches. (I except here the rather different question of the origin of life, to be discussed later, where molecular biology has a full conceptual role to play.)

In addition to this fact about the lack of conceptual impact of molecular biology on evolutionary work, we have the practical fact that, because ultimately the evolutionists' interests are directed toward the whole, living organism in nature (past or present), their work is often necessarily at one or more removes from the molecular level. Although an increasingly great amount of evolutionary work is being done that is directly dependent on molecular biology, there is still much pertinent work that has been and is being performed not directly dependent on molecular biology. Therefore, without apology, at this point in my defense of Darwinism I shall return to the more traditional biological concepts. Molecular biology is being held, but not forgotten.

Whatever its limitations compared to molecular biology, I need hardly say how powerful Mendelian theory really is in its own right. Regularities and quirks of heredity fall before its explanatory searchlight. From our viewpoint, one can say simply that it is the answer to a Darwinian's prayer. One can see a way leading to solution of all of Darwin's problems with blending. The genes are passed on from generation to generation in an entire state, and thus there is no question of physical characteristics being swamped out by reproduction, despite great adaptive value. If the phenotypic effect of a gene is blended through being matched heterozygously with another gene, or even if the gene has no effects at all for several generations through being masked by dominant partners, it remains intact, unsullied. When the time comes, it can again surface phenotypically and show its mettle in the struggle for reproduction. (Look back at Fig. 3.3 and see how the wrinkled peas vanished in the first filial generation and then reappeared, unchanged, in the second.)

And yet, answer to a prayer or not, what can be seen so clearly with hindsight was not at all obvious to those who were developing Mendelian theory. Somewhat naturally, in their studies the early geneticists tended to concentrate on nice sharp unambiguous variations, not to mention mutations that caused fairly significant breaks with what had gone before. Morgan and his associates were pushing into new ground. Sensibly, therefore, they sought and manipulated clear-cut, well-defined features in their experimental subjects. Unfortunately, however, this all led these geneticists and the many biologists who were influenced by them to feel that their neo-Mendelism was a *rival* to Darwinism, not a complementary part of the same true overall picture! Hence, among geneticists there grew a tradition of arguing for a saltationary evolutionary process, supposing that mutation gives rise to significant major organic changes — such changes being the prime cause of organic alteration. Selection was relegated to a minor, mopping-up role.

Fortunately this uneasy state of affairs was, comparatively speaking, not that long lasting. As the 1920s grew to a close, a number of thinkers started to sense that one could be both a Darwinian (that is, a believer in the evolutionary importance of natural selection) and a Mendelian (that is, one who accepted the theory of the gene presented in this section). Historians are still squabbling over who deserves most credit for this realization, the basic key to which is the insight that, if the variations caused by the genes are very small, all of the rules of Mendelian inheritance hold *and* natural selection can come into its own, with a full creative role. Commonly mentioned names in this context are Sir Ronald Fisher and J. B. S. Haldane in Britain and Sewell Wright in the United States. Without question, to these three should be added the Russian geneticist Sergei Chetverikov.

But, however the kudos really should be distributed, what matters is that ideas developed rapidly, and it was not long before a veritable flood of evolutionists started to produce work based on a Darwin-Mendel synthesis. The neo-Darwinian theory of evolution, or, as it is sometimes called, the "synthetic theory" of evolution, was born. In North America, undoubtedly, the crucial catalyzing work was that of the Russian-born, U.S.-residing biologist, Theodosius Dobzhansky: *Genetics and the Origin of Species* (1937, third edition 1951, revised and retitled 1970). (See Fig. 3.8.) This influenced the systematist Ernst Mayr, author of *Systematics and the Origin of Species* (1942, much augmented 1963); the paleontologist G. G. Simpson, author of *Tempo and Mode in Evolution* (1944, revised and retitled 1953); and the botanist, G. Ledyard Stebbins, author of *Variation and Evolution in Plants* (1950). At the same time, one had work going on in parallel and in series elsewhere. In Britain, for instance, one had Julian Huxley, author of *Evolution: The Modern Synthesis* (1942), in Germany, Bernhard Rensch, author of *Neuere Probleme der Abstammungslehre* (1947).

Drawing on these volumes, and on the great quantity of work done in succeeding years, let us now see how Mendelism is taken and fused with Darwin's insights. Just to give you a guide, for the rest of this chapter, I shall be looking at the theoretical side to the Mendelian-strengthened modern equivalent to what, in the last chapter, I characterized as the second part of Darwin's theory, the "core" causal mechanism. In the next chapter, I shall be looking at the empirical evidence for this core — very much the modern equivalent to the first part of Darwin's theory. In the final chapter of this section on "Darwinism Today," I shall consider the application of this core to the lower-level disciplines of the evolutionary spectrum — the equivalent to the third and last part of the theory of the *Origin*. (See Fig. 5.1 for a pictorial representation of the modern theory.)

Fig. 3.8
Theodosius Dobzhansky (1900-1975). (Reproduced by permission of Francisco J. Ayala.)

The Hardy-Weinberg law

The characteristic that most distinguishes Darwinism from all other theories is that evolution is seen as a function of *population* change, not of individual change (Ghiselin, 1969). Lamarckism, either the real variety or what has come to be called by that name, puts the emphasis on the isolated individual organism. Through interaction with the environment in some way we get change, and this is passed on. Lamarckism essentially could work, even if there were never more than one individual alive at any one time. Similarly, saltationism operates at the level of the individual. For Darwinism, matters are otherwise. Although variations indeed affect the individual, natural selection is a group concept — it is all a question of some in the group succeeding and others failing. With just one organism, one simply cannot have Darwinian evolution.

Now Mendelian genetics, as we saw it presented in the last section, deals with organisms at the individual level. Consequently, for those biologists who wanted to combine the insights of Darwin and Mendel, the first task was to make Mendelism applicable to the group level. Then, and only then, could one introduce Darwinian factors like natural selection, and thus build an adequate foundation to one's evolutionary theorizing — something that would function as the above-mentioned "core" to evolutionary studies, very much as Darwin's central arguments to and about natural selection functioned in the *Origin*.

This generalized analysis was indeed produced by evolutionists, who appropriately gave it the name of "population genetics." In our exposition of neo-Darwinism, we must therefore first look at it. As we go along, note how the modern approach to evolution, insofar as one is in the domain of theory, proceeds almost entirely at the level of the genotype. This is not because neo-Darwinians are uninterested in the phenotype. Obviously not! In an important sense, evolution begins and ends with the physical features of the organism. Rather, for conceptual ease, problems are worked out at the level of the genotype and then, as we shall see, their implications are translated into phenotypic phenomena and effects.

First in developing population genetics, one must generalize Mendel's laws, particularly the first law, up to the populational level from that of the individual. In fact, this is easily done, and formally the generalization, which after its two co-discoverers is known as the Hardy-Weinberg law, can be stated as follows. Assume a very large population of organisms (i.e., a population that is effectively infinite), evenly distributed between males and females and with random interbreeding. Assume also that at some locus one has alternative alleles A and a, in proportion $p:q$. Assume that there are no externally disruptive factors (e.g., no mutation). Then, whatever the initial distribution of genotypes, in the next and all succeeding generations the distribution of genotypes will be

$$p^2AA + 2pqAa + q^2aa$$

Moreover, in each generation the ratio of A to a alleles will stay constant at $p:q$. As corollaries, one has ready extensions of the law to deal with more alleles at the same locus, or, through Mendel's second law, with alleles at different loci. (See Fig. 3.9, for a proof of the Hardy-Weinberg law.)

The importance of the Hardy-Weinberg law for neo-Darwinian evolutionary studies simply cannot be overemphasized. It is the starting point for everything. As Dobzhansky has stated quite explicitly: "This law is the foundation of ... modern evolution theory" (Dobzhansky, 1951, p. 53). I am afraid, nevertheless, that it seems to be a general rule that the number of misconceptions of biological claims rises in direct proportion to the importance of the claim in question, and certainly the Hardy-Weinberg law proves no exception. It is frequently suggested, by those who know no better, that the law is a mere truism. After all, it seems to state that if nothing happens (e.g.,

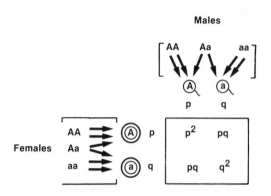

Fig. 3.9
The Hardy-Weinberg law: It can be seen easily how the specified ratios obtain. For instance, an AA homozygote must be the result of the union of an A sperm and an A ovum, and since there are (proportionately) p of each, there will be p^2 of AA. That the ratio of A to a stays at $p:q$, can also be seen readily. In any new generation there are (proportionately) $2p^2 + 2pq$ of type A alleles, and $2pq + 2q^2$ of type a alleles, and given that $p + q = 1$, this reduces to a $p:q$ ratio.

no selection or mutation) then nothing happens (i.e., gene ratios stay the same). But, this is a totally ill-founded objection. In fact, one needs virtually no biological knowledge at all to see that the law could be false. Given two alleles A and a, it logically could be that the more common allele A totally swamps the less common allele a in a few generations, and so $A:a$ goes to 1:0. Indeed, early geneticists thought that this would happen; and, as a matter of historical record, it took the pure mathematician G. H. Hardy, himself no biologist, to show his Cambridge high-table associates that they were wrong.

However, as is often the case with common misconceptions, I think this objection that the Hardy-Weinberg law is a truism hints at something interesting and important: that the Hardy-Weinberg law functions very much in biology as Newton's first law functions in mechanics. That law too is an "if nothing happens, then nothing happens" kind of law: if there are no forces, then motion or rest stays unchanged. But Newton's law is no idle truism; it is a very important law whose power lies in the fact that it provides a background of stability, against which physicists can introduce disruptive factors — forces — and measure them. If the law did not hold, then anything could go any which way, and one would have neither control nor explanation.

The same is true of the Hardy-Weinberg law; it is no truism, but a provider of background stability. Given the law, evolutionists are now in a position to introduce factors that might be expected to produce genetic change in populations, confident that the effects will occur and will not vanish due to random or other background factors. Thus, for instance, we can see even more clearly than before that, because the law is just Mendel's first law writ large, the Jenkin criticism is impotent: if even a very small percentage of a large population are bearers of a new, genetically caused variation, then, all other things being equal, the variations will persist indefinitely. They will not be swamped out of existence. Moreover, forestalling another common objection, the fact that "all other things" rarely are equal is no more of an invalidation of the Hardy-Weinberg law, than the fact that "all other things" never are equal is an invalidation of Newton's first law. Both laws are legitimately hypothetical, gaining status from the consequences that flow from them. (For a discussion of this kind of law, see Hempel, 1966.)

Models of change

Given the Hardy-Weinberg law, what happens next? For all the universality of the Hardy-Weinberg law, generally I think it is most accurate to say that today's evolutionists do not seek universal laws, applicable and actually at work in every situation — the kind of law I think Darwin sometimes thought he was after. Rather, what they try to do is build limited causal *models* — things that the population geneticist Richard Lewontin (1980) has perceptively referred to as sets of "as if" statements. There is no attempt to lay down universal claims about the way the world always works, once and for all. Instead, against a background of the Hardy-Weinberg law, evolutionists suppose different sets of possible or plausible initial conditions and disruptive factors — conditions and factors that will have certain effects on gene ratios. These little hypothetical pictures, or models, might then find actual empirical application in certain situations, according to the particular circumstances. They serve as "guides for perplexed experimentalists," to use another of Lewontin's felicitous phrases. In other words, presupposing a Hardy-Weinberg equilibrium, if all other things were equal, population geneticists build their models, introducing factors that might be expected to cause changes in gene ratios in actual populations; that is, cause changes that add up ultimately to evolutionary change.

But, there is a common pattern to these models. Specifically, in the Darwinian tradition, two causal factors above all others are taken to be of importance and analyzed as to their potential effects. On the one hand, we have the constant introduction of new genes into populations; that is, through *mutation* we have a process that leads ultimately to new kinds of phenotypes. This provides the Darwinian component of random variation. On the other hand, we have the fact that, because of their phenotypes, some genes can be expected to increase their representation in populations, at the expense of other genes; that is, we have a differential reproduction, or Darwinian *selection*. And, because of the quantificational precision that the Mendelian approach to genetics offers, evolutionists are in a position to examine this selection in controlled

detail, seeing how quickly a selectively favored or "fitter" allele might be expected to spread through a population, when for instance other factors affecting gene ratios (like mutation) might oppose or aid the selection, and so forth.
All of this is very much in the spirit of Darwin's work; but, I hardly have to say
how very much more mathematically sophisticated one can get than any of the
argumentation to be found in the *Origin*!

As noted in the Preface, it is neither my desire nor intention to reproduce
what can be found in virtually any elementary biology book. I do not therefore
feel bound to follow population geneticists, showing in detail exactly how they
quantify such factors as natural selection and mutation, and all the possible
models they can then build. At most, all I want to do is give a "flavor," so the
reader can follow my defense of Darwinism. With this end only in view, and
therefore making absolutely no apologies for the informality of my discussion
or for the totally biased and limited nature of my selection, in this section I
shall give a pair of very elementary results yielded by this formal approach to
evolution. Thus, I can illustrate the techniques used, show how evolutionists
build limited models rather than aiming for one universal axiom system all put
together, and perhaps convince that such an approach indeed confirms and
clarifies insights otherwise grasped only in a rather intuitive, fuzzy way. For
convenience, I shall concentrate just on the effects of selection, ignoring com-
plexities introduced by new mutation.

Remember that a model is a set of "as if" statements; so, to build our
first model and to get our first result, let us start off by pretending or supposing that we have a large population of organisms, with two and only two alleles
at some locus, A and a, and that a is recessive to A. If all other things are
equal, our population is assumed to be in Hardy-Weinberg equilibrium. A
question of some interest is what would happen were things no longer to be
equal and were selection suddenly to start favoring allele A over allele a; or,
considering selection as something operating on the phenotype rather than on
the genotype, what would happen were selection to start favoring an organism
with phenotype of a kind caused by genotype AA over an organism with
phenotype caused by genotype aa? One would expect that a would decline
relative to A; but, how rapid would the decline be? Would the decline be
quick, or would it be slow? Does the fact that a is recessive make much difference?

Let us introduce the notion of "Darwinian fitness" (or "adaptive" or
"selective" value), meaning the relative success or efficiency of a particular
gene or genotype against other genes or genotypes. We can arbitrarily give the
genotype AA the fitness 1, and the genotype aa, $1 - s$, meaning that (proportionally) for every AA that is produced through reproduction, selection wipes
out saa's, and thus only $(1-s)$ aa's are produced. (Remember that these are
proportions; we certainly do not want to say that every AA reproduces.) Adding the information that Aa is like $AA,$ we have therefore the following
assumptions defining our model.

Genotype	AA	Aa	aa
Fitness *(w)*	1	1	$1 - s$

Now, assuming that the initial distribution of A to a is $p{:}q$, $(p + q = 1)$, we can draw up the following matrix, using the information that initially our group was at Hardy-Weinberg equilibrium and that it would stay in such a state were selection not interfering.

	Genotypes			Total Population
	AA	Aa	aa	
Initial zygote frequency	p^2	$2pq$	q^2	1
Fitness, w	1	1	$1 - s$	
Zygote proportions after selection	p^2	$2pq$	$q^2(1 - s)$	$1 - sq^2$
Zygote frequencies after selection	$\dfrac{p^2}{1 - sq^2}$	$\dfrac{2pq}{1 - sq^2}$	$\dfrac{q^2(1 - s)}{1 - sq^2}$	1

I think this is all reasonably clear. The key line is obviously "zygote proportions after selection." All that we have done is simply to note that selection eliminates the specified proportion of expected aa homozygotes; and at the same time we have to note that these are lost from the total population as well. Hardy-Weinberg equilibrium gives us (proportionally) q^2aa individuals, and then according to one of the "as if" assumptions of the model, selection wipes out s of these.

Now, what we want to find is what happens to A. Does it increase proportionately in the next generation, after selection against a? Symbolically, what is the value of Δp, the increment in the value of p, the frequency of A? This will be found by subtracting p, the old frequency, from the new frequency, X. To calculate the new frequency, remember that there are two A's in each AA homozygote, one A in the heterozygote, and that every member of the group has two alleles. Hence

$$X = \frac{2p^2 + 2pq}{2(1 - sq^2)} = \frac{p(p + q)}{1 - sq^2} = \frac{p}{1 - sq^2}$$

Hence

$$\Delta p = X - p = \frac{p - p(1 - sq^2)}{1 - sq^2} = \frac{spq^2}{1 - sq^2}$$

Since both s and q are less than 1, this is a positive value. In short, expectedly, A will increase in the population, and we are now in a position to calculate the rate of increase.

By way of illustration, applying the model, we can suppose that selection against the homozygote ranges anywhere from $s = .01$ (the homozygote is at a 1 percent disadvantage) to $s = 1$ (the homozygote is lethal or fails to reproduce). If A and a start equal, $P_0 = Q_0 = 0.5$, then after one generation the frequency p_1 of A is:

Selection coefficient, s	0.01	0.02	0.1	0.5	1.0
Frequency of A, p_1	0.50125	0.5025	0.5128	0.574	0.67

Even with the weakest of selection, a is going to decline. What is interesting, and perhaps a little unexpected — even the most non-mathematical must have suspected that some decline would occur! — is how long the decline takes to reduce a to a virtual vanishing point, even when the homozygote aa never reproduces. If we start with a frequency $q = 0.5$, the frequency (given $s = 1$) drops to 0.1 in only 8 generations. But to get to 0.01 takes 100 generations, and to get to .001 takes 1000 generations! This could imply a comparatively long time, if one has a slow breeding organism like the elephant. In other words, just a few copies of a recessive gene could stay in a population, however deleterious it may be (especially if one takes into consideration other factors, like possible mutation to the deleterious gene).

Now, let us introduce a second model. What about the case where the heterozygote is a blend between homozygotes, and selection goes proportionately against it? Our model specifies:

Genotype	Aa	Aa	Aa
Fitness (w)	1	$1-s$	$1-2s$

Our matrix is:

	Genotypes			Total Population
	AA	Aa	aa	
Initial zygote frequency	p^2	$2pq$	q^2	
Fitness, w	1	$1 - s$	$1 - 2s$	
Zygote proportions after selection	p^2	$2pq(1 - s)$	$q^2(1 - 2s)$	$1 - 2sq$
Zygote frequencies after selection	$\dfrac{p^2}{1 - 2sq}$	$\dfrac{2pq(1 - s)}{1 - 2sq}$	$\dfrac{q^2(1 - 2s)}{1 - 2sq}$	1

And using the same kind of reasoning, we get

$$\Delta p = \frac{spq}{1 - 2sq}$$

For comparison with the first model, let us see just how much faster a disappears, when it has some effect on the heterozygote. Suppose that for every 100 successful AA homozygotes, there are 98 aa homozygotes. We compare the situation where a is recessive (i.e., where 100 heterozygotes succeed) with the situation where there is no dominance (i.e., where 99 heterozygotes succeed). We can calculate the number of generations needed to reduce the proportion of a as follows (Dobzhansky et al., 1977, p. 102).

From ➡ To		Recessive	No Dominance
0.25	➡ 0.10	710	110
0.10	➡ 0.01	9,240	240
0.01	➡ 0.001	90,231	231

One would certainly have expected some difference in the rate of decline. Without the mathematics, one would never have thought that the difference would have been as great as this.

It is obviously the case that being recessive helps a gene to withstand the ravages of selection. Conversely, if a gene is recessive and reasonably rare, it is less likely to harm its possessor (because it is unlikely to be homozygous). In fact, there is some evidence that organisms frequently "protect" themselves against harmful new mutants by ensuring that such mutants be recessive (because of various biological mechanisms). However, keeping matters in perspective, do note that even with a very weak selection, if a gene exposes itself at all in phenotypic effect, its frequency will (for most organisms) be drastically altered in at most a thousand years or two — a drop in the bucket of evolutionary time. A few copies of a deleterious gene may persist in a population, but most copies will be eliminated. Hence, neo-Darwinians feel that their mathematics justifies their assumption that the only explanatory models required for evolution are those positing small variations. One just does not need saltations to get major changes.

Balancing selection: Superior heterozygote fitness

Next, I want to make brief reference to the way in which neo-Darwinians approach and establish a result which has great importance in their evolutionary theorizing, but which may seem strange and unexpected at first. Natural selection can act not only to cause evolutionary change, in the sense that it can cause change in gene ratios, it can also act as a conservative force preventing change, that is keeping gene ratios stable!

Perhaps, indeed, this is not such a very surprising fact. If there were a selective value in rareness, suppose that predators had to learn to identify their victims and that consequently the more uncommon the victim the less the chance of attack, then selection might keep a population constant. If there were two forms, both equally vulnerable, then, so long as one form were less than 50 percent, it would be at a selective advantage and thus increase. But, at the 50 percent mark, neither form would have the edge on the other, and so one would expect a stable balance.

Another way in which selection could achieve such balance, and it forms my final example showing population genetics in action, involves "superior heterozygote fitness." The idea behind this is really quite simple, although it will be obvious that, without Mendelian genetics, one simply could never have conceived it. Suppose one has two alleles A and a and that the heterozygote Aa is fitter than either homozygote AA or aa. In other words, natural selection favors the Aa individuals over the AA and aa individuals. What is going to happen in the long run? Could it be that selection is going to eliminate neither the A nor the a allele, because the fittest organisms of all, the Aa heterozygotes, will always be contributing both A and a alleles to the next and succeeding generations? Would this then mean that AA and aa individuals will probably keep coming up, because when an Aa individual breeds with another Aa individual, by Mendel's first law, one quarter of its offspring will be AA and one quarter will be aa?

Let us formalize things and see if these suspicions are well founded. It would be nice to have precisely predicted ratios, so that when we go exploring for selection in nature, we come armed with some tools. This time our model is:

Genotype	AA	Aa	aa
Fitness (w)	$1 - s$	1	$1 - t$

Drawing up the usual table we get:

	Genotypes			Total Population
	AA	Aa	aa	
Initial zygote frequency	p^2	$2pq$	q^2	1
Fitness, w	$1 - s$	1	$1 - t$	
Zygote proportions after selection	$p^2(1 - s)$	$2pq$	$q^2(1 - t)$	$1 - sp^2 - tq^2$
Zygote frequencies after selection	$\dfrac{p^2(1 - s)}{1 - sp^2 - tq^2}$	$\dfrac{2pq}{1 - sp^2 - tq^2}$	$\dfrac{q^2(1 - t)}{1 - sp^2 - tq^2}$	1

Finally we calculate the rate of change.

$$\Delta p = \frac{pq(tq - sp)}{1 - sp^2 - tq^2}$$

Remember now our question: Could we ever get a stable situation, where the various selective pressures "balance" each other, so that gene ratios stay the same across the generations? In such a case, we would have $\Delta p = 0$, and it follows from the last equation that this will hold when

$$p = \frac{t}{s + t}$$

In other words, our premathematical suspicions are indeed true! When we have superior heterozygote fitness, we can expect the various selective intensities to hold gene ratios constant, according to this simple function.

Actually, there is a little bit more to the story than this. One should show, as in fact one can show, that not only will one have a stable balance when the ratio obeys the function, but that if the ratios do not fit the function initially, they will move toward it — that equilibrium frequencies are stable. Proving this point, suppose that p is greater than $t/(s + t)$. Then $sp > tq$. Therefore the value of Δp is negative, and so the proportion of A's moves down towards equilibrium. It will not drop below equilibrium, because then Δp turns positive.

My experience is that a taste for mathematics is like a taste for spinach: either you like it, or you don't! Some of my readers will just have their appetites whetted and be appalled at my informality. Others will have had quite enough symbols, thank you. Recognizing that no happy medium is possible, let me move on, hopeful at least that all readers appreciate in some sense the approach of population genetics, and are now convinced of a point I have been trying to show through the discussion: it is probably a mistake to think of modern evolutionists as seeking universal laws, at work in every situation. Because of the complexity and diversity of the organic world, today's evolutionists build limited models, trying to deal with particular problem situations: "If such and such is the case, then what results follow?" "If we have superior heterozygote fitness, then can we show that balance follows?"

Two controversies

Let me hasten to add that, for all this theoretical model building, one should not conclude that today's evolutionists are any less interested in the empirical world than Darwin was! I have suggested that probably Darwin himself sought universal laws, with the empirical content built right in, in the sense that they would be found to be working in all situations. Today's evolutionists find their empirical content in the attempt to apply their models to real-life situations. And this is obviously an important and nontrivial matter. Indeed, in a moment, we must certainly turn and look at some of the ways in which evolutionists try to put empirical flesh on their theoretical bones. But, before we do this, let me conclude my all too brief exposition of the theory of population genetics — the core of neo-Darwinian theorizing — by noting two important controversies that have attracted much attention in the past decade.

The first controversy concerns the extent to which the preceding model of heterozygote balance does actually apply to the real world. One school of thought, inspired by Dobzhansky, argues that balancing mechanisms like that based on superior heterozygote fitness are very common. Another school, inspired by H. J. Muller, argues that such mechanisms occur but infrequently. That this dispute between "balance" theorists and "classical" theorists has profound evolutionary importance can be seen right away from the fact that, if the balance hypothesis be true, then we should expect variation in populations to be the norm. At many loci one would expect two or more alleles to be represented, held in the population by selection. Hence, there would be no such thing as the standard genotype. All genotypes would be different, except for identical twins. Correspondingly, many phenotypes would be different or potentially different. In other words, one would not have to think of selection as waiting patiently for the occasional occurrence of a new mutation. Any population would contain massive variation, and if selection were to demand it, for instance, as the result of moving into a new ecological niche, it would be waiting there ready for use. (See Fig. 3.10.)

a. $+ + + + m + ... + + +$ $+ + + + + + ... + m +$
$\overline{}$
$+ + + + + ... + + +$ $+ + + + + + ... + + +$

Fig. 3.10a
Classical hypothesis: nearly all of the alleles at a locus are the same (" + "), with just the occasional mutant ("m").

b. $A_3B_2C_2DE_5...Z_2$ $A_2B_4C_1DE_2...Z_1$
$\overline{}$
$A_1B_7C_2DE_2...Z_3$ $A_3B_5C_2DE_3...Z_1$

Fig. 3.10b
Balance hypothesis: a wide range of different alleles usually occupies any given locus. For instance, at the first locus, there are three different alleles: A_1, A_2, A_3. (Adapted with permission from R. C. Lewontin, (1974). *The Genetic Basis of Evolutionary Change,* New York: Columbia University Press.)

I hardly need say that this consequence of the balance hypothesis gives a whole new perspective on the evolutionary process. Darwinism becomes a much more flexible, dynamic, opportunistic process than one might otherwise have imagined. In particular, the plausibility of natural selection as *the* creative process in evolution, as *the* cause of organic adaptation, is much enhanced. Rather than waiting for the solitary, rare, useful mutation, and building features up, step by laborious step, virtually all the time selection has a huge inventory of materials to draw on and can get to work at once should the need arise.

The metaphor that comes to mind is that of the difference between the scholar working in a center such as Cambridge, England or Massachusetts, with massive library facilities at his finger tips, and the scholar working at a very minor college, who relies on the intermittent and limited facilities of interlibrary loans for his basic source materials. Perhaps, even more accurately, since one can at least order the book one wants through interlibrary loans, and since mutation is random, we should liken the classical theorist's view to the situation of the poor isolated scholar, whose only source material comes through the Book-of-the-Month Club: there is nothing very directed towards scholarly needs about their offerings. (I hasten to add that the library at Guelph is not *that* bad!)

Obviously, it would be difficult to underestimate the importance of the truth-status of the balance hypothesis for Darwinian studies. And the same holds true for a second theoretical result which has caused perhaps even more controversy than putative balance mechanisms. Note that the Hardy-Weinberg law holds exactly only for large populations. What about the situation in small populations? One can, in fact, easily show that by chance, through sampling error, in small groups some genes could take over completely or be completely extinguished. Suppose, for instance, we had just two individuals, male and female, with genotypes AA and Aa. In a large population one would expect always to keep one quarter of the alleles as a, excluding disruptive factors. But in our case, purely by chance there may be no Aa offspring born, and thus the a allele would be totally eliminated.

I suppose in a way, one can think of drift as posing the modern equivalent of the Jenkin criticism to Darwinism. A solitary or very rare advantageous variant would not get blended out of existence, but if it were sufficiently rare or if the group were sufficiently small, then by chance it could get eliminated. The less fit character could become or stay the norm. Whether this "genetic drift" has been a significant evolutionary factor, or whether it even exists in nature at all, has led to some sprightly discussions between evolutionists. We shall have more to say about this matter later. The important point to remember now is that drift would not be controlled by selection. Therefore the characteristics it causes would not be expected to have adaptive value. Indeed, they could be mildly nonadaptive. And with a reminder that the Darwinian of today has certainly started into his model building no less convinced than the Darwinian of yesterday of the crucial importance of selection and adaptive advantage, this seems an appropriate point at which to end this chapter.

Chapter 4
The Evidence for Population Genetics

Theorizing is all very well. If population genetics is to be taken seriously as the foundation of evolutionary studies, what we need is some good solid evidence that it is more than just theory. Certainly we need something more than "theory" in the third of the senses given in the second chapter! Can we today do any better than Darwin, with his pretend examples of wolves chasing deer and of artificial selection which never really quite makes the grade? I think that we can, and in this chapter I want to give some of the reasons why I think we can.

I am not concerned here with the fact of evolution per se. That has already been argued for. What I am now interested in is the evidence that could put some empirical flesh on the theoretical skeleton given in the last chapter; or, less prosaically, do the theoretical causal models of population genetics find empirical exemplification, so that one might think that natural selection working on naturally occurring small variation could be a significant causal factor in evolutionary change? The models themselves prove neither the existence of selection nor that key variation is small. We need evidence that models specifying these, apply.

The Mendelian background

I shall assume here that the applicability of the general principles of Mendelian heredity can be taken for granted. I do not pass quickly over these principles because they are "obvious" — they certainly were not obvious to the pre-Mendelians! Nor do I pass them because they are not really important to the truth of neo-Darwinism — they could not be more important. Rather, I shall assume Mendelism because the absolutely massive evidence in its favor makes its essential truth incontrovertible, and therefore something which we can rely on without much discussion. In saying this, I do not pretend that no advances can be made on Mendelism — in my reference to molecular biology, I have already spoken of "advances" — but I do claim that the basic ideas of

Mendelism are true. In other words, we can expect to be able to apply to the living world models built on or presupposing Mendelism.

If one accepts Mendel's first law then one is at once committed to the Hardy-Weinberg law. Nevertheless, one might rather hope that there is some independent evidence showing that the law does in fact operate. It is true that we would not normally expect Hardy-Weinberg equilibrium to hold exactly in populations, because external forces like selection will normally be impinging. However, assuaging anxieties, where there are no obvious disruptive forces, there are some nice recorded cases of the Hardy-Weinberg ratios being exemplified.

One such case involves the human M-N blood groups. In a study of 1279 English people, the following ratios were observed:

M	MN	N
28.38	49.57	22.05

Were the law followed exactly, the ratios would have been

M	MN	N
28.265	49.800	21.935

To the untrained eye this is a pretty good fit! Indeed, the authors of the study allow that at best one would expect this agreement only one time in ten (Race and Sanger, 1954).

Obviously, as soon as one starts to introduce disruptive factors, the number of possible tests of basic populational genetical theory increases very dramatically. For example, one thing that our models of selection against a recessive allele lead us to expect is that, even where the allele has a very severe effect on the phenotype, because it is shielded, the allele might remain in the population at a certain level. Again, referring to humans, we find this expectation confirmed. For instance, one well-documented, human, genetically caused ailment is Tay-Sachs disease. The sufferer goes into a zombie like trance and dies at the age of three to four. Hence its bearers have zero fitness. Yet it is recessive, and expectedly within the group to which it is essentially confined, Ashkenazi Jews, there is a certain percentage of carriers. Indeed, as many as one person in thirty carries one of the offending alleles! (Kaback et al., 1974).

What about balanced superior heterozygote fitness? Are there cases of this model applying in nature? Recognizing that one or even a few cases would not establish the sweeping claims made by a balance theorist like Dobzhansky, one is happy to be able to report that there are well-documented, thoroughly analyzed instances of the phenomenon. Moreover, these instances show also very neatly the ability of population geneticists to translate their genetic speculations up to the level of the phenotype, where obviously forces like selection normally have to work. The most famous and best-analyzed case of such balance involves, once again, our own species, *Homo sapiens*. (No one thinks that humans are the only organisms to fit population genetics! It is just that medical needs have led to a bias in favor of study of our own species.)

In certain parts of West Africa, a small but fairly constant proportion of the children die in early years due to an inherited form of anemia. This "sickle-cell anemia" apparently is held in populations because, although the anemics who are homozygotes for a certain hemoglobin gene (*aa*) die without reproducing, heterozygotes (*Aa*) are not merely unaffected by the gene but have a natural immunity to a dreadful scourge of those parts, malaria. Homozygotes for the usual gene (*AA*), do not have such an immunity, and are thus at a disadvantage against the heterozygotes.

If we assume what appears to be a reasonable figure for the selective disadvantage for the homozygotes, namely that only three homozygotes reproduce for every heterozygote (i.e., $s = 1/4$), then given that no sickle-cell homozygotes reproduce (i.e., $t = 1$), we have $p = 1/(1/4 + 1) = 4/5$, where p is the frequency of the normal allele (i.e., A). It follows therefore that in *each* generation, for every 100 members of the population, we should expect that sixty-four will be AA homozygotes, thirty-two will be Aa heterozygotes, and four will be *aa* homozygotes and condemned to an early genetic death. And these ratios are in fact just about what we do find. Thus, through their abilities to link genotype with phenotype (e.g., *Aa* with malarial immunity), because of their theory, population geneticists give us an explanation. Conversely, there is supportive evidence for their position (Livingstone, 1971).

Let us grant the basic Mendelian background. We must now look somewhat more broadly, seeing if there is evidence that makes the overall claims of population geneticists compelling as valid descriptions of organic reality. Most particularly, if we have populations of organisms, does it seem that natural selection can operate and bring about change in the direction of adaptive advantage; can selection hold useful characteristics in populations; and could all the other things that are needed for full-blown evolution occur? For instance, what about something that is as yet unmentioned in the last or this chapter: speciation? Can new species be formed gradually, in conformity with selection, small variations, and the like? Remember, at this point we are talking just about the core, central mechanisms of neo-Darwinism, not the whole theory. Yet even here — especially here! — one would expect something to be said about so basic a phenomenon as speciation.

Taking a leaf from the book of physics, there seem to be two ways in which one might hope to answer questions such as these, thus proving the relevance of population genetics: one might run artificial *experiments* or one might look at *nature* (uncovering "natural experiments"). We find, in fact, that evolutionists have sought evidence from both of these sources. Without pretending to be exhaustive, let us see what has been discovered.

Experimental evidence

The experimental results have been particularly rich. I suppose that properly, like Darwin, one ought really start any survey with the successes of animal and plant breeders, showing the extent to which a selective force —

albeit artificial rather than natural — can indeed effect great phenotypic change. However, other than through one or two references, I will skip over this topic here. I have little to add to what was said earlier about Darwin's own reliance on the results of artificial selection. Such a phenomenon certainly does prove that a selective force can be effective, and this undoubtedly provides analogical support for natural selection. But selection as practiced by breeders can, at most, only incidentally show the nature and full power of a noncontrolled, natural selection. It certainly cannot show directly the natural production of adaptations. What we must look for are experiments in which evolutionists have tried to simulate conditions where, in the wild, natural selection might have been expected to operate. Does it and other posited forces indeed occur? What effect does it and the other forces have?

Let us start at the most basic level with natural selection hopefully operating in a straightforward manner. The models of population genetics point to the conclusion that a steady selective force will bring about change at the genotypic and phenotypic levels when we have two forms and no complicating factors like heterozygote fitness. We have seen this theoretically when selection works against a recessive gene, and obviously in theory selection is even more effective when promoting or reducing a fully dominant gene. There are no problems with blending. Hence, our first question can appropriately be whether such a selective force is, in fact, as effective as it claims to be in theory? Does selection work, promoting adaptations?

One elegant experiment reported by Dobzhansky (1951), aimed at showing how effective such a selective force could indeed be, and that population geneticists are right in thinking that the Jenkin criticism is powerless, attempted to simulate conditions found on oceanic islands. The insects on islands are often distinctive in being wingless or in having badly functioning wings. Normally this would be a highly deleterious feature, but there is a ready adaptive explanation: flies without wings are far less likely to be blown out to sea by cross-winds and lost than are flies with wings. Selection has favored wingless flies under these unusual circumstances.

Experimental cages of fruitflies (*Drosophila*) were therefore set up, mixing flies with wings and flies without wings — the difference being genetically controlled, and not involving distorting factors like heterozygote fitness. Under normal undisturbed circumstances, expectedly, flies with wings far outreproduced flies without wings. But, when a current of air was blown through the cages, removing flies caught in the stream, the result was reversed. Wingless flies became the norm!

Here, therefore, we had a case of selection in action, showing how adaptive features would become the norm, according to circumstances. Neo-Darwinians are right in thinking that natural selection can have a lasting effect. Moreover, in this experiment they have the added result that the kind of selective force involved is the kind to be expected in nature and led to the kind of effect found in nature. In other words, one has dual confirmation: the general models of selection seem to apply, and when one builds into the models certain causes of selection and expected effects, these also apply.

A similar experiment, which perhaps strikes a little closer to home for some of us, involved alcohol tolerance (McDonald et al., 1977)! Populations of *Drosophila melanogaster* which live around breweries and wineries generally tolerate alcohol far better than do flies of the species from more humdrum environments. They have special adaptations for the peculiarities of their circumstances. The Darwinian would expect that selection would have caused this. Those flies better able to tolerate alcohol in the appropriate circumstances would have been those flies that survived and reproduced. J. F. McDonald and colleagues selected for alcohol tolerance, breeding from one strain over twenty-eight generations, gradually increasing alcohol in their environment. As can be seen from Fig. 4.1, they were supremely successful in their endeavors. Flies thus selected had a far greater tolerance then unselected, control flies. Further study revealed the exact nature of the genetic control for alcohol tolerance in the flies. The products of a gene at an identifiable locus affect the workings of a gene at another locus, and the alcoholic tolerance of a fly is a direct function of the alleles the fly carries at the first locus.

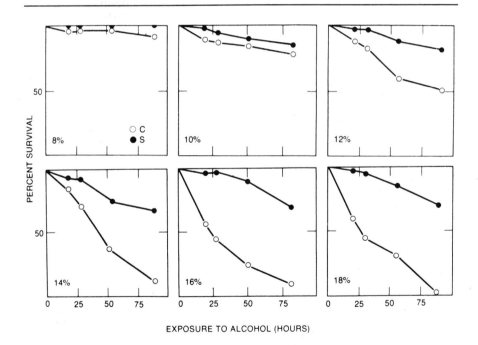

EXPOSURE TO ALCOHOL (HOURS)

Fig. 4.1
Percentages of *Drosophila melanogaster* flies which survive exposure to alcohol concentrations: Two strains were tested: those selected for alcohol tolerance (*S*), and those not selected (*C*). One can see a drastic difference in survival rates, especially as the alcohol concentration (given in lower left of graphs) gets greater. (Adapted with permission from J. F. McDonald *et al,* (1977). Adaptive response due to changes in gene regulation: a study with *Drosophila. Proc. Nat. Acad. Sci.* U.S.A., 74, 4562-4566.)

As I am sure a number of readers will have spotted, this experiment for alcohol tolerance is, in one respect, very much more powerful than the wing/wingless experiment, and consequently that much more supportive of the population geneticist's modeling. In the earlier experiment, selection worked, but only *after* the experimenters had artificially provided the required genetically based variations. In the later experiment, selection worked, ferreting out and collecting variation *which existed already* in the wild populations of *D. melanogaster* — populations that neither exhibited alcohol tolerance nor needed to! In other words, the experiment supported the claim of the balance hypothesizer when he argues that there are usually masses of variation held in any natural population, and that selection can get straight to work whenever the case arises. It is not necessary to wait for the appropriate new mutation.

All in all, a more beautiful interplay between theory and experiment could hardly be desired. In the interests of science, perhaps the only thing further that could be hoped is that there are plans underfoot to repeat the experiment with members of the species *Homo alcoholensis,* otherwise known as the common barfly. Possibly, however, Shakespeare had the final word:

Macduff. What three things does drink especially provoke?

Porter. Marry, Sir, nose-painting, sleep, and urine. Lechery, Sir, it provokes, and unprovokes: it provokes the desire, but it takes away the performance. Therefore, much drink may be said to be an equivocator with lechery. (*Macbeth,* Act 2, Scene 3)

Now let us see how Darwinians devise experiments designed to test rather more complex claims of population genetics — claims that go beyond assertions about straightforward, steady, selective forces. An experiment by Dobzhansky and his associate Pavlovsky, designed to test a consequence of the balance hypothesis and quite meaningless outside of the context of modern population genetics, has become somewhat of a classic in its own time. Remember, if the balance hypothesis be true, than there is no such thing as a standard member of a population. Virtually every organism is different.

Starting from this fact, Ernst Mayr (1942) has proposed a brilliant hypothesis, the "founder principle," about the evolution of a new group of organisms, isolated on an island or in some similar new niche. Mayr points out that a small group of founders, which might indeed be just one pregnant female, will necessarily be genetically atypical. They will not be like their parent population, because there are no standards! Thus, already, evolution to a new group will be on the way. Moreover, not only will there be all sorts of new selective pressures in the new home, but internal factors and pressures will cause rapid evolution. A gene, say, *A*, might be uncommon in the parental group, kept only because of its rarity value. In the offspring group, it might be the only gene! Thus, new selective forces might operate. Additionally, there could be a kind of domino effect in the genotypes of the new group, as the very limited variation "shakes down" into a cohesive genotype.

The overall consequence is that one expects rapid evolution and that something of a random factor is introduced. The chance sampling of the parental population will affect the future course of the offspring-group evolution. Obviously, however, "chance" must be understood in a somewhat limited sense here. There is no doubt in Mayr's mind that selection will be the major factor in the founders' evolution. I suspect that what Mayr envisions is a group of founders, faced with two or more viable evolutionary options. The founder principle tips them one way rather than the other, but selection forces the founders down the chosen path.

To test this principle, Dobzhansky and Pavlovsky (1957) started with twenty laboratory populations of fruitflies, *Drosophila pseudoobscura*: ten "large" populations (5000 individuals), and ten "small" populations (20 individuals). Initially, in all the populations a certain genetic constitution, represented as *PP*, had a frequency of 0.5. It was argued that, all other things being equal, *PP* on average should do equally well in a large or small population; but that, if the founder effect holds, one should find that time and new generations cause a much wider range of *PP* frequencies in the small populations. The large populations will yield much the same genetic background for the *PP* genotypes. The small populations will yield different backgrounds and this will affect the fitness of *PP*. (Note that the founder principle was tested only in part. Artificially Dobzhansky and Pavlovsky ensured that all the initial populations would be 50 percent *PP*, which the principle denies would happen in fact.) As the accompanying Fig. 4.2 shows very clearly, the prediction was triumphantly confirmed. After about eighteen generations, taking one and one-half years, overall in both large and small populations the average (mean) frequency of *PP* was the same, about 0.30, but the range in the small populations was far greater than that in the large populations.

By now, I trust you are starting to get some slight idea of how Darwinians can and do go about testing, experimentally, the claims of population genetics. The three examples I have given are but the tiniest tip of a very large and ever-expanding iceberg of experimental data. I myself shall be giving more examples of evolutionary experiments as the discussion proceeds. But, you can sense the way in which population genetics can be put to experimental test, and the strong positive response that has been recorded in the past decades, since the synthetic theory was first formulated. Without exaggeration, my own feeling is that an experimental result such as that obtained by Dobzhansky and Pavlovsky, in their test of the founder principle, is as strongly supportive of the evolutionist's case about the core of their theory as is Young's double-slit experiment supportive of the upholder of the wave theory of light. However, I will not bother to halt here and hymn the praises of the neo-Darwinians, but will turn next to look at results garnered from nature.

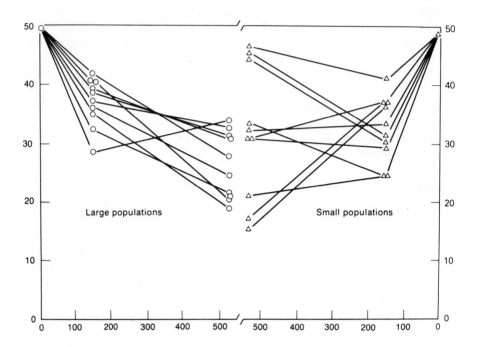

Fig. 4.2
The founder effect: The graphs show the fate of a certain genetic variant known as *PP* in laboratory populations of *Drosophila pseudoobscura*. Note that time goes from left to right for large populations, but is reversed for small populations. (Adapted by permission from T. Dobzhansky and O. Pavlovsky, (1957). An experimental study of interaction between genetic drift and natural selection. *Evolution,* 11, 311-319.)

The evidence from nature

At this point, it is the English, still continuing the great tradition of the early Darwinians, who come to the fore. It has never been a claim of Darwinism that *all* features must be adaptive. Remember, in fact, that Darwin himself argued for his own position precisely because some features do *not* have adaptive value: homologies and rudimentary organs, for instance. But broadly, Darwinism emphasizes adaptation and stresses that only selection could be behind it. Hence, we can and must ask whether, in nature, we actually do see selection holding certain characteristics in a population, because they confer an adaptive advantage on their possessors?

What would be particularly striking and convincing for the Darwinian case would be proof that selection preserves certain features that critics have identified as paradigmatic examples of nonadaptation: features outside of the Darwinian paradigm. In fact, just such convincing evidence is available! In the early years of population genetics, in North America particularly, genetic drift was very popular. If one could not think of an obviously adaptive function for a feature, then it was put down to drift. Virtually every one of those features has since been shown to be an exemplar of Darwinism! They are tightly controlled by selection.

Discussion of one case must suffice: that of the color of shells of the snail *Cepaea nemoralis.* Why is it that we find different colors of shell in different groups? Some are banded; some are not. Some are yellow; some are brown; some are pink. Some groups are uniform; some groups are mixed. Is this just chance? Answering these questions through careful study, the British evolutionists A. J. Cain and P. M. Sheppard (1952, 1954) were able to show that shell color has a vital adaptive role, providing camouflage against the most common predator, thrushes. Where the background is uniform, as on a heath, the shell tends to be unbanded. The reverse is true of a varied background like a ditch. And, we find intermediate groups against intermediate backgrounds. In like manner, color is also a function of background. A beechwood calls for a dark brown shell — and gets it! Moreover, color is additionally controlled by the seasons. Pink shells, for instance, are favored against the lighter background shades of the spring. (See Figs. 4.3, 4.4, 4.5, and 4.6.)

Fig. 4.3
Polymorphic forms of *Cepaea nemoralis:* yellow unbanded; yellow banded; brown unbanded. (Photograph by permission of John Haywood.)

Fig. 4.4
Banded and unbanded forms of *Cepaea nemoralis* in the grass. (Photograph by permission of John Haywood.)

Fig. 4.5
A "thrush stone": the broken shells of *Cepaea nemoralis* are left by the birds. (Photograph by permission of W. H. Dowdeswell).

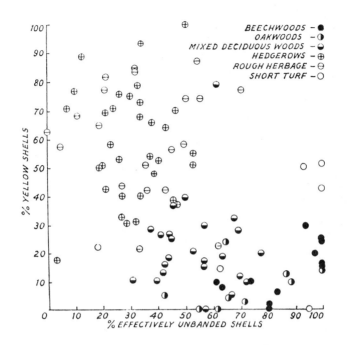

Fig. 4.6
Correlation of yellow shells and unbanded shells of *cepaea nemoralis,* showing habitats. (Adapted with permission from A. J. Cain and P. M. Sheppard, (1954). Natural selection in *Cepaea. Genetics, 39,* 89-116.)

Driving home the strength of their findings, the observers were able to show selection really in action. Fortunately the thrush is a good Darwinian. Making possible the naturalist's studies, conveniently he takes his prey to particular stones, "anvils," smashes the snail and leaves the broken, empty shell, ready to be counted! It was possible therefore to count living snails and to compare their numbers with those of the snails actually caught and killed by the thrushes. In one set of observations of snails found against a uniform background, Sheppard (1951) obtained the figures shown in Table 4.1.

It can be seen at once that there is a higher chance of death for the banded snail than the unbanded snail, and one can easily show that a selective force of this magnitude would soon eliminate unbanded snails. In all, one has a convincing picture of selection at work. I should add parenthetically that since the Cain-Sheppard work, a great deal more effort has been spent studying the variations in *Cepaea.* The importance of selection has been documented time and again, although it is now realized that there are many factors in addition

	Number of Shells			% Banded
	Banded	Unbanded	Total	
Living	264	296	560	47.1
Killed by thrushes	486	377	863	56.3

Predation of snails by thrushes.

Table 4.1
Predation of snails by thrushes. (Taken with permission from P. M. Sheppard, (1967). *Natural Selection and Heredity,* London: Hutchinson.)

to bird predation that control snail type. For instance, one important selective force is directly linked to temperature. (See Fig 4.7. Please consult Jones et al., 1977, for further references to *Cepaea* studies.)

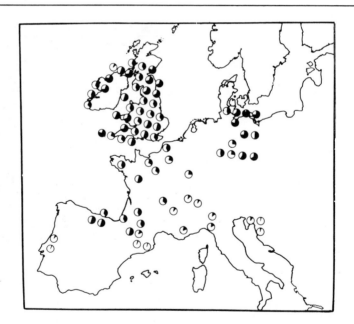

Fig. 4.7
Frequency of yellow shells (white sector) in European populations of *Cepaea nemoralis.* (Adapted with permission from J. S. Jones *et al*, (1977). Polymorphism in *Cepaea*: a problem with too many solutions? *Ann. Rev. Ecol. Syst.,* 8, 109-43. ©1977 by Annual Reviews Inc.)

What about observations of selection actually changing one form to another? Again we turn to Darwin's homeland, for the best-known sets of studies on natural selection in action are those by English evolutionists on the evolving melanic forms in moths. To take the most fully documented case, the moth *Biston betularia,* it has been recorded beyond doubt that in the past century the moth has evolved, from a uniformly mottled, light gray color to a dark "melanic" form. And, the reason is unequivocally a function of natural selection. The chief danger to the moths is predators, specifically birds that eat them. Against a clean, lichen-colored tree, the light mottled moths are well camouflaged, whereas the melanic moths are at a selective disadvantage. However, in the past 100 years, thanks to the rise of industry, the consequent air pollution and the soot-blackening of tree barks, the tables have turned. Now, it is the melanic forms that are camouflaged and at an adaptive advantage, and it is the gray forms that stand out and are picked off by predators. (See Figs. 4.8, 4.9, and 4.10.)

Fig. 4.8
The two forms of *Biston betularia* against a lichen-covered tree in Dorset. (Photograph by permission of the estate of the late Dr. H. B. D. Kettlewell.)

Not only has this process been actually seen to happen, but the conclusions have been backed up by experiment. The late H. B. D. Kettlewell of Oxford University released hundreds of light and dark moths in polluted and unpolluted areas of England (Birmingham and Dorset, respectively). Expectedly, it was found that birds in Birmingham could spot gray forms more easily, and that birds in Dorset could spot melanic forms more easily. These differences

Fig. 4.9
The two forms of *Biston betularia* against a dirty tree in Birmingham. (Photograph by permission of the estate of the late Dr. H. B. D. Kettlewell.)

Fig. 4.10
A robin holding in its beak the melanic form of *Biston betularia.* Can you see the other two moths on the tree (one is melanic and one is not)? (Photograph by permission of the estate of the late Dr. H. B. D. Kettlewell.)

were also dramatically underlined when moths were recaptured. Proportionately, far more melanic forms could be taken in Birmingham, and proportionately far more gray forms in Dorset. (See Table 4.2.) In short, everything points to the effectiveness of selection. Moreover, it is worth noting that *Biston betularia* is far from being an isolated case. At least a 100 different species of moth are known to exhibit industrial melanism. Expectedly, where strict pollution controls have been instigated, light moths have been found to make a come back! Selection once again favors them. (For full details, see Ford, 1971, and Kettlewell, 1955, 1973.)

Locality	Moths released		Moths recaptured	
	light	dark	light	dark
Birmingham	64	154	16(25%)	82(53%)
Dorset	393	406	54(13.7%)	19(4.7%)

Table 4.2
Briston betularia moths recaptured in two areas. Birmingham is dirty and Dorset is clean. (Taken with permission from H. B. D. Kettlewell, (1961). The phenomenon of industrial melanism in Lepidoptera, *Annual Review of Entomology*, 6, 245-62.)

It is sometimes argued that this well-documented and much-discussed example of natural selection in action does not prove enough. After all, we do not have an elephant being changed into a camel or anything like that. But, although this is undoubtedly true — after all, if we did see selection turning an elephant into a camel, I doubt I would have to write this book — I confess I find myself rather unmoved by the argument. What I am trying to show is how evolutionists have been able to establish that the kind of theoretical picture contained in population genetics actually finds a response in nature — the theory is about things that really occur. Examples like that of the melanic moth are obviously pertinent to this end. As the population geneticist claims, selection occurs and actually changes organisms according to adaptive needs. This obviously all helps to strengthen the case of the neo-Darwinian evolutionist about the relevance to nature of his core mechanism. Remember that at this point we are dealing with the central core; later we shall be turning to look at wider-scale changes.

The formation of species

Some readers may reasonably object: What about the kinds of queries that someone like T. H. Huxley was raising, just about as soon as the *Origin* was published? What about the creation of new species? The moth color changes certainly do not involve changes of this type or order of magnitude. Unless we have some evidence that today's evolutionist can throw causal explanatory light on this, we continue to have a major hiatus in the evidential case for neo-Darwinism. Happily, however, today we are able to go a very significant way toward countering the worries of Huxley. There is a rapidly growing number of experimental findings that selection-like forces can bring about reproductive isolation between subgroups of a population — the key mark of the making of a new species. (See Jones, 1981, for an excellent review.)

Reproductive isolation can be a function of many things, from simple disinclination of organisms to breed ("Do you have an erotic attraction towards cabbages?") all the way to hybrid sterility, the most famous case being the horse/donkey hybrid, the super-strong but totally sterile mule. For reasons to be explained later, both Darwin and modern evolutionists deny that hybrid sterility can be a direct function of selection. However, there is evidence that both artificial and natural selection can bring about isolating mechanisms not involving such sterility, and can strengthen them once they exist. I would have thought indeed that dog breeders have got very close to or achieved the required effect of isolation through artificial selection (Dobzhansky et al., 1977; Ridley, 1981). Reproductive isolation does not necessarily mean that no sexual desires exist, but rather that reproduction is impossible or prevented. A Great Dane and a Yorkshire Terrier would simply have great difficulty copulating. I doubt it could be done other than artificially. Of course, dogs are all one species, because interbreeding can go on between members on a gradated scale of size; but a barrier is a barrier. If one took away all the intermediates, one would be close to the production of two species.

Analogously, in some very well known experiments, J. M. Thoday and his associates were able to set up reproductive barriers between subgroups of fruitflies in a very few generations, by artificially selecting for extremes of body-bristle numbers (Thoday and Gibson, 1962). One should note however that Thoday was attempting to simulate sympatric speciation (i.e., speciation without geographical isolation), rather than allopatric speciation (i.e., speciation with such isolation). For this reason, he did not prevent his types of flies from interbreeding. The fact that the experiments have proven rather difficult to repeat (Scharloo, 1971), has underlined contemporary suspicion that, in nature, totally sympatric speciation is rare. (However, Paterniani, 1969, achieved results similar to Thoday's when artificially selecting corn.)

Some good experimental evidence that shows that selection can perfect isolating mechanisms was produced by Kessler (1969). The flies *Drosophila pseudoobscura* and *Drosophila persimilis* will sometimes cross breed, producing fertile females and infertile males. As Table 4.3 (Dobzhansky et al., 1977, p. 181) shows, expectedly, selection can strongly increase the degree of isolation.

Lines	pseudoobscura ♀ pseudoobscura ♂	pseudoobscura ♀ persimilis ♂	persimilis ♀ pseudoobscura ♂	persimilis ♀ persimilis ♂
Unselected	49%	6%	4 %	41%
High lines	39	2	0	59
Low lines	27	21	1.4	51

Table 4.3
Selection for reproductive isolation: The figures show rates of breeding. "High lines" were flies selected for eighteen generations aiming at showing no cross-breeding inclination, and "low lines" were flies selected to show cross-breeding inclination. (Taken with permission from Dobzhansky *et al*, (1977). Based on Kessler, (1969).)

Similar sorts of results have been achieved by other experimenters, working on isolation between groups from different species and within the same species (Knight et al., 1956; Koopman, 1950; Wallace, 1954).

But what about human run and natural experiments that show that, under the conditions supposed by neo-Darwinians, reproductive barriers will occur? Do we have direct evidence of the production of new species, or must we refer always to the analogy of artificial selection? Even though results like those just given, show that a selective force of some kind can lead to and perfect reproductive barriers, artificial selection never shows definitively that natural selection can do what is claimed of it.

To answer such questions as these just posed, we must first inquire a little more deeply into the neo-Darwinian position on speciation. The belief of most modern thinkers, like Mayr, is that generally reproductive barriers are a function of factors that occur as the incidental by-product of two isolated populations evolving apart under unrelated adaptive forces. The barriers can be strengthened by selection once the groups touch with each other again. Obviously this is all very much in the spirit of Darwin's position on speciation; although, many neo-Darwinians would probably emphasize the need for geographical isolation rather more strongly than did Darwin himself. (In fairness, I should add that this question is still a matter of ongoing debate; there is a vocal group of Darwinians who would agree with Darwin that ecological isolation can do all that is needed.)

Added to these views today, most neo-Darwinians think also that the founder principle is often a major factor in speciation. One popular hypothesis using this principle supposes that a small group of organisms find themselves in a new environment. Free from the competition of fellow species members, they might explode up in numbers (a "population flush"). But then, overextended, with an impoverished gene pool, numbers might collapse down again. And this cyclical process could happen several times, until (as it were) the group shakes down into a stable, cohesive unit. Were something like this to happen, it is suggested that speciation could occur rapidly (Carson, 1973, 1975).

It is sometimes suggested that a process like this rivals speciation which comes simply as a result of two isolated populations drifting apart as the consequence of unrelated adaptive pressures. However, although it is indeed true that one can emphasize the randomness in the founder principle almost to the exclusion of adaptive Darwinian change, as I hinted earlier when introducing the founder principle, it is probably better to think of speciation mechanisms as a continuum, with the founder principle going from nonimportance to crucial importance. For someone like Mayr, the direct effect of natural selection would always be a major factor. (But see Fig. 4.11.)

Certainly, it would be wise not to oppose the ends of the spectrum too starkly, for there is experimental evidence both that speciation can occur between groups coming apart when under the influence of different selective pressures and that it can occur when the founder principle with population flushes is operating. (Remember that we have already seen some experimental evidence for the founder principle alone.) Pertinent to the traditional view of speciation, one study showed that when isolated populations of *Drosophila melanogaster* were kept at different humidities and temperatures for five years, barriers to reproduction between population members were formed. Similar effects have been obtained with other species of *Drosophila* and with house flies (Kilias et al., 1980; see also Jones, 1981). Pertinent to the founder principle/population flush view, it was found that, after three cycles of expansion and contraction, populations of *D. pseudoobscura* started to show a definite disinclination to interbreed (Powell, 1978). In all of these studies it is worth emphasizing that, within experimental bounds, the forces at work were natural, rather than artificial. The experimenters did not breed from consciously chosen types in each generation. Rather, an attempt was made to simulate presumed naturally occurring conditions, and then nature was allowed to take its course without conscious, end-directed interference.

Turning from human-run experiments to natural experiments, we find several studies suggesting that something like the founder principle could be at work in nature. One clever study revealed that the northern elephant seal (*Mirounga angustirostris*), which at one point in the past century dropped to an effective breeding group of less than twenty, today (with a population of 30,000) has virtually no intragroup genetic variation. Thus elimination of variation is precisely the expected effect of the founder principle. *M. angustirostris* contrasts strongly with the southern elephant seal *M. leonina*

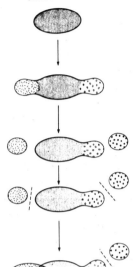

Conventional Model

First Stage.
A single population or series of similar populations in a homogenous environment.

Second Stage.
As the environment becomes partly diversified in physical or biotic factors, or as new populations are built up from migrants into new environments, the system of populations becomes diversified, giving rise to races with different ecological requirements but which nevertheless can still exchange genes at their boundaries, since no reproductive isolating mechanisms have developed.

Third Stage.
Further differentiation and migration produce geographic isolation of some races and subspecies.

Fourth Stage.
Some subspecies acquire genetic differences that cause them to be reproductively isolated from the remainder of the original population and from each other.

Fifth Stage.
Further changes in the environment permit some of the newly evolved species to enter the area still occupied by the original population. Because of past differentiation, the two sympatric species exploit the environment in different ways, and are prevented from merging by the barriers of reproductive isolation. Natural selection against the formation of sterile or ill-adapted hybrids promotes reinforcement of the isolating mechanisms and further differentiation in the ways the two species exploit their environment.

Quantum Model

First Stage.
Same as in the conventional model

Second Stage.
A few individuals of the original population, isolated in a new habitat, produce a secondary population with an altered gene pool

Third Stage.
A population crash reduces the secondary population to a few atypical individuals.

Fourth Stage.
Recovery accompanied by new selection pressures (resulting from the altered gene pool) produces a new population reproductively isolated from the original one.

Fig. 4.11
Origin of a new species according to the "conventional" and "quantum" models of geographic speciation. (Adapted with permission from Dobzhansky *et al*, (1977).)

which had no bottleneck and which has plenty of intragroup genetic variation (Bonnell and Selander, 1974).

But, perhaps most exciting and pertinent of all to the whole question of the creation of new species is a series of observations and inferences about a certain population of fruitflies (*Drosophila pseudoobscura*) to be found in Bogota, Columbia. Through a combination of luck and informed intuition, Prakash (1972) has been able to show that they are right in the middle of evolving into a new species, and that they exhibit just the characteristics one would expect were the principles of neo-Darwinism at work! In 1955 and 1956 extensive collection in Columbia yielded absolutely no members of *Drosophila pseudoobscura,* making it highly improbable that any existed. The nearest population was in Guatemala, 1500 miles away. However, *D. pseudoobscura* started to appear in Columbian traps in 1960, suggesting that somehow it had been transported to Bogota, and now in some localities it is one of the most common of fruitflies. Moreover, tests show that already Columbian *D. pseudoobscura* are starting to develop reproductive barriers with flies of the species collected from elsewhere. Although males from Bogota crossed with females from elsewhere produce normal offspring, females from Bogota produce totally sterile males when crossed with foreign *D. pseudoobscura.* New species are in the making!

The Bogota flies show strong evidence of a species being produced as the population geneticist would predict. In particular, they exhibit the features of a group affected by the founder principle. Chromosomal study suggests powerfully that the Bogota flies' closest relatives are those living in Guatemala. Expectedly, the Bogota flies show far less intrapopulation genetic variation than do those in Guatemala. This is a consequence of the founders bringing only a fraction of the total parental gene-pool. Where Guatemalan flies have no variation at a locus (or very little variation), then, expectedly, the Bogota flies tend to resemble the Guatemalan flies. And, expectedly and most significantly, showing that the founders could not have been totally typical (because no group is that), at least one allele which is very rare in Bogota (1–2 percent) is virtually the norm in Columbia (87 percent). In short, one has precisely what theory leads one to expect, and thus in turn one has evidence that what the theory claims about the evolution of new species actually and typically obtains in nature.

All in all, therefore, the neo-Darwinians can rightly point to a wide spectrum of evidence — experimental and natural — supporting their views on the mechanisms of speciation. In the next chapter, we shall see how this evidence is complemented by other findings in nature, as neo-Darwinians apply their mechanisms.

Molecular biology and the classical/balance dispute

Let me conclude this discussion of evolutionists' evidence for the central foundations of their theory by trying simultaneously to do two things. In the last chapter, I mentioned molecular biology, promising later to show it in action in the evolutionary domain. I suggested that its status seems to be less that of something that led to radical new insights into the evolutionary process and more something immensely helpful in resolving problems suggested by traditional biological theorizing but insoluble by traditional biological methods. To be candid, this is a matter of personal impression and not intended as a definitive claim. But, at least, I can show the great value of molecular biology in solving disputes by referring again to the classical/balance hypothesis dispute and seeing how far we are toward ending the controversy.

Remember that Muller's "classical" hypothesis supposes that the genetically caused variation occurring in natural populations is rare; whereas Dobzhansky's "balance" hypothesis sees variation almost as the norm, a function of such causes as balanced superior heterozygote fitness. No one denies that one does sometimes get causes like balanced heterozygote fitness at work: sickle-cell anemia is as well attested a case as one could possibly have. The crux of the dispute is over just how widespread and effective these causes are. That answers to this question are really important needs no justification. We saw in some detail just how much depends on the truth of the balance hypothesis. One's whole approach to evolution generally, and natural selection in particular, is bound to be colored by it. And, this is apart from the fact that crucial side mechanisms cherished by many neo-Darwinians, such as the founder effect, are meaningless if populations are absolutely uniform.

Unfortunately, if one tries to decide between the rival hypotheses using conventional techniques of breeding and so forth, definitive answers are just not forthcoming. Environmental factors and the like make direct results totally ambiguous — is a certain fly an efficient reproducer because of heterozygote fitness, or because of some design-quirk in the cage? One can certainly get some very suggestive hints, pointing towards the balance hypothesis. The alcohol tolerance experiment supports the hypothesis, for instance, as do all the natural findings about the importance of the founder principle. But the classical supporter can and will go on denying its universal validity.

Now, at one stroke, molecular evolutionists, most notably R. C. Lewontin, have cut through the Gordian knot. Using a technique known as "gel electrophoresis" (see Figs. 4.12 and 4.13), they have examined genes from a molecular perspective and have been able to show that there are indeed incredible amounts of genetically based variation occurring in natural populations. There simply is no such thing as a standard common member. The DNA molecules of the individuals of a group vary widely. (See Table 4.4.) In this sense, at least, the balance hypothesis of Dobzhansky is totally vindicated.

I am afraid that by now the reader must be realizing that, as in love and war, nothing in science runs very smoothly. Showing that there is molecular variation does not go all the way to proving Dobzhansky's strong claim, namely that the genetic variation of populations is held there by selection mechanisms, like that centering on balanced heterozygote fitness. I must therefore report that debate still continues among evolutionists. Some argue that, although there is molecular variation, it does not follow that much of this

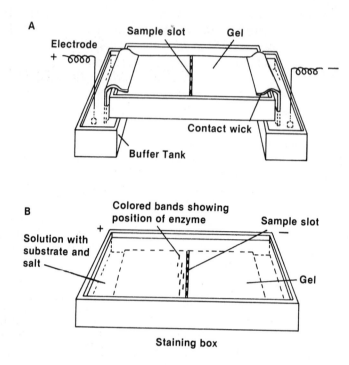

Fig. 4.12

Gel electrophoresis: The aim is to measure genetic variation in natural populations. As we have seen, different genes (*i.e.* different DNA molecules) produce different proteins, and the key to the technique of gel electrophoresis is that different proteins have different electrostatic charges. Thus by identifying these differences, one can infer back to the differences in genes. (At least, one can infer back to those differences which get reflected in the proteins.)

The technique is simple. One puts samples of protein, obtained from the tissues of the organisms being studied, on a tray of gel (as shown in *A* above); one runs an electric current across the gel for a few hours; and then through various chemical techniques one shows up how far the particular proteins one is studying have migrated down the tray *(B)*. The distance of migration is a function of electrical charge of the protein, and hence one can separate out the differences in the proteins. (Adapted with permission from Ayala and Valentine, (1979).)

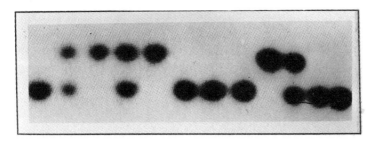

Fig. 4.13
A typical result obtained from a gel electrophoretic experiment: We are looking at the proteins obtained from tissue samples of 12 flies of *Drosophila pseudoobscura*, as they have migrated across the gel because of an electric current (running from bottom to top). It is believed, in fact, that we are dealing with two alleles Pgm^{100} and Pgm^{108}, and that proteins from the latter have migrated farther than proteins from the former. It can therefore be seen that (from left to right) the first fly was a $Pgm^{100/100}$ homozygote, the second a $Pgm^{100/108}$ heterozygote, the third a $Pgm^{108/108}$ homozygote, and so forth. (Taken with permission from Ayala and Valentine, (1979).)

Organisms	Number of species studied	Average number of loci studied per species	Proportion of polymorphic loci per population*	Proportion of heterozygous loci per individual
Invertebrates				
Drosophila	28	24	0.529	0.150
Wasps	6	15	0.243	0.062
Other insects	4	18	0.531	0.151
Marine	14	23	0.439	0.124
Land snails	5	18	0.437	0.150
Vertebrates				
Fish	14	21	0.306	0.078
Amphibians	11	22	0.336	0.082
Reptiles	9	21	0.231	0.047
Birds	4	19	0.145	0.042
Mammals	30	28	0.206	0.051
Average values				
Invertebrates	57	21.8	0.469	0.134
Vertebrates	68	24.1	0.247	0.060
Plants	8	8	0.464	0.170

*The criterion of polymorphism is not the same for all species.

Table 4.4
Genic variation in populations of some major groups of animals and plants. (Taken with permission from Ayala and Valentine, (1979).)

translates into different Mendelian genes, with their consequent different effects on phenotypes and their fitnesses. Because of redundancies, variants of
DNA molecules could all produce the same cellular products, or identically
functioning cellular products. It is suggested that perhaps much molecular
variation is therefore not controlled by selection, and, being adaptively
neutral, just drifts randomly in populations, subject only to the chance
vagaries of reproduction. (See, for instance, King and Jukes, 1969.)

Nevertheless, although one cannot say absolutely that this suggestion is
quite false, it is starting to seem highly improbable that it contains more than a
modicum of the truth. Increasing evidence shows that molecular differences
do indeed translate out as phenotypic differences, controlled by selection. In
other words, that the balance hypothesis applies widely in nature seems more
and more well established. One very pertinent series of observations, gathered
and analyzed by Francisco Ayala and his associates, showed that isolated
natural populations of fruitflies have virtually identical ratios of molecular
alleles, as revealed through their cellular products. This suggests that they are
under the control of selection. Were things otherwise, the ratios would have
drifted apart (Ayala et al., 1974a).

Additionally, given the fact that the evidential status of artificial selection
has suffered so much criticism since the *Origin* first appeared, it is nice to be
able to report that at this point artificial selection pertinently and helpfully
comes to support molecular biology. All of our experience, whether that of
breeders or of evolutionary experimenters, is that there is virtually no organic
characteristic that does not respond to artificial selection. For instance,
Lewontin observes of the fruitfly: "There appears to be no character — mor-
phogenetic, behavioral, physiological, or cytological — that cannot be selected
in Drosophila" (Lewontin, 1974, p. 92). This all points to great amounts of
genetically caused variation in populations, which variation expresses itself at
the phenotypic level. Hence, the classical theorist simply cannot conclude that
molecular variation hides down below the level that selection can touch. And,
since widespread drift at this upper level seems less and less probable, some
variant of the balance hypothesis seems more and more probable.

Conclusion

We have come full circle. The Darwinians' oldest form of support, artificial selection, touches hands with the Darwinians' newest form of support,
molecular biology. Appropriately, therefore, this survey of the evidential base
for population genetics, that body of knowledge which contains the core
mechanisms of neo-Darwinian evolutionary theory, can be concluded.

Leaving until the end of the next chapter an overall assessment of the
strength of neo-Darwinism, I would simply suggest here that things are very
much changed from the time of the *Origin*. That natural selection working on
small variations is a powerful mechanism, seems beyond doubt. Experimental
and natural observation confirms this. Furthermore, modern population

genetics, with its balance hypothesis perspective, with its subsidiary mechanisms like the founder principle, and with much much more, gives deeper and more adequate insights into the overall causes of evolutionary change than anything Darwin himself could give. There is continuity — and there is advance.

But our presentation of "Darwinism Today" is not yet complete. We have yet to see the core part of neo-Darwinian theory — population genetics — in action, as it is applied to the rest of biology. It is to this topic that we turn now.

Chapter 5
Neo-Darwinism: The Total Picture

I have been at pains to show the great changes that have occurred in evolutionary theorizing since the time of Darwin and the *Origin*: the coming of Mendelism, and the consequent substitution of population genetics, theory and evidence, for the rather informal central arguments of Darwin's theory. But now we start to sail into calmer and more familiar waters. Like Darwin himself, the neo-Darwinians recognize that throughout the living world there is a strong tendency towards overpopulation and that this sets up conflicting selective pressures. Hence, neo-Darwinians feel justified in turning to the theory that combines selection with modern principles of heredity: population genetics.

Thus, as Darwin's central arguments performed in the theory of the *Origin*, the modern causal mechanisms serve as a focus, uniting many different areas of biological thought, and conversely throwing explanatory light into all sorts of different corners. (See Fig. 5.1.) Paleontology, biogeography, embryology, systematics, instinctive behavior, and other disciplines are all brought beneath the umbrella. And it is shown how they are connected by the evolution of organisms, a causal function of Darwinian selection working on Mendelian (or molecular) genes within populations. Dobzhansky, as always, is beautifully explicit:

Evolution is a change in the genetic composition of populations. The study of mechanisms of evolution falls within the province of population genetics. Of course, changes observed in populations may be of different orders of magnitude. Experience shows, however, that there is no way toward understanding of the mechanisms of macroevolutionary changes, which require time on geological scales, other than through understanding of microevolutionary processes observable within the span of a human lifetime, often controlled by man's will, and sometimes reproducible in laboratory experiments. (Dobzhansky, 1951, p. 16)

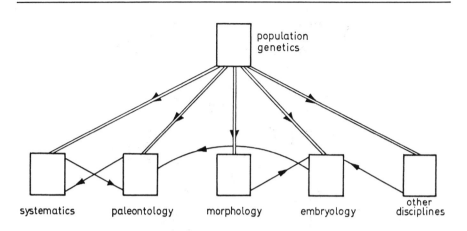

Fig. 5.1
The structure of the synthetic theory: In this figure, the rectangles represent various disciplines; the double lines the links between population genetics and other areas — such links are actually supposed to exist; and the single lines links between the subsidiary disciplines — although such links do exist, those shown in the figure are just illustrative, they do not necessarily denote particular instances. Compare this picture of neo-Darwinian theory, with the earlier picture of Darwin's theory in the *Origin* (Fig. 2.10).

Darwin's finches

As a paradigmatic example of neo-Darwinism in action, underlining both the continuity and advances since the *Origin,* I can think of no better candidate than that of the explanatory picture which is proposed for organisms on oceanic islands: a picture or model that is obviously inspired by, and intended to apply to, those very Galapagos finches which spurred Darwin to evolutionism and which deservedly held a prideful place in the *Origin.* (See Figs. 5.2 and 5.3.)

The overall claim by neo-Darwinians is that of Darwin. It is argued that the organisms (thinking now specifically of land-based organisms like animals and birds) come originally from the mainland, and then evolve in their new homes, such evolution reflecting new environmental pressures and the occasional movement of an organism from one island to another. Causally, as Dobzhansky states in the passage just quoted, it is assumed and argued that the evolution is controlled and directed by factors specified in population genetics. In other words, it is assumed that the organisms involved, the parent populations and those that go to the islands, are Mendelian in the sense that their members contain genes that function and are transmitted in the ways specified by Mendelian/population genetics.

Fig. 5.2

Darwin's finches; male and female of each species.

Scientific name	Descriptive designation
1. *Geospiza magnirostris* Gould	Large ground-finch
2. *Geospiza fortis* Gould	Medium ground-finch
3. *Geospiza fuliginosa* Gould	Small ground-finch
4. *Geospiza difficilis* Sharpe	Sharp-beaked ground-finch
5. *Geospiza scandens* (Gould)	Cactus ground-finch
6. *Geospiza conirostris* Ridgway	Large cactus ground-finch
7. *Camarhynchus crassirostris* Gould	Vegetarian tree-finch
8. *Camarhynchus psittacula* Gould	Large insectivorous tree-finch
9. *Camarhynchus pauper* Ridgway	Large insectivorous tree-finch on Charles
10. *Camarhynchus parvulus* (Gould)	Small insectivorous tree-finch
11. *Camarhynchus pallidus* (Sclater and Salvin)	Woodpecker-finch
12. *Camarhynchus heliobates* (Snodgrass and Heller)	Mangrove-finch
13. *Certhidea olivacea* Gould	Warbler-finch
14. *Pinaroloxias inornata* (Gould)	Cocos-finch

(Adapted with permission from D. Lack, (1947). *Darwin's Finches,* Cambridge: Cambridge University Press.)

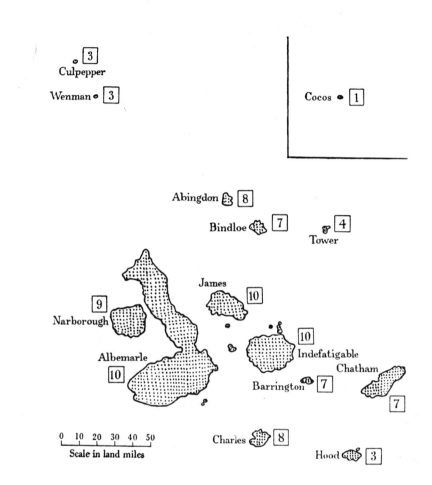

Fig. 5.3

Number of species of Darwin's finches on each island. (Adapted with permission from Lack, (1947).)

It is assumed further that the chief causal factor at work in the evolution will be natural selection, the differential reproduction of genotypes and phenotypes, operating on the different genetic/physical characteristics ranging through the populations involved — such variation ultimately being a function of nondirected mutation and, where selected, almost invariably small (at the phenotypic level). And of course it is presumed that the end result of selection will be adaptively integrated organisms, functioning adequately in their new homes.

Neo-Darwinians therefore expect to find, just about above all else, that the island organisms will reflect new selective pressures and adaptive needs. The prediction is that natural selection working on variations caused by random mutation will have been at work and will leave its mark. Because of the nonblending nature of Mendelian inheritance, adaptively valuable new features will not get swamped out. And, indeed, reflecting the fact that now we have far more empirical information than Darwin had, evolutionists feel happy that this prediction is strongly confirmed; that is to say, that the theorizing is exemplified in nature.

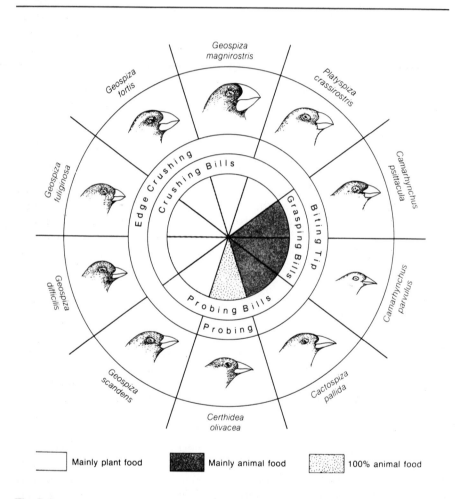

Fig. 5.4
The ten species of Darwin's finches to be found on Indefatigable Island, showing the adaptive evolution of their beaks for different feeding habits. (Adapted with permission from Dobzhansky *et al,* (1977).)

Thus, staying solely with the finches, we find that all the different species show the effects of selection — peculiar characteristic after peculiar characteristic has some special adaptive function. Some finches have evolved in such a way that they are ideally suited to the consumption of plant food; some mainly for the consumption of animal food; some solely for animal food. As Fig. 5.4 shows, there are beaks for cactus eating, beaks for insect eating on the wing, beaks for more general scavenging. One species has even developed the ability to probe with twigs for insects in hollow parts of trees! (So much for man, the toolmaker!)

Moreover, it seems that the finches have taken advantage of ecological vacancies due to the absence of other sorts of birds on the island. Thus speaking of the insectivorous tree-finches *Camarhynchus psittacula* and *C. parvalus* and of the woodpecker finch *C. pallidus* in a classic study, the ornithologist David Lack observed:

On James and Indefatigable all three species occur together. But on Chatham the large insectivorous tree-finch *C. psittacula* is absent, and here, . . ., the small species *C. parvulus* attains an unusually large size. But this is not all, for the Chatham form of the woodpecker-finch *C. pallidus* has a shorter beak than usual. This suggests that, in the absence of *C. psittacula,* there has been survival value to *C. pallidus* in becoming less specialized in beak, and that the Chatham form of *C. pallidus* takes some of the foods which on other islands are taken by *C. psittacula.*

The opposite situation perhaps occurs on Abingdon and Bindloe, where the woodpecker-finch *C. pallidus* is absent, and the large insectivorous tree-finch *C. psittacula* has a longer and straighter beak than usual, suggesting that it may take some of the foods normally taken by *C. pallidus.* (Lack, 1947, pp. 70-71. See also Fig. 5.5, which perhaps suggests that the causal connexion also goes in the other direction: when there is competition, organisms move away from direct conflict.)

I hope that now it is not necessary to go on stressing that results like these are precisely what Darwinians expect; conversely, they feel that their causal theory, as expounded in the last two chapters, throws explanatory light upon them.

Just very recently, a report has been published, documenting just precisely how selection in one instance has worked on the finches. A major drought occurred on the islet of Daphne Major in 1977. The medium ground finch (*Geospiza fortis*) suffered an 85 percent decline in population, and did not breed at all in that year. Survivors were larger than average and had larger beaks: they and only they were able to crack the large, hard seeds that predominated in the drought. This led to a lasting change in the group, as a Darwinian expects (Boag and Grant, 1981).

Obviously, in dealing with an explanation outside of the direct core, as in biogeography, one must add additional principles and information peculiar to the particular discipline at issue in order to work toward a complete explanation; that is to say, to provide a picture that is entirely applicable to the case at issue. In biogeography, for instance, Darwin went to great efforts to analyze natural methods of transportation and distribution around the globe, showing just how animals and plants might end up in strange and wonderful places.

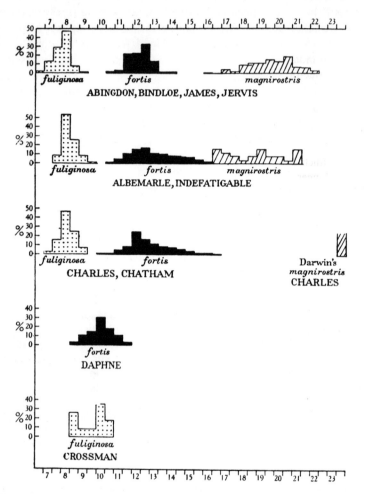

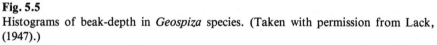

Fig. 5.5
Histograms of beak-depth in *Geospiza* species. (Taken with permission from Lack, (1947).)

Modern evolutionists follow Darwin in this, working toward natural causes of movement and trying to see that the suggestions apply in reality. (See Lack, 1947; Bowman, 1961.) Thus, in the Galapagos case, all agree that the birds will have been blown initially from the mainland, and then have made their way to the various islands. The more isolated the island, the less frequent a new invasion will be. In support of this, it is pointed out that, expectedly, the more isolated islands of the Galapagos group have a proportionately higher percentage of endemic species — a function of the unlikeliness of new arrivals.

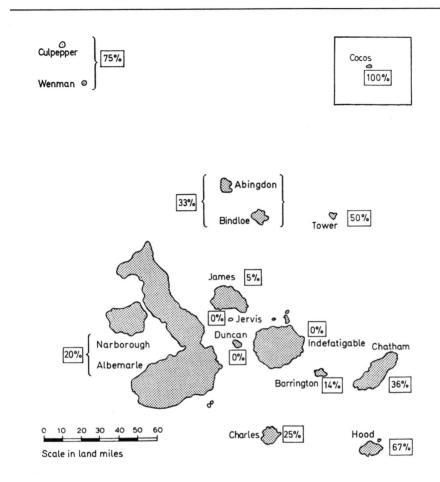

Fig. 5.6
Percentage of endemic forms of Darwin's finches on each island, showing effect of isolation. (Taken with permission from Lack, (1947).)

Referring to the map in Fig. 5.6, one might think from the figures that Charles, Chatham, and Hood would be more isolated than they are. Lack suggests that de facto they are more isolated, since the trade winds blow from south and southeast, making bird dispersal difficult in their direction.

All in all, therefore, following Darwin but working from greater information and with a far more secure theoretical foundation, neo-Darwinians extend their theory, explaining in areas like biogeography such phenomena as the distinctive state and nature of the Galapagos finches. Furthermore, they feel even more comforted about the correctness of their approach given that the

Galapagos finches are by no means unique. There are many similar phenomena, for instance, the incredible number of fruitfly species on the Hawaiian archipelago, which succumb to precisely the same principles of explanation. (Carson et al., 1970). In other words, their models apply again and again. (See Fig. 5.7.)

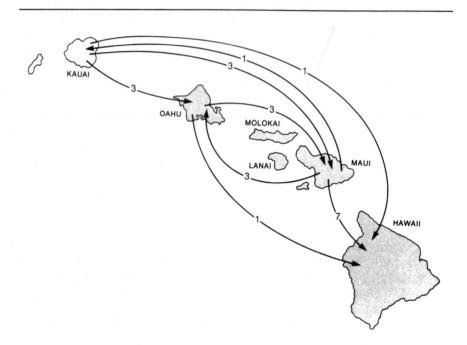

Fig. 5.7
Colonization of Hawaii by *Drosophila*: The arrows show the direction of migration, and the numbers give the minimum numbers of supposed separate colonizations. (Adapted with permission from H. L. Carson *et al,* (1970). The evolutionary biology of the Hawaiian Drosophilidae. In M. K. Hecht and W. C. Steere eds, *Essays in Evolution and Genetics in Honor of Th. Dobzhansky,* New York: Appleton-Century-Crofts, 437-543.)

Bringing this example to an end, let us not forget the founder principle. As we know, this is intended to apply most particularly to such cases as the Galapagos finches, explaining why they might have been expected to break up into so many species — why they did not stay as one uniform species from island to island. Since I have already said so much about this, I will say little more here, except to point out that, as with the Bogota fruitflies, one of the most distinctive marks of isolated groups is their lack of variability. This is just what the founder effect leads one to expect in such cases (Mayr, 1963, p. 211).

I hope that by now the reader is starting to get a feel for the way that modern evolutionary studies proceed. (I refer now to the application of the core area to problems within the subsidiary disciplines.) Obviously, as in Darwin's time, there is no total deductive rigor, in the sense that we can derive (say) all the statements we might want to make about island populations from initial premises, in a logically rigorous way. This means, therefore, that in dealing in particular cases like the finches, there is no question of gathering all the initial facts, popping them into the logical sausage machine, turning the handle, and having today's finches fly out of the other end!

What we do in fact find is that the neo-Darwinian presupposes his populational genetical core, and then he tries to draw some plausible account of what appears generally the case, or perhaps of particular events, consistent with and directed by his theory. He argues from known, controlled situations to hitherto unknown, uncontrolled situations, feeling that the sorts of theorizing and evidence given in the past two chapters applies directly to such phenomena as Darwin's finches. No one may have been around to test the initial, founding finches; but, because of what we know it is assumed by analogy that the founding finches will have been genetically atypical members of their parent population, and this assumption is then used in the explanation of today's finches. Similarly, with mutation and selection, and so forth. And clearly therefore, the neo-Darwinian is in a far stronger position than Darwin, not only because of the increased empirical information, but also because his more detailed knowledge of mechanisms gives a firmer base from which he can build his explanatory hypotheses. His models better exemplify what is going on in nature. Furthermore, the more sophisticated theory of this century can often throw explanatory light, where Darwin would have to stay silent. One thinks here of the insights stemming from the founder principle. (See Fig. 5.8.)

Premises: 1. Description of initial group of finches (e.g., small, with atypical genetic variation).

2. Biogeographical conditions and rules
   a) general to biogeography (e.g., ways of transport across water)
   b) special to Darwin's finches (e.g., trade winds, Galapagos climate)

3. Population genetical models of change, *common to all neo-Darwinian arguments,* (e.g., founder principle, effects of selection on a group).

Conclusion: Finches today, with distinctive features (e.g., adaptive characteristics, geographical distributions).

Fig. 5.8
Logic of a neo-Darwinian argument: biogeographical explanation of Darwin's finches.

But, ultimately it remains true to say that neo-Darwinian explanation parallels explanation in the *Origin*: the secret to the organic world is evolution caused by natural selection working on small, undirected variation. Today we can feel even more strongly than Darwin of the truth of this. Apart from the decline of religious objections, we know that there is sufficient time, that valuable features will not blend away and, perhaps most importantly, because of the truth of the balance hypothesis, we know that at any given time there are usually masses of variation already at hand.

Do not misunderstand me. I am not trying to say that Darwinian evolutionists today never disagree. In fact, there is still a very lively controversy about Darwin's finches! Some, like the late David Lack (1947), see the chief causal factor involved in driving the different species to different food as interspecific competition. They argue that were there no adaptive specialization, one or other species would wipe out other competitors. Others, like Robert Bowman (1961), think the chief causal factor is the positive one of the availability of different foodstuffs. This is still a matter of debate. But, a disagreement of this kind does not detract at all from the points I have made, about the overall structure and strength of the neo-Darwinian paradigm. In a vigorous science like quantum mechanics or evolutionary biology, one expects (and gets!) disagreements about the precise applicabilities of models. (See Abbott et al., 1977 for details of the debate about the finches. See Strong et al., 1979 for suggestions that many differences may not even be caused by selection; also see the effective reply by Grant and Abbott, 1980.)

Paleontology

Through the rest of this book I shall be giving many more examples of neo-Darwinian evolutionary explanations. Here, therefore, it is not necessary to attempt so comprehensive a survey of neo-Darwinian theory, as was given of Darwin's theory. The treatment of island organisms can stand as a paradigm. But, because of its importance, the reader is certainly owed some justification of my claim that population genetics functions in neo-Darwinian theory in the same *integrative* way as Darwin's core functioned in the *Origin*. Perhaps the best evidence for the claim can be garnered by a brief glance at the subject that comes to everybody's mind when one thinks of evolution: paleontology! If I can show that it stands within the neo-Darwinian fold, bearing the same logical relationship to population genetics as does a subject like biogeography, I am sure that all will agree that the case is made.

We shall, in fact, learn later that some paleontologists want to break free from neo-Darwinism. But, looking now at work that is intended to be part of neo-Darwinian evolutionary theory, one has no difficulty in showing that in example after example it is the Darwin-Mendel causal synthesis that guides, illuminates, explains, and confirms. Obviously the paleontologist cannot go out and study his subject organisms directly, analyzing distributions of Mendelian genes and the effects of selection and mutation upon them. Nevertheless, it is the same foundational theory that is presupposed — one that demands that organisms be understood in terms of change and adaptation.

Indeed, Simpson, in his pioneering works (1944, 1953), went so far as to give summaries of principal results of population genetics, and, although to-day paleontologists feel more secure, we find the practice has not vanished entirely! For instance, in a recent, much-used textbook on paleontology (Raup and Stanley, 1971), the authors are quite explicit in their Darwinian approach, stating that their central idea in evolution is that "species (or populations) evolve by natural selection and thereby adapt" (p. 155), giving elementary ideas of genetics, and even going so far as to quote Dobzhansky on the genetic background and constraints on organisms (p. 156). And, naturally enough, their actual explanations reflect this perspective. Let us sample some. (We shall see in Chapter 9 that both of the authors now have doubts about traditional Darwinism. This does not deny the Darwinian nature of the explanations to be given here. To show the general reader that even those evolutionists, who now in respects break with Darwinism, still continue to give factors like selection an important evolutionary role, I include here an absolutely beautiful example of selection at work, discussed in the second, less-Darwinian edition (1978) of their work.)

First, take explanations which are offered for a well-known generalization about the fossil record, formulated by the nineteenth-century paleontologist E. D. Cope: animals within a given group have a tendency through the ages to evolve toward greater size. (See Fig. 5.9.) About "Cope's rule" the authors write:

The reasons for an increase in size being advantageous to animals undoubtedly vary among lineages. Some animals may gain strength that permits them to attack other animals, or to ward off attacks, through size increase. [Again,] large animals keep warm in cool climates more efficiently than small animals. Another advantage of size increase is that, although large animals cannot run appreciably faster than small animals, they have greater endurance and can maintain a given speed for a longer period of time.... This factor may have been important in the phylogenetic size increase of grazing horses (Raup and Stanley, 1971, pp. 277-278).

And continuing, they write:

Instead of thinking of Cope's Rule as describing a tendency toward evolutionary size increase, we can reverse our viewpoint and think of it as describing evolution from small size. It is well known that many higher taxa have arisen from ancestral groups that are of relatively small size. In large part this is because such ancestral groups tend to be relatively unspecialized, and small individuals are much more likely to be unspecialized than large ones. Most large species within higher taxa have evolved so many special mechanisms for coping with their size that it has become very unlikely that they could give rise to a large new group whose morphologic features would be different enough for the group to constitute a major new taxon. For example, it is highly unlikely that an elephant genus could give rise to an entirely new quadruped order. The modification of evolving elephants, including greatly thickened limbs for supporting their massive

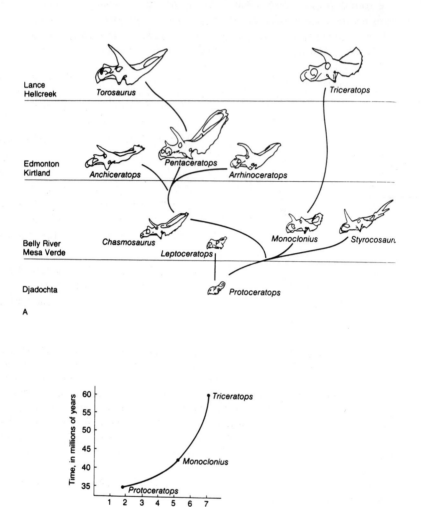

Fig. 5.9
Increase in size (body length) of a group of dinosaurs over time. A: Phylogeny of North American ceratopsians. B: Increase in body length in the lineage between *Protoceratops* and *Triceratops*. (Taken by permission from E. H. Colbert, (1948). Evolution of the horned dinosaurs. *Evolution,* 2, 14-163.)

bodies, a shortened neck to support the head, and a trunk to take the place of a long neck ... greatly limit their future evolutionary potential. New groups thus tend to arise from small unspecialized ancestors, rather than from large specialized ancestors, and this may be why Cope's Rule seems like a good description of nature (Raup and Stanley, 1971, pp. 278-279).

It is hardly necessary to stress that what is being presupposed in these passages is a background of stability, guaranteed by Mendelian population genetics. On top of this is natural selection at work controlling the particular features at issue, according to the kinds of models introduced in earlier chapters. These passages reek of an adaptationist perspective: "size being advantageous" to "attack other animals"; "large animals keep warm ... more efficiently"; "large species [have] mechanisms for coping with their size"; and so forth and so forth. Nothing makes sense outside natural selection and the randomness of variation (if not the latter, why cannot the elephants go in reverse?) Indeed, without laboring the point, I am sure it can easily be seen that the explanations can be set up in the form I have discerned in the case of the finch explanation (Fig. 5.8).

Next, moving from the general to a particular case of evolution, consider a well-known explanation by Simpson (1953) of the evolution of the horse, an example that the authors give as a typical sort of evolutionary phenomenon with a typical sort of explanation.

The early horses were browsers, and had teeth suitable for feeding on soft, leafy vegetation, but in the mid-Tertiary, apparently in response to the spread of abrasive siliceous grasses that began in the early Tertiary, some lineages developed more complex molars, adapted to grazing on abrasive, siliceous grasses. The primary changes in the molars were increase in the complexity of crown patterns, increase in the height of the crowns, and development of cement. The grazing horse was one of many new grazing lineages that evolved in the middle and late Cenozoic; a conservative, less successful phylogenetic group of browsing horses continued on into the Pliocene (Raup and Stanley, 1971, p. 274).

Here again we find the same theoretical principles infusing discussion — there was a Darwinian adaptive advantage in the ability to use new foodstuffs. Natural selection was the motivating force.

Third, consider the somewhat esoteric subject of vision in the trilobites, a well-known group of invertebrates that flourished from earliest Cambrian times until the Permian: 570 million years or earlier, until 230 million years ago. (See Fig. 5.10.) Trilobites had a compound eye, with many lenses packed in rows, using the most efficient geometric configuration possible. In many, many respects the trilobite eye shows evidence of selective forces, and is thus explained in terms of such forces, but nowhere is selection more dramatically illustrated and invoked than in the way in which the lenses avoid "spherical aberration" (the distortion caused in lenses by the focus of the light rays at the edge of the lens being different from that at the center).

Not until the seventeenth century did mankind overcome this problem, when Descartes and Huygens independently published designs for "aplanatic"

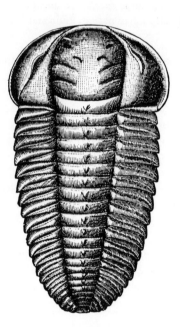

Fig. 5.10a
Trilobite

Fig. 5.10b
The eye of a trilobite showing the multiple lenses. (Taken with permission from E. N. K. Clarkson and R. Levi-Setti, (1975). Trilobite eyes and the optics of Descartes and Huygens, *Nature,* 254, 663–667.)

lenses (i.e., lenses that avoid the aberration). Now, compare the designs of Descartes and Huygens with cross-sections of trilobite lenses (Fig. 5.11). The

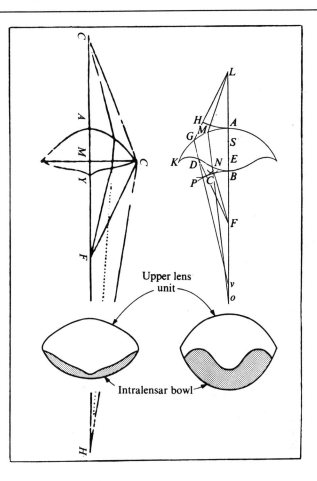

Fig. 5.11
Lens morphology of two trilobites (lower) compared with the original drawings for aplanatic lenses published by Descartes (upper left) and Huygens (upper right). (Taken with permission from Clarkson and Levi-Setti, (1975).)

resemblance is quite uncanny, and such apparent design is as avidly explained in terms of selection, working within a populational genetical context, as is any phenomenon from the still-living world. The only difference between the trilobite lenses and those of our seventeenth-century philosophers is that the former have a second (lower) lens. "But this is understandable when it is noted that the aplanatic lens was designed to operate in air. Calculations have shown that in the trilobite's aqueous environment the lower lens would be necessary to compensate for the relatively high refractive index of seawater" (Raup and Stanley, 1978, p. 182).

I hope there will be no dispute. Even though it cannot be denied that no one was around to check the Hardy-Weinberg law at work in the trilobites when they were alive, the very explanation of the nature of their eyes is meaningless outside the context of selection working on nonblending units of inheritance: the Mendelian gene! And in case there are those who still hesitate to accept what I say, I might add almost parenthetically that the Hardy-Weinberg law in action has in fact been observed in the trilobite fossil record! Best (1961), studying the Silurian trilobite *Encrinurus,* found that the spacing of its tubercles can most properly be interpreted as a function of two alleles, in Hardy-Weinberg equilibrium. (See Fig. 5.12.) What more could one ask?

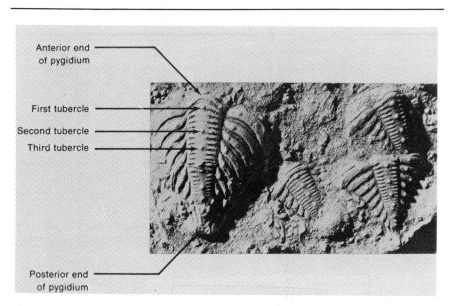

Fig. 5.12
The Hardy-Weinberg law among the trilobites! The spacing of the tubercles on the tail of the Silurian trilobite *Encrinurus varies.* Best shows that the exact positioning can be explained as a function of genes in Hardy-Weinberg equilibrium. (Used with permission of the Society of Economic Paleontologists and Mineralogists, from R.V. Best, (1961). Intraspecific variation in *Encrinurus ornatus. J. Paleont.,* 35, 1029-1040.)

My point is made: if the trilobites do not convince, nothing will! Undoubtedly, in a sense, the paleontologist usually has further to go than someone working on living organisms, like the biogeographer. The paleontologist is not in a position to watch and experiment with his organisms, where necessary performing direct checks on the genotypes. He frequently has to reconstruct the very phenomena he intends to explain. But the structure and form of his understanding is identical to that of the evolutionist working with living organisms. Models of understanding are devised, incorporating principles and findings from population genetics. Then, as in the case of other areas, to these models are added assumptions and principles pertinent to the particular subject under discussion. For instance, in the case of Cope's law we had certain elementary principles of thermodynamics, as in the case of Darwin's finches we had principles of transportation. Finally, the augmented models are applied to the reconstructed world of long-dead organisms, in explanation and in confirmation.

I conclude therefore that overall we see in neo-Darwinian evolutionary theory the same outstanding consilience of inductions that was so distinctive of Darwin's theory in the *Origin*. And with this, my direct presentation of "Darwinism Today" is completed. Admittedly, even allowing for material to be covered later, I can make no claim to having covered more than a fraction of the topics that engage today's evolutionists. Perhaps most regrettably, like Darwin himself, I have felt obliged to conserve my resources exclusively for discussion of evolutionary theorizing, leaving untouched all mention of current progress in discerning the actual paths of evolution, so-called "phylogenies." In part compensation for this omission, however, in future chapters I shall offer a limited amount of information on this score, touching on aspects of the actual course of evolution that are of particular interest to Darwinians. (See especially Figs. 6.9, 6.10, 6.11, and 6.12.)

Nevertheless I do trust that I have been able to give a fair sense of contemporary Darwinian studies — both of the structure of neo-Darwinian theory and of its relationship to the evidence. Unfortunately, however, before I can sum up and ask the key question that hangs over us at this point — "Have today's evolutionists really put the mechanism of natural selection on the foundation that eluded Darwin?" — there is a major critical objection to Darwinian evolutionary theory that must be faced and countered. Let us see what it is, why it is made, and why it fails.

Darwinism as metaphysics

The objection is as straightforward as it is popular and devastating, if well taken. It is claimed that Darwinian evolutionary theory — the critics usually lump together indifferently both past and present versions — is no genuine scientific theory at all. Despite appearances, it is just not about the empirical world; it is rather, at most, a speculative philosophy of nature, on a par with Plato's theory of forms or Swedenborgian theology. It is, in short, a metaphysical wolf masquerading as a scientific lamb. And, although the critics hasten to assure us that there is nothing wrong with metaphysics, it is usually not too long before words like "slight" or "inadequate" or even "dismal" start to slip into the talk. All in all, we are left with the impression that Darwinism says nothing, and even if it did say something, it would not be *that* worth listening to. "Evolution is not a fact but a theory" is a charitable epitaph.

Just how does this objection come about? Let us see by starting with some general thoughts about the nature of science. I am sure that all will agree that there is a distinction to be drawn between those bodies of information or ideas that we want to label "scientific" and those that we do not, even though it is not always clear precisely where the distinction should be drawn. We want to distinguish for instance between something like the wave theory of light (albeit that today we may want to modify it in respects) and other sorts of claims, like those of literary criticism, philosophy, or religion. It may well make sense to say that "God is love"; one may well believe it with all one's heart. But, important though it is, somehow it does not seem to be a claim of quite the same type as (say) Snell's law, $\sin i \,/\, \sin r = \mu$, or the claim that light goes in waves not particles.

It seems fairly clear that what distinguishes science from nonscience is the fact that scientific claims reflect, and somehow can be checked against, empirical experience — ultimately, the data that we get through our senses. The wave theory of light is about this physical world of ours; in some very important sense, God is not part of this world. We see light; we do not see God. But, how exactly does science reflect its empirical base? One might think that it is all simply a question of finding positive empirical evidence for scientific claims — evidence that is unobtainable for other sorts of claims. However, matters are a little more complex than this, because science does not deal with particulars, at least not directly and exclusively, but with generalities and universals. One's interest is not in this planet or that planet as such. Rather, one asks what each and every planet does, just as one asks what each and every light ray does.

But, this being so, simple checking and confirmation obviously cannot be enough. Suppose one has a general statement like Snell's law of refraction, and suppose also one has tested all kinds of light and all kinds of refracting media and found that the law holds. One can never preclude the possibility of a kind of light, or a type of medium, that violates the law. It is all a matter of simple logic; one just cannot definitively establish a universal statement by appealing to individual instances, however common or however positive they may be. Thousands of positive cases do not rule out one possible countercase.

Given this fact, many thinkers have therefore tried the opposite tack. Perhaps what distinguishes science is not that one can ever show it true, but that one can always knock it down! As T. H. Huxley was wont to say, the scientist must be prepared always to sit down before the facts, as a little child, ever prepared to give up the most cherished of theories should the empirical data dictate otherwise. Teasingly, Huxley used to say of his friend Herbert Spencer that his idea of a tragedy was that of a beautiful theory murdered by an ugly fact. Perhaps the edge to this quip reflects Huxley's belief that Spencer would go to any lengths to prevent murder being done — even to the extent of taking his theories out of science altogether (L. Huxley, 1900).

Recently, the thinker who has stood most firmly and proudly in Huxley's tradition has been the philosopher Karl Popper (1959, 1962, 1972, 1974). Starting from the logical point that, although many positive instances cannot confirm a universal statement, one negative instance can refute it, Popper argues that the essential mark of science — the "criterion of demarcation" — is that it is *falsifiable*.

I shall not require of a scientific system that it shall be capable of being singled out, once and for all, in a positive sense; but I shall require that its logical form shall be such that it can be singled out, by means of empirical tests, in a negative sense: *it must be possible for an empirical scientific system to be refuted by experience* (Popper, 1959, p. 41, his italics).

Now, armed with this criterion, apparently we can distinguish a paradigmatic statement of science, like Kepler's law that planets go in ellipses, from a statement of nonscience, "God is love." The former could be shown false by empirical observation and would indeed be shown false if one were, for example, to find a planet going in squares. The latter simply cannot be shown false by empirical data; it just is not falsifiable. In the face of the most horrific counterexamples — Vietnamese children screaming in agony from napalm burns — the believer continues to maintain that God is love. All is explained away as a function of freewill or some such thing.

Turning to science, or, more precisely, to claims that are made in the name of science, Popper and his sympathizers make short shrift of many areas of the social sciences. Freudian psychoanalytic theory is dismissed as incontrovertibly and irreparably unfalsifiable. But then moving on to biology, coming up against Darwinism, they feel compelled to make the same judgment: Darwinian evolutionary theory is unfalsifiable. Hence, the critical evaluation given at the beginning of this section: "I have come to the conclusion that Darwinism is not a testable scientific theory but a *metaphysical research programme* — a possible framework for testable scientific theories" (Popper, 1974, p. 134, his italics).

Since making this claim, Popper himself has modified his position somewhat; but, disclaimers aside, I suspect that even now he does not really believe that Darwinism in its modern form is genuinely falsifiable. If one relies heavily on natural selection and sexual selection, simultaneously downplaying drift, which of course is what the neo-Darwinian does do, then Popper feels that one has a nonfalsifiable theory. And, certainly, many followers agree that there is something conceptually flawed with Darwinism. (See Bethell, 1976; Cracraft, 1978; Nelson, 1978; Patterson, 1978; Platnick and Gaffney, 1978; Popper, 1978, 1980; and Wiley, 1975.)

Just how precisely do the various critics make their case? Simply, it is argued that there is no way, either in practice or in principle, to put Darwinism (for ease, let us concentrate here on neo-Darwinism) to the test. For a start, testing requires prediction. One predicts something on the basis of a theory, checks to see if the prediction turns out true or false, and then rejects or retains one's theory on the basis of the results. But how can one make genuine predictions with Darwinism? Who could possibly predict what will happen to the elephant's trunk twenty-five million years down the road? Certainly not the

Darwinian! And even if he could, there would be no one around to check out the prediction. Analogously, no one could step back to the Mesozoic to see the evolution of mammals and check if indeed natural selection was at work, nor could anyone spend a week or two (or century or two) in the Cretaceous to see if the dinosaurs, then going extinct, failed in the struggle for existence.

More importantly, argues the critic, even if one had a machine to go forward or back in time, it would make little difference! An essential claim of Darwinism devolves on the ubiquity of organic adaptation. The presumption is that physical characteristics have an adaptive value; they were preserved and selected because of their useful natures in the struggle for existence. But, in fact, it is easy to see that even in principle Darwinians guard themselves against counterarguments.

Take something much discussed by evolutionists: the sail on the back of the Permian reptile, *Dimetrodon*. (See Fig. 5.13.) The possibility that this may

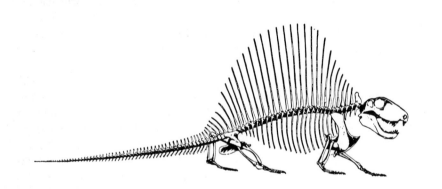

Fig. 5.13
Skeleton of *Dimetrodon*. (Adapted with permission from A. S. Romer, (1945). *Vertebrate Paleontology,* Chicago: University of Chicago Press.)

have absolutely no adaptive value is given no credence at all, as Darwinians plunge into their favorite parlour game: "find the adaptation." The sail was a defense mechanism (it scared predators), or it served for sexual display (not much chance of mistaking someone's intentions with that thing along one's backside), or, as many evolutionists (including Raup and Stanley) suppose, it worked as a heat-regulating device to keep the cold-blooded *Dimetrodon* at a more constant temperature in the fluctuating environment. The animal would move the sail around in the sunlight and wind, heating or cooling the blood in the sail, which could then be passed through to the rest of the body. In short, as this example shows, there has to be some reason for anything and everything. One can be sure that if the Darwinian can think of no potential value in the struggle for existence, then value will be found in the struggle for reproduction. Even the most absurd and grotesque of physical features are supposed to have irrepressible aphrodisiac qualities. Like the Freudians, Darwinians get a lot of mileage out of sex.

There must be something dreadfully wrong with Darwinism. How can it be that something, which seems at first sight to be so all-encompassing and so impressively empirical, fails so dreadfully when subjected to searching inquiry? The critics think they know the source of all the trouble. Darwinism is no genuine scientific theory because it rests on a bogus mechanism: natural selection. Far from being an empirically testable, putative cause of evolutionary change, *natural selection is no scientific claim at all: it is a vacuous tautology*. Consider that natural selection states simply that a certain proportion of organisms, by definition the "fitter," survive and reproduce, whereas others do not. But, which are the "fitter"? Simply they are those that survive and reproduce! In other words, natural selection collapses into the analytically true statement that those that survive and reproduce are those that survive and reproduce. No wonder all the subareas of evolutionary thought come apart on close inspection. They put their trust in an empty statement (Peters, 1976). Indeed, one might feel that Popper is charitable in describing Darwinism as "metaphysical." Like Freudianism, it tells us nothing about the real world and fraudulently pretends that it does!

Only one more nail is required to make the lid to the Darwinian coffin secure. Why is it that something so bogus, so clearly inadequate when judged by the stringent criteria of genuine science, should have gone so far? Why has Darwinism been such a success for 100 years, despite the sense of unease that so many clear thinkers have felt? It is simply because Darwinism has no rivals! It exists on its own, filling a gap, with no personal struggle for existence to fight. Indeed, when the occasional dissenter has suggested a possible alternative, it has always been dismissed out of hand, "possibly not on very adequate evidence" (Manser, 1965).

Darwinism as genuine science

I believe this whole line of objection to be mistaken, absolutely and entirely. Given the survey of hard empirical inquiry we have seen thus far, the suggestion that Darwinism is nonempirical strikes me as bordering on the ludicrous. Protestations notwithstanding, the critics' arguments look suspiciously like some of those of Darwin's religious opponents. Popper (1972), in fact, has been quite open about his inability to see how blind variation could lead to integrated, adaptive functioning in such a case as the eye or hand. Of this I am sure: there is an inability to grasp the implications of the balance hypothesis, with its claims about the ready supply of variation, available whenever selective pressures demand it. But, enough of what the critics can or cannot grasp. Onward, to the task of rebuttal! And, taking our cue from the critics, first let us make a few brief remarks of our own about science, before moving to direct defense of Darwinism.

The first point I want to make is that, although the major mark of science is undoubtedly the way in which it brushes against experience, and although undoubtedly falsifiability is important here, one must be careful not to take too literal or too narrow a reading of one's criteria. Otherwise one will end up by counting out just about every candidate for good science, including some that one obviously wants to include!

Put matters this way. There can be no doubt that Newtonian gravitational theory qualifies as genuine, good science. That it is perhaps now superceded does not touch this point. But, right through its career, in respects, it was unfalsifiable! There were always parts of the theory that did not work, in the sense that they led to predictions that went against the evidence (Kuhn, 1970). The perihelion of Mercury, for instance, was a glaring anomaly for centuries. But Newtonians did not reject their theory. They refused to let it be falsified, hoping that some day a solution within the Newtonian framework would be found — as almost invariably it was. And the same element of unfalsifiability emerges when we look at other claims, where the Newtonians speculated, but simply had no way of checking whether their speculations were true or false. Ad hoc hypotheses would be invented, or counterevidence denied or shelved, until things fell neatly into (Newtonian) place!

I do not want to exaggerate. The story of Newtonian theory in this century proves that ultimately the facts do prevail. My point is that the mark of science is not to be decided by pulling one or two claims from a theory and checking on whether scientists would let them be falsified, or whether they have even the first idea about checking them. In the Newtonian case, one had a paradigmatic instance of a theory which integrates from many different areas — which exhibits a consilience of inductions — and which therefore was judged as a whole. Newtonians could see many virtues in their overall theory, particularly in its integrating simplicity. They knew their theory was checkable in many parts — had planets gone in squares, everyone would have looked askance at the universal square law. However, Newtonians knew that their theory came through check after check with flying colors. Prediction after prediction was confirmed. Hence, Newtonians tolerated a certain amount of counterevidence, thinking up ad hoc face-saving hypotheses and the like, and they lived with a number of uncheckable claims. Indeed, one might almost say that one expects a really good, powerful theory to exceed its grasp, and to get a little out of focus at the edges! Unfalsifiability here is not a sign of nonscience. It is a sign of sensible tolerance.

Now, all I have just said obviously applies with a vengeance to Darwinian evolutionary theory. Given its consilient nature, one must judge as a whole, not on the basis of isolated claims. Most particularly, it is just not fair to pick out one or two isolated areas, and then to make final, definitive judgments on the basis of them. One must look at the total picture and see if the theory is protected, in fact or in principle, from any empirical phenomenon that might impinge and refute it. If this is so, then obviously the theory must go — it is not real science. But if real checks are available, then tolerance is justifiable and justified elsewhere. If claims seem to go a little against the evidence, or (perhaps more importantly) Darwinians seem determined to fit the facts into their own pattern, then before condemning one must judge the whole.

Enough by way of general prolegomenon. What of the critics' actual objections? Let us begin with the question of prediction. Now, I admit that no one can predict the future course of the elephant's trunk, or the giraffe's neck, or the camel's hump, or what have you. But, these inabilities have virtually no standing on the testability of Darwinism. First, remember a distinction we encountered already, namely that between the *causal theory* and the *path of evolution,* "phylogenies." Phylogenies, like the path of elephant evolution, depend on all sorts of unknown external factors. That we do not know these factors leaves untouched our quest for basic causal principles — principles that hold all the time. It is just not necessary to have monstrously long-range predictions to test basic causal claims like those about the founder principle.

Second, considering now the matter of causes, we can make predictions at this level! Dobzhansky and Pavlovsky (1957) forecast what would happen to their populations of fruitflies, when they began with large and small founding groups. Why should these "predictions" or "guesses" (or whatever you want to call them) be any less genuinely predictive or testable than what goes on in the laboratory of physical scientists? (Note, incidentally, that insofar as Darwinians are employing "as if" models, in the sense specified in Chapter 3, what is being tested is not the model in isolation, but the model insofar as we want to apply it to actual situations.)

Third, we can obviously test Darwinism in the overall theory by drawing out predictions, not about what we may find in the future, but about what we shall or should find in the present and in the record of the past. Darwinism predicts that the organic world, past and present, will be of a certain form, and this lays it open to check. For instance, unlike Lamarckian evolution, Darwinian evolution cannot repeat itself. The dodo is gone forever. Suppose one found a whole set of fossil mammals in the geological record, back about four billion years old, and then nothing until the mammals come back. Darwinism would be false.

Turning to the present, oceanic islands today appear to have all sorts of potentials for test. Analogously, something like systematics seems to support predictions. Since Darwinian evolution is gradual, one should find numerous ambiguous cases, which together make the life of the practising taxonomist one long headache: subspecies, semi-species, species nearly complete, species that may or may not be complete, and so on. This expectation comes right from the heart of Darwinism: if it proves false, then so also is Darwinism. It is as simple as that. In fact, the prediction is triumphantly confirmed time and again. The prettiest positive cases occur in the birds, with so-called "rings of races." One has a chain of populations of birds, right around the globe: each population interbreeds with its neighbor, but the end populations where they meet are reproductively isolated! (Mayr, 1963, see Fig. 5.14.)

Going on with the arguments against Darwinism, what about the objections based on the supposed impossibility of checking on claims about

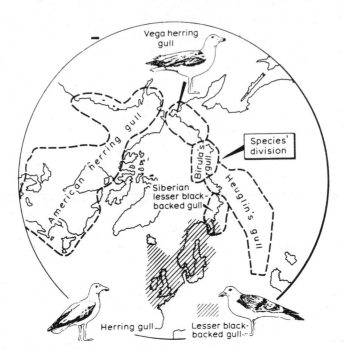

Fig. 5.14
A ring species of gulls surrounds the Pole. The change between neighbors is gradual, but in Europe the two ends of the ring are distinct species. (Adapted with permission from M. Ridley (1981). Who doubts evolution? *New Scientist, 90,* 830-2.)

dinosaur extinction or *Dimetrodon* sail function? Now, let me admit quite candidly that at this point in evolutionary theorizing one does get an element of speculation, and undoubtedly adaptive functions tend to be sought until they are found. Here I think the general remarks I had to make about science, Darwinism, and falsifiability have great importance. One looks for and expects adaptive function in the past, because *paleontology does not stand alone;* it is part of the greater whole.

And, from our evolutionary studies of the present, we have unequivocal, testable, empirical evidence about the importance of adaptation. The Cain-Sheppard study on snails, for instance, was open to falsification. Had the thrushes killed more banded snails from varied backgrounds and vice versa, their hypotheses about the adaptive value of shell color would have been shown false. It was not, nor were many, many similarly studied hypotheses.

Because of this, Darwinians feel justified — and, I would say, are justified — in interpreting areas less open to check, like the distant past, in the terms of their theory. Looking at, say, the sail of the *Dimetrodon,* the paleontologist is not working in isolation. He has the backing of Cain and Sheppard and all the other neontologists (students of living forms).

But do not let me give the impression that paleontology is a totally untestable cripple, parasitic on the rest of evolutionary thought for its scientific status. Take the dinosaurs. One recent hypothesis puts their extinction down to the dust cloud caused by a meteorite hitting Earth. Still very speculative, this hypothesis is open to check in that one expects evidence of the dust cloud in the geological record. Indeed, already some critics say the record falsifies the claim! (See Alvarez et al.,1980.) I myself incline to the suggestion that dinosaur extinction was linked to changes brought about by continental drift.

And, referring one more time to the *Dimetrodon* and its sail, although I doubt that so distinctive a feature of the sail would ever be dismissed as nonadaptive (unless there were reasons from living organisms), the actual suggestions are open to check. With respect to the temperature-regulating hypothesis, if the principles of thermodynamics are violated, then falsifying data is obtained. In fact, the hypothesis has been checked along these lines (Raup and Stanley, 1971). If the sail were indeed a device to control the animal's temperature, it then would have to have been proportionately larger in species with larger members. As body volume increased, sail area would need to increase at the same rate to perform at the same level of efficiency. But body volume increases with the cube of linear dimension, whereas body surface increases with the square of linear dimension. Hence, assuming body shape to have stayed more or less the same — which it did roughly — we have the following simple equations:

$$\text{sail area } \alpha \text{ body volume}$$
$$\text{body volume } \alpha \text{ body area}^{3/2}$$
$$\text{sail area } \alpha \text{ body area}^{3/2}$$

In reality, the observed relationship was:

$$\text{sail area } \alpha \text{ body area}^{3/2}$$

One really cannot hope for a much better fit than that! Conversely, surely at this point the paleontologist's claim was put to the test, with falsifying potential?

Incidentally, the paleontologist does not always say that everything absolutely has to be adaptive. Presumably Best's argument that trilobite tubercle spacings were in Hardy-Weinberg equilibrium presupposed that the relative spacings had little or no adaptive value. Adaptive value is presumed for those sorts of things that we know from today's experience are likely to have such value. Here the paleontologist stands with other Darwinians.

Is natural selection a tautology?

We come now to the strongest and most crucial objection of all, namely that natural selection is a tautology, and that consequently the whole Darwinian edifice collapses into a truism. I believe that this objection is as wide of the mark as it is possible for an objection to be. In at least three respects, there is an empirical, nontautological, falsifiable basis to the mechanism cherished by Darwinians. That is to say, inasmuch as Darwinians want to apply models containing their mechanism to the living world, they commit themselves to at least three testable claims.

First, there is the claim that in the organic world there is a struggle for reproduction. Not all organisms that are born can and do survive and reproduce. Many fall by the wayside. This claim is undoubtedly true, but it is not a tautology. If everyone were identical, lived exactly the same length of time, and asexually produced one and only one offspring at the same point, there would be no struggle, no selection, and no evolution. Darwinism would be false; that is, any attempt to apply Darwinian models to the world would be fallacious.

Second, there is the central claim of Darwinians that they can apply their theory throughout the organic world, because success in the struggle is, on average, not random, but a function of the distinctive characteristics possessed by organisms. This is why we get adaptations. Again this is an empirical claim and could be false. Indeed, fairly obviously, supporters of the notion of genetic drift think that at times the claim is false. Drift is a highly contentious notion, but not even its strongest detractors think it a contradictory notion — which it would be were selection a tautology. It is logically impossible to apply to the world a model containing a contradiction. If drift is contradictory, why then was it necessary for Cain and Sheppard to spend as much time as they did out in the countryside looking at snails and thrushes?

Third, there is the claim that selection is systematic — what selection favors in one situation will be what selection favors in identical situations. In other words, one can apply a model with certain specified parameters again and again. A characteristic that helps an organism at one time and place can be expected to offer similar help in the same circumstances at different times and places. Thus, upon finding an arctic mammal with a white coat, an evolutionist confidently puts it down to an adaptive response to the snowy terrain, because this has been found to be the case for other arctic organisms. In a sense, this claim about the systematic nature of selection is the inductive element built into selection and is no doubt the reason why so many people think selection tautological. (When one has a common fallacy, it is important to show not merely why it is fallacious, but also why it is common.) It may be "obvious" that same causes in the same circumstances lead to same effects, but as the great Scottish philosopher David Hume (1740) showed us, it is not a logical necessity.

No doubt, some will complain that this last claim embodied in selection is all very well; but, how do we know when we have identical or nonidentical situations and when we are simply making our claims true by fiat? I would not deny that we have here a difficulty, but I would point out that this is a difficulty common to all science. It is certainly no cause for picking out Darwinian selection as peculiarly inadequate. As Darwin's one-time friend Whewell (1840) made very plain, scientists of all stripes constantly have to make judgments about whether circumstances are similar or different and whether counterexamples hold or not. The boomerang does not obey Galileo's laws; but, we do not take its existence as a refutation of the laws. We judge that the circumstances are not the same as those of a cannonball falling from the tower of Pisa.

Similarly, we must and can make judgments about the circumstances surrounding selection. If the situation seems similar, we are justified in expecting and looking for similar characteristics being effective; otherwise not. And, of course, for all the difficulties, we do have sufficient *empirical* success in this

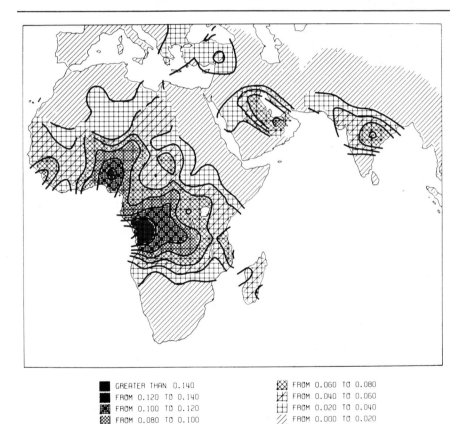

■ GREATER THAN 0.140	▧ FROM 0.060 TO 0.080
■ FROM 0.120 TO 0.140	⧗ FROM 0.040 TO 0.060
▦ FROM 0.100 TO 0.120	⊞ FROM 0.020 TO 0.040
▨ FROM 0.080 TO 0.100	⫽ FROM 0.000 TO 0.020

Fig. 5.15
Distribution of hemoglobin-S gene in the Old World: This computer-generated map shows the frequency of the sickle-cell gene *S*. (Courtesy of D. E. Schreiber, IBM Research Laboratory, San Jose.)

regard to justify optimism or suspension of judgment about apparent counterexamples. The uncanny extent to which the malarial regions of the world are isomorphic to those regions with human populations carrying the sickle-cell gene shows clearly one instance of how genes causing physical characteristics of a certain kind have a uniformity of action and success — a uniformity embodied in the third empirical element to natural selection, or rather to applications of theory containing it. Would anyone seriously want to say that the isomorphism is a necessary truth? (See Figs. 5.15 and 5.16.)

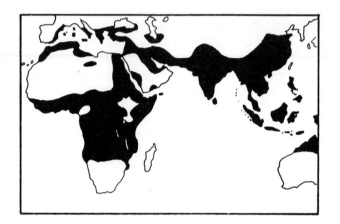

Fig. 5.16
Distribution of malaria in the Old World: The map indicates the areas where there is a significant incidence of *Plasmodium falciparum* malaria.

On three points, therefore, natural selection transcends the tautological; that is to say, claims that the theory containing natural selection applies to the world require empirical, testable assertions. Additionally, within the core of modern evolutionary theory we have many other claims, and application of these latter is certainly not tautological. I have already dealt with the charge that the Hardy-Weinberg law is a truism, and so shall not bother to retread ground. The charge of unfalsifiability merits no more attention. Neither the central mechanism, nor Darwinian theory taken as a whole stand outside of the bounds of genuine empirical science. To go on arguing otherwise is to put ideology and ignorance above reason and experience.

Darwinism's rivals

With the collapse of the critics' case, the call to defend Darwinism against the claim that it succeeds simply through lack of rivals seems far less pressing.

But, to complete the case, a few brief remarks might appropriately be made on the subject. It would be a pity if so ill-founded a charge left any lingering suspicion. Also, we can add one or two details to complete our own picture of neo-Darwinian evolutionary theory.

As we know already, it simply is not true to say that, through its history, Darwinian evolutionary theory never faced any rivals, or that alternative evolutionary mechanisms to natural selection have never been proposed. For a start, there was *Lamarck's* theory, both in the main form intended by Lamarck himself and in the sense of the inheritance of acquired characteristics. I am not sure that anyone ever wanted the whole of evolutionary change put down to the inheritance of acquired characteristics; but certainly Lamarck, Darwin, and many others in the nineteenth century thought the phenomenon might be an important factor in evolutionary change. There are times, perhaps, when Darwin's contemporary Herbert Spencer got very close to making it the sole foundation for his evolutionism. (See, for example, Spencer, 1864.)

Then, again, as a rival to Darwinism there was *saltationism* in its various forms: the belief that evolution proceeds, not by the small variations favored by the Darwinians, but through large changes. In this century, some supporters of saltationism have spoken of it as being fueled by "macromutations" (Goldschmidt, 1940, 1952). Also, there was a theory which we have not yet encountered: *orthogenesis* (Bowler, 1979). Some paleontologists at the end of the nineteenth century noted that one sees many "trends" in the fossil record where certain features of organisms seem to evolve for a time in a particular direction. Cope's law, for instance, notes the frequent trend towards larger size. These paleontologists suggested that, towards the end of a trend, carried forward by a kind of evolutionary momentum, one gets features that are nonadaptive, not caused by selection. The gigantic antlers of the "Irish Elk" were taken as prime evidence for the case. (See Fig. 5.17.)

And finally, without trying to give a complete list of Darwinism's rivals, we have the *drifters,* seeing much evolutionary change as a function of the random effects of breeding, especially in small populations. It will be realized that one might hold a modified or partial version of the drift hypothesis; or indeed simultaneously hold bits and parts of any or all of the just-listed mechanisms. As in Darwin's time, even the severest critics of Darwinism have usually given selection some role, albeit a minor one.

Running quickly through the various rival options, one can say simply that the evidence against them is massive. *Lamarck's* original theory is totally negated by the fossil and living world (Bowler, 1976). Leaving until the next chapter matters to do with spontaneous generation, we have seen that there is absolutely no reason to think that organisms conform essentially to a chain of being or that long-dead organisms will reappear. All the evidence of the fossil record is that once something is gone, that is it. Living trilobites will never be seen again. Lamarckism in the sense usually understood, the inheritance of acquired characteristics, is absolutely refuted by modern genetics. There is neither place nor need for bodily characteristics impinging on the genes in the sex cell — indeed, in the female mammal such genes are set aside before birth,

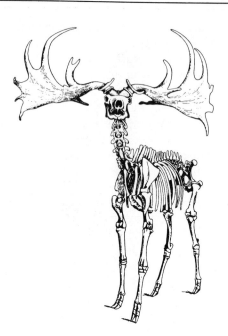

Fig. 5.17
The Irish Elk, really a cervine deer, *Megaloceros.* (Taken with permission from S. J. Gould, (1973). Positive allometry of antlers in the "Irish Elk," *Megaloceros giganteus, Nature,* 244, 375-376.)

and so acquired features just could not affect them. And all of this is quite apart from the physical evidence against the theory. Let us repeat Mivart's question: Why do the Jews have to keep circumcising?

For some reason, Lamarckism has a strong grip on the popular imagination. I suppose it is because some features seem so obviously to be the effects of a Lamarckian process: the stretched neck of the giraffe and the callused bottom of the ostrich. (See Fig. 5.18.) Defenders constantly spring to Lamarckism's aid. It is argued that Mivart's counter is no true counter, because circumcision is a mutilation and not of adaptive value. Although, the adaptive merits of a foreskin aside, why some features acquired by the body should get ingrained genetically and not others is never made very clear.

One prediction one can surely make about evolutionary studies, if not about evolution itself, is that periodically the popular press will announce that Lamarckism is "proved." Indeed, they are all agog at the moment about claims, supposedly to this end, made recently by two Canadian researchers. (See Robertson, 1981; Steele, 1979; and Tudge, 1981.) All one can say about new "confirming" cases is that they rarely show anything remotely resembling that which Lamarck or Darwin supported, like callused ostrich bottoms.

Fig. 5.18
View of the ventral surface of an ostrich, to show the callosities. (Adapted by permission from J. E. Duerden, (1920). Inheritance of calosities in the ostrich. *American Scientist*, 54, 289.)

Those claims that are not totally fraudulent, and I am afraid that the honesty index in this respect is not high, purport to prove some esoteric aspect of heredity that has little or nothing to do with the traditional beliefs. The most recent claims, for instance, which are already being treated with skepticism, are about rather subtle ways in which immunological responses might be acquired and transmitted. Essentially, the idea is that changes in the somatic cells, involving ribonucleic acid (RNA), could get picked up and incorporated in the DNA of sex cells, and thus passed on. Even if such a process does occur, there is no violation of basic principles of molecular biology.

I take it that nothing more need be said here about religiously inspired *saltationism*. As far as nonreligious saltationism is concerned, my comments here must necessarily be brief and limited, because I shall have more to say on the subject later. However, three points can be made now. First, there is no direct evidence in nature of the massive useful variations supposed by someone like Huxley. All the evidence points the other way, to small variations. That sophisticated adaptations (something that Huxley minimized, it will be remembered) come through chance jumps seems implausible and quite unrecorded. As Darwin himself noted, whenever we do get a large variation, almost invariably it brings no joy to its possessor. The stumpy limbs of the achondroplastic dwarf, the product of a single mutation, are good examples.

Moreover, we have very strong evidence from studies of groups today that change within and across species barriers is gradual, not sudden. Foxes do not change into dogs at one leap. Ayala and his associates have made this point strongly through a fine series of studies of speciating fruitflies in South America. (See Figs. 5.19 and 5.20.) The flies are evolving into new species

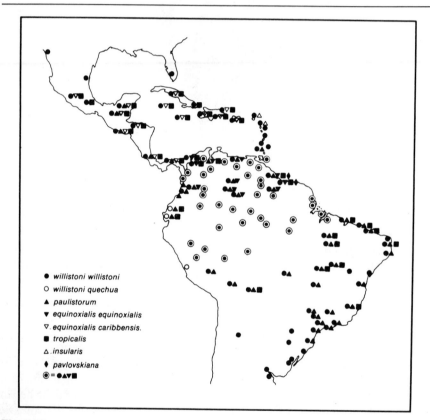

Fig. 5.19
This, and the succeeding figure (5.20) show the several stages of *gradual* speciation of South American fruitflies: Above we see the geographical distribution of six closely related species of Drosophila. *D. willistoni* and *D. equinoxial* are broken into subspecies, separated by natural barriers. Already, slight isolating mechanisms have appeared. Then in the next figure we see semi-species of *D. paulistorum.* Some of these groups are now back in contact with each other, and where (but only where) such contact has been reestablished, full isolating mechanisms have been developed. Finally, in the above figure, we see the full species of *Drosophila,* which are quite isolated from each other. (Adapted with permission from Ayala and Valentine, (1979).)

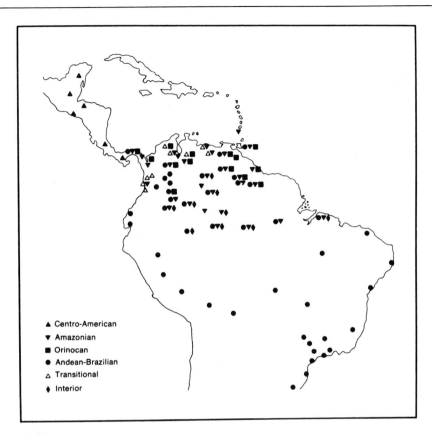

Fig. 5.20

Semi-species of *Drosophila paulistorum*. (Adapted with permission from Ayala and Valentine, (1979).)

away from each other, and all the evidence is that the process is gradual (Ayala and Tracey, 1974; Ayala et al., 1974b, c). There are many more recorded cases like these. And if all of this were not enough, there is the problem of mates that the saltationist must face. If a *saltus* takes an organism into a new species (and if it does not, it is not much of a *saltus*), then with whom does it mate? Not with the parent species, obviously. In other words, one needs two or more macromutations at a time. If one is improbable, how much less probable are two? (Dobzhansky, 1951; but see chapter 9.)

Second, if one takes seriously both the theory and findings of population genetics, particularly with respect to the balance hypothesis, then the urge for saltations is much reduced. One simply does not need them. The elementary models of the population geneticist show that even weak selection on minor change has quick effects in the evolutionary time-scale, and the balance hypothesis guarantees lots of ready variation. Agreed, all this does not make saltationism false; but, if we add redundancy to the implausibility proved in the first point, the whole position starts to seem even more transparent. To revert to my library example of early in the chapter, saltationism is rather like supposing that a complete set of books from a whole area of study, say, zoology, would without cause come together and thus be ready for use.

Third, let me now backtrack somewhat. In the plant world, there is a well-known and widespread phenomenon, known as "polyploidy," which is certainly saltationary of a kind. Further, it is believed important in the evolutionary process, particularly that of flowering plants. (Stebbins, 1950) Normally in reproduction, as we know, offspring get a haploid set of chromosomes from each parent. In polyploidy one gets more than two half sets going on to the offspring. One can get three or four sets, and the parents might not even be of the same species! Occasionally such offspring are fertile, although not with parents. One has a new species in one generation — a *saltus* indeed! Moreover, what happens in nature is often duplicated in the laboratory.

It hardly needs saying, however, that this is not really traditional saltationism of the fox-into-dog variety. If it occurs, it occurs very rarely in the animal world. Hence, the correct way to view it is, not as a refutation of Darwinism, but as a supplemental method of speciation. Here, recalling again that I shall be returning to the question of saltationism, let me simply conclude this brief discussion by noting that, generally, there is as much evidence for Darwinism in the plant world as there is in the animal world. Plants are a product of random variation, sifted and molded into adaptations by natural selection. And this is so even where polyploidy is common.

Orthogenesis is not really so much an evolutionary mechanism as a highlighting of a number of phenomena in the fossil record, which supposedly cannot be given a Darwinian explanation and therefore call for some nonselective but directing cause (Simpson, 1953). As with Lamarckism, the coming of modern genetics makes the hypothesis totally implausible. Additionally, every feature held up by the orthogeneticists as a paradigm of non-Darwinian evolution has fallen into selective line! For instance, Gould (1973) has shown that the Irish Elk, really a cervine deer, belongs to a group where antler size is a direct (logarithmic) function of body size. Far from being atypical, the size of this elk's antler's are a paradigm for the whole group. (See Fig. 5.21.)

But, is there an adaptive reason for the size of the elk and its antlers? Remember the explanation for Cope's rule. A recent commentary on the elk, using similar ideas, is as follows:

Larger body size has many advantages: strength in capturing prey, fleetness in evading predators, and success in mating competition are examples. So long as increasing size does not entail offsetting disadvantages, such as an inordinate food requirement, it might be favored by selection....

[Also] Cervine deer frequently use their antlers in display to promote success in mating, rather than in combat, and it is reasonable that *Megaloceros* did also. Indeed, their large body sizes may have evolved partly because of selection for increased antler size through reproductive success for well-endowed stags (Dobzhansky et al., 1977, p. 245)

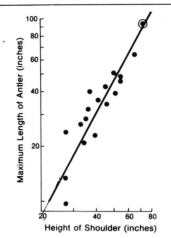

Fig. 5.21
Relation between body and antler size in cervine deer. As can be seen, the Irish "elk's" antlers are precisely in line with the antlers of the rest of the group. (Adapted by permission from Gould, (1973).)

In short, like the snail-shell colors, what was taken as a definitive counter to Darwinism turns out to be supportive. One cannot hope for better evidence for a theory than that facts, once taken as counterevidence, prove themselves to be precisely what the theory (and only the theory) predicts. To quote Darwin's old mentor, Herschel, on the subject:

The surest and best characteristic of a well-founded and extensive induction, however, is when verifications of it spring up, as it were, spontaneously, into notice, from quarters where they might be least expected, or even among instances of that very kind which were at first considered hostile to them. Evidence of this kind is irresistible, and compels assent with a weight which scarcely any other possesses (Herschel, 1831, p. 170).

Finally, there is *drift*. I have little more to say here than has been said already in the last chapter. Paradigmatic examples of drift turn out to be paradigmatic examples of selection in action. It is true that some still argue that nonadaptive random processes are important factors, operating now at the molecular level (specifically the level of the proteins) — below the effect of natural selection (Kimura and Ohta, 1971; King and Jukes, 1969). As we have seen, the claim is that much molecular variation is adaptively neutral. Let me just say two things about this hypothesis.

First, this is a case that is yet to be proven. We ourselves have seen that there are facts that belie its universal truth. One much publicized claim by the "neutralists" was that nonadaptive molecular variation would yield a very exact "molecular clock." If cellular molecules are changing (because of mutation) at a reasonably constant rate and if this change lies below selection, one should be able to make accurate calculations of times since organisms split from others. Members of a species will evolve together, away from other organisms. But, without denying that, taken at an average level, this insight has led to some very suggestive findings, it is clear from the fossil record that such a "clock" is not overly accurate. This suggests that selection is at work at all biological levels. (See Fig. 5.22.)

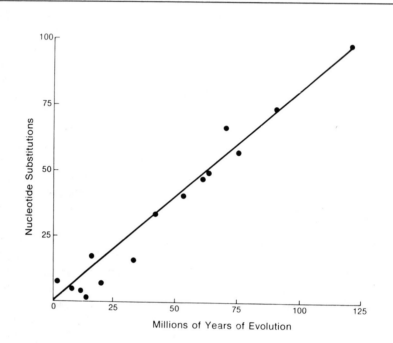

Fig. 5.22

The rate of molecular evolution: The graph plots total nucleotide substitutions of seven proteins for several pairs of species whose ancestors separated at the times indicated in the abscissa. (Based by permission on W. M. Fitch, (1976). Molecular evolutionary clocks, in F. J. Ayala ed., *Molecular Evolution,* Sunderland, Mass., Sinauer.) Obviously, on average, the rate of substitution seems fairly steady, although it is certainly not uniform. The lower points below the diagonal represent primate pairs, suggesting that primate protein evolution is slow. It could, of course, be that we overestimate the time since primate species diverged. (See Chapter 10 for more on this point.)

Second, even if molecular random evolution should appear widely true, it is hardly a refutation of Darwinism in its all-important sense — that the organisms we see around us are physically and behaviorally the result of natural selection. Darwinism really says nothing about any molecular evolution that has no effect at all on the phenotype.

No lengthy conclusion is required. Darwinism has had its rivals. They have been tested, and they have been found wanting in the fire of experience.

Darwinism evaluated

What is the status of natural selection? Is neo-Darwinian evolutionary theory a well-confirmed scientific theory, the sort of thing that can sit proudly at the table with the great theories of physics and chemistry? My answers are loud and clear. Natural selection is a genuine, widespread, powerful mechanism of evolutionary change, past and present, and neo-Darwinian theory is a well-proven theory. Judged as a body of science, Darwinism is indeed a theory, but no less of one than Einsteinian astronomy, quantum mechanics, or (to take another area closer to home) plate tectonics.

One should not overstate the case. Neither Darwin nor any of his followers, past or present, has ever wanted to claim that absolutely every facet of the organic world is totally adaptive, tightly controlled by selection. Today even the most loyal Darwinian would probably not deny some chance factors — in the founder principle, if not in drift. Additionally, as noted, there are vestigial effects of evolution, like useless homologies and the like. Then, given the randomness of variation, one cannot expect always that nature will devise the best and most efficient "solution." Also, there is the problem of what one might call basic biological "engineering": how does one put all the parts together and get them to work? Most certainly, there will be features of no great functional value. (Gould and Lewontin, 1979; but see also Cain, 1979, and the discussion in Chapter 9.) And so forth.

But these factors are only background noise against the main evolutionary tune. Time and again we have seen evidence of selection on small variation bringing about adaptively valuable features in the ongoing struggle for survival and reproduction. There simply can be no adequate non-Darwinian answer to the tight relationship between the distributions of sickle-cell anemia and malaria. Therefore, given the overall functioning nature of the organic world, the only reasonable conclusion is that neo-Darwinian theory, centering on natural selection, holds the secret to evolutionary change.

Part III
Darwinism Tomorrow?

Chapter 6
The Origin of Life

Many people think that scientific theories are a little bit like the ten commandments: written on tablets of stone. It is presumed that one can lay out a theory clearly, stating the principle premises, conclusions, and evidence, and that is the end of matters as far as that particular theory is concerned. Apart from a certain amount of polishing around the edges, slightly more elegant ways of deriving proofs, and the like, a scientific theory is something one discovers, elaborates, and uses, period.

Fortunately for the sanity of scientists, this view of science, one rein- *Conclusion* forced by the confident tone of elementary textbooks and by so many works on science written by philosophers, is about as far from the truth as it is possible for any myth to be. In fact, scientific theories are much more like organisms or species: they are born, grow, live, reproduce, and die. Above all, they never stay still.

This constant motion is almost the defining mark. The theory of evolution through natural selection has changed and moved continuously, since its first full public appearance in the *Origin of Species* — and *that* represented a development over Darwin's earliest formulations of his theory. Projecting forward, it would be foolhardy in the extreme to assert categorically that the theory has finished growing and developing. Whether the next 100 years will see changes of the order of the past 100 years is a moot point; but, undoubtedly we can expect to see many alterations, developments, and extensions.

I am afraid that philosophers are notoriously bad forecasters of the future progress of science. I have colleagues who are still "proving" that the biological sciences will never interact meaningfully with the physical sciences! However, since philosophers also find it very difficult to learn from experience, here I want to try my hand at predicting the future course of Darwinian studies. I realize that my insistence at playing the seer could easily degenerate into an exercise in self-indulgence; hence, I shall do more than simply list my "likely prospects." I shall rather choose several areas of investigation, which have a historical interest for Darwinians, where some very exciting work has been done recently, and where perhaps we might expect to see even more exciting developments in the future. I am *not* saying that these are the only areas in which good evolutionary work is being done, or that anyone else today or 100 years from now would say that I have made the wisest of choices. But I do think that by looking briefly at these areas we can get some sense of the thrill of contemporary evolutionary work and prospects — why a bright young graduate student might be tempted into evolutionary studies.

Spreading my net as widely as possible, I begin with recent advances regarding the origins and development of early life. In a way, these are not so much part of Darwinian theory, as an important *complement* to the theory. Then I move on to work in ecology, where I think we start to see important refinements and additions to the *core* of neo-Darwinism. Next comes the explosion of work, theoretical and experimental, in animal social behavior: the development of one of the *subdisciplines* of the Darwinian synthesis. Concluding, we will look at a recent *challenge* to Darwinism coming from the paleontological end of the evolutionary spectrum.

Ultimate origins

Darwinism is a theory about causes in the biological world. It tries to give answers to questions about the way in which organic types develop and change over time, showing also why organisms today are as they are. But, although Darwinism is a theory of biological causation, it invites questions beyond its own strict domain. Naturally — almost inevitably — one is led back in time to ask questions about ultimate origins: where did life come from in the first place? Thus, at a very minimum, complementing Darwinism, as it were, we could use a theory of the first production of life: a theory of chemical evolution perhaps?

However, even if this theory is produced, questions will remain. We are going to want some way of linking up the chemical and the biological. Can the history of life on this globe plausibly be interpreted as one of continuous transition, or should we seek other causes? For instance, even if we eschew miracles, believing that life can be created naturally, would it make more sense to think of the earth itself as having been "seeded" from outer space?

It is to this twofold problem that I turn in this chapter. Is it reasonable to think that life was created naturally, and do we seem to have a smooth transition from ultimate beginnings to a fully populated earth? Setting a pattern to be repeated, I shall begin my story by going back in time.

Spontaneous generation

"Spontaneous generation," the idea that living organisms are produced naturally at one stroke from nonliving substances, has a long history. Most people think it was Aristotle who first popularized the idea, stating that flies and maggots appear spontaneously from rotting meat; eels and the like from mud; and frogs and worms from the earth. Then after 2000 years of total acceptance, supposedly the idea fought a drawn-out rearguard action, against ever refined experimental techniques. First came Francesco Redi, in 1688, showing that, if flies are prevented from laying their eggs, then maggots do not appear on meat. Next came Lazzaro Spallanzani, in the eighteenth century, showing that sterilized broths do not putrify. Finally, in 1862, Louis Pasteur took experiment right down to the smallest possible organisms, showing definitively that life only comes from other life. And, the truth of this historical account appears to be reinforced by its almost perfect mesh with Darwin's tactics in the *Origin*. I do not know if you noticed, but he did not discuss the ultimate origins of organisms at all! Surely, by 1859 Darwin realized that spontaneous generation was on very shaky ground indeed, and so wisely (and fortunately) he stayed away from something that was soon to receive its death blow.

In fact, the true history was not quite like this at all. It is indeed true that experimental evidence was brought to bear critically on the spontaneous generation question, often with great effectiveness. As we ourselves have seen, Lamarck's reliance on spontaneous generation was strongly faulted on empirical grounds. But, typically for ideas that so capture the popular imagination, much of the opposition to the concept came more from extra-scientific sources, particularly from those of religion. Redi, for instance, was quite explicit in his religious distaste for spontaneous generation. It runs counter to the idea of God having created in a Biblical fashion, at the end of which He sat back with the satisfied feeling that His work was done.

And, this kind of objection persisted right down to the nineteenth century. Indeed, such Genesis-based opposition was part of the reason for the enthusiastic reception of Pasteur's work, in the very conservative French Third Republic. Additionally to opposition based on revealed religion, there was hostility to spontaneous generation on grounds of natural religion, namely that it runs counter to God's design. Instantaneous creation of life from nonlife is the paradigm of order coming from randomness. Undoubtedly it was this fact that led to much British opposition to spontaneous generation. With reason, spontaneous generation was taken to be materialistic and a step towards atheism.

Conversely, correcting the popular impression, we find that the history of spontaneous generation, in the years from Redi to Pasteur, was far from one of continuous smooth decline. In fact, in Germany, at the beginning of the nineteenth century, at the very time that the French were criticizing Lamarck for promoting spontaneous generation, spontaneous generation flourished as never before! The reason for this was the widespread popularity of the metaphysics known as *Naturphilosophie*: a philosophy that sees order and symmetry throughout the universe. The *Naturphilosophes* seized on such phenomena as organic homologies as evidence for their position — the repetition of order from organism to organism was just what they expected to find

— and, as can be imagined, given the repetitive order one finds in such inorganic phenomena as minerals, they saw nothing remarkable in the supposition that the nonliving might spontaneously change into the living. It was simply a transition from one state to another — the underlying order was present, before and after.

These two factors, the opposition of religion to spontaneous generation and the support of *Naturphilosophie*, led to a rather paradoxical situation in Britain around the time of the publication of the *Origin*. Darwin himself could not accept the traditional notion of spontaneous generation, because like his teachers and elders he saw the concept denying or ignoring the design-like appearance of the organic world. Additionally, simply for reasons of prudence, he determined to keep even mention of so controversial a notion out of the *Origin*. He had troubles enough as it was! However, by the end of the 1850s, in respects, time had started to pass Darwin by. Partly as a function of the loosening grip of orthodox religion, partly as a function of the rise of a materialistic way of thinking, and partly as a function of a growing popularity of certain elements of *Naturphilosophie,* by that time in Britain, if anything, belief in some form of spontaneous generation was *on the increase*!

Hence, given the way that biological evolutionism points towards ultimate origins, when the *Origin* was published, many thinkers naturally saw that evolutionism (Darwinian or otherwise) and spontaneous generation were part and parcel of the same picture — just at the time when Pasteur supposedly was sounding the death knell of spontaneous generation! Moreover, countering the results coming out of France, in both Britain and Germany there was optimism that more positive evidence was coming in to support the doctrine. In particular, dredging experiments on the sea-bed revealed a layer of "transparent gelatinous matter," a substance that Huxley and others took to be composed of primitive organisms and to which the name *Bathybius haeckelii* was given (after Ernst Haeckel, of biogenetic-law fame). Here indeed seemed to be the link between inert matter and sophisticated living organisms. (See Fig. 6.1.)

Unfortunately, however, the enthusiasm was relatively short lived. In the 1870s, *Bathybius haeckelii* was shown to be no organism at all, but simply a chemical precipitate. Consequently, with the growing recognition of the importance of the experiments of Pasteur and others, traditional beliefs in spontaneous generation went into a general decline. But it was a decline with tension: for all that Darwin himself said nothing publicly, most scientists and educated thinkers felt that evolutionism required some kind of natural production of the living from the nonliving. Consequently a good many of the later Victorians favored a compromise position, supposing that at some point in the distant past life had been naturally created, but that because of changed conditions this creation is no longer possible.

Indeed, in a private letter Darwin himself espoused a view like this:

It has often been said that all the conditions for the first production of a living organism are now present which could ever have been present. But if (and oh! what a big if!) we could conceive in some warm little pond, with all sorts of ammonia and phosphoric salts, light, heat, electricity, etc., present, that a protein compound was chemically formed ready to undergo still more complex changes, at the present day such matter would be instantly devoured or absorbed, which would not have been the case before living creatures were formed (F. Darwin, 1887).

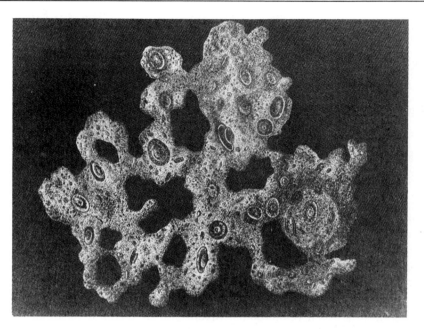

Fig. 6.1
Bathybius haeckelii: From C. Wyville Thomson, (1873). *The Depths of the Sea,* London.

Obviously, what Darwin had in mind here was some sort of gradual chemical evolution. He never accepted that integrated functioning could be instantaneously produced from randomness.

It was not until this century was well under way that real progress was made on the origin-of-life question, and, with hindsight, Darwin gets full credit for his speculations. As the complex workings of the cell were uncovered, it became more and more obvious that the idea of life having appeared spontaneously, fully fashioned, from inert matter, and on a continuous basis simply was not reasonable. However, at least two thinkers in the 1920s, J. B. S. Haldane in Britain and A. I. Oparin in Russia, realized that the more that was learned about the chemistry of the cell and of life itself, the more reasonable it is to suppose that life could have originated naturally, by a slow process of chemical evolution — piece by piece — from inorganic matter to fully functioning organisms. And, as Darwin supposed, this would be a nonrepeatable process, in the sense that the natural creation of life would so alter environmental conditions that it could never occur again. Most particularly, such evolution could not occur in nature today.

Somewhat anachronistically, let us now jump straight to the present, and let us see what fruits this supposition about nonrepeatable chemical evolution has borne. We shall see some very interesting work, backed by impressive evidence. Already, those sure indicators of scientific orthodoxy, elementary textbooks, almost automatically include discussions of the origin of life in their overall treatments of the evolutionary synthesis. Nevertheless, enough unanswered questions remain to suggest that evolutionary studies in this area have the prospect of ongoing work and expansion. (What follows is much indebted to Dickerson, 1978.)

Chemical evolution

The basic unit of the living organism, the cell, consists primarily of long macromolecules, "polymers," which in turn are chains of smaller unit molecules, "monomers." As we learned earlier, there are two important kinds of polymer. First, there are the "proteins": chains of "amino acids." The proteins serve either as structural building blocks for the cell or as catalysts ("enzymes"), driving the chemical processes of the cell. Second, in the cell, there are those macromolecules that contain and transmit the information of the cell, the key molecule in most cells being deoxyriboneucleic acid (DNA). These macromolecules are made up of smaller molecules of sugars and other substances. (Refer back to Chapter 3, for full details.)

Taking the cellular polymers as a reference point, any putative chemical evolution of a primitive unicellular organism must therefore have fallen into about five stages. First, the earth must have gotten to such a state that it contained the appropriate raw materials for life. Second, the monomers must have been formed. Third, monomers must have connected up into polymers. (Today, DNA is involved in making proteins and vice versa. Presumably, to escape from this chicken and egg situation, original polymers of one or both kinds must have been formed independently.) Fourth, polymers must have devised ways of separating themselves and their functioning off from the rest of the world. Fifth, such proto-cells must have developed the ability to reproduce.

A key finding about the putative evolution of life, one due to Haldane, is that, if the first stage involved an Earth as it is today, specifically one containing 20 percent oxygen in its atmosphere, then the second stage could not have occurred! Had there been so much free oxygen, the monomers essential for the creation of life could simply not have formed and persisted. Fortunately this fact does not bring chemical evolutionary hypothesizing to an abrupt end. The evidence is that at the time of Earth's cooling to a point at which the evolution of life could begin, the surface would have carried oceans surrounded by an atmosphere very unlike today's. There would have been no free oxygen. However, the atmosphere would have satisfied the first stage of chemical evolution, for it contained the ingredients for organic life in the form of such gases as methane (CH_4), ammonia (NH_3), carbon dioxide (CO_2), and hydrogen sulfide (H_2S). Additionally, there was a rather promising source of energy. Since there would have been no ozone (O_3) layer, far more ultraviolet radiation than at present would have come from the sun to the Earth's surface. (See Kerr, 1980, for recent thought on this subject.)

Now, under conditions such as these, could the process of chemical evolution have actually started? Answering this question brings us to what is perhaps the most exciting item of all pertinent to the origin of life, that which convinced many that the idea of a natural chemical evolution is a real possibility. This was an experiment performed by Stanley L. Miller and Harold C. Urey, at Chicago, in the 1950s. Assuming that one would have a cooling Earth like the one just described, they attempted to simulate the conditions, and to see if they could produce experimentally the monomers necessary for life. In other words, they tried to reproduce the second crucial stage in the evolution of life.

As is well known, Miller and Urey succeeded beyond all expectation! They ran their simulating apparatus (see Fig. 6.2) for a week or so at a time,

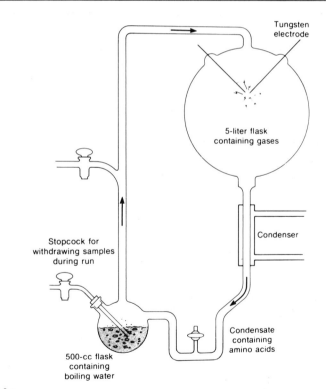

Fig. 6.2
The apparatus used by Stanley Miller to produce amino acids "naturally": Appropriate gases were circulated through the tubing and the hoped-for compounds were formed. (Adapted by permission from Dobzhansky *et al.*, (1977).)

and, by varying the initial mixture, they were able to produce all kinds of amino acids, the essential building blocks of proteins — the matter of the structural materials and catalysts within the cell. This is still a long way from establishing the natural production of fully functioning life; but, the fact that, under the most likely conditions, so crucial a step can indeed proceed naturally rightfully has proven a keen stimulus to research and to a confidence that a full solution is there to be found. Confidence has been further increased by the fact that now parallel progress has been made on the natural production of the constituents of DNA.

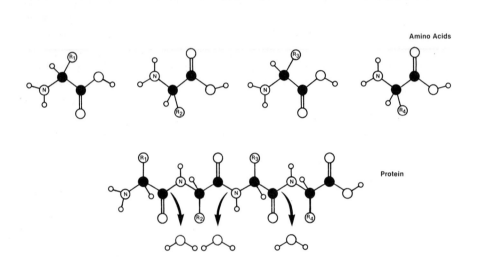

Fig. 6.3

In order to make a protein (a "polypeptide" chain), one must link up amino acids by removing water molecules. Construction of DNA also involves the removal of water.

The third putative stage in the evolution of life, "polymerization," presents some interesting problems. As can be seen from Fig. 6.3, polymerization involves the linking up of monomers by removing water molecules, thus creating bonds. But, could this have happened naturally in the early existence of the globe? If, as supposed, amino acids and the like are first created in some primeval ocean, then with all the water around, the last thing that the monomers will do is give up a water molecule. It is much more likely that polymers will take up water, thus breaking up into individual monomers! However, there are suggested solutions to this dilemma, some obvious and some rather less so. Evaporation of the early organic "soup" by the sun is one obvious possible way in which the troublesome excess water might have vanished. Conversely, freezing may have been important! Like evaporation, this can serve to concentrate substances that are dissolved or contained in water. Yet another possibility, less obvious but one that excites interest today, is that the organic molecules might have been absorbed into clays and other minerals, concentrated and bound there by the catalytic effects of the minerals themselves, and thence through natural processes slowly leached back into the waters of the Earth.

As we move along through the stages of the putative evolution of life, increasingly we enter the realm of the hypothetical. Many queries remain about the formation of polymers, and the same is even more true of the fourth and fifth postulated stages of the evolutionary process. Oparin himself worked for a long time on the fourth stage, the separation of the cell off from the outside world. He tried to show how aqueous solutions of polymers will tend to form self-contained droplets that can, as it were, function as individual entities. To be frank, neither his work nor that of others has made much attempt to replicate the exact conditions and precise polymers that might have been expected to exist at the end of the third evolutionary stage. However, realistic or not, some fascinating effects have been obtained, with minute droplets forming, having wall-like coverings, and even growing and budding in an almost bacterium-like fashion. If analogy counts for anything, some progress has been made. (See Fig. 6.4.)

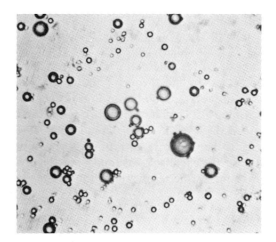

Fig. 6.4a
Self-contained droplets produced in Moscow by A. I. Oparin.

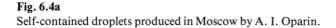

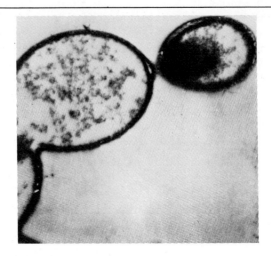

Fig. 6.4b
Self-contained droplets produced in Miami by Sidney W. Fox. These droplets can be made to grow and bud. (Photographs taken by permission from R. E. Dickerson, (1978). Chemical evolution and the origin of life. *Scientific American,* September, 70-86.)

Unfortunately we do not really even have analogical models for the fifth stage of chemical evolution — the development of the apparatus of replication, ensuring that the genes get passed on from cell to cell and from individual to individual. At most we have untried speculations. But I think by now that enough ground has been covered to justify the claim that, although spontaneous generation as traditionally conceived has gone the way of the dodo and the 10 cent cup of coffee, the major question about the origin of life, presupposed if not asked by the theory of the *Origin,* has started to yield positive and exciting answers and bodies of knowledge. We have very far to go. Apart from anything else, much of the work so far occurs less at the level of theory and more at the level of simulated modeling. Also, at this point to date, concern seems to be primarily with tracing sequences. Presumably, at some point, some sort of "chemical selection" must be invoked to make the processes work. But, for all the reservations, the first steps have surely been taken.

Life's early history: The outline

We come now to the second part of our inquiry about origins, presupposed and invoked by a biological evolutionary theory like Darwinism. Suppose we grant that some progress has been made towards the understanding of the origin of life. Suppose that we even grant, what is not yet proven, that we have a full understanding of the natural production of simple one-cell organisms.

Presumably, at this point, the Darwinian will argue that his *biological* theory can take over. Through a process of mutation and natural selection, biological evolution has brought us up to our present state. The theories of chemical evolution and biological evolution are not rivals, but complementary parts of the overall picture.

However, with reason, the disinterested critic might wonder if all the gaps have been filled. When we left Darwin, it is true that we had nothing on the ultimate origins of life; but, also, if memory does not deceive, it is true that we had nothing very much at all until the explosion of life at the beginning of the Cambrian, a point that we now know to be about 600 million years ago. But, if anything is certain in evolutionary studies, this much is certain: if one posits a process of gradual change like Darwinism, one does not expect life to explode instantaneously from simplest forms to the sophisticated record that we find in the Cambrian! Natural selection positively forbids a one-step move from single-celled organisms to something like the trilobites.

Hence, to complete our story of origins — what we have learned and what we have yet to learn — we must now look at today's knowledge about the actual course of evolution. Does it support the idea of a smooth, Darwinian transition, up from beginnings to the teeming state we find recorded in the Cambrian? And, what about some of the other queries left over from earlier discussion? For instance, where did all the oxygen come from, if it was not present when life was first formed?

Taking Darwin as our starting point, remember that, although he kept ultimate beginnings out of the *Origin,* he did not dare to do the same with the nonexistent pre-Cambrian fossil record.

Consequently, if my theory be true, it is indisputable that before the lowest Silurian stratum was deposited, long periods elapsed, as long as, or probably far longer than, the whole interval from the Silurian age to the present day; and that during these vast, yet quite unknown, periods of time, the world swarmed with living creatures.

To the question why we do not find records of these vast primordial periods, I can give no satisfactory answer ...

The case at present must remain inexplicable; and may be truly urged as a valid argument against the views here entertained. (Darwin, 1859, pp. 307–308.)

Remember also that, ever ready with an answer, Darwin suggested that perhaps the earliest organisms lived where today there are seas, but that unfortunately all traces of their remains will now be metamorphosed by the incredible weight of water above them! Unable to grasp at fossils, Darwin grasped at straws.

Obviously the discussion of the *Origin* was far from satisfactory; friends and critics alike realized this. It was therefore with some relief to evolutionists that, shortly after the *Origin* first appeared, new evidence was unearthed (literally) that apparently went some considerable way towards solving the dilemma of the appearance of life (O'Brien, 1970). A number of strange objects were discovered in pre-Cambrian rocks of Canada, and these were identified by Sir William Dawson, world-leading authority on the subject, as remains of a species of formanifer. It was promptly labeled *Eozoon canadense,* and known informally as the "dawn animal of Canada." (See Fig. 6.5.) Darwin and his supporters immediately seized on it as the very missing link they had sought, and as might have been expected, it was not long before *Eozoon canadense* was making a star appearance in new editions of the *Origin!*

Fig. 6.5
William Dawson's reconstruction of the Pre-Cambrian 'fossil' *Eozoon.*

Beautifully illustrating the very large gap that exists between empirical discoveries and cherished hypotheses, we find that Dawson — to the end of his life an ardent opponent of all kinds of evolutionism — drew entirely the opposite conclusion from the existence of *Eozoon canadense*! He saw it as the paradigm of an isolated organism — one without predecessors or immediate successors. In other words, he saw the gap between the dawn animal and the next life on earth as the gap to end all gaps, or rather all evolutionism! For him, it was proof positive of God's creative interference in Earth history.

In fact, it turns out that both sides had built their houses on sand — metamorphic sand. Before long, *Eozoon canadense* was seen to be no true organism at all, but an object produced inorganically by great heat and pressure on limestone. And that was the end of that. The mysterious appearance of life on this planet remained as mysterious as ever.

What we know now — But not the lower

This uncomfortable state of affairs persisted well into this century. Indeed, only recently have we started to make real progress in finding out about life's early history, and much work still remains to be done. But, trying to be as positive as possible, let us see what we do know. The most important fact is that today we have increasing fossil evidence testifying unambiguously to pre-Cambrian life (Schopf, 1978). Much of this evidence is microscopic, and thus previously escaped paleontological attention; but, there is no longer any doubt as to its widespread existence and genuine validity. It is not going to vanish in a limestone vapor, along with *Eozoon canadense!* Furthermore, the oldest-known sedimentary rocks date back to over 3 billion years ago, and at least two of them (the Fig Tree and Onverwacht deposits, 3.2 and 3.4 billion years old respectively) contain bacteria-like microfossils.

In other words, since the earth is 4.6 billion years old, we have traces of life from about a billion years after Earth was formed; or, putting matters another way, we have a record of organic life for about three quarters of the Earth's history. Presumably, therefore, the chemical evolution of life must have occurred by then. And, as if in confirmation of this fact, it was indeed in, and only in, the very early stages of Earth history that the atmosphere had the form that (we have seen) could apparently have fueled this life-creating evolution.

Following the earliest discovered organisms of all and coming down through the ages, we get more and more evidences of life. (See Fig. 6.6.)

Fig. 6.6
(Left) Fossil stromatolites found in limestone about 1,300 million years old in Glacier National Park.
(Right) Living stromatolites photographed at Shark Bay in Australia. (Photographs taken by permission from J. W. Schopf, (1978). The evolution of the earliest cells. *Scientific American,* September, 110-138.)

back to Darwin

Moreover, as we edge close to the Cambrian, we start to see the kinds of advance in development that a Darwinian or, indeed, any other variety of evolutionist would expect. For instance, we get our first evidence of animals in the late pre-Cambrian era (some time after 700 million years ago), and apparently these were rather primitive forms. They had hydrostatic skeletons, that is to say they had bodies filled with fluid working against muscles. One can infer this much about them from the traces left by their burrows, as they dug into the sea bed. (See Fig. 6.7.)

Fig. 6.7
Late pre-Cambrian soft-bodied animals: *A, Cyclomedusa. B, Marywadea,* which resembles some annelids. *C, Tribrachidium,* a triradiate form of unknown affinities. (Taken from M. Glaessner and M. Wade, (1966). The late precambrian fossils from Ediacara, South Australia, *Paleontology,* 9, 599-628. Used by permission of the authors and the Palaeontological Association.)

Life's early history: Details

It can therefore now be stated with some confidence that, in outline, we know how life evolved from its earliest beginnings. Let us turn next to the ways in which one can try to put some flesh on the bare bones of this picture. There are several possible sources of information. One can study living organisms for possible clues; one can examine the fossil record in even greater detail; or one can look at the inorganic record, trying to find clues pertinent to one's story.

LIFE'S EARLY HISTORY: DETAILS   169

The study of living organisms has proven particularly fruitful. There are two basic kinds of organism: those that consist of cells that do not have nucleii ("prokaryotes"), and those that consist of cells that do ("eukaryotes"). In many respects, the eukaryotes seem far more sophisticated. All the "higher" organisms have cells with nucleii, only the eukaryotes can reproduce sexually, and indeed almost all prokaryotes are unicellular, which in itself limits their overall abilities and potentials. An obvious implication therefore is that the first organisms were prokaryotes, and only later did these evolve into eukaryotes. A great many studies of the chemistry of the cell bear out this supposition. Often one finds that prokaryotes and eukaryotes do not work in fundamentally different ways, but rather that eukaryotes do what prokaryotes do, plus something more. In other words, eukaryotes seem as if they started as prokaryotes and then evolved by adding stages on.

The most significant point of overlap of this kind involves the ways in which the two kinds of cell get their energy from foodstuffs — their metabolisms. For eukaryotes, their central process of metabolism is respiration, which involves the burning of glucose in oxygen, thus producing energy. This is far, far more efficient than the metabolic mechanism of most prokaryotes, fermentation, which involves the simple breaking down of the glucose molecules, thus releasing energy. What is of vital interest is that the early stages of respiration almost exactly parallel those of fermentation — then an oxygen-using sequence is added on. In other words, one seems to have a primitive prokaryote stage and then a far more sophisticated stage added.

What this all suggests, of course, is that the coming of oxygen was an important point in life history, whether as cause or effect or more probably as both. One looks for evidence of prokaryotes arriving first on Earth; next, somehow, free oxygen becomes plentiful; and then come oxygen-using eukaryotes. Coincidentally and consiliently, this sequence would mesh neatly with what we have learned already, namely that life itself could not have originated in an atmosphere filled with oxygen. And, in fact, living organisms do seem to bear testimony to such a sequence! We find that although eukaryotes all need oxygen, there is great variability in oxygen needs among prokaryotes, ranging all the way from those for whom oxygen is a poison to those who need oxygen to survive. This certainly hints that the first prokaryotes appeared in an oxygen-free environment, and then along with a rise in atmospheric oxygen, some evolved both tolerance and ability to use the gas.

In addition, we find that some prokaryotes, the blue-green algae (known as the "cyanobacteria"), can perform photosynthesis. That is to say, they produce oxygen! In other words, cyanobacteria probably evolved from other prokaryotes, these then filled (or started to fill) the atmosphere up with oxygen, and this in turn paved the way for the evolution of the eukaryotes. Supporting this hypothesized sequence is the fact that the metabolism of cyanobacteria seems to be intermediate between non–oxygen producing prokaryotes and oxygen using eukaryotes. Many species of cyanobacteria operate most efficiently at half of present oxygen levels (i.e., they work best at around a 10 percent oxygen concentration), suggesting that they evolved at a time before the Earth arrived at present levels. (See Fig. 6.8.)

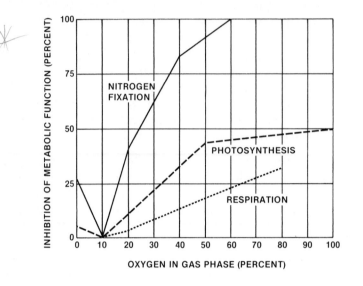

Fig. 6.8
This figure shows dramatically how cyanobacteria function most efficiently when oxygen concentration is about 10 per cent (i.e., about half the concentration we have today). Does this imply that cyanobacteria evolved at a time when oxygen concentrations were less than they are today? (Adapted by permission from Schopf, (1978).)

How do all of these inferences about the possible evolution of early life fit in with other evidence, namely that gathered from the fossil and inorganic records? The answer seems to be that, although there are as many questions as answers, everything fits reasonably well. One cannot tell directly from studying most of the pertinent microfossils whether they are prokaryote or eukaryote remains. But, working indirectly from such factors as size (eukaryote cells tend to be larger than prokaryote cells) and complexity, it seems fairly certain that the earliest identifiable eukaryote-type fossils are no more than one and a half billion years old. In short, as study of today's organisms suggests, prokaryotes came first, and eukaryotes followed later.

If this sequence is correct, then we would hope to find evidence that, around two billion or so years ago, oxygen levels in the atmosphere rose sharply. Happily, sedimentary rocks of this period suggest that such a rise did indeed occur. For instance, uraninite (UO_2) is a mineral that oxidizes readily in the presence of oxygen (to U_3O_8). In fact, so readily does it oxidize that it is unlikely that uraninite would be deposited, were oxygen concentrations in the atmosphere above 1 percent. Expectedly, in sediments older than two billion years we find uraninite, but it is absent from younger deposits! Likewise, but in a converse fashion, we find iron oxides deposited after the two billion year mark, but not before. Biologically generated oxygen was probably a major causal factor.

Enough has been said to make the point. We are on the way to finding and understanding the full history of life on Earth. (See Fig. 6.9.) We have plausible hypotheses about the beginning of life; we are working out the long early history of life; and this can then be linked to what we know of life once it exploded into action around the beginning of the Cambrian. (See Figs. 6.10, 6.11, and 6.12.) Darwin left us with many questions. Answers are now starting to come forth, although obviously there is still much work to be done. I am sure that, 100 years from today, scientists will look back with pity at our ignorance. But then, would we really want to deprive our grandchildren of an emotion that gives us such pleasure, when we look back in time?

Events in biosphere	Time (billions of years)	Events in planetary environment		
Permian – Triassic extinctions	0.22			
First well-mineralized skeletons	0.57		(Plate tectonics)	
First body fossils	0.70			
First metazoans?	1.0			Free oxygen in atmosphere
Possible early eukaryotes	1.3			
		Cranial sediment, chiefly oxidized	(Plate tectonics probable)	
Possible early eukaryotes	1.91			
		Most banded iron formations		
	2.21			
(Prokaryotes becoming diverse)				
		Cratonal sediment, chiefly unoxidized	(Global tectonics unlike present)	Chiefly anoxic atmosphere, probably reducing
Oldest dated fossils (prokaryotic autotrophs)	3.31			
		Rocks chiefly granitic and gneissic, sediments extensive		
	3.81	Oldest dated rocks		
		Record not known		
	4.61	Origin of Earth		

Fig. 6.9
Major events in the history of the earth. (Adapted by permission from P. Cloud, (1974). Evolution of ecosystems, *American Scientist,* 62, 54-66.)

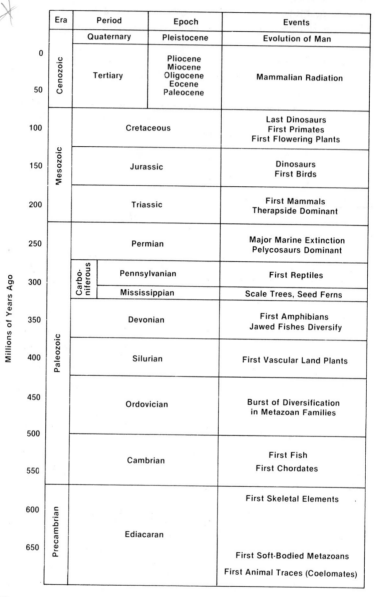

Era	Period	Epoch	Events
Cenozoic	Quaternary	Pleistocene	Evolution of Man
Cenozoic	Tertiary	Pliocene Miocene Oligocene Eocene Paleocene	Mammalian Radiation
Mesozoic	Cretaceous		Last Dinosaurs First Primates First Flowering Plants
Mesozoic	Jurassic		Dinosaurs First Birds
Mesozoic	Triassic		First Mammals Therapside Dominant
Paleozoic	Permian		Major Marine Extinction Pelycosaurs Dominant
Paleozoic	Carboniferous Pennsylvanian		First Reptiles
Paleozoic	Carboniferous Mississippian		Scale Trees, Seed Ferns
Paleozoic	Devonian		First Amphibians Jawed Fishes Diversify
Paleozoic	Silurian		First Vascular Land Plants
Paleozoic	Ordovician		Burst of Diversification in Metazoan Families
Paleozoic	Cambrian		First Fish First Chordates
Precambrian	Ediacaran		First Skeletal Elements
Precambrian	Ediacaran		First Soft-Bodied Metazoans First Animal Traces (Coelomates)

(Vertical axis labeled "Millions of Years Ago" with markings: 0, 50, 100, 150, 200, 250, 300, 350, 400, 450, 500, 550, 600, 650)

Fig. 6.10

Major events in the evolution of multicellular life. It is interesting to compare this picture with Owen's corresponding 1860 picture (figure 2.5). The older picture stands up surprisingly well. (Adapted by permission from J. W. Valentine, (1978). The evolution of multicellular plants and animals. *Scientific American,* September, 140-158.)

The next two figures tell in more detail about particular facets of life's history, and in themselves are interesting exercises in ways of conveying information.

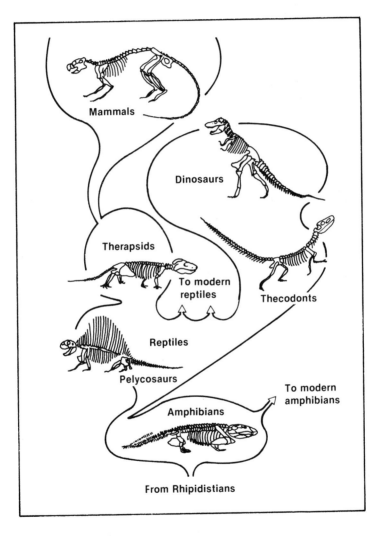

Fig. 6.11

Some tetrapod (land vertebrate) types. Ancient amphibians gave rise to reptiles, which in turn gave rise to therapsids (the ancestors of mammals), to modern reptiles, and to the dinosaurs. The amphibian shown here, *Ichthyostega,* dates from the late Devonian. (Taken by permission from Ayala and Valentine, (1979).)

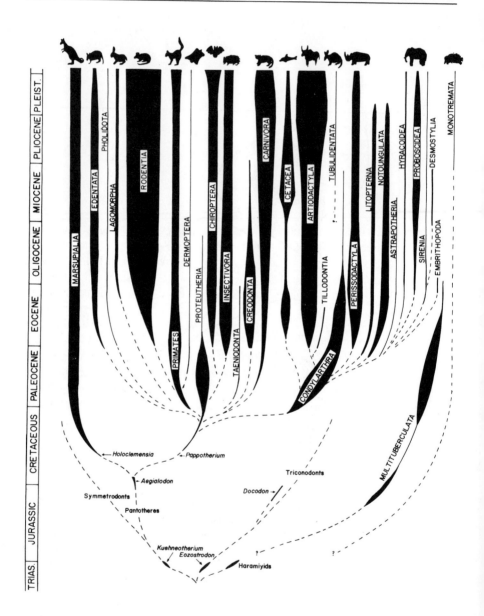

Fig. 6.12
Radiation of the mammals: the width of the shaded area gives a rough estimate of the (relative) numbers of genera in the fossil record. (Taken by permission from P. D. Gingerich, (1977), Patterns of evolution in the mammalian fossil record. In A. Hallam ed, *Patterns of Evolution As Illustrated by the Fossil Record,* Amsterdam: Elsevier, 469-500.)

Chapter 7
Population Ecology

I come to the second point at which I forecast a bright future for "Darwinism Tomorrow." My choice may occasion some surprise. For most of us, the term "ecology" summons up thoughts of an environmentalist movement opposed to acid rain, artificial fertilizers, and the Newfoundland seal-hunt. Since many in this movement are violently opposed to science and technology, the prospect of there being a worthwhile interaction between evolutionary theory and ecology seems remote indeed. One would think it the last thing that most evolutionists would want.

And yet, I believe that within neo-Darwinian studies the coming of ecology represents the most important event of the past decade, perhaps even since the coming of Mendelism: only now are we sensing the incredibly fertile prospects. I suspect that both theoretically and experimentally evolutionary ecology will infuse and transform virtually all aspects of neo-Darwinism.

Population ecology

First, clearing up any misconceptions, it must be realized that the sense of "ecology" involved here, that which interacts with evolutionary thought, is but distantly connected with the social philosophy of that name. What I am talking about is what is generally known as "population ecology": the science concerned with populations or organisms, their growth, their internal differences and physical distributions, and with their interactions, one with another and with the environment, through competition and predation.

Now, as soon as I characterize ecology in this sort of way, things start to seem a little more familiar and less paradoxical. Indeed, one might wonder why all the fuss. Contrary to the impression just given, surely evolutionists have been acknowledging and using ecology for a long time. In fact, through the *Origin* there are repeated ecological hypotheses, digressions, and discussions. Take the following famous passage, for instance:

I am tempted to give one more instance showing how plants and animals, most remote in the scale of nature, are bound together by a web of complex relations ... I have ... reason to believe that humble-bees are indispensable to the fertilisation of the heartsease (Viola tricolor), for other bees do not visit this flower. ... The number of humble-bees in any district depends in a great degree on the number of field-mice, which destroy their combs and nests. ... Now the number of mice is largely dependent, as every one knows, on the number of cats. ... Hence it is quite credible that the presence of a feline animal in large numbers in a district might determine, through the intervention first of mice and then of bees, the frequency of certain flowers in that district! (Darwin, 1859, pp. 73–74)

Generations of evolutionists have joked that the main fault with this passage is that it is incomplete. Darwin should have noted that lonely spinsters are fond of keeping cats, and that thus the clover in the fields is a direct function of the number of old maids in the district! No one thought that a discussion like this had no place in the *Origin*. Ecology of this sort fitted comfortably and appropriately into Darwin's analysis, and it has done so ever since in evolutionary work.

In fact, one can apparently completely turn the tables on my claims about the novel importance of ecology for evolutionary thought. Going back to my paradigm example of an evolutionary explanation, namely island speciation, it turns out that Lack (1947) openly acknowledged that one of the key influences on his position was a well known ecological hypothesis, Gause's principle. This postulates that, whenever one has two very similar species competing, eventually one will win out over the other. In light of this hypothesis, Lack decided that the crucial evolutionary force driving co-existing species apart had to be the negative one of competition, rather than the positive one of available, alternative foodstuffs. How much more important could ecology be?

Nevertheless, although evolutionists have certainly acknowledged and used ecology, traditionally there was no attempt to incorporate ecological thought in any systematic, formal way into evolutionary theorizing. Thus, for instance, when someone like Dobzhansky or Ayala considers balanced heterozygote fitness or a like mechanism, the selection coefficients s or t are introduced (indicating how much less fit the homozygotes are compared to the heterozygote), and then the formal or experimental machinery takes over. No one is too much perturbed about whether the inadequate fall by the wayside as infants or adults, as the result of the environment or competitors, or as a fact of behavior or physiology. In other words, the ecological background is ignored in the theory. One needs to find out the ecological facts, of course, but not as important items in their own right. Rather, such facts help to determine and make reasonable the essential ingredients in the genetic machinery; they fill in the basic outlines.

Conversely, traditionally, ecologists have been just as indifferent towards the incorporation of evolutionary factors into their theorizing. Theoretical population ecology had its start in the 1920s — exactly the time of the start of theoretical population genetics — but no attempt was made to see organisms as the products of evolution. Certainly, no attempt was made to see organisms as the product of selection. And why should there have been? At the time, most people did not dream that selection working on small mutations could be sufficiently powerful to cause significant change, and that this could happen relatively rapidly.

Thus, we find one of the founders of formal population ecology quite explicitly dissociating his work from anything of interest to and analyzable by the evolutionist: "It is characteristic of inter-group evolution that it can, and at times does, proceed at a rapid rate, ... Intra-group evolution, on the other hand, usually proceeds at a rate which, measured in our habitual standards, seems very slow" (Roughgarden, 1979, p. 311, quoting Lotka, 1945). As a consequence of this attitude, ecologists tended to treat organisms as genetically identical and unchanging, and they based their modeling on this assumption.

Since formal population ecology is undoubtedly unfamiliar to many readers, an example might be appreciated, showing both the general approach and underlining this very point about the absence of any kind of evolutionary perspective. As an illustration let us refer briefly to one of the classical analyses of formal ecology — that proposed for predator-prey interactions by the two ecologists, A. J. Lotka and V. Volterra. The ideas behind their approach are simple and intuitive. Suppose we have a species (the prey), for instance, the snails of the Cain-Sheppard study. Undisturbed, as good Malthusians these multiply in numbers quite happily. Now, however, let us introduce another species (the predators), which live on the prey-species. In the Cain-Sheppard study these were the thrushes. The questions of interest are how these two species interact and what effect this all has on their population numbers.

We can formalize our problem at an elementary level without too much trouble. (I follow the simple treatment given in Wilson and Bossert, 1971. See alternatively Maynard Smith, 1974; or Roughgarden, 1979.) Let us suppose that the size of the predator population is N_1, and that of the prey population N_2. Now, starting with the predator population, its birthrate will (as an approximation) vary directly with the size of the prey population: more snails mean more thrushes get born. Hence, the predator birthrate is B_1N_2, where B_1 is a constant. The death rate is assumed to be less dependent on the size of the prey population, and so can be set as a constant D. Therefore, the rate of growth of the predator population with respect to time is given by the following simple equation:

$$dN_1/dt = \text{(individual birthrate} - \text{individual death rate) } N_1$$
$$= (B_1N_2 - D)N_1$$
$$= B_1N_1N_2 - DN_1$$

By a similar line of argument, we can obtain the prey population growth, assuming here that birthrate is independent of the predator, but that, since more thrushes mean more snails get eaten, death rate is a linear function of predator population size:

$$dN_2/dt = \text{(individual birth} - \text{individual death rate)}\ N_2$$
$$= (B_2 - D_2N_1)N_2$$
$$= B_2N_2 - D_2N_1N_2$$

where B_2 and D are constants. (Those readers unfamiliar with the calculus should not panic. The terms dN_1/dt and dN_2/dt are expressing the idea that population numbers, N_1 and N_2, change at a certain pace according to time, just as acceleration expresses the idea that velocity or speed changes at a certain pace according to time.)

These two formulas are the Lotka-Volterra equations. They are obviously very idealized, ignoring all sorts of possible disruptive factors. Nevertheless, they do rather capture one's intuitions about the course of many predator-prey relationships, namely that the predator is continually playing "catch-up" on the prey. The prey multiplies in size; the predator multiplies because of this. Eventually the prey is overcropped and starts to drop in number; the predators' numbers drop as a consequence; and then everything starts again! (See Figs. 7.1 and 7.2.)

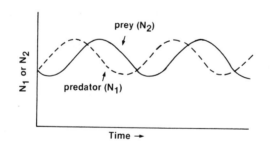

Fig. 7.1
Predator-prey interaction as predicted by the Lotka-Volterra equations. The graph plots the numbers within the species as a function of time.

Since I have been so rude about the popular kind of ecology, perhaps I can make amends by pointing to one rather surprising consequence of the equations, which does have important implications for human well-being: Volterra's principle. Suppose one indiscriminately wipes out a proportion of both predator and prey populations. Suppose, for instance, through insecticide one halves an insect pest population, but simultaneously does the same to its insect predators. Since the product N_1N_2 is reduced so much more than either N_1 or N_2 taken alone (1/4 compared to 1/2), the effect is to slash the birthrate of the predator and the death rate of the prey. Hence, very soon the prey population numbers will bounce back, perhaps to even higher levels than before. In short, beware before you drench everything with killer chemicals!

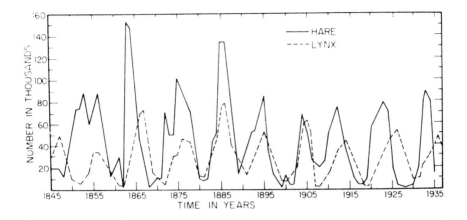

Fig. 7.2
Population cycles in the lynx and its principal prey, the snowshoe hare, in Canada. The vertical axis gives the number of pelts received by the Hudson Bay Company. (Taken by permission from E. P. Odum, (1971). *Fundamentals of Ecology,* Philadelphia: W. B. Saunders.)

Population ecology meets population genetics

Returning now to our direct concern, namely the present state and future prospects for neo-Darwinism, two things stand out from the kind of little model just introduced. First, as forecast, no attempt is made to fit the interactions being analyzed into an evolutionary framework. The organisms are treated as genetically uniform. Second, one surely should be moving towards an evolutionary approach! The Cain-Sheppard analysis showed clearly how things like predator-prey interactions set up selective pressures and leave their marks on the genotypes. What is going on in such cases cries out for neo-Darwinism. Conversely, neo-Darwinism is impoverished if it cannot use formal analyses such as that of the predator-prey model.

About ten or so years ago, a number of biologists realized that something had to be done. Evolution theory needs ecology, and ecology needs to be seen against evolution. Hence, increasing efforts were made to bring the two together. It has not been easy. Apart from anything else, whereas population genetics is fairly well standardized, population ecology has all sorts of different competing analyses, and so many would-be combiners of evolutionary theory felt mystified as to where they should begin. As the perceptive author of, what I am sure is destined to be, a landmark survey and synthesis of the field writes:

The fusion of population genetics with population ecology can be compared to a prearranged marriage between partners who speak different languages. Although both families agree that the marriage is advantageous, it is somewhat difficult to achieve because of cultural differences between geneticists and ecologists (Roughgarden, 1979, p. 297).

Revealingly, when this work was reviewed in the major journal of the field, *Evolution,* two biologists divided the task: an evolutionist dealing with the population genetics, and an ecologist dealing with the population ecology.

I do not think that, even now, anyone would want to claim that population genetics and population ecology have been completely fused, thus making a comprehensive population biological theory. But, already, significant progress has been made, with every promise of more exciting work to come. Moreover, this new theory holds every prospect of moving right into the core position of neo-Darwinian evolutionary studies. Let me therefore complete my coverage of the new evolutionary ecology by giving a brief (but exciting) example to show how the fusion takes place and with what result. We can look at a matter of great ecological interest, namely what happens to organisms when they get crowded or run out of room and resources. We can see how this "density dependent" situation can be spelled out in evolutionary terms, particularly those involving selective forces that cause changes in genotypic ratios within populations. (I follow the discussion in Roughgarden, 1979.)

Let us start with the simplest sort of case, namely with a population growing without limit, supposing that each individual always multiplies at the same rate. Given the population size $N(t)$ at time t, we can say the *rate* of change of the population size is given by the simple equation:

$$dN(t)/dt = \left\{ \begin{array}{c} \text{an individual's} \\ \text{contribution to} \\ \text{population growth} \end{array} \right\} N(t)$$

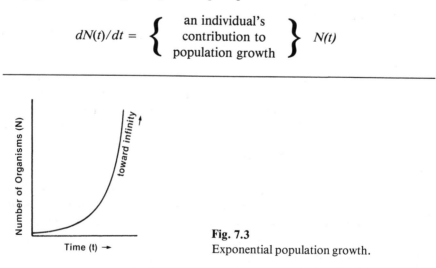

Fig. 7.3
Exponential population growth.

For the individual's contribution let us introduce the constant r, known as the "intrinsic rate of increase." Thus we have:

$$dN(t)/dt = r\,N(t)$$

Graphically the situation is as in Fig. 7.3. This is known as "exponential growth." (Observant readers will note that the term B_2 in the exposition of the Lotka-Volterra equations is in fact the prey population's r. Usually the equations are given using this more familiar terminology.)

But, of course, this picture of exponential growth is unrealistic. There comes a point where the environment can hold no more of that species of organism. A much more realistic picture is given in Fig. 7.4. This is known as "logistic growth." What we have here is the population exploding up and then slowing down as it approaches the maximum number of organisms the environment can hold. Traditionally, we use the symbol K to represent this maximum, and it is known as the "carrying capacity" (of that environment with respect to the maximum number of that species of organism). Basically, therefore, what we are saying in the logistic case is that, as $N(t)$ approaches K, the effect of an individual's contribution to growth drops away to zero.

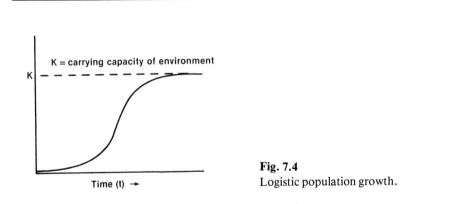

K = carrying capacity of environment

Time (t) →

Fig. 7.4
Logistic population growth.

Intuitively, I am sure it can be seen that the following equation captures the situation we are analyzing:

$$dN(t)/dt = r[1 - N(t)/K]\,N(t)$$

When $N(t)$ is small, $N(t)/K$ is small, and growth is virtually exponential. When $N(t)$ approaches K, $N(t)/K$ is nearly 1, and growth virtually vanishes. At the individual level, we are saying simply that if population size is N, then:

$$\left\{ \begin{array}{l} \text{individual's contribution} \\ \text{to population growth} \end{array} \right\} = r - \frac{rN}{K}$$

(Do not get confused here: r is the "individual's contribution to population growth" when there are no restraints, and growth can thus proceed exponentially. Now we are finding "individual's contribution to population growth" when restraints make the growth logistic.)

At this point bells start ringing. If you cannot hear them, listen a little harder! Surely, an individual's contribution to population growth has something to do with selection, *a concept in population genetics?!* Remember back to when we talked of such things as balanced superior heterozygote fitness. We were talking there of the contribution of one type of organism as compared to another kind. In particular, we set the fitness (w) of an organism as equal to 1 less the selective value against it.

$$w = 1 - s$$

Now, we can regard $- s$ as the individual's contribution to the overall growth of the group, which is obviously a negative contribution when selection is against some genotype, as it was in the cases we discussed. But clearly we can generalize and say that

$$w = 1 + \text{individual's contribution to population growth}$$

where we can consider an organism as adding either more or less than its share to the group. And, with this move taken, we are in a position to link genetics with ecology, for the last term of this just given population genetical statement occurs as the first term in this repeated population ecological statement:

$$\text{individual's contribution to population growth} \ = \ r - \frac{rN}{K}$$

Therefore:

$$w = 1 + r - \frac{rN}{K}$$

In short, with logistic growth we are saying that the fitness of an individual decreases as a linear function of population size.

Density dependent selection

Again, I am afraid I am going to disappoint my mathematical readers because, having made the link-up between genetics and ecology, I am going to miss out all the calculations and jump straight to some results that one can generate about this "density dependent selection" (i.e., selection that is a function of population sizes and the room available for them).

Essentially, one is going to set up a number of models of populations containing different genotypes, in the simplest case considering just two alleles A and a. Then, using these models, one will try to see how the gene ratios in such populations vary, assuming that they give rise to phenotypes with different intrinsic rates of increase (r) and different carrying capacities (K). And in order to do this, one makes the general assumption, borne out time and again in nature, that there is a tradeoff between r and K; a phenotype may have a large r or have a large K, but cannot have both simultaneously. A large r comes about only by sacrificing K, and vice versa.

This assumption is justified by considering in more detail which phenotypic traits produce a large r and which a large K. To obtain a large r, an organism must rapidly allocate the energy it has acquired to the production of offspring. Recall that r controls the initial rate of population growth. If an organism initially allocates energy to other purposes and only later to seed or egg production, then the initial growth of the population will not be as rapid as if organisms immediately allocate their energy to seed or egg production. However to obtain a large K, an organism must defer the allocation of energy to seeds and eggs and instead develop the facilities to survive under crowded conditions. For example, a plant that allocates energy to leaves will be able to survive under low light conditions. Hence a population of plants each of whom defers allocating energy into seeds until many leaves are produced will ultimately attain a larger population size even though the initial growth of the population may be slower. Similar arguments can be developed for animals. The point is that an organism cannot do both. An organism has a finite amount of energy and time during a growing season, and it can be allocated in favor of producing a high r or a high K but not both (Roughgarden, 1979, p. 313-314).

Now, given this assumption, we are in a position to see how selection works, specifically whether it favors a phenotype with high K or one with high r. Suppose we start with two alleles, A and a, assuming that A is completely dominant over a, and that we have the following numerical values:

$$r_A = .8 \qquad\qquad K_A = 8000$$
$$r_H = .8 \qquad\qquad K_H = 8000$$
$$r_a = .6 \qquad\qquad K_a = 12000$$

(in other words, A confers high r and low K, and a confers high K and low r. H stands for the heterozygote.)

First, we have the situations where one or other allele is completely fixed, that is where only A or a exists in the population. Here we get the standard growth curves (Fig. 7.5). Next, let us consider the case where both alleles are in the population, with A having an initial frequency of p. Using a computer to do the arithmetic, we obtain the picture in Fig. 7.6. What does this mean? Essentially it tells us that initially the allele with high r increases at the expense of the allele with high K (i.e., A over a). But then, no matter what the initial frequency, the allele with high K wipes out the allele with high r completely! A vanishes from the population.

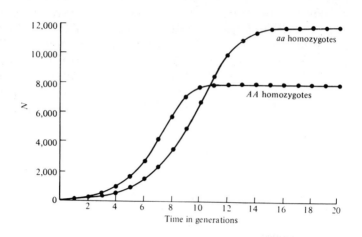

Fig. 7.5
Curves comparing population size (*N*) against time, when the *A* allele and the *a* allele are fixed (*i.e.*, when populations consist entirely of one or the other). Here $r_A = .8$, $r_a = .6$, $K_a = 12,000$. (Taken by permission from J. Roughgarden (1971). Density-dependent natural selection. *Ecology*, 52, 453-468. Copyright 1971 by the Ecological Society of America.)

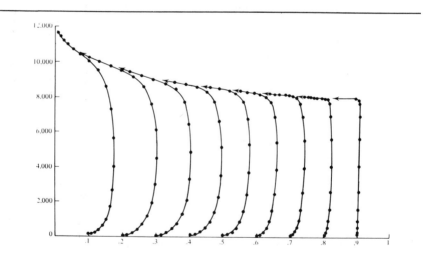

Fig. 7.6
Trajectories showing the effects of density-dependent selection, and how population size and allele frequency change together. The *aa* genotype has the highest *K* and the *AA* genotype has the highest *r*. Density-dependent selection leads to fixation of the *a* allele. Here $r_H = .8$, $r_A = .8$, $r_a = .6$, $K_A = 8000$, and $K_a = 12,000$. (Taken by permission from J. Roughgarden, (1971).)

Changing the situation slightly now, putting in other figures, we have two more possibilities. First, there is the case where the heterozygote has the highest K. Perhaps expectedly this leads to a balance (Fig. 7.7). Note that, again, the final outcome is not a function of the initial p or the r's of the two alleles. What counts are the K's. Finally we have the case where the heterozygote is the one with the lowest K (Fig. 7.8). Here what seems to count is the initial ratio of A to a. Below a certain frequency, and the A's get wiped out; above that frequency, and it is the a's that go. But, note one more time that the r's are irrelevant.

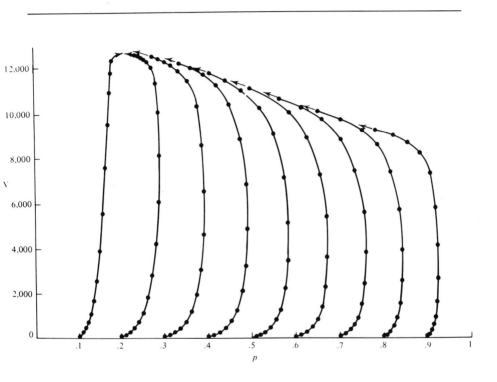

Fig. 7.7

Trajectories of density-dependent selection. The heterozygote has the highest carrying capacity and a stable polymorphism results. Here $r_H = .7$, $r_A = .8$, $r_a = .6$, $K_H = 15,000$, $K_A = 8000$, and $K_a = 12,000$. (Taken by permission from J. Roughgarden, (1971).)

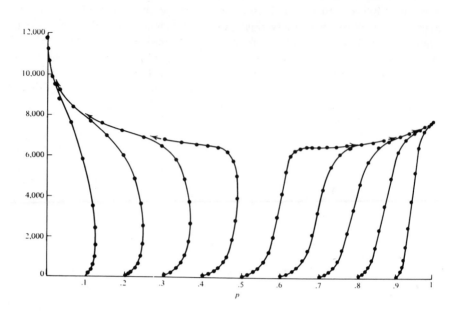

Fig. 7.8
Trajectories of density-dependent selection. The heterozygote has the lowest K. Trajectories fix on either allele depending on the initial position. Here $r_H = .7$, $r_A = .8$, $r_a = .6$, $K_H = 5000$, $K_A = 8000$, and $K_a = 12,000$. (Taken by permission from J. Roughgarden, (1971).)

The overall conclusion therefore is as interesting as it is unexpected. It does not matter what the rate of increase (r) of a phenotype is; the only factor of importance is the carrying capacity (K). But, note something that is equally interesting: this conclusion holds *only* in a stable environment where a population can go up to its maximum and stay there. If the environment is unstable and the population is frequently decimated, then what we shall have is growth and selection governed by the lower parts of the trajectories. But, here, it is the alleles conferring high r that count! The slope of the curves is always first towards the right, that is in the direction of increase for the allele A, which confers the highest r. In other words, in an unstable environment it turns out that selection favors high r over high K, the very opposite to the result in a stable environment.

We have here one of the fundamental results of evolutionary ecology. In a stable environment, selection will favor features that maximize the ability of organisms to achieve the highest possible population numbers. In an unstable environment, selection will favor features that maximize the ability of organisms to reproduce as rapidly as possible. Appropriately these two forms of selection are known as *K*-selection and *r*-selection, respectively. A classic *K*-selected organism is (or rather was) the elephant, which reproduces relatively slowly, but which can and does keep its numbers fairly high relative to its resources. A classic *r*-selected organism is the herring, which produces millions of fertilized eggs, very few of which survive to maturity. Humans, generally, are *K*-selected. Although, given our present population growth, brought on by modern technology, it would seem that we have altogether too many *r* characteristics for our own good these days.

Finally, let me mention a beautiful experimental test of this whole theory. Solbrig (1971) considered populations of dandelions containing four genotypes (*A* through *D*), growing in three sites: first, heavily disturbed by mowing, in full sunlight and with dry soil; second, occasionally disturbed and in moderate shade with damp soil; and third, virtually undisturbed and in much shade with very damp soil. He found that the genotype ratios varied among the sites, obtaining the figures shown in Table 7.1 (Roughgarden, 1979, p. 318).

Population	A	B	C	D
1. Dry, full sun, highly disturbed	73	13	14	0
2. Dry, shade, medium disturbance	53	32	14	1
3. Wet, semishade, undisturbed	17	8	11	64

Table 7.1
Percentages of four different genotypes from three populations of dandelions, *Taraxacum officinalis*. (Data from O. Solbrig, (1971). The population biology of dandelions. *American Scientist,* 59, 686-694.)

There are two ready hypotheses. First, conventionally, we assume that adaptation is a function of heat and dryness versus cold and wetness. If this is so, since the scale *A — D* seems to be correlated with the scale hot/dry — cold /wet, we should find that *A always* does better than *D* in hot dry conditions, and vice versa. Second, we assume that *r*- and *K*- selection are at work, and that the crucial causal factor is density independent mortality (i.e., the extent to which external environmental factors impinge on population growth, causing some plants to die). Here, when types *A* and *D* are grown under undisturbed conditions, we expect *A* to show high *r* features and *D* to show high *K* features. This would presumably mean that *A* would produce seed well before *D*, but that *D* would produce many leaves and eventually predominate over *A*. So long as conditions remain undisturbed, these patterns should hold — no matter what the soil and water characteristics.

Putting the alternative hypotheses to the test, Solbrig found that it was the second hypothesis that was confirmed. In a greenhouse, where there were no disturbing factors but where the soil conditions could be varied, although type

A dandelions always got off to the faster start, without exception, it was the type *D* dandelions that eventually became the norm. In short: "dandelion populations evolve a high *r* and low *K* under conditions of high density independent mortality and a low *r* and high *K* in undisturbed conditions" (Roughgarden, 1979, p. 319).

I shall say no more by way of exposition. Evolutionary ecology is exploding in content — leading to all sorts of metaphors about the growth of science and *r*- and *K*- selection! Work is going on, linking genes and selection to relative ages of members of populations, to competition and predation, and to niche theory and the ecology of island populations, to name but a few areas of interest and research. All I can hope is that the very brief introductory treatment I have just given conveys some of the excitement of the field.

Moreover, I trust the reader will agree with my surmise that what we have just seen is not the expansion of one of the subdisciplines of the evolutionary synthesis, but a development of the very *core* of neo-Darwinism. The models for density-dependent natural selection can apply right through the evolutionary spectrum, as can other models going back to the Hardy-Weinberg law and its disrupting factors. Thus, for instance, in paleontology we expect fossil organisms to show *r*- and *K*-selected features. Analogously, in some other area like the study of instinct, we expect to find such kinds of selection to have been at work.

All in all therefore, I argue that as Darwinism heads toward its future, we see the central causal heart being extended into a mature all-encompassing population biology, synthesizing relevant parts of both genetics and ecology.

Chapter 8
Animal Sociobiology

A natural but irritating fault of Darwin scholars is to see, in Darwin's own writings, the seeds of every important development in the subsequent history of evolutionary theory. One even finds those who hopefully suggest that "really" Darwin had grasped the essential ideas of Mendelian genetics. At the risk of sounding a little smug, I hope the reader will not accuse me of this error. Although Darwin had interesting ideas about the ultimate origins of life, and although Darwin properly saw the evolutionary importance of ecology, the very last thing I would claim is that all the work of the present can be found within Darwin's own thought and writings. However, turning next to one of the subdisciplines of the evolutionary synthesis — the theory of animal behavior — I believe we shall really see that in important respects Darwin was very much ahead of his time. Darwinism's past reaches forward to the present, and together they face the future. Let us start by going back in time.

Darwin and the level of selection

Darwin argued that organisms have the features that they have because these are of adaptive value in the struggle for survival and reproduction. Darwin realized also that, when one speaks of organic features, these must extend to the behavioral sphere: physical features directly involved in behavior and behaviors themselves. Even in his crucial notebooks kept just while he was on his way to this theory, Darwin devoted much space and attention to what animals do and to why they do what they do. Not surprisingly, therefore, there was never any doubt in Darwin's mind that natural selection applies to behavior, and that such behavior and related organic features must be analyzed in terms of adaptive advantage.

In the *Origin,* many aspects of behavior gave Darwin little trouble, since they flowed naturally from his main principles. Like such phenomena as organic geographical distributions, the instincts and actions of animals fell easily within the evolutionary consilience. Remember the very first example Darwin gave of selection in action, namely that of a wolf running faster and faster in order to capture its prey, and of the probability of different groups of wolves with different prey evolving different behaviors and associated features. Here, obviously, Darwin was explaining behaviors and behavior-related features in the light of his evolutionary principles. At least, conceding that the example was hypothetical, he was showing how behaviors could be explained by selection.

However, it cannot be denied that some behavioral patterns gave Darwin much food for thought. We saw, in our discussion of the *Origin,* that Darwin raised the question of very complex behaviors, such as the cell-making abilities of the bee. These abilities are obviously not learned, but in some sense are programmed into the animal's instincts. Could they have been formed through selection working on chance variation? And, as we saw also, Darwin agreed that they could. Indeed, Darwin treated complex behaviors in the way he treated all complex features, arguing, first, that selection working on minute variations could indeed maximize behavioral skills; and, second, that the existence today of gradations of animals showing skills from lesser to greater degrees implies the possibility of such gradations from past to present.

Much more troublesome for Darwin were the behaviors and associated features of organisms that devote themselves entirely to the welfare of others. In particular, Darwin ran up against difficulties caused by the sterile castes of insects. Could something that was physically and behaviorally "altruistic," foregoing its own sex life, have been forged by a process that begins with a struggle for reproduction? Could selection have made a being that does nothing for itself — not even having children? At first, Darwin had no answer to this question. Indeed, it appears that he did not have a solution for many years. It was only by the time of the *Origin* that he had really worked things out to his own satisfaction, and even then friends and critics kept him defending his position.

Why did sterile workers give Darwin so much trouble? To answer this question, it will be useful to introduce two new terms. By "individual selection," let us imply a selection ultimately rebounding exclusively to the benefit of the individual organism. All features and behaviors can be analyzed in these terms. By "group selection," let us imply by contrast a selection that can work towards the benefit of the individual's group, say, the species, at the individual's expense. Features and behaviors may therefore be exclusively for fellow species members. Fairly obviously, if one is a group selectionist, sterile workers give one no trouble at all. The workers are the same species as everyone else, and so their altruistic features can be explained in terms of group benefits. But, if one is an individual selectionist, then sterile workers are a major problem. In some way, one must relate their sterility to self-benefit, and this seems impossible.

It is here that we find the source of Darwin's troubles, for *he was a totally committed individual selectionist.* Even with the first introduction of the struggle for existence, Darwin was at pains to point out that the struggle operates at all levels, including that existing between members of the same species. Hence, selection can and does work to produce features of value only to the individual — features that are set against other members of the species. Furthermore, the very point of Darwin's subsidiary mechanism of sexual selection was that selection works for the individual, not the group. Sexual selection only operates between members of the same species, and consequently everything it produces goes against the benefits of the whole!

Nor should one presume that Darwin drifted idly into an individual selectionist position — something that came about almost by chance and that he would be prepared to deny on occasion. He made sacrifices for his position and defended it against attack. Take the phenomenon of hybrid sterility, something that seems almost to beckon a group selectionist approach. Hybrids are sterile because this benefits both parent groups, whose regular offspring will not then be competing with offspring that are literally neither fish nor fowl. (See Fig. 8.1.) Darwin refused to accept this answer, arguing rather that such sterility is simply a by-product of other changes. And he continued to do so, despite the

Fig. 8.1
The mule is incredibly strong and a hard worker; yet it is quite sterile. (Photo of the Thomas 12 mule hitch, used by permission of *The Small Farmer's Journal*.)

urging of natural selection's co-discoverer, Alfred Russel Wallace, who felt that putting so pervasive a phenomenon as hybrid sterility down to chance side effect was almost to invite criticism (Ruse, 1980). (See Fig. 8.2.)

Fig. 8.2
Alfred Russel Wallace
(1823–1913).

Why did Darwin feel so strongly on the subject of individual selection? Simply because he thought *group selection contradicts the very notion of selection.* Suppose we have two organisms, one with a characteristic ϕ that benefits only itself, and another with a characteristic $-\ominus-$ that benefits its species but is a burden to itself. Which one will reproduce? Obviously, Darwin argued, the individual with characteristic ϕ! While this individual is getting on with reproduction, the second individual is wasting time helping others. Thus in the case of hybrid sterility, however much it may benefit the parent groups that the hybrid not breed, selection could never act on the hybrid itself to stop it breeding. (Of course, Darwin accepted that selection can and will promote the disinclination to breed hybrids in the first place.)

Given his strong position, how then did Darwin finally deal with sterile castes of insects? As always, he turned to the domestic world for guidance, and there he saw that characteristics could be selected vicariously, as it were, *through close relatives.* The bullock will never breed, but one can select for desirable features in bullocks by choosing the appropriate fertile relatives. Similarly, Darwin argued that the features and behaviors of sterile workers could in some way be selected and transmitted through fertile relatives. That the relatives themselves may not have these characteristics is no more a bar to the effect of natural selection than the fact that a bull may not have the docile nature of his castrated sibling is a bar to the effect of artificial selection.

In a sense, therefore, Darwin considered colonies or hives of social insects, all closely related and with sterile workers helping fellow colony members, as kinds of supra-organisms or *supra-individuals!* Hence selection can work on these as a whole, just as selection can work on a normal individual, without requiring that each element of the body be capable of independent reproduction. Individual selection is preserved.

I have such faith in the powers of selection, that I do not doubt that a breed of cattle, always yielding oxen with extraordinarily long horns, could be slowly formed by carefully watching which individual bulls and cows, when matched, produced oxen with the longest horns: and yet no one ox could ever have propagated its kind. Thus I believe it has been with social insects: a slight modification of structure, or instinct, correlated with the sterile condition of certain members of the community, has been advantageous to the community: consequently the fertile males and females of the same community flourished, and transmitted to their fertile offspring a tendency to produce sterile members having the same modification. And I believe that this process has been repeated, until that prodigious amount of difference between the fertile and sterile females of the same species has been produced, which we see in many social insects (Darwin, 1859, p. 238–239).

The neglect of behavior

Darwin acquitted himself well in his discussion of animal behavior. He had no doubt, whatsoever, that behavior and related features must be brought right within the evolutionary synthesis; he looked squarely at the major problems raised by behavior; and he invoked subtle arguments to avoid compromise of his carefully considered thought on the nature and action of natural selection. There was no equivocation on the individual/group selection question. And yet, in the hundred years following the *Origin,* no part of the evolutionary spectrum was so neglected as that dealing with animal behavior. It lagged right behind. Why?

There were at least two major reasons for this neglect and consequent lack of growth. First, there was the simple methodological fact that behavior is hard to observe, quantify, and measure. It is far, far easier to study, say, skeletal differences in kangaroos, than the way in which the males interact and compete for females, if that is indeed what they do. Even when one is dealing with experimental animals, behavior is hard to handle — indeed it is particularly hard to handle in experimental animals, because the artificial environments cause all sorts of distorting factors. Does a certain species of

Drosophila do what it does because this is an adaptive function preserved by selection, or does it do what it does because being in a cage upsets it? For reasons like these, biologists tended to put their efforts into the study of gross morphological features, their evolution, and their adaptive functions. Behavior was put on one side until the general ideas and hypotheses were more fully developed.

A second reason for the neglect of the evolutionary nature of behavior was the rise of psychology, particularly behavioristic psychology. Many social scientists are ignorant of, and perhaps even hostile toward, biological science. No doubt this is partially a function of a felt need to create independent disciplines, ones that are not simply footnotes to other sciences. But, whatever the motives of social scientists, the fact of the matter was that most pioneering psychologists started with the a priori assumption that an animal begins life as a behavioral tabula rasa. One can choose any animal one likes, and one can teach it pretty much anything that one wishes. Many psychologists therefore worked with and only with rats, assuming that any results they obtained apply without qualification to the rest of the animal world. But what this obviously all meant was that any evolutionary implications for behavior were dismissed as nonexistent before discussion even began! And, although biologists are certainly not psychologists, one suspects that this attitude must have encouraged biologists to put their own energies into areas other than those dealing with behavior.

There were other reasons for the neglect of behavior by evolutionists. For instance, Darwin's sexual selection was always thought a little suspect — as something steering too close to anthropomorphism. Hence sexual activity was not subjected to intensive independent examination. But, whatever the full causal picture, behavior went unstudied. It is true that, after the coming of the neo-Darwinian synthesis, things changed a little. In Europe, particularly, the "ethologists" (Konrad Lorenz, Niko Tinbergen, and others) started to look systematically at animal behavior from an evolutionary perspective. But, it was not until around 1960 that evolutionary study of animal behavior really started to explode — in theory, through controlled experiment, and because of detailed and extended observation of the natural behavior of wild animals.

One major factor in the rapid progress of "sociobiology," to use now the term that seems to have established itself for the evolutionary science of animal behavior, was a thorough rethinking of the individual/group selection question, with a strong return to a Darwinian position, from which many biologists had started to stray. What sparked this was the publication of V. C. Wynne-Edwards' *Animal Dispersion in Relation to Social Behaviour* in 1962, in which a consistently group-selectionist stance was taken toward many facets of the animal world. Unhappy with Wynne-Edward's claims, a number of biologists, most notably G. C. Williams in his *Adaptation and Natural Selection* (1966), were led to Darwin's arguments: group selection simply will not work. But, if one is an individual selectionist, then all of Darwin's problems reassert themselves. Indeed, if anything, they are more pressing. Thanks particularly to the work of the ethologists, it was realized that sterile worker insects are but the extreme form of all kinds of stylized and cooperative behaviors, which run right through the animal world.

Nothing draws a scientist like a problem: more and more biologists turned to the study of behavior, and almost overnight one got a flood of new theoretical ideas, together with massive amounts of valuable empirical data. Without any attempt to follow things through historically, I shall now review some of the recent important work in animal sociobiology. At this point, except tangentially, I shall not touch upon possible implications of biology for humans. This is all being left for discussion in the next part.

Parenthetically, as I leave direct treatment of the individual/group selection controversy, I should remark that some biologists today are still trying to formulate viable group selection models. Although, at best, the scope of the models seems limited. (See Wade, 1978.)

The sociobiology of aggression

In the spirit of Darwin, what really engages the attention of evolutionists is behavior which in some sense involves social interaction — something that in some way transcends "nature red in tooth and claw." An ideal place for us to start our survey and to see how this attention is engaged and with what consequences is with the topic of *aggression*.

Prima facie, one might think this an odd choice. When the lion chases the deer, there is nothing very social about the interaction. But, this is not quite the kind of aggression that concerns the sociobiologists. Their interest centers on the kind of restrained or otherwise complex aggression often seen between members of the same species. I am sure we have all seen cases where two dogs fight, one obviously wins, and yet the victor fails to kill the loser. Why should animals hold back from the ultimate *coup* in cases such as these? Surely Darwinism implies all-out combat? A dead rival is no threat in the struggle for existence and reproduction. Analogously, in intragroup conflicts, why should some animals be very ferocious whereas others of the same species are very timid? And, why should an animal sometimes be savage and sometimes cowardly? (See Fig. 8.3.)

Obviously, if one is an individual selectionist, then in order to explain phenomena such as these one has to invoke some sort of hypothesis involving "enlightened self interest." One supposes that restraint benefits the winner, as well as the loser; one supposes that being timid has its virtues, as well as being ferocious; one supposes that cowardliness, like savagery, has evolutionary attractions. Probably, the most exciting work addressed to these issues has been produced by a number of British evolutionists who have borrowed ideas from game theory. (See, for instance, Maynard Smith, 1972, 1976.) Basically they consider situations where there are both benefits and risks in conflicts, and they ask whether there is an "evolutionary stable strategy": is there a state, favored by selection, resulting in a stable balance between all-out aggression

Fig. 8.3
Subordinate male bison (left) acknowledges his lower status by turning his head away
from the dominant male. (From D. P. Barash, (1977), *Sociobiology and Behavior,* New
York: Elsevier. Used by permission of the author.)

and all-out avoidance of aggression? Can the kinds of complex, restrained-
aggressive situations just mentioned be selection-favored stable states? They
think that there frequently are such stable states, as the following simple little
model, given by Dawkins (1976), shows.

Take a population within a species, and let us suppose that there are
potentially two types or forms, which we can appropriately nickname
"hawks" and "doves." (These are ideal types; apparently, in fact, doves are
rather nasty, aggressive creatures!) Putting some figures on things to make the
discussion as clear as possible, suppose that, when faced with a rival, a hawk
fights flat out until it wins or loses. A dove fights in a ritualized noninjurious
fashion with other doves but runs away before hard fighting when faced with a
hawk. A victory is worth fifty points (cashable at the avian supermarket in
terms of mates, territory, and so forth), a simple loss zero points, wasted time
costs ten points, and a serious injury or death means a one hundred point loss.
Given such conditions, one can readily calculate that it would not pay to be a
hawk in a population of hawks. That is to say,unrestrained aggression is not
an ESS (evolutionary stable strategy) — all-out violence simply does not pay.
Natural selection would favor genes that turned a population-member away
from hawkish behavior.

To see this fact, pretend that two members of the group meet and compete. Since they are both hawks, they will fight to the kill or serious injury. The probable benefit/cost to an individual in such an encounter is therefore $(+50 - 100) \times 1/2 = -25$. It pays to be a dove in such a situation, where all the fellow species members are hawks. It does not gain anything, but then again it does not lose anything (i.e., benefit/cost = 0). In other words, selection would favor any process that increased the proportion of doves in the group. On the other hand, we can see why some aggression pays. Suppose one had a population of doves. Any encounter would be lengthy, but without serious cost. Hence the cost/benefit = $(+50 - 10 \times 2) \times 1/2 = +15$. But a solitary hawk gains in such a situation: cost/benefit = $+50$. Hence selection now favors hawks!

Fortunately our little model does not imply that the population will career erratically back and forth between total dove and total hawk. In fact, one can show that, when the ratio of doves to hawks is 5:7, we have an ESS. The average pay-off to both hawks and doves is 6-1/4, and thus no one would be better off by changing sides. Or, more prosaically, there would be no reproductive advantage to an organism's being a hawk rather than a dove, or vice versa. In other words, in a case like this, we can have selection holding some aggressive types and some nonaggressive types stably in a population.

Instead of having two different types in a group, one can also use the model to show that an ESS can be achieved if all organisms sometimes show hawk behavior and sometimes show dove behavior. Moreover, one can develop more sophisticated models with different kinds of strategy. For instance, given the potential costs, it may not be in an organism's interest to escalate the fighting straight up to the maximum — at least, one can try to find out what the opposition will do. Moreover, bearing directly on the problem of restrained aggression which spurred this discussion, given the fact that every one is liable sometimes to be the weaker (in youth, old-age, sickness, and the like), models can be devised showing that even where some aggression pays, all-out aggression to the death is not necessarily an ESS. Evolution can in theory benefit the individual if it restrains its aggressiveness — the benefit of winning may not outweigh the potential cost of losing. It may pay to kill one's opponent; it may pay even more to avoid the possibility of being killed oneself!

Of course, the key phrase behind all of this model building is "in theory." Is there empirical evidence to back this line of theorizing, or is it all unrestrained speculation? It cannot be denied that we are very far from having anything like a tight fit between theory and fact — the given figures have as much substantial basis in reality as do those of utilitarians when they start calculating which course of action leads to the most happiness. On the other hand, fresh observation after fresh observation suggests that ESS models may apply to real-life situations. Time and again, we find organisms competing, trying to maximize their own benefits and to minimize the costs. Thus, for instance, John Maynard Smith, to whom goes much credit for developing the

ESS approach, writes as follows about the Siamese fighting fish, *Betta splendens:*

Ritual conflicts between males are usually followed by escalated fights, in which one or both rivals may be seriously injured. Conflicts between females however often end (typically after five-fifteen minutes) with the surrender of one fish, without escalated fighting. Simpson followed such conflicts in detail, measuring the frequency and timing of particular components of the ritual. He found no significant difference between the frequencies with which eventual winners and eventual losers performed particular acts, except during the last two minutes of a contest, when the eventual winner could be recognized from the fact that her gill covers were erected for a larger proportion of the time. The fact that the winner could not be distinguished from the loser until close to the end of a contest fits well with the prediction from game theory (Maynard Smith, 1972, p. 24).

Concluding this discussion of aggression, mention should be made of one very important, pertinent observation, now repeated many times. Under a group selective force, organisms would *never* intentionally kill conspecifics (members of the same species) simply for their own benefit. It can never benefit the species to lose members in this way. Under an individual selective force, including one based on game theory, although all-out "selfish" aggression may be rare, it is certainly not barred absolutely. If it pays an organism to kill in this way sometimes, despite the risks, then selection will favor this propensity. And, what observation has now established beyond all doubt is that animals do sometimes kill conspecifics just for their own benefit. Indeed comparatively, some do it a great deal. (See Fig. 8.4.) It is apparently absolute nonsense to suggest, as a great many people from the Nobel Prize winning biologist Lorenz on down have suggested, that man and only man has the mark of Cain: the killer lust. In fact, we are a peaceable species. The murder-rate of lions far exceeds that of humans in Detroit! (Wilson, 1975a).

One may ask why this fact about animal violence has so long escaped attention. Part of the reason is that people only see what they want to see, but the main reason is that such facts about animal behavior emerge only after days, weeks, months, of patient study of organisms in their natural habitats. And, only now are we getting these studies. After all, if one took a walk through Detroit, it is highly improbable that one would see one person kill another: one needs 24-hour, 365-day-per-year vigilance to get the full story. The same is true of other animals.

The sociobiology of sex

Next, let us look at the question of *sex* and mating. Once again we find a return to the ideas of Charles Darwin himself (Campbell, 1972). After years of neglect, sexual selection now is a high-profile concept, as sociobiologists try to understand the biology of sexual behavior. Indeed, taking Darwinism even beyond Darwin, almost all possible types of competition within a species are

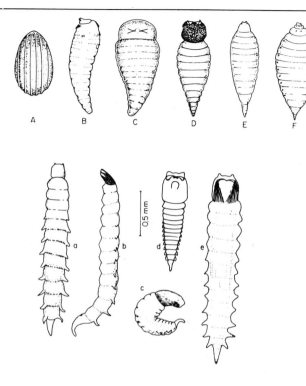

Fig. 8.4
These two series show the successive developments of the larvae of two species of
parasitic wasp (upper *Poecilogonalos thwaitesii,* lower *Collyria calcitrator*). They show
graphically how one stage (upper D, lower c-e) has adaptations specifically for killing
the larva's conspecifics. (Taken with permission from C. P. Clausen, (1940). *En-
tomophagous Insects,* New York: McGraw-Hill.)

seen to be a crucial part of the evolutionary scenario: this includes competition
between members of the same sex and even competition between members of
opposite sexes!

The basic premise behind the sociobiology of sex is that male and female
represent two opposed reproductive strategies: quantity, with hopes of great
success but risk of total failure, versus quality, with guaranteed moderate
gains but no hope of hitting the reproductive jackpot. What one might call the
"gold-mine-shares" versus the "government-bonds" approaches to reproduction. Thus, on the one side, we have males. Reproduction per se costs them virtually nothing, and potentially they can reproduce more or less indefinitely.
They are not the ones who get pregnant. In other words, if evolutionary success is tied to reproductive ability, the average male is ideally poised to spread
his genes far and wide. Just two things stand in the way. First, there are other
males, all of whom are trying to do exactly the same thing! This means that
males must compete for females, developing features and behaviors that

enable them to outrace other males along the path to success. Hence, as Darwin rightly pointed out, we get such things as the grossly powerful bodies of the male walrus.

Second, there are the females who are apt to be choosy about the male who mates with them, supposing that the male gives them (or cannot prevent them from having) any choice. Males must therefore develop adaptations, physical and behavioral, that make them attractive in the females' eyes. Putting together these two obstacles in the way of unrestricted reproduction by any particular male, what we therefore can expect to find is that probably some males will be incredibly successful at reproduction, and probably many will not reproduce at all. Hence there will be strong selective pressure on the features that bring about success.

On the other side of the battle of the sexes — a metaphor in that no outright hostility need be shown or felt, but literal in the sense that there is competition and compromise between different evolutionary ends — we have females. Generally speaking, female animals in the wild are almost certain to get inseminated. Not only are there all those eager males around, but insemination is obviously in the females' own reproductive interests. However, balancing this fact is the additional fact that pregnancy can mean a great deal of effort for the female. It is she who has to raise the baby!

Hence sociobiology predicts that the female will not play a totally passive role in insemination, indifferent as to her mate. From the female perspective, two virtues in her would-be inseminator are particularly desirable. First, given the fact that it is the female who gets pregnant, if it is needed she would like from the male some willingness to take part in child-rearing duties. Second, even if paternal help is not really needed, it is in the female's interests to have the putative father possessing the sorts of characteristics that will in turn make the female's children very fit and, most particularly, that will make the female's male offspring attractive! All that effort in raising children goes to naught, if there are to be no grandchildren.

Thus, the sociobiology of female sex dictates that selection will favor features and abilities in the female that maximize the attainment of these ends. One writer (Dawkins, 1976) has descriptively referred to the two paths toward such realization as the "domestic bliss" and "he man" strategies, respectively. The female seeking help with child-rearing will dole out sexual favors in return for effort by the male, with respect to such tasks as nest-building and so forth. The female seeking top-quality children, especially sons, will be turned on only by the gaudiest, sexiest males, and so forth.

The net result of all of these male and female sexual selective forces has been summed up by E. O. Wilson in a work that has rather taken on the status of the "Bible" of the newly extended science of animal behavior: *Sociobiology: The New Synthesis*. Wilson writes as follows:

Pure epigamic display can be envisioned as a contest between salesmanship and sales resistance. The sex that courts, ordinarily the male, plans to invest less reproductive effort in the offspring. What it offers to the female is chiefly evidence that it is fully normal and physiologically fit. But this warranty consists of only a brief performance, so that strong selective pressures exist for less fit individuals to present a false image. The courted sex, usually the female, will therefore find it strongly advantageous to distinguish the really fit from the pretended fit. Consequently, there will be a strong tendency for the courted sex to develop coyness. That is, its responses will be hesitant and cautious in a way that evokes still more displays and makes correct discrimination easier. (Wilson, 1975a, p. 320)

What about proof for all of this theorizing? The sociobiologists argue that the empirical evidence is overwhelming. Right through the animal world we see the most incredible male/female dimorphisms in features and behaviors. Males tend to be big, bullying, colorful, and lazy; females tend to be active, submissive, drab, and careful — just what the sociobiology of sex predicts. Males are out to impress and dominate; females are out to work and to avoid silly mistakes. (See Fig. 8.5.)

Fig. 8.5
Stellar sea lion surrounded by his harem. (From Barash, (1977), by permission of the author.)

Moreover, particular aspects of male/female behavior fall in line with sociobiological predictions. For instance, according to theory, the places where females are most likely to have success in getting males to help with the duties of child care are those very places where such help is probably in the males' interests also! There is no point in doing a lot of inseminating, if the females cannot raise the offspring unaided. Hence theory dictates that at such points the males help their own reproductive prospects by helping the females.

And, this is what we find happens in nature! Consider the differences between birds, where males do much work in nest-building and child care, and most mammals, where males do virtually nothing. If one is stuck up a tree with a limited breeding season, then rapid child growth is at a premium. Help from the males can make all the difference. However, if one lives in a hole in the ground (or whatever) and is not going to move that much with the seasons, then males can afford to leave most of the work to the mothers — and they do (Barash, 1977).

Finally, talking of the evidence for the sociobiology of sex, it is worth noting the interesting case of the fish, which is the exception proving the rule. Here, frequently males raise the offspring, and females compete for the males, having all the attributes that one usually associates with male competition. The suggested reason for all of this is that, unlike land animals, it is the male who is left holding baby! Because of external fertilization, males are the ones who necessarily have the final dealings with the zygote; as a result, it is they who take on the responsibility for offspring care, and so forth (Dawkins, 1976).

I suspect that with this argument we have crossed the border into the realm of speculation. Hence this is an appropriate place to break off and move on. Probably even now we are merely scratching at the surface of the sociobiology of sex. However, thanks to this scratching, some sort of coherent picture is beginning to emerge from beneath the surface covering.

The sociobiology of the family

Following sex, one has *parenthood* and the *family*. I suppose one's automatic assumption — my automatic assumption! — is that the evolutionary interests of parent and child are one and the same. After all, the child is carrying on the biological torch for the parent — they share the same genes. Thus, one might think that parent and child would cooperate and work harmoniously to the same end — the parent helping the child selflessly, and the child doing all that it can to lighten the load of the parent.

This picture of domestic bliss is not at all the one painted by the sociobiologists. In fact, parents and children are not genetically identical, and they do not have the same evolutionary interests. Parents and children have only a 50 percent genetic overlap, since each child has *two* parents. (I talk now of sexual organisms, and speak only of those alleles that vary in a group.) Furthermore, it is usually in the parents' interests to maximize the successful development of *all* their children, not just the development of one individual.

Hence, one is liable to get points of tension, when the child's evolutionary interests and the parent's evolutionary interests do not coincide (Trivers, 1974; Alexander, 1974). That extra morsel of food or those extra months in the maternal burrow may just make some particular offspring that much fitter. But, for the parent, it may be more advantageous to give the food and attention to another offspring — two reasonably fit offspring could be preferred to one very fit offspring and one very unfit offspring. (See Fig. 8.6.) Also, it may

Fig. 8.6
Adult female burro refusing to let her foal nurse. (From Barash, (1977), by permission
of the author.)

pay the parent to give differential help to the sexes. Given that females are very
likely to get impregnated, whatever their state, it may be in a parent's
reproductive interests to give extra attention to sons who will probably succeed
far better if they are in the peak of health.

Of course, the parent-child relationship is not the only place where one
gets genetic overlap within a family. By Mendel's first law, full siblings have
just as tight a relationship (50 percent), and there are lesser bonds between
other sorts of relatives (e.g., an uncle and nephew have a 25 percent relationship). Since parents do help offspring, presumably because of the genetic
bonds, one is led to ask whether it can ever be in an individual's evolutionary
interests to aid other relatives, even at the individual's own direct reproductive
expense. Can one thus find some clues to the all-out cooperation, the
"altruism," one sometimes gets in the animal world, the explanation of which
Wilson has labeled "the central theoretical problem of sociobiology" (Wilson
1975a, p. 3)? In particular, without necessarily detracting from Darwin's
work, can one throw new light on that most extreme case of animal altruism
where sterile worker ants give their whole lives to their fertile siblings?

In what are surely some of the most exciting moves in evolutionary
thought since Darwin, the English biologist W. D. Hamilton (1964a, b) addressed himself most fruitfully to these questions. At the general level,
Hamilton showed that, if one increases one's own genetic representation in the
next generation more effectively by helping relatives than by helping oneself,

then selection will favor instincts and actions that lead to such relative help. In reproduction, one is passing on *copies* of one's own genes. Relatives share copies of genes. Therefore, the offspring of relatives have copies of some of the genes of all the relatives, not just of their own parents. Hence, theoretically, selection could promote features that ensure copies of one's genes, not in one's own offspring but in the offspring of relatives. In other words, the possibility exists of some kind of reproduction by proxy, as it were!

When might selection, known in this kind of situation as "kin selection," favor an organism's helping relatives at the expense of its own reproduction? Take siblings. Since siblings share half one's genetic makeup, one can see fairly readily that kin selection should come into effect when the number of extra nephews and nieces one makes possible is more than double the number of children one would have oneself. One is half related to one's own children, and one quarter related to nephews and nieces. Hence, if one could have one child oneself, but through aid could cause three extra children for one's siblings, vicarious reproduction would thereby cause more copies of one's own genes in the next generation.

Analogous reasoning holds for all other relationships. One expects kin selection to come into play, causing altruistic behavior, whenever helping a relative causes more copies of one's own genes, than does direct personal reproduction. Obviously, the less closely related one is to individuals, the greater the number of offspring they must have to compensate for the personal genetic loss in not having children of one's own. Technically, the crucial formula showing when kin selection might be expected is $k > 1/r$, where k is the ratio of gain to loss in fitness, and r is the average coefficient of relationship of benefiting relatives (i.e., as the relationship goes down, the gains must go up proportionately). One should not confuse the r and k of the sociobiologists with those of the ecologists. The symbols are the same, but the concepts are not.

So much for the theoretical background. Next, in one brilliant stroke, Hamilton used the concept of kin selection to throw bright new light on Darwin's problem: social insects and their sterile castes. Hamilton pointed out that almost all the social insects are Hymenoptera — ants, bees, and wasps — and that a distinguishing feature of the Hymenoptera is that they have a haplo-diploid reproductive system. Females are produced by the usual sexual process of a male's sperm fertilizing a female's egg; males, however, are produced directly from the female's unfertilized egg. They have no father! Consequently, whereas females have the customary two sets of chromosomes, one from each parent, males have only a half set, that from the mother.

This all leads to fascinatingly unusual sets of genetic relationships between family members. (See Fig. 8.7.) Mothers and daughters have the typical 50 percent relationship. However, unlike the conventional 50 percent, sisters have a 75 percent relationship! This is because half their genes come from their father, and these are the same for each daughter. In other words, females are more closely related to sisters than to daughters. This holds between all sisters, fertile and infertile, because sterility is caused by differential treatment during

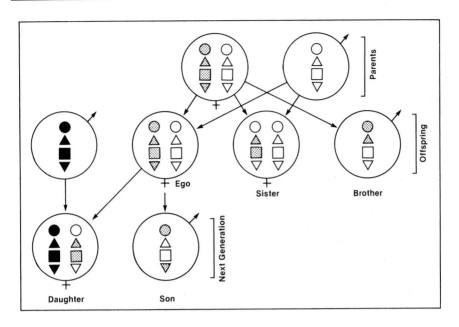

Fig. 8.7
A diagrammatic representation of the genetic relationships in the Hymenoptera.
Females are diploid; males are haploid. Only females have fathers. It can be seen that
sisters have a 75% shared genetic relationship, whereas mothers and daughters have only a 50% shared genetic relationship. Kin selection therefore favors the raising of fertile
sisters rather than fertile daughters. Males have no such special relationships, and
therefore do not form sterile worker castes. (Adapted by permission from J. Maynard
Smith, (1978). The evolution of behavior. *Scientific American, 239*, September,
176-192.)

development and is not a direct function of genetic difference. Males do not
have the females' extra-close relationship, to their brothers, to their sisters, or
to their daughters (they have no sons).

Hamilton therefore hypothesized that kin selection favors the development of altruism in female Hymenoptera, and this is the reason for sterile
castes. Paradoxical as it may seem, females can better serve their own future
genetic representation by raising fertile sisters than by raising fertile daughters!
Males do not have this spur, and this is the reason why one does not find male
worker castes in Hymenoptera. Although very much within the Darwinian
tradition, Hamilton obviously takes the whole question of the evolution of the
social insects a major step beyond Darwin himself. For Darwin the whole colony was to be seen as a unit. Hamilton treats the individual members as having
separate genetic interests. Individual selection is pushed right to the limit.

Of course, theory is one thing; confirmation is another. On today's
evidence, general consensus is that kin selection has played some important

role in evolution, particularly in the Hymenoptera (Oster and Wilson, 1978). There surely has to be some reason why sociality and sterile castes have evolved an estimated *thirteen* separate times in the Hymenoptera, but not otherwise in the animal world, with the sole exception of the termites (which exhibit striking differences from Hymenoptera sociality). Moreover, if kin selection was not involved, then many other aspects of Hymenoptera social life remain puzzling. For instance, if one ignores the fact that females and only females have something to gain by raising their sister's children, then why does one always get working females and idle males?

Some researchers have put Hamilton's hypothesis about kin selection and the evolution of the Hymenoptera to direct experimental test. They started from the fact that, if kin selection is at work, then one ought to find a nest functioning in such a way as to maximize the workers' genetic interests. Moreover, this functioning could be in opposition to the genetic interests of the queen. These implications can be tested by checking sex ratios: normally it is in a parent's genetic interests to have an equal balance of male and female offspring, and this holds true for the queen. But, because of their special relationships to siblings, the optimum ratio maximizing workers' interests shifts to a 75:25 female to male ratio. By counting and weighing the ratios of males to females in nests, Robert L. Trivers and Hope Hare (1976) were able to show that the predictions indicating worker nest control hold very tightly. Hence the conclusion was drawn that the active presence of kin selection is moved from the possible to the plausible. (Actually, the experiment by Trivers and Hare was slightly more complicated than just implied. When more *effort* is required to produce an offspring of one sex rather than the other, this is reflected in optimal ratios. They took this fact into account.)

Prospects

Enough ground has now been covered to show the scope and success of animal sociobiology. We are obviously looking at an exciting and rapidly forward-moving field. Almost daily one gets new theoretical suggestions and pertinent reports on experiments and field work. Insects were the first kinds of organisms to get detailed study, but now much interest centers on birds, who make ideal subjects for study. Birds are relatively easy to observe, and, given their rapid breeding time, they show far more social behavior than do many other types of animals, like mammals.

I do not want to pretend that there are no disputes or controversies. These occur, as they do in any healthy branch of science. For instance, the Trivers-Hare findings and interpretations have not gone unchallenged (Alexander and Sherman, 1977). But, overall, it is true to say that one of the slower areas of the Darwinian synthesis has now really started to catch up on its more developed siblings. I am sure that in years to come, in the sphere of animal behavior, we are going to see many more exciting evolutionary developments. Here, indeed, one looks forward to Darwinism tomorrow.

Chapter 9
The Challenge from Paleontology

Sociobiology sets one to thinking in terms of kin! Perhaps, therefore, I might be allowed to continue the metaphor of Darwinian theory being a family, with the various subdisciplines as offspring. If, as I have suggested, sociobiology is a late developer which is only just now starting to move up on its siblings (but, as is often the case with late developers, with prospects of being one of the adult stars), then I think it is true to say that paleontology is the rather difficult child. It has always (or nearly always) been the one that did not really fit in properly, and that caused awkwardness or problems of one kind or another.

I do not suggest that paleontology is unimportant or thought of little consequence by evolutionists. Often, one has a special affection for the troublesome child! But, paleontology does have a history of uneasy relationships with orthodox evolutionary theorizing, particularly Darwinian theorizing. And this continues today. Let me explain, beginning as always in the past and then coming up to the present. Because of paleontology, will we see significant modifications to, or perhaps even limitations in, the Darwinism of tomorrow?

The fossil record and evolutionary theory

Back in the first chapter, we had plenty of evidence of the funny relationship between paleontology and evolutionary theorizing. Although today one can see that the fossil record almost begs for an evolutionary interpretation, Lamarck was virtually indifferent to the record, including any notions of progression that one might want to read into it. Indeed, inspired by Cuvier, it was the catastrophists — those who were most opposed to evolution — who most ardently championed both the record and a progressive interpretation: fish, reptiles, mammals. They saw the record, not as evidence of evolution, but as proof positive of God's intervening creative powers (Coleman, 1964). Indeed, so greatly did the catastrophists take the record and its supposed progressiveness to their hearts, this was undoubtedly a major reason why Charles

Lyell adamantly denied that there is any such pattern to the record! He wanted no truck with such God-intoxicated speculations.

The Believers stressed progression; Lyell denied it; finally, the evolutionists stole it. However, as we know, the progression appropriated by Darwin was far from a simplistic undirectional rise, from the earliest primitive forms to today's sophisticated flora and fauna. There is no place for absolute progression in Darwinian evolutionism. His fossil progression contained branchings, irregularities, and other interesting features, such as embryonic forms early in the record. Indeed, Darwin's picture of evolution is so different from old-fashioned progression that, with reason, many of his followers prefer not to talk of "progression" at all. But, whatever one calls the pattern of the record, it seems true to say that, by the time of the *Origin,* the overall paleontological picture was in many respects as Darwin's theory supposed. Admittedly there were a number of problems — gaps in the record, the absence of pre-Cambrian life, and so forth. Hence, the definitive case for evolution was certainly not made on the fossils. But, because of the positive features, it would be unfair to conclude that the record destroyed Darwin's theory. Perhaps, therefore, the fairest verdict is that Darwin wrestled paleontology to an uneasy draw (Bowler, 1976; Rudwick, 1972).

As we move on from Darwin and the *Origin,* we find that virtually all paleontologists followed the rest of their biological bretheren into the evolutionary fold. Not only was there the influence of extra-paleontological arguments, but the fossil record itself started to produce many more of the sorts of things that an evolutionist predicted. Indeed, in 1861, just two years after the *Origin* was published, the limestone quarries of Solnhofen in Bavaria yielded what is still the greatest of all evolutionary links: *Archaeopteryx,* the bird/reptile. (See Figs. 9.1 and 9.2.) Equally impressive were discoveries in the 1870s by American paleontologists, who were able to form an exquisitely detailed picture of the course of equine evolution. But, as we know only too well, evolution is one thing; natural selection is another. From the day that the *Origin* was published, paleontologists were in the forefront of opposition to Darwin's mechanism. Whereas paleontologists to a person were evolutionists, it was they, more than any other evolutionists, who most vigorously trumpeted nonselective causes as the major mechanisms of evolutionary changes.

Some, like Huxley, became saltationists. The full story behind Huxley's preference for saltations is complex; but, undoubtedly, the step-wise nature of the fossil record was crucially influential. Riding a slightly different track, other paleontologists became full-blown Lamarckians, vigorously pushing the inheritance of acquired characteristics as the chief reason for change. And, showing that not only Christians split into many opposing factions, yet other paleontologists endorsed orthogenesis. They argued that once a trend has started, it might carry over into the positively nonadaptive and harmful. The reader will remember that the supposedly burdensome antlers of the Irish Elk were the orthogeneticists' favorite counterexample to Darwinism.

This state of affairs lasted well into this century. Given the extent to which Darwinism was under continual attack from other biologists, there is little

Fig. 9.1
The most famous fossil of them all: the Berlin *Archaeopteryx,* found in 1877 in Bavaria.
Note the feathers.

wonder that paleontologists continued their own orthogenetic trend of opposition to natural selection. But then, like everyone else, the paleontologists succumbed to the charms of neo-Darwinism, particularly as it was purveyed by Theodosius Dobzhansky in his *Genetics and the Origin of Species.* In 1944 paleontology was at long last brought into the Darwinian fold. In a brilliant tour-de-force, George Gaylord Simpson argued in his *Tempo and Mode in Evolution* that there is nothing in the fossil record that positively bars neo-Darwinism, and that, conversely, by taking seriously the major tenets of neo-Darwinism — particularly the core principles of population genetics — much illuminating light can be thrown on the organic past and its record.

Such was the influence of this powerful book (and its successor in 1953, *The Major Features of Evolution*) that, with very few exceptions, paleontologists began to think and reason in exactly the same way as their fellow

Fig. 9.2
Artist's reconstruction of *Archaeopteryx*. There is, in fact, debate today over whether
the *Archaeopteryx's* wings were for flying or insect catching.

evolutionists. One cannot see genes and natural selection actively at work in
the past, but these very genes were and are the key to all evolutionary
understanding. Major evolutionary events of the past, "macroevolution," are
simply the summation of many, many minor evolutionary events,
"microevolutions" — events of a kind that are going on all the time today. A
mile is simply 63,360 inches, end to end, and the evolution of mammals from
fish is simply a multitude of small random variations, sifted by selection, end
to end. Thus paleontologists happily set to work producing explanations of a
kind that we saw in illustration in the final chapter devoted to "Darwinism Today."

The challenge to Darwinism

The harmony was too good to last. In the past decade, paleontology has
again grown fractious, and again we find voices being raised against the Darwinian synthesis. A number of articulate and informed paleontologists, Niles
Eldredge, Stephen Jay Gould, and Steven M. Stanley, to name but three, have
thrown a large rock — a large saltationary rock — into the still waters of
unanimity. (See bibliographic essay for references.) It is argued that the gaps

against

in the fossil record are just too real merely to be dismissed as an unfortunate effect of incomplete fossilization. At the very least, evolutionists have no right to conclude without proof that the gaps are no true reflection of what really happened, and that (as Darwinism supposes) evolution took a smooth gradual path. Moreover, argue these critics, when one looks at such fossil deposits as one does have, one finds clearly defined species or groups with no appreciable internal change. Eventually, such groups always vanish abruptly and they are followed by the next set of forms. Predecessors and successors may be quite similar, but there are always unambiguous differences.

In the early days of the attack, I think it is true to say that the critics were in a conciliatory mood toward paleontological orthodoxy. They were obviously breaking with evolution as Simpson saw it. But, when they turned to causal speculation, the critics wanted to argue that theirs, and only theirs, was the true application of neo-Darwinism to the fossil record! Seizing on Mayr's hypothesis of the founder principle, it was pointed out that orthodox evolutionism supposes that new species caused by geographic isolation ("allopatric speciation") will move rather rapidly from the parent forms. Such a process, the critics noted, would be over in a geological instant. Hence a jump in the record is what already accepted neo-Darwinism leads us to expect! Paradoxically, considered from the time perspective of the paleontologist, the course of orthodox Darwinian evolution is saltationary! (See Fig. 9.3.)

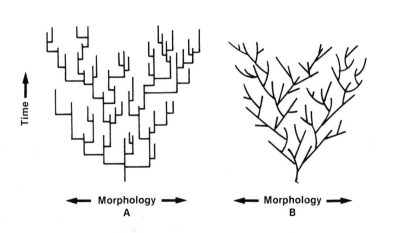

Morphology
A

Morphology
B

Fig. 9.3
The saltationary or "punctuated" model (A) and the Darwinian or "gradualistic" model (B) compared.

It is a good policy always to look skeptically upon people's declared intentions. Whatever they may have said, the critics' position certainly represented a change of emphasis from conventional neo-Darwinism. The theory of "punctuated equilibria" rather downplays any gradual changes of one form to another — changes that occur without allopatric speciation. In this, the would-be reformers opposed most neo-Darwinians, who had assumed that gradual change — "phyletic gradualism" — was common. (See Fig. 9.4.)

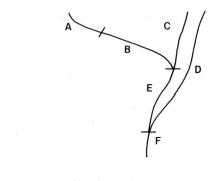

Morphological and other differences

Fig. 9.4
Classification: Loosely associated with the debate over the nature of the fossil record is an even-more-heated debate over classification. The traditional evolutionary taxonomist (*e.g.* Mayr) relies on common descent for classification. Thus, horses are put with cows rather than fishes, because they belong to closer branches of the tree of life ("clades"). However, if morphological change occurs very rapidly, evolutionary taxonomists take account of this. Thus, in the figure above, A and B would be separated because of the great change which has occurred, even though they both belong to the same clade. A new school of taxonomy, "cladism", classifies entirely on the basis of branching. Thus A and B could never be separated. Conversely, C and E would be separated, even though change is minimal. Naturally, cladists are attracted to punctuated equilibrism, given the latter's downplaying of gradual change (as in the transition from B to A), and its supposing that branching does lead to significant change.

And, in another sense, I believe the critics started to move well beyond Darwinism. The Darwinian sees trends as smooth, *systematic* moves toward greater adaptive advantage. Thus, remember how it was argued that the move toward increased size that one often sees in successive groups of animals

(Cope's rule) has selective virtues. Hence, all other things being equal, one expects any particular group within a trend to go with the trend. Why indeed would it go against the direction of selection unless there were special reasons? But, whatever the punctuated equilibrists may have thought of the overall adaptive values of trends, they certainly did not see individual species events as being particularly adaptive. The chance factors involved in the operation of the founder principle make the forms of any new species essentially random with respect to the forms of the parental species. Therefore, the reforming paleontologists felt one should find, as they suggested one does find, that new groups of organisms will as often go against the trend, as with it. Only considered overall does one see a trend emerge. (See Fig. 9.5.)

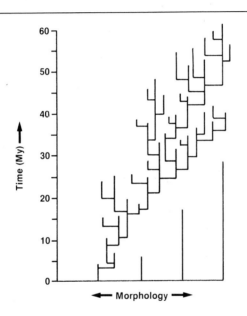

Fig. 9.5
Species selection. Note that the morphological trend is from left to right, even though there are as many speciation events moving to the left as there are events to the right. (Adapted by permission from S. M. Stanley, (1979). *Macroevolution: Pattern and Process*. San Francisco: W. H. Freeman.)

Elaborating on this last idea, Stanley suggested that we ought to recognize a new kind of selection: "species selection." He argued that, just as we have conventional natural selection sitting between individuals in a group, so also we have a selective process deciding which species proliferate and then survive. New species, like new variations, just occur, almost by accident, with or without special advantages: "I believe speciation to have a strongly random aspect" (Stanley, 1979, p. 185). Some groups are more given to speciation than others. And then some species survive and others do not. This is species selection.

The concept should not be confused with group selection; there is no question of certain members altruistically laying down their lives for others. It is just that some species are better fitted for reproduction and for survival than others. Stanley suggested, incidentally, that species selection gives a reason for the common occurrence of sexuality in species. It is not that sexuality gives an immediate adaptive benefit, as is commonly supposed. Rather, sexuality lends itself to speciation (sex is a key factor in the founder principle), and thus one simply gets more sexual species than asexual species.

Stanley points out that asexual clones do not speciate easily, while sexual clades more readily divide themselves into separate species because interacting individuals form interbreeding populations that often split into geographically isolated subgroups. Thus, sexual species are not more numerous because sex itself provides strong adaptive advantages. Asexual species are just as successful and abundant by number of individuals. Sexual species predominate simply because they maintain a high capacity for speciation, while asexual clones do not. (Gould and Eldredge, 1977, p. 140)

Of this much I am certain. Insofar as it has endorsed the notion of species selection, the theory of punctuated equilibria has always represented more than just a change of emphasis within neo-Darwinism. For all that there may be a random element within the founder principle, a Darwinian stalwart like Ernst Mayr never saw it supporting or implying the totally chance effects that the paleontologists supposed. The position of the punctuated equilibria theorist seems to be that, with respect to any particular feature, speciation could take an organism in virtually any direction. The orthodox Darwinian could not accept this: there may be options, but they would have to be within clearly defined adaptive limits. (See the discussion in Part 2.)

Whatever the original intentions may have been, in the past ten years the reforming paleontologists have continued to move away from Darwinism. Whether this has been done gradually or through sharp steps, I will leave to the reader to decide. One presumes that Stanley today can hardly be that enthusiastic about any of the principles of neo-Darwinism, since he tends "to agree with those who have viewed natural selection as a tautology rather than a true theory" (Stanley, 1979, pp. 192–193).

Gould (1980a) is quite open in his dissent. He argues that the basic ground plan of any given organism — why a mammal has four limbs rather than six — does not necessarily have any particularly adaptive value. Instead, he thinks that fundamental patterns may just be accidents, brought on by random factors in evolution. Often, they are constraints brought about by the sheer "mechanics" or "architecture" involved in putting together a living organism. (See Fig. 9.6.) Again, the particular combination of genes in a founding population might lead to a drastic morphological shakeup, with a new form being created — a form not in any way caused by external selective necessities. Additionally, Gould endorses a version of Stanley's concept of species selection, making its nonadaptive nature even more explicit. And, even long-term trends are now seen as things that occur very much more by chance than by any orthodox selective design (Fig. 9.7).

Fig. 9.6
One of the spandrels of St. Mark's (in Venice). It exists as a matter of architectural
necessity, to keep the building up! That it can be used for decoration is a by-product.
Gould and Lewontin argue that many Darwinians commit a fallacy akin to thinking the
decoration the primary purpose. They feel that many things in the organic world, which
seem as if they have immediate function (like decoration), are in fact essentially nonadaptive by-products of the overall "architectural" or "engineering" constraints of a
working organism. (Taken by permission from S. J. Gould and R. C. Lewontin, (1979).
The spandrels of San Marco and the panglossian paradigm; a critique of the adaptationist programme. *Proc. Roy. Soc. Series B,* 205, 581-598.)

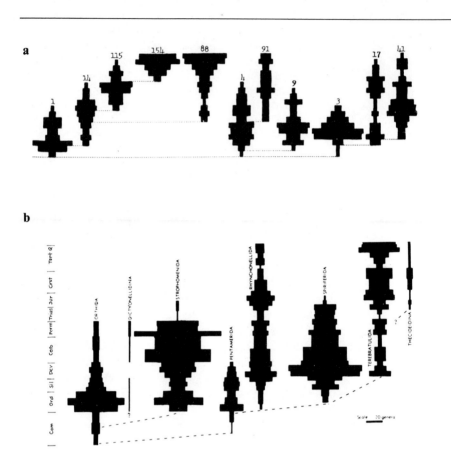

Fig. 9.7
Remember: a "clade" is a branch of the tree of life, which will in fact consist of a
number of taxa all descended from some particular ancestral taxon. One can readily
diagram the "success" of the clade, using a horizontal bar made as many units wide as
there are members of the clade. At any succeeding time, the bar will shrink or expand
according to the then number of extant taxa. Figure *b* above thus shows pictorially
several clades produced by genera of brachiopods. (Much paleontological work uses the
genus as the lowest level of classification, because the fossil evidence is not really sufficiently sensitive for more refined division.)

A number of paleontologists (including D. Raup and S. J. Gould) have tried manufac-
turing "artificial" random clades with computers. They programme the computer to
divide ("speciate") or end ("make extinct") any particular lineage at random. They
claim that the "clades" thus generated (as in figure *a* above) are remarkably similar to
real clades. Thus, it is concluded that the course of evolution is far more random than
hitherto thought; in particular, the role of selection is downplayed.

Other evolutionists disagree, including S. M. Stanley who sees the position as an attack
on his concept of species selection. They do not get random clades which look like real
clades! To get real clades, they feel the need to feed in factors which they think are of

evolutionary significance (like important adaptive innovations leading to many new species). At the moment, therefore, conventional Darwinians can relax, until paleontologists can decide on what the fossil record is really telling us! Certainly, some events in life history seem to transcend the random: the occasionally great bursts of diversity, when many groups appear at the same time (for instance, that which occurred in the Ordovician), the occasional mass extinctions of species (for instance, that which occurred in the Permian), and the long-term persistence of some clades with very few members. The Permian extinction, for instance, seems associated with the linking of all main land masses into one giant continent, Pangaea, and the consequent loss of suitable environment for many species of marine organism. (Figures taken by permission from S. J. Gould *et al,* (1977). The shape of evolution: a comparison of real and random clades. *Paleobiology,* 3, 23-40.)

Relatedly, at the basic level of the creation of new species, perhaps distrustful of even the modicum of selection that might be smuggled in via the founder principle, Gould explores and warmly responds to alternatives. We know that a major objection to saltationism is that, if a saltation takes an animal to a new species, then it is liable to perish through lack of a mate. The new kind of organism, formed by a rare macromutation, has no fellows, and yet it cannot breed with the species of its parents. Gould suggests that perhaps chromosomal rearrangements or multiplications *in just one animal* give rise to a whole family with such novelties. Then the siblings inbreed, thereby concentrating the novelties, as it were. However, perhaps at the same time, the members of this small group of relatives remain fertile, one with another, and thus we have the founding members of a new species! (Here he adopts ideas put forward by White, 1978.)

In one of his most recent discussions of evolutionary thought, Gould quotes Mayr on evolution as follows:

The proponents of the synthetic theory maintain that all evolution is due to the accumulation of small genetic changes, guided by natural selection, and that transspecific evolution is nothing but an extrapolation and magnification of the events that take place within populations and species (Gould, 1980a, p. 120, quoting, Mayr, 1963, p. 586).

He then comments:

I well remember how the synthetic theory beguiled me with its unifying power when I was a graduate student in the mid-1960's. Since then I have been watching it slowly unravel as a universal description of evolution. The molecular assault came first, followed quickly by renewed attention to unorthodox theories of speciation and by challenges at the level of macroevolution itself. I have been reluctant to admit it — since beguiling is often forever — but if Mayr's characterization of the synthetic theory is accurate, then that theory, as a general proposition, is effectively dead, despite its persistence as textbook orthodoxy (Gould, 1980a, p. 120).

Need more be said?

Phyletic gradualism versus punctuated equilibrism

What is the response of orthodox Darwinians to the theory of punctuated equilibria? The following counterarguments are particularly important.

First, there is objection to the way in which the punctuated equilibria supporters extrapolate from causal models derived with today's organisms (Lande, 1980). As might be expected from comments that I have made already, strong exception is taken to the use made of the founder principle. All accept that the principle supposes evolution to take place very quickly, and that a random factor is involved; but, this is hardly warrant for suggesting that totally new forms of animals or plants might be produced, as the reforming paleontologists suppose.

Take something presumably formed (in part) by the action of the founder principle, for instance the finches of the Galapagos or the earlier-discussed fruitflies of South America. These organisms hardly give rise to thoughts of drastic change, even if the founder principle is effective. Certainly there is no question here of organisms with fundamentally modified ground plans: four wings and the like. Again, if one looks at some of the proposed chromosome species mechanisms that so excite Gould, one suspects that orthodox evolutionists would like more proof as to their universal nature. Gould never mentions Darwin's finches, the paradigm of the Darwinians. Do they not fit his theory?

The second defensive line protecting neo-Darwinism is one manned by orthodox paleontologists. Although it is conceded that there are many gaps in the fossil record, it is countered, nevertheless, that there is a sizable number of well-established gradual changes to be found in the record. Hence, given all the factors making fossilization improbable, Darwinism remains totally plausible. To ask for more than this from the fossil record is unreasonable.

Thus, for example, Kellogg (1975) studied the microfossil radiolarian *Pseudocubus vema,* taken from a single antarctic deep-sea core. She argues that we see a long-term gradient (two million years) towards increased size. In other words, we have the "long-term phyletic trend" supposed by orthodox Darwinism. Again Ozawa (1975) has studied the Permian verbeekinoid foraminifer *Lepidolina multiseptata.* He finds continual change, particularly in prolocular diameter size. (See Fig. 9.8.) Likewise, Gingerich (1976, 1977) has sought trends in higher organisms, for example, the primate *Pelycodus.* He believes that his search has ended in success.

Discussion on the merits of these claims is ongoing, but apparently they are sufficiently strong to have persuaded even the sternest critics of neo-Darwinism that we do get some gradual changes. Of Ozawa's results, Gould and Eldredge write: "We are delighted with these results, and believe that they reflect well upon our model" (Gould and Eldredge, 1977, p. 129). Frankly, in view of some of their other comments, I suspect that the authors are putting on a little bit of a brave face in both of these conjuncts. But, no matter! Everyone now accepts that there is more to macroevolution than punctuated equilibria — although how much more is of course still debatable. As might be

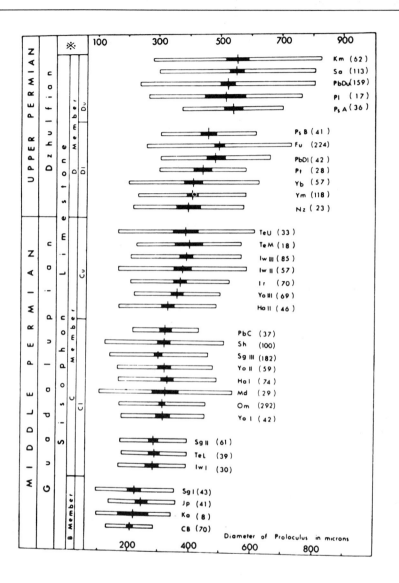

Fig. 9.8
Increase over time of the diameter of the proloculus (first chamber) of the foraminiferan *Lepidolina multiseptata*. The white rectangle shows the range of sizes for each population, the black rectangle the 95 per cent confidence limits for the mean. The six clusters are in stratigraphic succession (*i.e.,* go from early to late), but ordering within clusters is arbitrary. (Taken by permission from T. Ozawa, (1975). Evolution of *Lepidolina multiseptata* (Permian Foraminifer) in East Asia. *Mem. Faculty of Science, Kyushu University*, 23, 117-164.)

expected, not all of the claims have been accepted as supportive of Darwinism. It is agreed that Kellogg's radiolarian size changes are all in the same direction (thus countering species selection). But, whereas Kellogg takes her results as supporting gradual change, Eldredge and Gould take them as supporting punctuated equilibria! There is, therefore, no question yet of surrender by the critics on the fossil record.

A third objection by Darwinians to the would-be reformers is that the latter have not yet proven, on the basis of the fossil record, that really major changes, say, from reptiles to birds, occur instantaneously or so quickly as to be virtually instantaneous. Admittedly, Gould and Eldredge write: "Smooth intermediates between *Baupläne* [i.e., organisms with different ground plans] are almost impossible to construct, even in thought experiments; there is certainly no evidence for them in the fossil record (curious mosaics like *Archaeopteryx* do not count)" (Gould and Eldredge, 1977, p. 147). But, with respect, this is no argument. Why does *Archaeopteryx* not count? We have seen it to be firmly intermediate between reptiles and birds.

One suspects, of course, that every time a Darwinian produces a counterexample to a supposedly unbridgeable gap, the response will be that the bridged organisms do not have genuinely different *Baupläne*. Perhaps, therefore, at this point argument is best suspended, until the reformers can define *Baupläne,* until they can prove that Darwinians want to make the links (no one wants to link horses and cabbages), and until they can show that there are absolutely no plausible intermediaries. In passing, we might recall Darwin's point that, even though we may have many gaps in the fossil record, in living organisms we frequently find trends, say, from possession of rudimentary eyes to the most sophisticated of eyes. These trends show the possibility of the kind of gradual temporal evolutionary process supposedly caused by natural selection (Lande, 1980).

Also, note that we do have strong evidence that absolutely massive changes can be brought about by the additive effect of mutations causing minor changes. The cob on Indian corn or maize, with the husks surrounding it and the very long styles or silks which receive the pollen, is about as novel a structure as any among wild species of flowering plants. Indeed, until genetic analysis was performed on it, Indian corn (*Zea mays*) was considered to be in a genus on its own, distinct from the nearest wild relative, teosinte (*Euchlaena mexicana*) (de Wet et al., 1978). But now it is realized that it is basically the product of a gradual process of artificial selection, from something like teosinte, which does not have any ears or cobs at all! (See Figs. 9.9 and 9.10.) Analogously, consider one of the most bizarre and striking variations in *Drosophila,* the headshape of the Hawaiian species *D. heteroneura* (Fig. 9.11). Apparently this is something sufficiently novel to set up reproductive barriers with other *Drosophila*, because the females of other groups will not respond sexually to such strange males. Yet, genetic analysis shows that the oddness of *D. heteroneura* is simply the additive effect of mutations at about eight different loci. In other words, the evidence points to a gradual, rather than abrupt, evolution (Templeton, 1977; Val, 1977).

Fig. 9.9
Teosinte, the closest relative of maize. (Taken by permission from P. C. Mangelsdorf, (1974). *Corn: Its Origin Evolution and Improvement,* Cambridge, Mass.: Belknap Press.)

Fig. 9.10
Corn cobs illustrating an evolutionary sequence from about 5000 B.C. to A.D. 1500.
(Taken by permission from Mangelsdorf, (1974).)

Of course, as the punctuated equilibrists themselves used to point out, to a certain extent one has a bogus conflict at this point. To the paleontologist, a change that takes, say, 50,000 years is very fast, given the over half billion years he has to play with since the pre-Cambrian. To the geneticist, 50,000 years is a long time! Hence, it could be that, in many cases, after semantic confusions are cleared, the punctuated equilibria theorist and the neo-Darwinian have little disagreement about the gradualness/rapidness of evolutionary change.

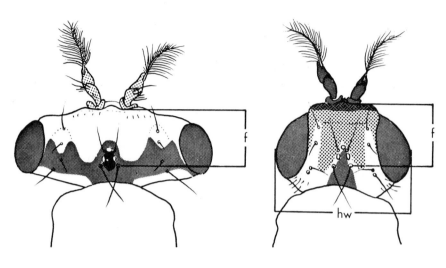

a. *D. heteroneura* male   b. *D. silvestris* male

Fig. 9.11
The strange shape of the *D. heteroneura* male's head is suffcient to prevent females of other species from breeding with it, and yet it is known to be the additive effect of several genes with small phenotypic effects. (f = frons or head length; hw = head width) (Taken by permission from F. C. Val, (1977). Genetic analysis of the morphological differences between two interfertile species of Hawaiian *Drosophila. Evolution,* 31, 611-629.)

Coming now to the final argument that the neo-Darwinian makes to the punctuated equilibria theorist, we return to familiar but crucial ground. The Darwinian complains that the new paleontology seriously underestimates the overwhelming evidence that we have for ubiquitous or near-ubiquitous adaption in the organic world. Listen once again to A. J. Cain, who still finds it necessary to say what he said thirty years ago:

Various excellent biologists at various times have pointed to various characters as trivial, or neutral, or unimportant to their possessors. In every case, when such characters have been properly investigated, quite large selection pressures have been found to be acting, or functions have been discovered which imply them (Cain, 1979, p. 599).

Similarly, Maynard Smith (1981) argues that supposedly nonadaptive features either have or have had selective causes. Take, for example, a popularly cited nonadaptive feature, the four-limbedness of vertebrates. Is this just a matter of chance, or a by-product, or was selection at work? Maynard Smith suggests that there was a simple adaptive reason, namely that when the vertebrates evolved they were fish, and quite simply, four limbs, two balanced at the front and two at the back, made for the most efficient swimming design. The principle was the same as that for airplanes, with two wings at the front and two tailfins at the back. From then on, as is so often the case, selection has simply worked with what it already has.

Hence, for these, and for all the sorts of reasons presented in earlier chapters, the deemphasis of adaptation that occurs in the writings of punctuated equilibria theorists seems untenable. Organisms like the Galapagos finches are so definitely a case of evolution occurring for adaptive reasons, notwithstanding "chance" factors involved with geographical isolation, that any "revision" of current thought that minimizes or denies selection's power and importance is a step backwards.

Revolution or assimilation?

What can a nonbiologist say in conclusion, looking at matters from the outside? One thing does seem clear: we are hardly at the point where we must start preparing the obituary notices for Darwinian evolutionary theory. At most, the reforming paleontologists have put forward exciting and stimulating hypotheses, which only now are being subjected to hard examination and test. Even were the Darwinians sitting back passively, the extreme position of someone like Gould would be far from well-established theory. But, in any case, the Darwinians are *not* sitting back passively, and they give at least as good as they get.

Already some of the sweeping claims about the absence of intermediaries have been tempered, and this could be the prelude to other compromises. Most particularly, the critics of neo-Darwinism are going to have to engage far more strenuously with the problem of adaptation than hitherto, if they are to win many converts. So long as a leading critic like Stanley continues to argue that natural selection is a tautology, it is hard to imagine that punctuated equilibria theory will remain much more than a fad, espoused by one particular clique of paleontologists.

However, let me make one final point, ending both this discussion and the chapter. We all tend to think of the progress of science in terms of "revolutions." Supposedly, one has a particular theory, which everybody holds and which functions happily for a while. Then, lo and behold, this first theory is smashed to smithereens, and in comes another theory. Thus, once we had Newtonianism, and now we have Einsteinianism; once we had Special Creationism, and now we have Darwinism; once we had a static world, and now we have plate tectonics.

Scientists themselves rather like this picture, which has been heavily reinforced in recent years by Thomas Kuhn's attractive book, *The Structure of Scientific Revolutions,* with its talk of "paradigms," changeable only through the efforts of a few geniuses. After all, the picture holds out the hope that you too might be a Copernicus, or a Newton, or a Darwin! It is interesting, although not surprising, to see that already supporters of punctuated equilibria talk in terms of revolutions. Indeed, the not-so-very subtle suggestion is floated that they are founders of a new "paradigm"! "Considering the central position that the concept of the sufficiency of microevolutionary processes to account for macroevolutionary differences holds in evolutionary theory . . ., a paradigm shift rather than a modification may be the more apt descriptor" (Stidd, 1980, p. 167).

In fact, like so much of the popular talk about science, most of the claims about revolutions have a very tenuous connection with reality. Certainly, major changes occur with science, and in this sense one has revolutions. But rarely, if ever, does one get abrupt breaks with the past. Rather, old ideas influence and merge with new positions, and very often, supposedly radical proposals get toned down, perhaps redefined, and then absorbed into the old. The course of science is far more like a gradual Darwinian change than like that supposed by the hypothesis of punctuated equilibria!

In the light of all this, with respect to the current controversy about the fossil record, it seems highly unlikely that the theory of punctuated equilibria will simply wipe out orthodox Darwinism. What one will find, rather, is that some of the major insights, if they prove valuable, will be incorporated or melded into existing theory. The course of science will proceed in a continuous fashion. Let us not minimize disagreements. Despite some possible semantic confusion over what is meant by "gradual" evolution, we have seen that there are real differences between paleontologists. Somebody has got to give way. Nevertheless, reminding you again that philosophers are notoriously bad forecasters of the future course of science, let me simply say this. I, for one, would be very surprised if the arguments of the paleontologists brought about too much more than a modification of some elements of neo-Darwinism. Already there seem to be some elements of compromise on whether there are ever gradual changes.

On the other hand, lest this all sounds just too condescending to be true, remember that vital science never stays still, it will always be open to fresh ideas and perspectives. I sense that punctuated equilibria theorists are causing many neo-Darwinians to reconsider parts of their theory. For instance, it is known that over and above "structural" genes, which cause cell products, there are "regulatory" genes, which control the workings of structural genes. Although not exclusively because of the challenge of dissident paleontologists, there is today great interest in the evolutionary importance of regulatory genes, including their potential to effect major phenotypic changes quite rapidly (Ayala and Valentine, 1979).

Again, although some Darwinians feel that their theory is already quite powerful enough to explain any changes seen in the fossil record, they do agree that punctuated equilibria theorists are right to emphasize the *lack* of change ("stasis") that often characterizes long-lasting fossil types. There are a number of orthodox possibilities for this, including developmental constraints and "normalizing" selection (i.e., selection that favors average population types, relative to extremes). But, more work needs to be done on this topic. Note, incidentally, that as in the case of the rate of evolutionary change, with respect to the question of biological constraints and evolutionary "engineering," there is a certain amount of cross talk between Darwinians and critics. All agree that such constraints may give rise to nonadaptive features; the dispute is one of emphasis about importance and occurrence (Stebbins and Ayala, 1981).

The prospect for the future, therefore, seems to be one of compromise and gradual development, rather than revolution. Perhaps some readers are disappointed. Predictions of violent change are far more thrilling than predictions of stable continuity. Do not despair! This discussion of future prospects for neo-Darwinism has surely shown that really exciting science does not necessarily demand a repudiation of ideas that have been accumulated carefully over the years. Neo-Darwinism is a theory with a proud past, a secure present, and prospects of an even more glorious future. There is promise of quite enough action to attract even the most ambitious of graduate students. Building on what has been achieved by Darwinism Past and Darwinism Present, let us look forward eagerly to Darwinism Tomorrow.

Part IV
Darwinism and Humankind

Chapter 10
Missing Links

Remember Darwin's comment at the end of the *Origin*: "Light will be thrown on the origin of man and his history" (Darwin, 1859, p. 458). Nobody was fooled by the seeming casualness of this throw-away remark. It was what everyone was waiting for and what many took to be *the* key question in the evolutionary debate. What about man? What about ourselves? Are we little more than glorified monkeys, if that? Is the wretched ape really our brother? (See Fig. 10.1.) Copernicus had driven us from the security of our home. Was

Fig. 10.1
Cartoon of Darwin as monkey (published in 1871, just after the appearance of the *Descent of Man*).

Darwin now about to drive us from the security of our bodies? Fortunately none suspected that Freud lurked, just around the corner, ready to drive us from our minds!

Because I am a human, and because you my readers are humans, I intend now to turn the discussion exclusively to this one species that so excited the Victorians: *Homo sapiens.* What exactly is the relationship between Darwinian evolutionary theory and humankind? I begin in the past, and then move towards the present.

"Going the whole orang"

From the time of the Ancient Greeks and before, it has been obvious to everyone that there are major similarities between humans and the animals, particularly between humans and the so-called higher animals, like cows, sheep, and horses. A tradition dating back to Plato saw all animals as falling into an ordered scale, from the lowest to the highest: the *"scala natura"* or, the "great chain of being." Man was placed at the top end of the scale, thus emphasizing our superiority, but also acknowledging our similarities with the animals. By the eighteenth century, thanks to all the reports and finds of hairy, ape-like beings that world discoverers were bringing back to Europe, the gap between humans and other animals had grown ever smaller. (Refer back to Fig. 1.1.) The great Swedish taxonomist Linnaeus had no hesitation in putting man, together with the apes, into the zoological order of primates: Anthropomorpha (Greene, 1959).

None of this speculating and classifying was, in any way, taken as implying that man was just an animal; nor did people see the Linnaean classification as the first step to evolutionism. As we know, this insight, if that is the correct word, was due to Lamarck, who temporalized the chain of being — seeing it as a kind of evolutionary escalator — and who drew the conclusion that since man (at the top) stands just above the orang-utan, it must therefore be from the orang-utan that we have all evolved. Thus Charles Lyell's quip, quoted at the head of this section, that, thanks to the evolutionists, it now seemed that we should have to "go the whole orang!"

As we also know, reaction to Lamarck was predictable. For the British particularly, the claim that humans had evolved from the apes was quite unacceptable. Revealed religion had no place for human evolution. The Bible stated that God had created man on the sixth day, in His own image. There was nothing in the first book of Genesis about the orang-utan. Similarly, natural religion seemed to bar human evolution. Man's unique attributes — particularly his powers of speech, his intellect, and his moral and religious sense — were taken to be self-evident proof of man's distinctive place here on Earth. And, if this were not enough, man's absence from the fossil record seemed to echo his special status as the last-arrived creature on earth. Uniformitarians and catastrophists came together, affirming man's direct link to God.

It is against this background that we must judge the Darwinian debate, and how it impinged on the "monkey question." On the side of orthodoxy, we find Richard Owen, undoubtedly Britain's leading biologist. (See Fig. 10.2.)

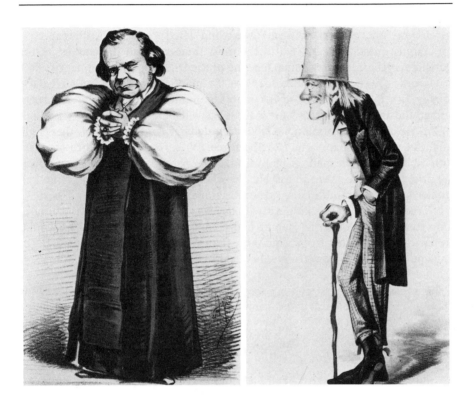

Fig. 10.2
Samuel Wilberforce, Bishop of Oxford.   Richard Owen.
                                        (Caricatures from *Vanity Fair*.)

He put himself firmly in the camp of the critics by declaring that man's special nature is underscored by the uniqueness of his brain — man and only man has that organ known as the hippocampus major (Owen, 1858). Obviously, possession of this organ does not deny the possibility of evolution, which by this stage Owen did not really want to deny anyway. But he and his fellow critics felt that the more difference they could find between man and the apes, the less plausible a totally natural evolutionary history would seem. And, this implausibility applies particularly to a history that bases its case primarily on natural selection. In their minds, it simply did not make sense to think that man, that most wonderful of organisms, was merely the product of random, chance variations, picked out in the struggle for existence.

On the side of the Darwinians, Huxley made the evolution of man his special crusade. He contradicted Owen flatly, claiming that man's supposedly unique brain is a chimera. Owen's case had been based mistakenly on dissections of pickled ape brains. If one works from fresh specimens, the hippocampus major can be found in some nonhuman species. Hence, Huxley concluded that man's special status can no longer be maintained (Huxley, 1861).

It was this quarrel between Owen and Huxley, over the "great hippopotamus question," that led to the most famous of all the clashes in the Darwinian debate. At the annual meeting of the BAAS, in the summer of 1860 in Oxford, Owen firmly made his case for man's uniqueness, and Huxley, equally firmly, made his case for man's nonuniqueness. Infuriated, Owen primed the Bishop of Oxford for a subsequent debate with Huxley. (See Fig. 10.2.) He chose a formidable ally: arch-debater and leader of the High Anglican party, "Soapy Sam" Wilberforce. Wilberforce warmed to his task with vigor, but then made a bad mistake. Apparently charmed by his own rhetoric, he went so far as to ask Huxley whether he claimed descent from the monkeys "on his grandfather's side or his grandmother's"?

Trading quips of this kind with Huxley was not a wise move, as the bishop soon found to his chagrin. Rumor had it that Huxley replied that he would prefer to be descended from a monkey, than from a bishop of the Church of England. Hardly less powerfully, Huxley probably replied that

Would I rather have a miserable ape for a grandfather, or a man highly endowed by nature and possessed of great means and influence, and yet who employs these faculties and that influence for the mere purpose of introducing ridicule into a grave scientific discussion — I unhesitatingly affirm my preference for the ape (Letter to F. Dyster, 9 Sept. 1860).

Ladies fainted! Fitzroy, Darwin's old friend from the *Beagle,* stormed around the hall, brandishing a Bible, crying: "The Book! the Book! We must have the Book!" And, the Owenites retired from the field, crushed.

Going on the offensive in print, in his best-known work, *Man's Place in Nature* (1863), Huxley examined in detail the physical similarities and differences between man and the apes. He felt able to argue strongly for man's simian origin because, although there is a larger gap between man and apes than between any two succeeding type of ape, there is less gap between man and ape than between highest and lowest ape, which latter Huxley felt confident had come from common stock. (See Fig. 10.3.) And, this seems to have been the end of this line of argument. The hippocampus's moment in the limelight was over. (Neither Huxley nor anyone else wanted to argue that man is descended from an ape that exists today; rather, man and today's apes descend from some extinct, joint ancestor.)

But, as can be imagined, this was not the end of the debate about man's position in nature. A cry which went up from many critics at that time was for evidence of the "missing link" between man and apes. If we are no more than

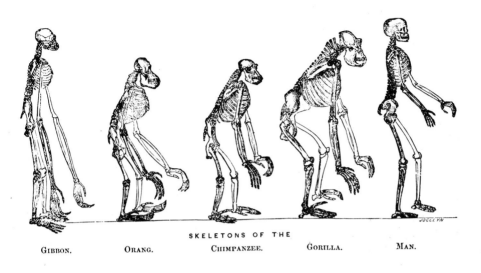

SKELETONS OF THE

GIBBON. ORANG. CHIMPANZEE. GORILLA. MAN.

Fig. 10.3
Huxley's picture of man and the apes, underlining our similarity. Taken from *Man's Place in Nature,* written by Huxley in 1863.

modified monkeys, then where is the fossil evidence? Unfortunately unambiguous evidence was not forthcoming at the time. Although, to be quite honest, one wonders if any empirical evidence would have satisfied these critics. Nevertheless, the fossil record (including here the recent record) did not fail the evolutionists entirely. In the late 1850s, the first specimens of "Neanderthal man" were unearthed (Oakley, 1964). This being was very close to man. Some, like Huxley, thought that it was too close to be separated from *Homo sapiens;* others, rather more optimistically, declared it to be more primitive than man and placed it in its own species, *Homo neanderthalensis.*

But, whatever its true status, Neanderthal man did at least give the evolutionists hope that more definitive bridging links could be found. And, in the meantime, minor but significant victories were being scored. By the 1860s what was becoming established beyond doubt is that man's history stretches back beyond the very recent past. In the face of discoveries of man's remains together with those of organisms indubitably extinct, even Sedgwick had to admit to man's great age. Admittedly this concession was a very thin end of the wedge, but it was a very big wedge!

In the decade after the *Origin,* most scientists moved towards a compromise. They accepted evolution, even for man. The general case that Darwin had made was just too strong to be resisted, and it was clear that Huxley had got the better of Owen over hippocampus major. However, most scientists then drew back. They argued that the changes involved in evolution are not random, that they are guided by God. Most particularly, it was claimed, that in the case of man — to make his mind, his intelligence, his moral and religious sense, and his soul — God intervened in a special creative way.

Wallace and Darwin on human evolution

Darwin himself had expected that many would take this path. What surprised and shocked him, was that natural selection's co-discoverer moved in this direction also! As a young man, Wallace had had little or nothing by way of religious belief, and he was certainly untroubled by any such belief in his quest for an adequate evolutionary mechanism. However, in the 1860s, on his return to England, Wallace got more and more enmeshed in the beliefs and practices of spiritualists, soon becoming quite convinced of the reality of some God-like life force.

This soon led Wallace to doubt the total efficacy of natural selection in the evolution of our own species (Smith, 1972). For such things as human hairlessness, he could see no direct adaptive function, nor could he see how something like human intelligence could have evolved naturally. He pointed out that the average savage uses hardly more than a modicum of his intelligence. How then could such a potential have evolved? Most particularly, how could it have been selected in the struggle for existence? Unable to answer his own questions, Wallace turned his back on natural causes, feeling driven to suppose some kind of special, divine intervention, coming at the last step between ape and man: "a superior intelligence has guided the development of man in a definite direction, and for a special purpose, just as man guides the development of many animal and vegetable forms" (Wallace, 1870, p. 359b).

Appalled at Wallace's apostasy, Darwin would have no truck whatsoever with attempts to take man's origins out of the natural world. Nor was this a hastily taken decision. Indeed, as noted earlier, the very first time that he ever put on paper his beliefs about natural selection, just a month or so after he realized its significance, Darwin was speculating about how natural selection might bring about the evolution of human mental powers! "An habitual action must some way affect the brain in a manner which can be transmitted. — this is analogous to a blacksmith having children with strong arms. — The other principle of those children which chance produced with strong arms, outliving the weaker ones, may be applicable to the formation of instincts, independently of habits" (Gruber and Barrett, 1974, N, p. 42). For Darwin, man was never ever anything but another animal.

In response to Wallace and like thinkers, Darwin was finally spurred into detailed public discussion of the origins of man. In 1871 he published a major study on the subject, the *Descent of Man, and Selection in Relation to Sex*. Expectedly, there are no major surprises in this work; man's connections and similarities with the animal world are argued for with forceful vigor. And, as always, Darwin saw the main force behind evolutionary change to be natural selection. Those apes who were brighter, more active, and better able to feed and defend themselves were those who survived and reproduced with such success that eventually *Homo sapiens* appeared on the face of the Earth: "in the rudest state of society, the individuals who were the most sagacious, who invented and used the best weapons or traps, and who were best able to defend themselves, would rear the greatest number of offspring" (Darwin, 1871, 1, 247).

Nevertheless, the *Descent of Man* is a curious book, for despite its main title and subject, more than half of it was not directly about man at all! Rather, Darwin devoted much space to a very extended discussion of his secondary selective mechanism, sexual selection. He showed, in a careful survey of the animal world, how it is that the dual forces of male combat and female choice can bring about the evolution of the strangest and most complex of sexual dimorphisms.

Now, this is all very well! But, why do we get this discussion, right in the middle of an analysis of the evolution of man? The full answer comes only toward the end of the book. In sexual selection, Darwin thought he had the key to many human racial differences, and most especially, to those very features that Wallace itemized as inexplicable on natural selection! Why are humans hairless? Simply because hairlessness was an attractive feature in the eyes of other humans. Why do the women of some native tribes have big bottoms? For no other reason than that the successful warriors had the pick of the maidens who were most amply endowed! "According to Burton, the Somal men are said to choose their wives by ranging them in a line, and by picking her out who projects farthest *a tergo*. Nothing can be more hateful to a negro than the opposite form" (Darwin, 1871, 2, 329–330). And, why do we have many of the mental attributes that we do? Because they too were desired and valuable in the struggle for sex.

In making use of sexual selection in this way, Darwin was certainly giving a new emphasis to hitherto minor parts of his theorizing, but he was not introducing new concepts. Sexual selection appeared in the *Origin*; and, indeed, it is mentioned quite fully in Darwin's first draft of his theory, something that dates back to 1842. In other words, Darwin really did try to stay true to his resolve not to treat his own species as in some way special or out of the usual course of nature.

Indeed, in only one respect have I been able to find that Darwin wavered in the *Descent* from formerly held principles. We know, from earlier discussion, how committed Darwin was to an individual selectionist perspective. But, when faced with man's moral nature, Darwin confessed that he did not really see how the altruistic person would be a better reproducer than the selfish person.

It is extremely doubtful whether the offspring of the more sympathetic and benevolent parents, or of those which were the most faithful to their comrades, would be reared in greater number than the children of selfish and treacherous parents of the same tribe. He who was ready to sacrifice his life, as many a savage has been, rather than betray his comrades, would often leave no offspring to inherit his noble nature. The bravest men, who were always willing to come to the front in war, and who freely risked their lives for others, would on an average perish in larger number than other men. (Darwin, 1871, 1, 163)

Perhaps, therefore, because of human peculiarities, it might be possible to have here some group selective mechanism at work.

But, Darwin did not really like this conclusion. At once, he covered himself by pointing out that man's evolution probably occurred among small bands of kin — hence, like the sterile worker, the altruistic person is helping his/her extended family. Moreover, Darwin suggested that altruism might be enlightened self-interest: "each man would soon learn that if he aided his fellow-men, he would commonly receive aid in return." Right to the end, Darwin set an example to the thinker who refuses to make an exception of his own species. (Today's evolutionists, revealingly, refer to Darwin's mechanism as "reciprocal altruism.")

The path of human evolution

Against the background of the nineteenth century, let us now come up to our own day and age. What have we learned in the years since Darwin? Do we know how man evolved from the apes? Do we know why? Was it a process consistent with — implied by — natural selection? We must try to answer these questions.

Obviously what we all want to get to is the fossil record. But, just before we do so, let us recall once more what has been emphasized time and again: the case for evolution does not succeed or fail exclusively on the record. Indubitably from the record we can learn things about phylogenies that are unobtainable from other sources, but the overall fact of evolution rests on much, much more. And this applies to our own species also. Most importantly there is the matter of the similarities between man and the apes.

Let us not exaggerate. Men are not apes, and there are major differences. *Homo sapiens* walks upright; humans have very large brains; they can manipulate and use complex tools as part of their material culture; they talk in developed speech; they have small teeth (especially the canines); they have distinctive sexual habits (tight bonding, extreme male parental care, nonstop sexual activity); and so forth. But, from a biological perspective, the differences are swamped by the similarities. Huxley's comparisons between ape and human skeletons go far towards establishing our simian origins. Why should there be these fantastic similarities, given our different life-styles, if we are not descended from common ancestors? Without evolution, the homologies just do not make sense.

And, the same goes for the many other correspondences between man and ape. For instance, at the molecular level we find that α and β hemoglobin chains in humans contain 141 and 146 amino acids, respectively. Chimpanzees have exactly the same chains, and gorillas differ by only one acid in each chain. Generally, it has been calculated that man and chimpanzee differ by about only one in every hundred amino acids in their proteins. Similarly, at the genetic level, the differences are very few. Again comparing man and chimpanzee, one form could be changed into the other by making about only one allelic substitution for every three loci.

Put matters this way. There is less genetic difference between man and chimpanzee than between fox and dog! Chromosomes also are similar. The only difference is that two chimpanzee chromosomes are fused into one human chromosome, thus giving chimpanzees forty-eight chromosomes and humans forty-six. In short, the facts are rather sobering for those who would argue for complete human uniqueness. If one is genuinely prepared to accept a natural explanation, one just has to accept that man and ape evolved from a common ancestor. No other explanation makes sense. (See King and Wilson, 1975, for more details of the fantastic molecular similarities between man and chimpanzee.)

But, what about the fossils? Let us now look at these. Caveats aside, it seems true to say that the quest for human origins is something that has had a very checkered history. Until recently, there were a few, important, brilliant discoveries, but progress was spasmodic and marred by long barren periods, misunderstandings, failures in interpretation, professional rivalries and jealousies, and, on more than one occasion, outright dishonesty.

From the perspective of the mid-1860s, this sorry tale might seem surprising. We have just seen how, at first, the search for human origins seemed promising. Neanderthal man had been discovered. However, even then the discerning thinker might have sensed future trouble, for already there was inconclusive debate. What was the true status of this early man? Was he a real, independent species, or, as Huxley surmised and as now seems accepted, a form, perhaps a subspecies, of our own species? In the absence of fresh evidence, nothing could be settled in any definitive way. Hence, the early promise of progress on man's origins fast petered away, replaced by repetitive debate, which went on inconclusively generating far more heat than light.

But, ten years after Darwin died, inquiry took a major step forward (Oakley, 1964). At the beginning of the final decade of the nineteenth century, the first real claimant to "missing link" status was uncovered. A young Dutch army doctor, Eugene Dubois, unearthed a skull cap and thigh bone of a human-like animal, which was nevertheless very much less advanced than modern *Homo sapiens.* Somewhat naturally, whenever anyone discovers a possible human ancestor, there is a tendency to magnify its importance. Therefore, it is made as unique as possible and given its own fancy name. Dubois' discovery, "Java man," was first called *Pithecanthropus,* but it has since been realized that this name conceals Java man's very close similarities with modern man. Dubois' find has therefore been reassigned to the same genus as us, *Homo,* but given its own specific name, *Homo erectus.* This shows that it is like us, but not completely! Although a specific name need not convey any information, obviously in this case the name points to the fact that Java man walked around on his back limbs, just like us. (See Fig. 10.4.)

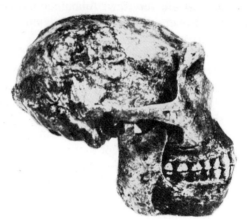

Fig. 10.4
Homo erectus, or Java Man, unearthed in 1891 by Eugene Dubois.

Since Dubois' work, many more specimens of *Homo erectus* have now been found around the world — in Asia, in Africa, and in Europe. To appreciate *H. erectus* to the full, it is obviously instructive to compare it both with us and with living apes. With respect to the key question of its brain, we find that its cranial capacity falls between the ends of the scale: *H. sapiens* (1400 cc), *H. erectus* (900–1000 cc), gorillas (500 cc). One cannot read too much into these figures. *H.s. neanderthalensis* has, if anything, a slightly larger cranial capacity than we. Also, remember, no one wants to claim that *H. sapiens* is descended from living apes. But, these and similar types of comparison have convinced people that *H. erectus* is a direct human ancestor. As more specimens were found and as it became possible to infer the habits of *H. erectus,* its human-ancestor status has become even more probable. For instance, it used fire (the first known user) and made stone tools.

As this century began, the inquiry into human origins went very badly indeed. It was put right off track by one of the worst scientific frauds of all time: "Piltdown man." In 1912 in England, a supposed potential ancestor was unearthed by the amateur scientist Charles Dawson. Having been authenticated by leading authorities, it was given the name *Eoanthropus dawsoni* (Dawson's dawn man). What made Piltdown man such a damaging phenomenon was the way in which it so positively misled. The upper part of the skull is much more like the skull of *Homo sapiens* than that of *H. erectus,* whereas the jaw is far more primitive even than *H. erectus.* We saw that a major difference between man and the apes is that man's teeth, especially the canines, are much smaller. *H. erectus* is like *H. sapiens* in this respect, whereas Piltdown man was like the apes! Hence, much time and effort was wasted on trying to place Dawson's find — an impossible task, since it is now known that Piltdown man was indeed a fabricated male-ape hybrid. (See Fig. 10.5.) People still disagree about who was the perpetrator of the fraud. One who may have been involved was the French scientist/theologian, Teilhard de Chardin (Gould, 1980c).

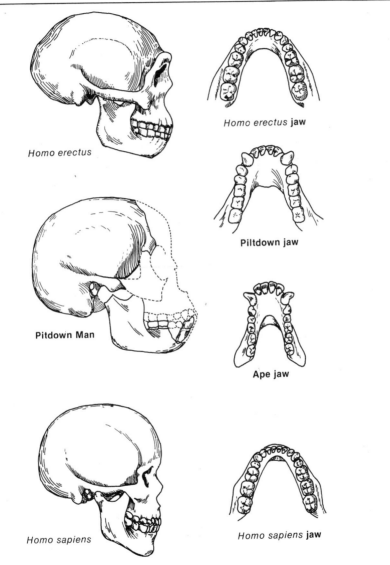

Homo erectus

Homo erectus jaw

Pitdown Man

Piltdown jaw

Ape jaw

Homo sapiens

Homo sapiens jaw

Fig. 10.5
It is easy to see from this figure why Piltdown man was such a problem for evolutionists. His cranium is just like that of a modern man and nothing like as primitive as that of *Homo erectus*. He simply did not fit! (Adapted by permission from an original drawing by Luba Dmytryk.)

Returning to the true course of discovery, the next major genuine find, one of a creature much more primitive than *Homo erectus,* occurred in 1924. This discovery was of the well-known "Taung baby," found by Raymond Dart, a South African anthropologist, at a site north of Kimberly, in South Africa. This animal, labeled *Australopithecus africanus,* had a brain of about 500 cc and was rather smaller than modern man (about four to four and a half feet tall); but it too walked upright (was "bipedal"). Its features were a mixture of ape and man: ape-like forehead, but rather human-like teeth. Other species of australopithecine which have since been discovered include *Australopithecus robustus* and *A. boisei.* These are rather more hardy than *A. africanus,* and some authorities include them in the same species (*A. robustus* has been found in South Africa, whereas *A. boisei* hails from East Central Africa).

In recent years, the pace of discovery has really started to pick up, and, together with the new finds, far more sophisticated and accurate ways of dating fossils and their surroundings have been developed (Reader, 1981). Much credit must go to the various members of one single world-renowned family group, the Leakeys. Especially worthy of note is Mary Leakey's discovery in 1961 of the first known intermediate between *Australopithecus africanus* and *Homo erectus.* This specimen, bipedal, with more human-like teeth than *Australopithecus* and with a brain size (700 cc) almost exactly between *A. africanus* and *H. erectus,* was named *Homo habilis.* It was a major user of tools; although, expectedly, its tools were rather more primitive than those of *H. erectus.*

Obviously, a pattern is starting to emerge, and this fits in with best-calculated estimates of the absolute dates at which these creatures flourished. Earliest records of *H. sapiens* go back to about 500,000 years, or a little less. *H. erectus* appears to have lived around the one to one-half million year mark.

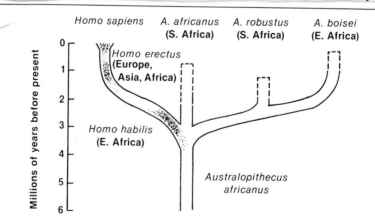

Fig. 10.6
Tentative reconstruction of hominid phylogeny. (Adapted by permission from Ayala and Valentine, (1979).)

After some controversy, *H. habilis* has been dated as having a span which straddles the two million year mark. *Australopithecus robustus* (and *A. boisei*) overlaps with *H. erectus* and *H. habilis,* and seems therefore to be on a line (or lines) off on its own. *A. africanus,* which goes back from around two million years, apparently therefore is the ancestral species for all the others. Putting all together, a reasonable reconstructed phylogeny would seem to be as in Fig. 10.6.

However, this is to reckon without what are possibly the most brilliant discoveries of all, those made in the last decade in Ethiopia by Donald Johanson and his associates. Thanks to one find after another, they have been able to extend the record right back, so that now we can trace human ancestry to almost four million years ago (Johanson and Edey, 1981). Most particularly, because of "Lucy" and similar finds (see Fig. 10.7), we now know that,

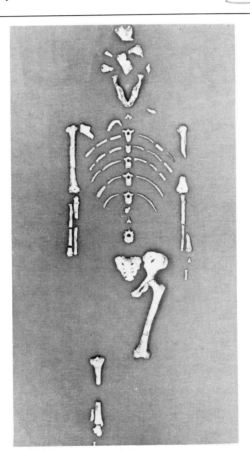

Fig. 10.7
Australopithecus afarensis: "Lucy." (Photograph used by permission of the Cleveland Museum of Natural History.)

named Lucy

in Africa all that time ago, there existed a little creature (three and a half to five feet tall) with a tiny brain (about the size of a chimp), which apparently was not tool using (there is no evidence of tools), and which walked! Moreover, this was a creature that walked properly — there was no shuffling or dropping down on all fours when it got tired.

One could not desire a more beautiful example of a "missing link" — something that is truly a being evolving up from the apes to the humans. Johanson and his colleague, Tim White, have given it the specific name, *Australopithecus afarensis,* and they suggest that it (not *A. africanus*) is the true ancestor of all the known hominids (members of the genus *Homo* and the genus *Australopithecus*). They reconstruct our family tree as given in Fig. 10.8.

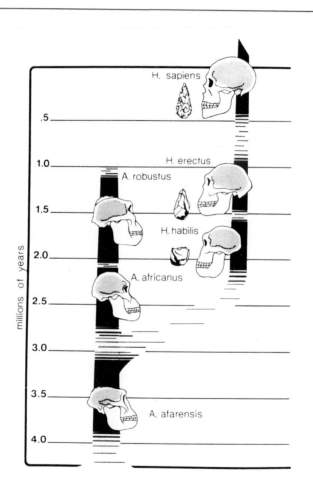

Fig. 10.8
The latest family tree. (Used by permission of Steve Misencik.)

Judging by the past history of "paleoanthropology," we have certainly not yet heard the final word on matters. There are many more gaps, even in this picture, to be filled, and undoubtedly others will want to give *their* views on the proper reconstruction. Nevertheless, a satisfying full picture of the course of human evolution, in the past four million years, is starting to emerge. But, where did *Australopithecus* come from? Can we go back, thus eventually linking up *Homo sapiens* with *Pongo pygmaeus* (orang-utan), *Pan troglodytes* (chimpanzee), and *Gorilla gorilla* (gorilla)? Unfortunately, although improving, the fossil record before *Australopithecus* is still very poor. It is believed that the oldest discovered ancestor of man that is *not* also an ancestor of the great apes is *Ramapithecus*, which lived rather more than ten million years ago, and which has been found in fragments in Africa and India (some authorities think *Ramapithecus* a side branch of this ancestor).

Going before this to the common human/ape ancestor, the likely candidate is *Dryopithecus*. This came from Africa, but spread to Europe and Asia. It was a true ape, flourishing from about twenty million years ago, a tree dweller and a fruit eater. Its brain size was about that of modern apes. The crucial split occurred about fifteen million years ago, with the apes going their way and with us going ours. (See Fig. 10.9.) Before *Dryopithecus*, around twenty-eight million years ago, we find *Aegyptopithecus*, which is probably the last common ancestor of man, great apes, gibbons, and siamangs (collectively put in the superfamily Hominoidea, the "hominoids").

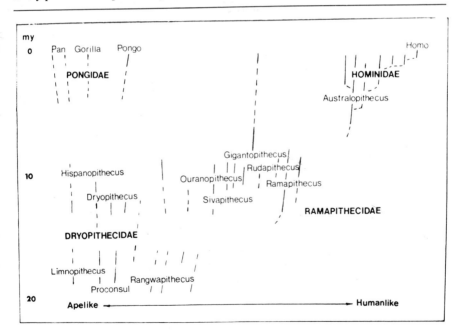

Fig. 10.9
Our knowledge, so far, of human ancestry. (Used by permission of David Pilbeam.)

We have gone far enough back. There are many many questions still to be answered, and there are many controversies yet to be ended. For instance, those scientists who concentrate on the molecular features of humans and apes are convinced that the differences are far less than one would expect, had the ape/human split happened fifteen million years ago. Indeed, judged purely on the basis of the molecules, it has been suggested that man and the apes diverged less than five million years ago! Almost literally, Lucy's parents would have to be something like chimpanzees. Alternatively, perhaps as has been speculated recently, perhaps the apes descended from us, or at least from our near-ancestors (Cherfas and Gribbin, 1981; Gribbin and Cherfas, 1981). Clearly, some crucial questions, theoretical and empirical, must be asked and answered. But, let us emphasize the positive. For all the gaps and tensions, already we have learned a great deal about the course of human evolution. And this, obviously, leads us straight to the question of causes.

Why did humans evolve?

Why? Why? Why? Probably the most exciting question that the Darwinian faces! Why was it that humans evolved in the way that they did, with all of their unique features: their upright stance, their large brains, their small teeth, their ability to manipulate and use tools, and so forth? There are almost as many answers as there are scientists who have addressed themselves to the question!

One thing that does seem fairly well agreed on is the phenomenon responsible for triggering the sequence, which ended ultimately in *Homo sapiens*. Some fifteen or so million years ago (in the Miocene) there were long, drawn-out, climatic changes in Africa. Until this point in history, one had lush rain forests as the norm, and the extant hominoid apes were well adapted for an arboreal existence. But then, the rains started to dry up, and gradually the forests started to give way to grasslands: savannahs. Some apes stayed with the dwindling forests. Their descendants are the great apes of today. Other apes, our ancestors, took an alternative strategy. They started to make the move toward the open spaces. And it was this move that directed animals down the path to *Homo sapiens*.

At this point, given the poor fossil record, we enter the great unknown, and the story can only really pick up again some four million years ago, with the arrival of *Australopithecus afarensis*. But, knowing where we are going gives us some clues and helps to reduce the number of competing explanations for human evolution (Lovejoy, 1981). Most particularly, thanks to Lucy and her friends, we can rule out one of the most popular hypotheses — one that began with Darwin and that until this day has had a strong body of supporters. It can no longer be argued that the key factor in human evolution was the use of tools — that using tools meant the redundancy of the canines (which the apes use for fighting), and that such tool use led our ancestors to move up onto their hindlegs for ease of manipulation, simultaneously putting pressure on brain size development. This hypothesis must be false because *A. afarensis* has everything backwards! It was a creature that walked and had small teeth, yet it had a small brain and apparently no tool use (certainly no extensive tool use).

We must therefore start the other way around, with bipedalism and (at some point) with the reduction of tooth size. A number of candidates have been suggested for bipedalism. Some evolutionists have hypothesized that it may have been a direct function of the move to savannah life, and the consequent advantages in being able to stand upright in the tall grasses and look out for predators and possible objects of prey. Others point out that, although a being on two feet cannot run as fast as a being on four, it does nevertheless seem to have more stamina for extended forays, which may have been of advantage in pursuing limited food sources. And yet another evolutionist recently has linked bipedalism directly with the freeing of hands, which in turn enables a being to carry foodstuffs a great distance.

Chimpanzees are fully capable of short-range bipedal walking and a variety of hindlimb stances . . ., but because they lack the pelvic and lower limb adaptations characteristic of hominids, bipedal walking leads to rapid fatigue. . . . It appears likely that the skeletal alterations for bipedality would be under strong selection only by consistent, extended periods of upright walking and not by either occasional bipedality or upright posture. While primitive material culture does not impose this kind of selection, carrying behavior. . . does. It is likely that the need to carry significant amounts of food was a strong selection factor in favor of primitive material culture (Lovejoy, 1981, p. 345).

Although, to the nonspecialist, the shrinking of the teeth is hardly as dramatic as the move to two legs, it too has to be fitted in somewhere. (See Fig. 10.10.) Furthermore, if one is a Darwinian, one wants to steer clear of the

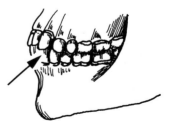

Chimpanzee mandible   **Human mandible**

Fig. 10.10
Human and chimpanzee teeth compared. Look at the difference in canines! (Adapted from an original drawing by Luba Dmytryk.)

rather Lamarckian tones of Darwin's own explanation (!), which saw tooth-reduction as a function of loss through disuse. The most likely causal candidate is a selective pressure brought on by a change of diet, possibly also connected with the move to savannah life. One suggestion, by the anthropologist Clifford Jolly (1970), tries to link tooth reduction directly with the evolution of bipedalism. He proposes that, as our ancestors moved into grasslands, they started to use grass seeds and the like as food. In such a situation, canines could be a positive burden, and selection would favor their reduction. Simultaneously, suggests Jolly, there would be pressure to keep standing, in order to gather the seed. Thus, in what was probably a kind of feedback situation, one would get the evolution of *Australopithecus*.

As can be imagined, everyone has good reasons why theirs and only theirs is the correct explanation, and why all the others will not do. The simple fact of the matter is that we shall not be able to give definitive answers until the fossil record beyond four million years is opened up. Then, and only then, will answers start to flow. If there seems to be no connection between the coming of bipedalism and tooth reduction, then presumably Jolly's suggestion must go.

Moving on from the arrival of *Australopithecus afarensis* and down through the *Homo* line, the reasons for distinctively human evolution do seem a little clearer. With the hands freed, for whatever reason, the way is open for an advanced use of tools, especially sticks and stones — something that occurs only in a relatively rudimentary form in other primates. Sophisticated tool use has incredibly great adaptive advantages, especially for the kind of creature that we are now considering. Food can be rooted out more efficiently, and animals can be chopped up. Probably at the earlier points we are dealing less with hunters and more with scavengers; but, even for scavengers, tools are valuable. Something like a hippopotamus is as inaccessible dead as it is alive, without crude stone cutting implements. No doubt, in later points of human evolution, tools could be and were used as weapons, either in attack or defense.

In Darwinian evolution, when two things occur together, as often as not, one does not have simple cause and effect. Rather, one has a reciprocal feedback process, with improvement in one thing leading to improvement in the other and vice versa. This was probably the case for the increase and development in human tool making and use, and for the growth of the brain with the corresponding rise in intelligence. The creature that was more intelligent made more efficient tools, which led to more favorable prospects of survival and reproduction. There was then a strong selective pressure back to increased abilities at tool making, and to yet higher intelligence. Certainly this fits the pattern that we find in the fossil record. *Homo erectus* is ahead of *H. habilis*, in both brain size and tool use, which latter in turn apparently was ahead of its ancestors.

With this increase in brain size in what was already a bipedal creature, it is probably appropriate to start thinking of other distinctive human features, particularly our slow individual development and our sociosexual structures and characteristics. It may indeed be the case that these, what many of us would think of as the most human of all features, are almost a by-product of the move to bipedalism and increasing brain size. Why should this be so? Simply because an animal adapted to an upright stance, just cannot give birth to large babies. Even though the female pelvis did broaden in response to this need, there was an upper limit beyond which it could not go.

Hence, because of this impasse, there was an evolutionary move toward minimizing development before birth and maximizing it after birth. In short, in hominids offspring were born needing more and more attention after birth. This meant that females had to give a great deal of time and effort to their helpless children, and that we all take a long time to mature. Quite possibly this led to more and more of a division of labor between the sexes: men scavenging and hunting, especially animals, and females child-rearing and looking for vegetable food.

It is plausible to suggest also that this move by hominids toward offspring requiring atypically large amounts of care simultaneously set up selective pressures which would end with males being involved in child care. Like the birds, humans require special amounts of child care; like the birds, human males are involved in child care. Perhaps the causal sequences are the same! And, completing the story, no doubt somewhere along the line, the various selective pressures came together to bring about the evolution of the peculiarly human sexual behavior. Males and females copulate the whole year around, rather than restricting such behavior to times when the female is in heat and ready for fertilization. This is an awfully big waste in energy, if there is no good reason. However, continuous copulation helps to cement bonds between male and female. Thus, both sexes cooperate on the needs and demands of survival and reproduction; jointly they supply food and help with child care, and so forth.

If pair bonding was fundamental and crucial to early hominid reproductive strategy, the anatomical characters that could reinforce pair bonds would also be under strong positive selection. Thus the body and facial hair, distinctive somatotype, the conspicuous penis of human males, and the prominent and permanently enlarged mammae of human females are not surprising (Lovejoy, 1981, p. 346).

It may also be that bonding plays some important role in helping to reduce intragroup strife. If males were frequently off foraging, away from the females, having a special mate could reduce the tensions and fighting that such absences could otherwise cause. Obviously, this is all very much bound up with the male being involved in child care. It is not in his evolutionary interests to help raise children, if he cannot be sure that his mate is faithful.

Enough is enough! We have already skated onto very thin ice. Before we fall through, let us stop, with the arrival of something at least vaguely human!

I am sure that some of the causes suggested so far in this section will stand the test of time; I am equally sure that some will not! But, notwithstanding all the reservations that one must make, my own feeling is that the general causal picture is starting to emerge from the mists of the past. We must hope that further fossil discoveries will help fill out the picture.

The same should also be true of more detailed studies of the behavior of today's apes, and of ever more refined methods of extracting information from the pertinent objects we do presently have. One potentially exciting area involves ways of inferring the nature of brains from castes of fossil skulls. Another involves detailed microscopic studies of teeth, to infer foodstuffs and eating habits. Of course, there will undoubtedly always be argument about all of the exact causal forces that led to the evolution of *Homo sapiens* (particularly about such things as speech), which are at least one step removed from the fossil record. But, perhaps instead of regretting the inevitable areas of ignorance and speculation, we should give thanks that we know as much as we do.

We come of age

Let us therefore now turn our attention from our past towards our present. Around 40,000 years ago, representatives of our own subspecies *Homo sapiens sapiens* appeared in Europe. They were responsible for the "upper Paleolithic culture," and with them we start to get the explosion up from primitive tools toward today's fantastically sophisticated human culture. We find more subtle instruments, careful cooperation in hunting, art and elaborate concern with the dead. (There is some evidence that Neanderthal man, 100,000 years ago, cared about his dead, and perhaps had some cult of animals, especially bears). Then, around 10,000 years ago, we get the invention of agriculture; we get the change of many peoples from hunting and gathering to this far more efficient method of food production, and, as a consequence, we get increases in human numbers and population densities. The Malthusian explosion was well under way, and man was on the course towards Beethoven's ninth symphony, Auschwitz, and walking on the moon.

But, stop a moment! How can we possibly let such a list as this pass by without comment? How can the same being soar to such incredible heights and plunge to such abysmal depths? We pride ourselves on being a unique species, distinguishable from the brutes by our culture: our laws, our institutions, our religions, our artifacts, and much, much more. How is it that we are able to do all of this? How is it that we cannot do other things, like eliminating strife and prejudice and poverty? Is it the case that, in looking at the human present, we should still have one eye turned behind, looking at the human past? Can important clues to human behavior and achievements, triumphs and failures, be found in the legacy of our simian ancestry? We have seen that, biologically, in many respects we are like our living ape relatives. Do the similarities go much deeper into that which we think makes us unique? It is to this all-important question that we must turn next.

Chapter 11
Human Sociobiology

Charles Darwin had little doubt that modern man — in his behavior, in his emotions, in his social attitudes — is very much a product of his evolutionary past. But, moving on from Darwin, we have the already mentioned rise of the social sciences. And, as can be imagined, an enterprise that denied the importance of evolution for the brutes was not about to allow it for man! Hence, there grew up a powerful ideology, denying almost entirely the relevance of biological thought to human social behavior. Even those influential figures who indeed thought human biology important tended to have their work "revised" by their followers to bring them into line. Freud, for instance, always stressed that biology influences human behavior — sometimes entirely determining it — but many post-Freudians labored to show that this was an inessential, removable part of his position. (See, for instance, Bieber et al., 1962. The definitive work on Freud's biological roots is Sulloway, 1979.)

It is true that a number of thinkers, particularly anthropologists, have turned to evolutionism to guide their theorizing about cultural change. But, it has always been emphasized that what they seek from biology is analogical insight, not directly applicable theory. Man as an animal is taken as a tabula rasa, and indeed analogies have been sought more in Lamarckism than Darwinism (Sahlins and Service, 1960). It is true also that, from time to time, some people have argued vigorously that humans, in their behavior, are but partially transformed apes. But, until recently, such arguments on the subject have tended to fall into the semi-popular, "blood lust" genre. They have veered toward speculation and sensationalism, rather than toward informed opinion (e.g., Ardrey, 1961).

However, in the past decade, things have changed drastically. We know full well that Darwinism now has entirely revitalized the study of animal social behavior. Perhaps, expectedly, the explosive growth of this new subject of "sociobiology" has made itself felt on studies of our own species. We find now that many biologists, joined by an increasing number of social scientists, openly endorse Darwin's own stance towards *Homo sapiens*. They argue strongly that the only way to understand human beings, referring here particularly to human beings as social entities, is as products of our evolutionary past. And, as good Darwinians, an evolutionary understanding of human social behavior is taken to imply an understanding in terms of our genes, as fashioned in the long evolutionary process by natural selection.

It is this new, or revitalized, movement that I intend to study now — the human dimension to the neo-Darwinian discipline of sociobiology.

The biology in society

If one were an alien from another world, I imagine the one thing that would strike most forcibly in looking at human societies — virtually any human society — would be the diversity within them. Even in those countries that supposedly have a strong commitment to equality, for example Russia and China, one finds that different people do different things, play different roles, get different rewards, and have different statuses. Some people lead, some people follow; some people teach, some people learn; some people work, some people play; some people make lots of money, some people do not; some people cure the sick, some people are adminstrators. In some societies, like Feudal Europe and nineteenth-century India, people's relative positions are made very explicit; in other societies, less so. But differences always exist. Think for a moment of Christianity, with its powerful message about the ultimate equal worth of every human being, and then think of the hierarchy of the Catholic Church.

Why should there be these differences? Most sociologists would argue that it is all simply a matter of nongenetic culture. Some people are born in more favorable circumstances than others, some encounter environmental factors that spur them to greater or lesser effort, some are lucky and some unlucky, and so forth. Now, the sociobiologists certainly do not want to deny the importance of any of these factors. Indeed, at one point E. O. Wilson (1975a), the leading spokesman for human as well as animal sociobiology, goes so far as to say that "the genes have surrendered most of their sovereignty." Nevertheless, the sociobiologists feel that, perhaps at a distance, people's different genetic constellations cannot be discounted as pertinent causal factors, in determining social status and the like. There are probably genes influencing people's general intellectual abilities — the extent to which they can or cannot puzzle out different abstract and concrete problems. Similarly, there will be genes influencing such factors as drive, tenacity, extroversion and introversion, innovativeness, and all the other personal elements that contribute to one's rise or fall within society.

This is not to say exactly how the genes influence makeup or performance in society. There is certainly no direct one-to-one correspondence between genes and social role. There is not, for instance, a single gene that makes one person a doctor, and another gene that makes another person an administrator. "Even so, the influence of genetic factors toward the assumption of certain *broad* roles cannot be discounted" (Wilson, 1975a, p. 555, his italics). In a sense, therefore, the position of the sociobiologists is very much like that of the social scientists themselves. First-born children tend to be high achievers. This is not to say that every first-born is a high achiever, or that no later-born children are high achievers. Rather, the social scientist would suggest that there is a broad causal correlation between the environmental circumstances and one's social fate. The sociobiologists suggest that the same is also probably true of the influence of the genes.

Apart from diversity, another noteworthy factor about any human society is its members' fear and mistrust of outsiders. This applies whether one is speaking of foreigners or of distinctive minorities within the overall population, like Jews, or blacks, or homosexuals. People outside the fold are the "spicks," "wops," "yids," "niggers," "fags" — the terms speak for themselves. One must not exaggerate. As remarked earlier, humans show a lot less aggression and hostility than many species of animal. Nevertheless, like other animals, we do tend to be wary of, and unfriendly toward, strangers and others who are "different." And again, the sociobiologists see a genetic foundation. Xenophobia (fear of strangers) "has been documented in virtually every group of animals displaying higher forms of social organization" (Wilson, 1975a, p. 249).

Moreover, it is suggested that these attitudes were preserved and strengthened by selection in our recent evolutionary past. The greatest threat to man's ancestors were other groups of hominids, striving for the same territories and foods. Conversely, however, there would be pressure to cooperate *within* small groups. As another articulate sociobiologist, Richard D. Alexander, has written: "I suggest that, at an early stage, predators became chiefly responsible for forcing men to live in groups, and that those predators were not only other species but larger, stronger groups of men" (Alexander, 1971, p. 116).

Such broad cultural phenomena as religion, art, and morality are also related to biology. For instance, approvingly, Wilson quotes the anthropologist Robin Fox, who poses the question of what would happen were a group of children raised in isolation, insulated from human culture.

If our new Adam and Eve could survive and breed — still in total isolation from any cultural influences — then eventually they would produce a society which would have laws about property, rules about incest and marriage, customs of taboo and avoidance, methods of settling disputes with a minimum of bloodshed, beliefs about the supernatural and practices relating to it, a system of social status and methods of indicating it (Wilson, 1975a, p. 560).

As we know, Darwin himself suggested that moral behavior was perhaps caused and maintained by reciprocal altruism: "You scratch my back, and I'll scratch yours." The only change that the sociobiologists make is to bring Darwin up to date, casting the hypothesis in terms of selection working on the genes. Those of our ancestral species whose genes predisposed them to help others got help in return, and thus survived and reproduced. The unfriendly species members went without help, and thus did not survive and reproduce. As one of the more provocative writers on the subject, Robert L. Trivers, puts matters: "Given the universal and nearly daily practice of reciprocal altruism among humans today, it is reasonable to assume that it has been an important factor in recent human evolution and that the underlying emotional dispositions affecting altruistic behaviour have important genetic components" (Trivers, 1971, p. 48).

Finally, let us bring to an end our brief survey of the supposed sociobiology of humans by turning to individual human beings and to their personal behavior. Here, sociobiologists make their strongest and, they believe, best justified claims. First, there is the matter of sex. There are two sexes, and, as everyone acknowledges, within virtually every society we see males and females playing different roles. Males tend to be more promiscuous, more dominant, and generally the powers in society. Females tend to be more reserved sexually, more "domestic," and generally controlled by males. Feminists and social scientists argue that these differences are a function of males having and holding the reins of power; they are not reflective of innate differences. Theoretically, with a fairly straightforward relaxation of the status quo, one could turn everything around. The sociobiologists argue otherwise.

The building block of nearly all human societies is the nuclear family. The populace of an American industrial city, no less than a band of hunter-gatherers in the Australian desert, is organized around this unit. . . . During the day the women and children remain in the residential area while the men forage for game or its symbolic equivalent in the form of barter and money. The males cooperate in bands to hunt or deal with neighboring groups. . . . Sexual bonds are carefully contracted in observance with tribal customs and are intended to be permanent. Polygamy, either covert or explicitly sanctioned by custom, is practiced predominantly by the males (Wilson, 1975a, p. 554).

And all of this goes back to our genes, as selected during the evolutionary path up to *Homo sapiens.* It is not to say that there is no overlap between males and females. There is. Nor is it to deny that, through careful (and perhaps extremely artificial) environmental manipulation, one might be able to make males and females more similar in emotions, attitudes, behaviors, and achievements. One could. It is to say that, as we are, our biology makes us as different psychologically and behaviorally, as it does physically and physiologically. On average, males are bigger than females, because of the genes. On average, males are more dominant than females, because of the genes.

The sociobiologists believe that biology also extends down through the family. Much human cooperation is seen as a function of kin selection, just as it is seen as a function of kin selection in, say, the bird world. Supposedly, close relatives aid and support each other, insofar as this rebounds to personal genetic advantage. But, where the returns are absent, cooperation fails.

Moreover, we can expect conflict within the family when genetic interests clash: "Conflict during socialization need not be viewed solely as conflict between the culture of the parent and the biology of the child; it can also be viewed as conflict between the biology of the parent and the biology of the child" (Trivers, 1974).

One particular thing about family life attracts the attention of sociobiologists, as indeed it has attracted the attention of social scientists before them. If life is a battle for reproduction, with evolutionary success going to the winner, one might anticipate that sex would go on whenever and wherever it could. And yet, within the family sex is curiously absent, except between the parental partners. Parents and children, brothers and sisters, uncles and nieces, and other close relatives, rarely engage in sex. Moreover, virtually every society has and respects such barriers against "incest." The practice is looked upon with emotions ranging from incomprehension to revulsion.

Why should this be so? Following in the footsteps of the nineteenth-century anthropologist Edward Westermarck (1891), the sociobiologists argue simply that incest barriers are rooted in human biology: those of our ancestors who did not copulate with close kin were fitter than those who did. Inbreeding leads to all kinds of genetic ailments, because deleterious recessive genes are thus made homozygous and so affect the phenotype. Hence, in the past, there was selective pressure against intrafamilial intercourse, and hence today, for genetic reasons, we simply do not feel the desire to copulate with relatives.

By now you will be getting the general picture of our species that the sociobiologists try to paint. I am not denying of course that there are those students of animal behavior who prefer not to touch on the human realm. But, it is true to say that the position just sketched is representative of many biologists, who believe that only by application of Darwinian principles to human social behavior can we hope to reach a full understanding of our own true nature.

Moreover, let me emphasize a point to which I shall be returning. The sociobiologists think that what they have to say applies to *all* societies and to *all* humans. We in the Western world may be farther from the exposed elements than the Tierra del Fuegan; but biology counts for us all. In this total commitment, one can say without exaggeration that the human sociobiologists are the most Darwinian of Darwinians.

The question of evidence: The broad claims

Just about every claim made in the name of human sociobiology has been subjected to withering criticism. Many of the objections have centered on what is perceived as an objectionable right-wing ideology permeating the whole enterprise. I shall defer until later (Chapter 12) examination of these charges. Here, I want to move straight to what surely is the most crucial question one can ask about human sociobiology. Does the enterprise bear any resemblance to the true state of affairs, or is it about as solidly grounded in reality as spiritualism and astrology, and possessing the same seductive aura to the gullible?

I am afraid that one starts the response on a rather negative note. It must be conceded that, with respect to most of the broader claims about societal functioning, much of the discussion is very hypothetical! There is, for instance, absolutely nothing that backs up the speculations about the links between genes and religion. Again, although Trivers explores in some detail his supposed links between genes and morality, showing that the kinds of consequences do obtain that one would expect were the genes at work, he has to concede that he has no direct evidence of such genes.

Sadly, not much is offered on the much-touted subject of xenophobia. It is true that Wilson makes reference to animals that supposedly reflect human behavior in disliking strangers and outsiders, the implication being that since animal behavior is innate, so also is human behavior. But, there are certainly no rigorous studies showing that human behavior and animal behavior in this respect are so similar, that it simply is not plausible to think they have different causes. Nor are we shown that all human behavior is so similar, that one genetic mechanism (if such a mechanism there be) will suffice. Really, at most, we get some ideas and not a great deal more.

What about the whole question of social roles and presumed genetic etiologies? The key issue of the supposed links between the genes and intelligence is highly controversial. For every argument in favor of such links, one can find another argument against such links, not to mention an accompanying argument to the effect that there is no such thing as intelligence anyway! One is reminded of the man accused of a crime who said that he didn't do it, and, even if he did, he's very sorry. (See Block and Dworkin, 1974.) On balance, there is probably now sufficient positive evidence to validate a definite genetic factor in those things we normally associate with intelligence: mathematical ability and so forth (Ruse, 1979b). There are, for instance, some striking adoption studies, showing that adopted children veer more toward the abilities of their biological parents (same genes, different environment) than toward the abilities of their adoptive parents (different genes, same environment). It is hard to see how these correlations could have come about, were the genes not making some sort of causal input (Munsinger, 1975a, b). (See Fig. 11.1.)

However, even though this obviously counts as positive evidence for the sociobiologist — a random sample of university professors presumably would differ in pertinent respects from a random sample of farm laborers — it hardly makes the whole case. As Wilson admits, there are many other factors influencing one's social role, and there is certainly not much by way of genetic information on these. Perhaps the most common form of mental illness is schizophrenia, and this certainly has a genetic component. Identical twins (i.e., people with the same genotype) are far more likely to be alike with respect to schizophrenia than are nonidentical twins (i.e., people with genotypes no closer than those of ordinary siblings). But, even though it is true

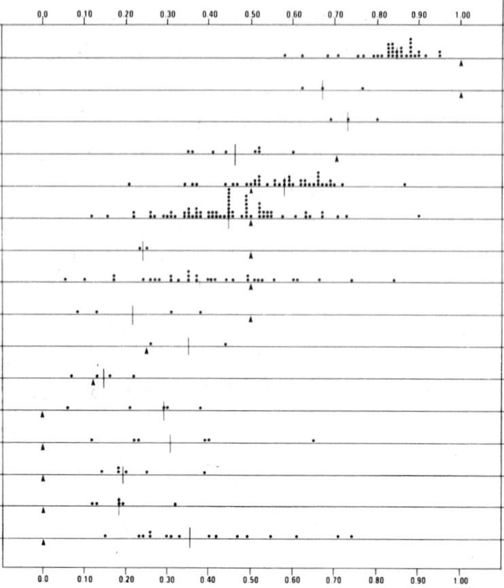

	NO OF CORREL ATIONS	NO OF PAIRINGS	MEDIAN CORREL ATION	WEIGHTED AVER AGE	x² (d f)	x²/d f
MONOZYGOTIC TWINS REARED TOGETHER	34	4672	85	86	81.29 (33)	2.46
MONOZYGOTIC TWINS REARED APART	3	65	67	72	0.92 (2)	0.46
MIDPARENT-MIDOFFSPRING REARED TOGETHER	3	410	73	72	2.66 (2)	1.33
MIDPARENT-OFFSPRING REARED TOGETHER	8	992	475	50	8.11 (7)	1.16
DIZYGOTIC TWINS REARED TOGETHER	41	5546	58	60	94.5 (40)	2.36
SIBLINGS REARED TOGETHER	69	26,473	45	47	403.6 (64)	6.31
SIBLINGS REARED APART	2	203	24	24	.02 (1)	.02
SINGLE PARENT-OFFSPRING REARED TOGETHER	32	8433	385	42	211.0 (31)	6.81
SINGLE PARENT-OFFSPRING REARED APART	4	814	22	22	9.61 (3)	3.20
HALF-SIBLINGS	2	200	35	31	1.55 (1)	1.55
COUSINS	4	1,176	145	15	1.02 (2)	0.51
NON BIOLOGICAL SIBLING PAIRS (ADOPTED/NATURAL PAIRINGS)	5	345	29	29	1.93 (4)	0.48
NON BIOLOGICAL SIBLING PAIRS (ADOPTED/ADOPTED PAIRINGS)	6	369	31	34	10.5 (5)	2.10
ADOPTING MIDPARENT-OFFSPRING	6	758	19	24	6.8 (5)	1.36
ADOPTING PARENT-OFFSPRING	6	1397	18	19	6.64 (5)	1.33
ASSORTATIVE MATING	16	3817	365	33	96.1 (15)	6.41

Fig. 11.1

This chart shows, at a glance, results of studies on possible IQ correlations between relatives. The vertical bars show the median correlations in each study, and the arrows, the correlations one would expect were IQ simply a direct function of the genes. It would seem that the genes do indeed have some effect on IQ, although clearly not total effect. (Taken by permission from T. J. Bouchard and M. McGue, (1981). Familial studies of intelligence: a review. *Science,* 212, 1055-1058.)

that schizophrenics tend to have lower status jobs in society, no one could seriously suggest that this is a major reason why people play different roles. Apart from anything else, there simply are not enough schizophrenics to make that kind of difference. One needs to suppose all sorts of other factors at work also influencing role behavior and achievement.

Overall therefore, looking at the broad claims made by the socio-biologists, they have really not yet given us too much more than speculation. We certainly do not have anything approaching a definitively established case. We have some interesting and suggestive hints, particularly with respect to social roles, but there is no solid proof. However, having now looked at the weaker side and certainly having shown how far we are from successful execution of the program, let me turn to the area where sociobiologists themselves feel that they are making some solid advances. I refer to the more individual sphere of human social behavior, particularly the domain of sex and the family. Is there enough promise here to justify confidence in the general human sociobiologist picture? I shall pick out two items to look at in depth: male/female sexual differences and incest barriers. If the sociobiologists make some progress on these items, then we should continue to take them seriously; otherwise, not.

The question of evidence: Sexuality

We start with sex and with the differences between male and female. The sociobiologists argue that there is a genetic foundation to many of the behavioral and attitudinal differences that we see distinguishing males and females, both in our own society and in others, including preindustrial, preliterate groups. Is this so? Since many different pieces of evidence are offered in support of the sociobiological claim, in order to structure discussion, let us follow the path of Darwin. When he was asked why one should accept his theory, he argued that there are three kinds of evidence: direct, analogical, and indirect.

What *direct evidence* does the sociobiologist offer for the claims about sex? There are at least three things. First, the sociobiologist points out that, at a physiological level, humans fit the required pattern for sex differences as closely as any animal. The key to the sociobiology of sex is that males and females have different reproductive "strategies." Males can inseminate many females, behaviorally therefore they should be directed to this; females bear but a few offspring, and behaviorally they should be directed to this. Humans satisfy the antecedents, therefore the consequents should follow. (See especially Wilson, 1978, Chapter 6)

Second, not only do we find sex differences actually manifested in societies, but we find that deliberate efforts to eliminate them tend to fail. This suggests that the differences are more than just "cultural." The Israeli kibbutz, for instance, was supposed to eliminate male/female roles. What we find, however, is that, in the kibbutz, such roles have crept (nay marched) right back in! Males do the heavy work and make the decisions. Women cook, launder, and look after babies. Moreover, before one rushes in and starts talking about male "power plays" and the like (although this very explanation confirms sociobiology rather than refutes it), note that it was females who led the drive to be back with their children, and so on. The genetic influence was not to be suppressed (van den Berghe, 1979, pp. 71–72).

Third, in direct support of the sociobiology of sex, there is the physiological evidence that aggression and other kinds of behavior generally associated with one sex rather than the other are linked to hormonal levels. In particular, if the testosterone level is high at the time of hypothalamus development (3–6 months of fetal life), one gets male type behavior; and not otherwise. And, it is males and males alone who typically do get the pertinent high testosterone levels. On those rare occasions when testosterone levels are altered — female fetuses get high levels and male fetuses get low levels — we get significant switches in male/female behavior and expectations. (See Fig. 11.2.) There is certainly no question of turning boys into girls, or vice versa, but overall Wilson feels able to seize on such findings and to conclude that, by birth, "the twig is bent a little." Clearly, completing his explanation, Wilson believes that the testosterone levels are controlled by the genotypes, and that these in turn have been selected and maintained because of their Darwinian value. (See also Money and Ehrhardt, 1972.)

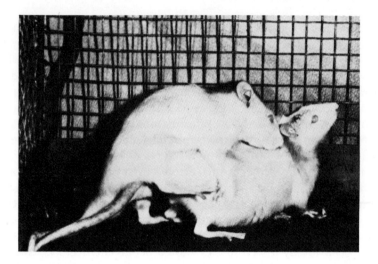

Fig. 11.2
Thanks to hormonal manipulation, what we have here is a female mounting a receptive male. How far examples like this can be used to throw analogical light on human attitudes and behavior is obviously a moot point. (Taken by permission from G. Dörner (1976), *Hormones and Brain Differentiation,* Amsterdam: Elsevier.)

Putting together the three items just given, how should one rate the direct evidence for the sociobiology of sex? A strong case has been made, even though all counterargument is hardly closed. The evidence of the kibbutz is somewhat tenuous. Even in nonreligious kibbutzim, one wonders if the strong male orientation of the Jewish religion is entirely without effect. Are none of the members affected by the attitudes of fellow Jews? Again, although impressive, the natural experiments on testosterone levels are not that many. Certainly some people have challenged their sweeping application. But for all that, particularly given the extent to which our physiology does fit the pattern, there is good direct evidence for the sociobiological case.

We move next to *analogy*. To what extent can we argue from animal sexual behavior to human sexual behavior? I am afraid that the answer seems to be: "not very much!" In experiments, one can change animal behavior back and forth on the male-female spectrum by appropriate hormonal manipulation, particularly that involving the sex hormones and the hypothalamus. What this proves about humans, arguing from the case of rats, is a moot point, given the great hormonal differences between humans and rats. Perhaps more suggestive is the fact that higher primates similarly respond to such manipulation. Appropriately treated females are far rougher and more aggressive than untreated females. They do the sorts of things more usually typical of male monkeys and apes. This certainly fits in with expectations for human sexuality, although obviously no proof can be attempted. And the same seems true of the analogies that can be drawn with animals in a natural, wild state. Generally, in the higher primates, males are more dominant and aggressive than females. But, in many respects, there are so many gaps in our knowledge, and so many possible exceptions, that at this point one cannot really say more than that humans fit the general pattern. (See Dörner, 1976; Goy and Phoenix, 1972.)

We come third to the *indirect evidence* for the sociobiology of sex. Here, we seek confirmed predictions from the central hypotheses about sex. Some of the most interesting and impressive work pertinent to this quest comes from anthropologists studying power and sex in preliterate societies. Do not be misled. No one would want to claim that preliterate societies are culture-free. They certainly are not. However, such societies almost necessarily tend to be closer to the environment than most. Consequently there is more scope for the operation and influence of selective forces, undistorted by environmental effects. Hence, here, if anywhere, we expect to find evidence for the truth of human sociobiology. In particular, since theory predicts that all men try to maximize their reproduction, in preliterate societies we might expect to find the clearest evidence that powerful men reproduce more than most.

One anthropologist who tested this prediction was Napoleon Chagnon, who studied certain Indian tribes in southern Venezuela, the Yanomamö. The prediction was dramatically confirmed, as can be seen in Table 11.1 (Chagnon, 1980, p. 553).

Marital and reproductive performance of headmen compared to other males 35 years old or older.

Status of Male	Number	Wives	Average Number of Wives	Offspring per Wife	Mean Number of Offspring
Headmen	20	71	3.6 ± 1.9	2.4 ± 2.5	8.6 ± 4.6
Nonheadmen	108	258	2.4 ± 1.4	1.7 ± 2.0	4.2 ± 3.4
			$p = .007$	$p = .238$	$p > .001$

Table 11.1
The Yanomamö Indians: Marital and reproductive performance of headmen compared to other males 35 years old or older. (Adapted from N. Chagnon, (1980). Kin-selection theory, kinship, marriage and fitness among the Yanomamö Indians. In G. W. Barlow and J. Silverberg eds. *Sociobiology: Beyond Nature/Nurture?* Boulder: Westview, 545-572.)

It is clear that power in a Yanomamö village translates into having more offspring than average. Note, also, that it is in a female's genetic interests to be the wife of a headman, as she too will then have more children than average.

One could not hope to have a nicer case of prediction and successful confirmation. Furthermore, this is just one study of a growing number. For instance, relatedly, a number of people are working on marriage customs in preliterate and more advanced societies. It does not take much imagination to see that human sociobiology leads one to expect an asymmetry. Whereas polygyny (one man, multiple wives) should be common, polyandry (one woman, multiple husbands) should be very rare, and probably directly linked to abnormal circumstances. And again, the predictions hold! No less than 85 percent of human societies allow and encourage polygyny; less than 1/2 percent of human societies contain polyandrous relationships, and these tend to be cases (like the Eskimos) where the environment makes it very difficult for one unaided man to support a wife (van den Berghe, 1979; Alexander, 1979).

I could go on giving examples of the indirect evidence for the sociobiology of sex, but the case is made. No one would want to contend that this area of human sociobiology is completed. However, taking all of the indirect evidence into account and adding to it now the direct and even the analogical evidence, I would suggest that this is one point in human sociobiology, where work has moved well beyond the hypothetical and into the plausible.

The question of evidence: Incest barriers

The sociobiologists claim to give us all sorts of insights into the family, showing how the various genetic relationships lead to familiar and universal behavioral patterns. What sort of evidence do they offer? Do they lay themselves open to check? Let us turn to our test case, namely the matter of incest, again seeking direct evidence, analogical evidence, and indirect evidence. Do incest barriers have a genetic foundation?

Interpreting the notion of *direct evidence* as broadly as possible, there are at least three items that sociobiologists forward in support of their position. First, there is the evidence for the deleterious effects of close inbreeding, which is very strong indeed. Study after study shows that when close relatives have offspring, the proportion of deformed and otherwise handicapped children is very high indeed (e.g., Adams and Neel, 1967) Hence the selection pressures toward incest barriers will be correspondingly high. (Charles Darwin married his first cousin, Emma Wedgewood, and one of their children was feebleminded. It has been suggested that this could have been a result of inbreeding.)

Second, there is the fact that even the most grotesque and abnormal of human societies respect incest barriers. Since human variability is something one associates with environmental causes, whereas human constancy points to genetic causes, the sociobiologists again think they have a clue hinting at the genetic basis of incest barriers. Consider the unbelievably revolting Kogu cannibals of New Guinea.

Kogu women are routinely gang-raped, before and after death — dismembered alive limb by limb and eaten. Sick relatives and acquaintances are killed so that their meat can be enjoyed before it is wasted away by disease. A special culinary delicacy is putrid human meat cooked with its maggots (van den Berghe, 1979, p. 39).

As the anthropologist Pierre van den Berghe wryly observes: "The Kogu are clearly not the sort of chaps most people in most cultures would want their daughters to marry." And yet, they have incest barriers. It is considered terribly bad form to copulate with or eat close relatives. Surely, argue the sociobiologists, were incest all a matter of culture, these savages would observe no such barriers. Since they do, there must be a genetic basis to incest barriers.

Third, once again the kibbutz provides a natural experiment (Shepher, 1979). Children of the kibbutz are brought up together, regardless of blood relationship. Yet, it is a very well-documented fact that those who were reared in one group, particularly those reared together between the ages of three and seven, feel no sexual attractions towards each other, despite very close emotional attachments. And this occurs, even though there are neither explicit nor implicit barriers to such sexual attachments. The sociobiologists argue, therefore, that this situation supports their case. The kibbutz fools the genes, who are unable to distinguish between social siblings and biological siblings. Because of one's biological heritage, incest barriers go up where close biological links might be expected — even though, in some special cases, no such links actually exist!

Reserving comment on some traditional objections which are inevitably raised against putative biological foundations of incest barriers, let me say simply that direct evidence for the sociobiological case on incest barriers is most impressive. Given the diversities in societies, were there no genetic causes, it is most improbable that such barriers would hold universally. Furthermore, the evidence of the kibbutz — backed incidentally by similar evidence from similar cases — is a powerful support of the sociobiological case.

What about the analogical evidence? I have already expressed my general feeling about the value of analogical arguments from animals to humans. At most, they are a source of insight rather than definitive justification. However, having recognized the restricted scope of analogy, it is worth pointing out that more and more studies show phenomena in the animal world that very closely parallel human incest barriers. The higher apes, for instance, rarely or never couple with close relatives, and the same apparently holds as one goes down the scale.

Turning third to *indirect evidence,* as in the case of sexuality, once again the sociobiologists use their central hypotheses to throw light on common anthropological phenomenon, suggesting that if one adopts their position, then certain important predictions can be made, tested, and confirmed (Alexander, 1979). In this particular case of incest, they believe their general approach helps one to understand the distinction that is frequently drawn in societies between different kinds of cousins, together with the reasons for the marriage customs and prohibitions based on the distinction.

Even the distinction may be a little strange to some readers, so let me explain both it and the problem which is at issue. In our own society, a cousin is a cousin is a cousin. But, many societies make a clear distinction between two kinds of cousin. On the one hand, one has *parallel* cousins: cousins whose related parents are siblings of the same sex. On the other hand, one has *cross* cousins: cousins whose related parents are siblings of the opposite sex. The first question that arises is: "Why is this distinction made?" Then, relatedly, one has the fact that societies that make the distinction usually go on to prohibit parallel cousin marriages. (See Fig. 11.3.) Therefore, one has the secondary question: "Why should there not be a similar ban on cross-cousin marriages?"

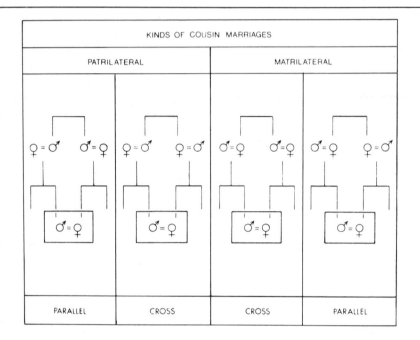

Fig. 11.3
The four possible kinds of cousin marriages: Often cross-cousin marriages are permitted or even encouraged, whereas parallel-cousin marriages are barred. Sociobiologists argue that the asymmetry may have a genetic foundation. (Adapted by permission from R. D. Alexander, (1979). *Darwinism and Human Affairs,* Seattle: University of Washington Press.)

Prima facie one has here a counterexample to the sociobiological position. The degree of relatedness is the same between both parallel and cross cousins (12-1/2 percent). Hence, it would seem that there can be no biological basis to the asymmetrical treatment of cousin marriage; the causes must be found in culture. The sociobiologists argue, however, that the asymmetry does not disprove their case. Rather, it confirms it, triumphantly! They suggest that the parallel/cross distinction could be a manifestation of incest avoidance, if it turns out that parallel cousins might systematically be more closely related than cross cousins. How could this be? Most obviously, if mothers had the same husband, or if fathers had the same wife! In other words, if parallel cousins were also possible half-siblings, then we would have a biological case for distinguishing parallel and cross cousins. And, obviously, we would have a case for prohibiting marriages between the former.

Under what societal situations might we expect to find parallel cousins also being half siblings? The most probable occurrence would be in a society that practiced sororal polygyny, that is where sisters married the same man. Given the male's objection to sharing a mate, other potential causes are far less likely. So what do we find in human societies? Strong support for the sociobiologists! Where sororal polygyny is practiced, there is far more probability that parallel cousin marriage will be banned and vice versa. There is a confirmed prediction from sociobiological theorizing about incest barriers.

As before I see no reason to deny the sociobiologists their triumph. The logic of their argument differs in no way from the method of prediction and test in the physical sciences. Direct evidence, analogical evidence, and indirect evidence all point in the same direction: incest barriers have a genetic basis. But, of course, this is just the positive side to the picture. What about the supposed objections to the biology of incest? What about the Pharoahs?! Brother and sister were required to mate. How can one support biological causes promoting incest avoidance in the face of such a counterexample?

To be honest, my first reaction is to say that, if the Pharoahs are the best (or worst) that the critics can throw at the sociobiologists, then the sociobiologists have little to fear. Just think how few Pharoahs there were, compared to the rest of humankind. Most physicists would welcome such little evidence against their theories! Perhaps the easiest thing is to let the sociobiologists speak for themselves. van den Berghe writes:

There are three well-known cases of institutionalized brother-sister incest and all three are extraordinarily alike. In the Hawaiian, Incan and Egyptian royal family, the king has, at least in certain periods, been permitted or even expected to marry his sister. ... Why the exception for royalty? [The] explanation is that dynastic incest restricted the number of legitimate claimants on the most important resource in those societies, supreme political power. The possible reduction in biological fitness of one's children-nephews was more than made up for in the monopolistic retention of extraordinary resources, especially when those resources gave one access to innumerable lesser wives and concubines who, although they could not bear future kings, could certainly bear children. (van den Berghe, 1979, p. 78).

I will waste no time in detailed summation. The case for the sociobiology of incest is strong. The onus is certainly now on those who would deny biological causes to prove their case.

Limits

One cannot pretend that even two swallows make a summer, or that sex and incest make a definitive evidential case for human sociobiology. All that one can claim — certainly, all that I would want to claim — is that there is now enough evidence about some parts of human sociobiology, to warrant taking seriously the whole enterprise as a program for further scientific research.

But even if human sociobiology proved successful beyond E. O. Wilson's wildest dreams, how far it would go toward providing a full understanding of human beings is still a very open question. Perhaps the ideas on xenophobia can throw some light on the enormities of Auschwitz. Perhaps the importance of tools in human evolution tells us something about present-day technological triumphs, like walking on the moon. I have seen nothing yet that even scratches at an explanation of how a transformed ape could produce the magnificence of Beethoven's choral symphony.

In short, this all rather suggests that, whatever the success of human sociobiology, there will still be plenty of room for other students of that fascinating, fractious organism: *Homo sapiens*. Whether we be humanists or scientists, there is place for us all as we try to understand ourselves. And in partial confirmation of this surmise, I intend to conclude my direct discussion of Darwinism and humankind by turning now to the interactions between Darwinism and my own subject, philosophy. I want to see if, together, we can achieve a mutually illuminating perspective on human moral behavior: a topic which has certainly engaged philosophers since the time of Socrates.

Chapter 12
Evolution and Morality

Many Victorians hated evolutionism, because they saw it as being grossly immoral — something that would undercut the social system and leave everything in a morass of animal bestiality. One who was explicit and eloquent on the subject was the Scottish self-made geologist and religious controversialist Hugh Miller (1847). He declaimed at length against all varieties of evolutionism, pointing out that, if we evolved from fish, the implication is either that fish have souls or that we have none. But, without souls, why indeed should man "square his conduct by the requirements of the moral code, farther than a law and convenient expedience may chance to demand?" (Miller, 1847, p. 14). Apparently, Miller never took seriously the thought that the spirit of his breakfast kipper might be enjoying some fishy paradise.

The Darwinians themselves, as people, went a long way toward stilling fears about the immoral implications and effects of their ideas. Had they been eighteenth-century rakes, fornicating, drinking, fighting, swearing, leading dissolute lives of total idleness, their critics would have taken gloomy satisfaction in seeing their worst fears realized. But, the Darwinians were not like this at all. In fact, to a man, they were archetypal Victorians of the most serious, earnest, and rather boring kind. They were dedicated family men with never the slightest hint of sexual impropriety. They were hard-working to the point of neurosis — day after day, they labored at their studies. And, they were complete public servants. Huxley even served on the London School Board, urging the moral value of compulsory Bible study! In the face of such paradigms, it really was not easy to keep up the claim that Darwinism leads down to hell by way of the gin tavern and the whore-house. Certainly, as the years went by, the social behavior of Darwinians aided their cause.

Nevertheless, the topics of evolutionism and ethics, the systematic bases of moral behavior, have continued to impinge and react with one another from those days to these. In one sense, this is hardly surprising. It is obvious that evolutionism, Darwinism in particular, has relevance to questions about morality. Suppose that one subscribes to some particular ethic, whether it be a religious one like that given in the Sermon on the Mount or a secular one like utilitarianism, which urges us to maximize human happiness. Unless one has some awareness of the way that the world is and works, one has no hope whatsoever of actually putting one's moral beliefs into practice.

And, this awareness must extend to biology. Take, for example, a matter that has received a great deal of attention in the press in the past ten years, "genetic counseling." This refers to the attempt to eliminate genetic diseases: for instance, by identifying defective fetuses and aborting them. Now, whatever the ultimate rights and wrongs of this practice may be, it is clear that its very existence and success depends ultimately on facts and causes of evolution. For instance, one sometimes hears suggestions that all genetic disease be eliminated by a once-and-for-all detection program. Clearly, such suggestions would not be made, if the makers were aware of their biological futility. Such phenomena as mutation are always leading to new instances of disease, and so one could never eliminate all disease for all time.

Again, one might wonder at the moral worth of a world-wide program to eliminate the sickle-cell anemia gene, if one consequence was that many more people would now suffer and die from malaria. And, generally, if one subscribes to the balance hypothesis, any proposed "eugenics" programs, aimed at making a race of genetically pure supermen, looks very suspect. Neo-Darwinian theory shows that there is so much variation in populations, and that it is held for so many adaptive reasons, that most judgments of "better" and "worse" are really rather meaningless (Ruse, 1981).

Undoubtedly, as one looks at particular cases where facts and principles of evolutionism are pertinent to ethical questions, one will encounter great complexity. As is so often the case, the right course of action will be hard to see. But, the general point seems fairly simple, and, I trust, relatively uncontroversial. However, this is only one of the ways in which Darwinism has been thought relevant to ethics, and controversy starts almost with the mention of the most notorious of the supposed connections between evolutionism and ethics. I refer, of course, to the belief that the very foundations of moral codes can be derived from the facts and causes of evolution, because these facts and causes are in themselves, morally good things! That which is good and to be cherished is that which evolves and that which brings such evolution about.

Evolutionary ethics

Even before the *Origin* was published, there were those who looked to the content of evolutionism itself, in its various forms, as something that could provide the intellectual basis for morality. Herbert Spencer (1857), the father of sociology, was one. (See Fig. 12.1.) He saw everywhere an "inherent tendency of things towards good," and "at work an essential beneficence." He approved of the struggle for existence, because in an important sense this meshed nicely with his a priori beliefs about laissez-faire economics: human

Fig. 12.1
Herbert Spencer (1820–1903).

happiness is maximized by unfettered business competition in the marketplace. And, overall, he thought the course of evolution to be a good thing, and that humans should take their cue from it.

What was the reaction of the Darwinians themselves to this line of argument? Darwin felt rather mixed emotions. As the grandson and financial beneficiary of Josiah Wedgewood, one of Britain's leading industrialists, Darwin was not about to deny the virtues of capitalism or to suggest that the struggle for existence is an unmitigated horror.

In all civilised countries man accumulates property and bequeaths it to his children. So that the children in the same country do not by any means start fair in the race for success. But this is far from an unmixed evil; for without the accumulation of capital the arts could not progress; and it is chiefly through their power that the civilised races have extended, and are now everywhere extending, their range, so as to take the place of the lower races. (Darwin, 1871, p. 169)

On the other hand, although Darwin felt very uncomfortable about the way in which such things as vaccination allow the (biologically) unfit to survive and reproduce without limit, he could not bring himself to argue that such intervention is a morally bad thing.

T. H. Huxley (1901) was much more explicit and definite in his opposition to any such evolutionary ethicizing. For him there was nothing in evolution, the struggle for existence, or natural selection that implied anything about what one ought or ought not do. Indeed, the struggle seems directly opposed to morality: "Cosmic evolution may teach us how the good and the evil tendencies of man may have come about; but, in itself, it is incompetent to furnish any better reason why what we call good is preferable to what we call evil than we had before" (T. H. Huxley, 1901, p. 80).

But, Huxley did not have the final word. It was all very well for him to produce his fancy arguments; but, what then did *he* intend to substitute for religion? Many people felt that there had to be some of world force which gives life meaning, whether the force be sacred or secular. Hence, the twentieth century has seen much effort aimed at putting ethics on an evolutionary basis, more specifically on a Darwinian basis. Of all people, T. H. Huxley's grandson, the late Julian Huxley, was one who argued in this way! One presumes that in that special corner of heaven reserved for evolutionists, debate on the subject continues with all the vigor and sparkle for which the Huxley family is justly noted.

Recently, biologicized ethics has been given a major boost, for it has found favor with some of the leading sociobiologists. At times, Wilson sounds almost Spencerian in his enthusiasm. Consider the following passage, with which Wilson opens *Sociobiology*:

The biologist, who is concerned with questions of physiology and evolutionary history, realizes that self-knowledge is constrained and shaped by the emotional control centers in the hypothalamus and limbic system of the brain. ... What, we are then compelled to ask, made the hypothalamus and limbic system? They evolved by natural selection. That simple biological statement must be pursued to explain ethics and ethical philosophers, if not epistemology and epistemologists, at all depths. (Wilson, 1975a, p. 3)

And, almost paradoxically, similarly based sentiments can be found in the writings of those who probably most abhor sociobiology! For instance, in the recent controversy about recombinant DNA work, a popular argument by the critics was that one ought not tamper with the course of evolution, simply because it is the course of evolution. What has evolved is, in itself, a good. As one critic asked rhetorically: "Have we the right to counteract, irreversibly, the evolutionary wisdom of millions of years, in order to satisfy the ambitions and the curiosity of a few scientists?" (Chargaff, 1976, p. 940.)

Biologists of all persuasions think that their theories hold the key to ultimate questions of conduct; organisms are of value simply because they are the result of evolution, and the mechanisms of evolution are worthy things. Long live natural selection!

Why evolutionary ethics is wrong

Who was right: Grandfather Huxley or Grandson Huxley? One group that one might turn to for advice is that of professional philosophers. After all, it is their job to worry about the foundations of morality (not to be confused with being particularly moral). For once, one finds near unanimity. Almost without exception, professional philosophers have dismissed evolutionary ethics with brief contempt, because supposedly it makes an invalid move, of a type first identified by the Scottish philosopher David Hume (1740). One violates the *is/ought* barrier. One goes from the way that things are, to the way that one thinks things should be. And, in the opinion of almost everyone, from professor down to first-year undergraduate, that is that. Evolutionary ethics falls into the trap that Hume identified, and that the early twentieth century philosopher G. E. Moore (1903) labeled: it commits the "naturalistic fallacy."

At the risk of sounding somewhat priggish, let me say that I never found this quick dismissal that satisfying (Ruse, 1979b). It is all-too-easy to give a dog a bad name. Why is it a fallacy to derive "ought" from "is?" The result may be surprising, but that is no good reason. We derive pretty surprising things in mathematics, but that is thought no reason to cry "fallacy." And, at the risk of sounding somewhat smug, let me report that recently a number of philosophers have been worrying about whether the naturalistic fallacy is really that fallacious (Hudson, 1970; Quinton, 1966). Expectedly, since philosophers are like scientists in wanting their Great Men to be forever without blemish, we find that, in the wake of these counterarguments, there is no shortage of voices ready to proclaim that really Hume meant the very opposite to what everyone has taken him to mean for the past 200 years!

Fortunately we can side-step the involuted arguments of philosophers and their rewritings of history. No fancy arguments or pretty names are needed to show that, whatever the true size and status of the is/ought barrier, there is indeed something awfully fishy about all efforts to derive morality from the course or causes of evolution. Any attempt to do so leads to obviously false conclusions or forces one to assume, in a circular fashion, the very conclusion one is trying to derive. A simple topical example will make the point. It seems that, after great effort, with justifiable pride, the World Health Organization has finally eradicated smallpox from natural human populations. For all intents and purposes, smallpox now joins the dinosaurs and the dodo as an extinct species. The course of evolution has obviously been changed by man. But was this an immoral act? Obviously not! The very opposite in fact. And, the same will be true of acts that eliminate TB, measles, poison ivy, and tobacco. To talk of "evolutionary wisdom" at this point is callously stupid. We judge matters by independent, moral criteria, like the promotion of happiness or conformity to the Christian ethic.

It is of course true that, as a general conservative rule, one should be careful about fooling around with the course of evolution. But, this is not because evolution in itself is a good thing. It is rather because such tampering, as often as not, leads to unhappiness, most particularly the unhappiness of humans. Using DDT was not wrong because it eliminated mosquitoes, but because it affected humans and other animals. Thus, the appeal is not to evolution per se, but to an independent morality: one that exhorts one to put human happiness above other ends, or some such thing. There is nothing sacrosanct about evolution. What is good, or what one ought to preserve or encourage, is not necessarily what has evolved or is evolving, even if this evolution is along Darwinian lines.

At this point, in order to save the general argument, one might be tempted to argue that what ought to be cherished is *human* evolution and its (Darwinian) process. Thus, apparently, one is not committed to the absurdity of giving moral worth to the continued existence of the smallpox virus. But, this move fails for at least three reasons. First, one is already now veering from a straight connection between evolution and ethics. It looks very much as if one is smuggling in as premises, other principles about the intrinsic worth of human beings and their happiness. Hence, one is caught in the kind of circularity I have just mentioned. Second, the moral worths of smallpox and measles slip right back in! There is little doubt that smallpox and measles were factors in human evolution. A major reason why so many primitive people died when confronted by the white man was that, unlike Europeans, they simply had not built up a genetic immunity to these diseases. Hence, if we are valuing human evolution, and its causes, as things in themselves, it seems that we ought to cherish these diseases. They made us what we are.

Third, countering the notion that morality can be defined in terms of human evolution, there are many aspects of people's basic biological nature that are not very morally praiseworthy. Presumably, there is some adaptive value to aggression — those humans who struck out and fought back survived and reproduced more efficiently than those that did not — but whether aggression is always an unqualified good is another matter, indeed. Both aggressor and victim can be rendered very unhappy. And, if something makes everyone unhappy, its moral value is certainly in question. Indeed, Wilson himself notes this fact, observing that, "it is possible to be unhappy and very adaptive" (Wilson, 1975a, p. 203). Need I say more?!

As yet another move to save Darwinian evolutionary ethics, one might be tempted to argue that what really counts, what is really of ultimate moral value, is that in some loose sense the human species be preserved and encouraged on its course. But, although such a sentiment has a general appeal, yet again the overall position collapses. If Darwinian evolution teaches us anything, it is that the key to success lies in reproducing as many of one's kind as one possibly can. From an evolutionary perspective therefore, what we humans ought to do is to have just about as many offspring as the world can possibly hold. But, would we really want to say that this is a morally good thing?

I would have thought a much stronger case could be made for the moral desirability of fewer people, who thereby have a higher material standard of living, and who can also have a fuller life, with respect to the arts and science and so forth. And, since this is so, it seems fairly clear that we are not deriving morality from evolution, but evaluating evolution in the light of morality. Human life is worthwhile, only under certain extrinsic conditions. (Even this argument is rather weaker than it could be, since I have left unchallenged the defense's group-selective approach to human reproduction. I cannot believe that it would be morally a good thing for some people to have many children, and for the rest of us to have none, even though this seems to be the consequence of unfettered biology.)

But, would we not want to say that the very existence of human life is a moral absolute? Whatever form it takes, and whatever numbers there are, surely we should try to preserve it? Again I agree, but again I doubt that this claim comes from Darwinian biology. Rather, it is something we impose on biology. Suppose astronomers showed us that, in a hundred years, Earth will collide with a comet, and that everyone on Earth will die a terrible, painful death. Even those who cannot accept euthanasia might agree that it is morally acceptable (if not desirable) to avoid all future reproduction. The human race may die out; but, at least, we shall avoid the pain and distress of the natural calamity. If nothing else, I am sure you will agree that, in such a case, it is debatable whether we ourselves should actively seek its end. And this being so, once again we see the failure of traditional evolutionary ethics. Evolution, even Darwinian evolution, is not the ultimate source of moral judgments.

Perhaps I can best end this discussion by giving the floor to Wilson, whom we have already encountered as one of today's proponents of Darwinian evolutionary ethics. He writes:

The moment has arrived to stress that there is a dangerous trap in sociobiology, one which can be avoided only by constant vigilance. The trap is the naturalistic fallacy of ethics, which uncritically concludes that what is, should be. The 'what is' in human nature is to a large extent the heritage of a Pleistocene hunter-gatherer existence. When any genetic bias is demonstrated, it cannot be used to justify a continuing practice in present and future societies (Wilson, 1975b, p. 50).

I am glad to find that it is not only philosophers who are capable of contradicting themselves!

The evolution of ethics and ethical relativism

At this point, you may be gripped by a sense of despair. I am supposed to be defending Darwinism; and yet, rather, I am pointing to limits to Darwinism. What kind of a defence is this?

I find myself relatively unconcerned. The failure of traditional evolutionary ethics is no limit to Darwinism. Darwinism is a scientific theory, not a metaphysical basis for morals, and that is all there is to it. Indeed, I suggest that the limitation is a strength. Beware of anything that claims to be able to explain everything. Nevertheless, having been so modest and self-effacing about Darwinism's scope, let me say that I do not really think that Darwinism has nothing of value to say about human conduct and the moral code! In fact, properly understood Darwinism will surely prove to have great relevance.

Most pertinently, it seems highly improbable that chance was responsible for so pervasive a human phenomenon as ethics and the moral capacity. Along with everything else, ethics was a product of evolution. It is true that we do not yet have direct evidence for this surmise. But, we have indeed seen suggestive hypotheses directed toward the putative evolution of morality: how it occurs and what adaptive advantages it brings. That people should be nice to relatives, giving without necessarily hoping for return, follows readily from kin selection hypotheses. And, it is easy also to see why evolution might promote the moral sense, leading us to give help for "altruistic" reasons, that is to say without conscious hope of return. Most of us perform far more efficiently, if we believe in what we are doing, than if we are consciously scheming to get the greatest returns for our actions (Alexander, 1979).

The explanation of friendliness and warmth to nonrelatives, which of course is where morality really starts to have some bite, has caused Darwinian evolutionists more trouble. As Darwin himself noted, it is all too easy to drop into group selection explanations. But, as we know, the way out was seen by Darwin himself. Cooperation between nonrelatives can be explained as a case of, what today's sociobiologists call, "reciprocal altruism" (Trivers, 1971). You help me and I will help you; but not otherwise.

One cannot pretend that, even now, we know very much about the evolution of morality. We certainly do not. However, evolutionists are past the first stage of unbridled speculation, and well into the task of analyzing actual cases, where moral and moral-like behavior is involved. Hence, it does seem reasonable to predict that Darwinism and ethics will prove to have important connexions.

Does Darwinism imply ethical relativism?

Unfortunately, at this point, the hard-line evolutionary ethicist might be tempted to return to the fray. Let us grant, our not so hypothetical critic might argue, that ethical claims cannot be justified by evolution *per se*. However, even in suggesting that moral capacities and so forth might be a product of Darwinian evolution, you undercut the very independence of ethics, for which you have argued so strenuously! Given the truth of your suggestion, we would see that ethics is no more than an illusion, brought about by what is evolutionarily expedient. It would be no objective reality. It would be simply a self-deceptive gloss on human behavior, to maximize our efficiency as gene-producing machines.

Wilson takes this line, into total moral relativism. Different people have different evolutionary interests: old and young, male and female, powerful and weak. There is simply no way of deciding between them, and, indeed, the subjectivity of morality is underlined by the fact that everyone has different explicit desires (Wilson, 1975a, p. 564). In short, it might have been better to have accepted traditional evolutionary ethics, because now we have virtually nothing. Anything goes!

Let me make three comments in reply to this argument. First, as a matter of linguistic fact, what this argument is showing, if anything, is not so much moral relativism, but really that there is no morality at all! We are being reduced to naked conflicting desires. I want the cake; you want the cake. Whosoever is stronger, or trickier, or less of a fool, gets it. That is the end of the matter. There is no morality here. No real right and wrong, whatever anyone may say.

Second, even given conflicting genetic interests, it is not really fair to say that everything is quite so relative and subjective as the preceding argument implies. Suppose that two people (say a man and a woman) have different genetic interests. This causal fact could easily mesh with the phenomenal fact that, as far as behavior and emotions are concerned, they work in loving unison (say, in raising their children). Moreover, even when people have different desires, they can share a moral code. I want the cake; you want the cake. We may both agree that we ought to give the cake to a third person, who is far hungrier than either of us.

Nor is the critic's case saved by pointing out that different societies have different moral codes, thus pointing to the relativity of ethics. Apart from the fact that sociobiology emphasizes the unity of humankind, thus hardly providing a genetic backing for such differences, there are many common patterns underlying the moral diversity of different peoples. Two societies may have quite different customs, and yet have the same fundamental moral rules. Suppose one society practices polygamy and the other monogamy. At a higher level of abstraction, one may well see that both subscribe to some such rule as: "Everyone who so wishes ought to have a reasonable opportunity to get married, compatible with environmental factors and so forth." I suggest that a great deal more argument is needed before one can conclude that societal differences justify moral relativity (Taylor, 1978).

The third point is the most important. The critic may still feel that morality is undermined, simply because morality is now shown to be a function of evolution. It has no objective reality. As Trivers (1976) pointed out, natural selection is far more powerful than any mere politician: it could be fooling all of the people all of the time. Morality could just be a farce played out by the genes to serve their own ends. However, there is an obvious tu quoque reply to this line of argument: sauce for ethics is sauce for science. Not only do we get ethics because of evolution, through organs perfected by selection, but also we get science because of evolution, through organs perfected by selection. Ethics, therefore, is no less objective, or whatever, than science. One certainly cannot point to the evolution of ethics and the moral sense, in order to downplay ethics, because the very same points apply to our claims about evolution itself, including the parts which teach us about the origins of ethics!

Nor is ethics intrinsically weaker, or more fickle, than science, and so, more at the mercy of the genes. In fact, ethical claims are far more stable than scientific claims. One can still follow Plato in ethics. One would look pretty silly following Ptolemy in science. In short, the objection fails, because the scientific premises on which the objection is based are no less subject to the objection itself than is the target of the attack, ethics! Of course, if you press me, I have to admit that, in some ultimate sense, I cannot get outside of myself and prove that ethics "really" does have an objective reality. Here, I would appeal to some sort of pragmatism. Ethics works and I believe in it. I can say no more. Nor do I feel the need to say more.

I should add that, in respects, somewhat paradoxically, the kind of position I am favoring here seems not entirely unlike that of the great German philosopher, Immanuel Kant (1929, 1949). Kant argued that our thinking and our very experience, including our moral thought and experience, are governed by certain mind-given restraints: "categories of the understanding," which imply that we can only think and reason in certain rule-bound ways. It was these restraints (today, often called "regulative principles") which lay behind Kant's famous necessary statements of science and ethics, the so-called "synthetic *a priori*". (See Körner 1955, 1960.)

Kant thought that the necessity of the synthetic *a priori* came from the fact that we can think in no other way. We must think that "2 + 2 = 4" and we must think that "To every action there is an equal and opposite reaction". If the facts seem to say otherwise, we know we have made a mistake. In a world of non-Euclidean geometry and non-Newtonian physics, I am not sure about this. But, I do believe with Kant that, in ethics, we think and evaluate according to certain mind-given rules. For us, these rules are ultimate and not capable of further justification, other than a pragmatic one; if ethics made us all dreadfully unhappy, then it would simply fail to work, because we would ignore it. Unlike Kant, I refer the origin of our ethical beliefs and constraints to our evolutionary heritage.

I feel comforted and assured that the kind of position I am endorsing has merit, because having arrived at it through philosophical argument, I find that it is consilient with biological thought on this matter. In their recent book, Lumsden and Wilson (1981) have argued that culture is strongly governed by what they call "epigenetic rules". These are regularities during growth that channel "the development of an anatomical, physiological, cognitive, or behavioral trait in a particular direction" (Lumsden and Wilson, 1981, p. 370). In other words, they are constraints or parameters on what we are or believe or sense.

Lumsden and Wilson distinguish primary rules from secondary rules. As far as culture is concerned, primary rules affect the very act of sensing. Thus, in every act of seeing, the brain processes or acknowledges contour, "the spatial rate of change and huminance and . . . the shapes of objects," and color, "information about the surface of objects" (Lumsden and Wilson, 1981, p. 43). Similarly, for hearing: "The infant begins life with built-in acoustic behavior that helps to shape its subsequent communication and social existence" (Lumsden and Wilson, 1981, p. 49).

Secondary epigenetic rules set strong constraints on thinking and belief. They structure the very way we make judgments: about causality, probability, and so forth. And, with respect to these notions, the fit between a Kantian regulative principle and a secondary epigenetic rule is very close indeed. Moreover, Lumsden and Wilson explicitly cite moral rules as examples of secondary epigenetic rules: they give the incest taboo as an example.

Not insensitive to the delights of quoting Wilson against himself, can I simply invite the sociobiologists to make proper philosophical use of their biological findings? Morality is indeed rooted in evolution, but not in the crude way supposed by traditional evolutionary ethics. We think ethically because of our evolution; it works; and, no higher justification can be found or asked for. Furthermore, no simplistic ethical relativism is implied here. Because of our common evolutionary heritage we share an ultimate moral code, and can indeed make judgments of right and wrong, distinguishing them from personal preference. The man who says that it is morally acceptable to rape little children, is just as mistaken as the man who says that 2 + 2 = 5. Moral standards are upheld by evolution; not destroyed by them.

The ideology of evolutionism

At this point, many outraged critics of modern Darwinism will be able to contain themselves no longer. They will accuse me of deliberately skirting around the periphery of the issue of evolutionism (specifically Darwinism) and morality, avoiding the very real and pressing questions that simply must be answered. I have treated evolution as a fact, and Darwinism as a scientific theory that does not itself have moral connotations. But, the critics will claim, this is to miss the wood for trees. Scientific theories, Darwinism in particular, are not value-free descriptions of absolute reality, whatever that might be. They are human constructs, models, about the world. Thus, through the creative element that enters into them, there is ample opening for the introduction of wishes, hopes, ideologies, and so forth. And, evolutionists, particularly neo-Darwinian students of humankind, have taken full advantage of this opening. They have smuggled in all sorts of non-empirical elements, reflecting their racist, capitalist, sexist prejudices.

Hence, the critics will cry, the really important discussion of evolution and ethics should center on this fact: human sociobiology is morally pernicious ideology parading as disinterested, objective science. All human actions are portrayed as "selfish," directed towards individual gains. Peoples and races are considered different, and the not so subtle implication is that some (e.g., blacks and Jews) are inferior. And, above all, hangs the greasy pall of sexism. Women are portrayed as inferior, as inadequate, as "feminine," and as altogether different and secondary to men. Deprived by nature of the right genes, they have to resort to such subterfuges as the "he man" and "domestic bliss" strategies.

And, as we all know, cry the critics, disclaimers notwithstanding, having given this picture of humankind, the implied next step by Darwinism is a justification and cherishing of the *status quo*.

For more than a century, the idea that human social behaviour is determined by evolutionary imperatives and constrained by innate or inherited predispositions has been advanced as an ostensible justification for particular social policies. Determinist theories have been seized upon and widely entertained not so much for their alleged correspondence to reality, but for their more obvious political value, their value as a kind of social excuse for what exists (Allen et al., 1977, p. 3).

Obviously, no defence of Darwinism would be complete without some response to this charge. Even though one might protest that no course of social action is implied by one's scientific claims, the critics are surely right in suggesting that scientific claims do frequently direct one toward certain actions. Most particularly, although I have argued that science per se cannot yield moral norms, I have also agreed that, as a general conservative position, one should hesitate before tampering with the product of evolution. More happiness might be reached by leaving well enough alone. Hence, if Darwinism is all of the things that the critics claim, I am certainly pointing the reader in the direction of immoral action.

The most obvious defence, one that I am sure would be adopted by most philosophers, is a stout denial that science can in any sense be ideological, influenced by wishes and the like. To use Howard Cosell's memorable phrase, science "tells it like it is," and that is all there is to it. To accuse a scientific theory of being, say, sexist, is just a logical absurdity: nature is neutral on the quality of the sexes (See Nagel, 1961, for arguments in this vein.)

But, neither logic nor history will let me take this path. I have argued that scientific theories are not mirror images of objective nature. They are indeed sets of models, which abstract and try to capture limited facets of the world. There is therefore plenty of scope for nonempirical elements to intrude. And, who could doubt that some claims could be primarily a function of the kind of world the modeler would like, rather than a function of anything else?

Moreover, if the history of evolutionary thought convinces one of anything, it is that people's wishes and prejudices play more than a minor role in their finished products. Consider, for a moment, Herbert Spencer's views of evolution, which supposed a kind of Lamarckian progression up from the brutes to *Homo sapiens*. Spencer (1852) argued that life's difficult conditions cause a striving, which brings about more sophisticated characteristics, which are then in turn passed on to future generations in a Lamarckian fashion. Coupled with this progressive rise, one gets a drop in fertility (and thus a weakening of Malthusian pressures), as vital nutrients go to the brain, rather than waste away in reproduction.

Spencer had little difficulty in fusing this theory with a curious amalgam of Victorian views on sexuality and the lower (i.e., non-English) races, particularly the Irish. Major proof of the connection between fertility and intelligence is provided by the "obvious" fact that overproduction of sperm cells, however caused, leads initially to head-aches: "This is followed by stupidity; should the disorder continue, imbecility supervenes, ending occasionally in insanity" (Spencer, 1852, p. 493). And, evidence for the progressive rise comes clearly from our own species, what with the "civilized European" showing greater development "than does the savage," and the pitiful Irishman with his huge families standing in stark contrast to the restrained, successful Englishman.

It seems to me that this picture of evolution is as typically Victorian in its attitudes and ideology, as an essay by Carlyle, a sermon by Newman, or a poem by Tennyson. Certainly, it and like views were taken by many to be a "justification" of what their gut feelings had long suspected. (See Fig. 12.2.)

Fig. 12.2
This cartoon of an Irishman (from *Puck* 1882) clearly illustrates the extent to which evolutionary speculations about human links with the apes color Victorian views of "lesser races." The Irish are less evolved than the English; hence they are portrayed as more ape-like.

Nor should we think that only our forefathers were capable of building their dearly held beliefs into their science. Gould, for instance, is quite explicit that his opposition to conventional Darwinism is, in part, Marxist-inspired. He argues for punctuated equilibria, because he is attracted to the revolutionary aspects of the position (Gould and Eldredge, 1977). He argues against what he sees to be the excessively adaptationist thrust of conventional Darwinism, because he wants a more holistic, historical perspective on the organism. He wants to argue that one cannot cut up an organism conceptually and consider each part independently, but must see it as an integrated whole, within an ongoing historical process (Gould, 1980a, see p. 512). And, with respect to our own species, he likes his position because he believes it implies the essential sameness of humankind. There was no gradual progression up to *Homo sapiens,* with all sorts of implications about inferior and superior races. Rather, humans appeared more or less at once, on the scene, in fully finished form.

At times, indeed, even orthodox Darwinians have based their models rather less on the dictates of nature, and rather more on the dictates of conscience. We have seen that no one in the 1930s could really say how much variation there is in natural populations. Hence, given what is known of his

religious yearnings, it seems plausible to suppose that Theodosius Dobzhansky's early attractions to the balance hypothesis were probably as much a
reflection of a religious commitment to the existential worth of us all, as things
dictated by brute fact.

Although all men now living are members of a single biological species, no two persons,
except identical twins, have the same genetic endowment. Every individual is biologically unique and nonrecurrent. It would be naive to claim that the discovery of this
biological uniqueness constitutes a scientific proof of every person's existential
singularity, but this view is at least consistent with the fact of biological singularity
(Dobzhansky, 1962, p. 219).

Why human sociobiology is not morally pernicious

At this point, the critics will be rubbing their hands with glee. I seem to
have given them their case completely. Not quite so! Having poured water all
over the altar of Darwinism, let me now try to relight the fire. There are at least
two ways in which one might defend the integrity of sociobiology. First, one
might show that, in fact, it was never based on the pernicious ideology the
critics impute. Second, one might show that it has gone beyond ideology to
confirmed science. The balance hypothesis now has solid empirical backing —
it transcends Dobzhansky's Christian sentiments. Both of these points rescue
human sociobiology from the critics, establishing it as good, morally acceptable science.

First, it is clear that the picture of humankind painted by human
sociobiology is anything but one of unrestrained barbarism. For all that they
use terms like "selfishness" and "enlightened self-interest," there is no vision
of the kind espoused by the industrialist John D. Rockefeller, who assured a
Sunday-school class that Darwinism is a good thing, because the weakest firms
go to the wall (pushed there by Standard Oil!) In fact, as we have seen,
sociobiology argues that people will usually do things for the most honorable
of reasons, if only because biology works better that way! The average altruist
is not like Uriah Heep, forever thinking about ways in which he can better
manipulate people to his own end. Rather, he does what he does because he
thinks it right, and because he has a general empathy for other human beings.
Of course, sociobiology thinks there are underlying causes, but this does not
destroy the genuine nature of human emotions and sentiments. After all,
would we want to deny the virtues of a saint, because her parents conditioned
her with strict discipline as a child?

Again, there is no suggestion in sociobiology that blacks are genetically
inferior. If anything, the emphasis is on the unity of humankind. Nor is there
real suggestion that women are not as good as men. Does sociobiology imply
that women are less intelligent than men? Or more lacking in a sense of
humor? Or less sensitive? Or whatever else it is that makes one admire and
love one person rather than another? I rather think not. If anything, it is males

who are being portrayed as the lesser beings, with their chest-thumping, macho, adolescent attitudes. And finally, let me ask why, in heaven's name, it should be thought morally pernicious to suggest that incest barriers have a genetic foundation?! I cannot even think of a reason.

The second potential line of defence supports the first. We saw in Chapter 11 that there is empirical evidence for at least some of the sociobiological claims. Frankly, were anyone today to deny some truth to the claims about the genetic basis to incest barriers, I would suspect them of putting ideology above the facts. Again, I find it hard to imagine that the genes play no role whatsoever in human intellectual achievement. Similarly, in the case of sexual differences. Hormonal studies are very suggestive. Are testosterone levels in no way connected to the genes? And do the prenatal testosterone levels have no effect whatsoever on adult attitudes and performance? It seems quite incredible to suggest that we could have *total* reversal of sexual roles in human societies. Women have several husbands; women do the fighting; women are constantly the sexual aggressors and men almost invariably are reticent, wanting to limit sex and to dispose of favors selectively; women read and are turned on by *Playgirl,* men are relatively indifferent to pornography (at present, the largest readership of *Playgirl* is the male homosexual community); and so forth (Symons, 1979).

Going further down the scale, I admit we risk sinking into the morass of unbridled speculation. But, taken as whole, and regarded with many reservations, there obviously is some empirical support for human sociobiology. At least, enough to warrant taking it seriously. Hence, I suggest that it is unfair to accuse the sociobiologist of unrestrained prejudice. In this respect, neo-Darwinism is not simply an epiphenomenon of filthy facist ideology.

Furthermore, I would point out that sociobiology does not say that change in human behavior can never occur. Moderate change is obviously possible, given appropriate changes in attitude, child-rearing, education, and so forth. And even drastic change is probably possible. If, in the name of some kind of equality, one aspires to total human androgeny, one probably faces no insuperable barriers erected by the sociobiologist. He warns that purely environmental manipulation may prove inadequate, it could well be that one would have to resort to hormonal treatment; but, identity for the sake of equality is not a logical impossibility.

Of course, the sociobiologist wonders at the wisdom of this course of action. Would so drastic a tampering with human beings really make us happy? But, such queries are no more than those raised by conventional sexologists, who show in great detail the unhappy nature of people without a firm sense of sexual identity (Green, 1974; Money and Ehrhardt, 1972).

Conclusion: The ideology of Darwinism

In bringing this chapter to an end, I must make one point very clear. I have shown that values and ideologies have influenced evolutionary theorizing from before Darwin to the present. Personally, I find Spencer's ideas rather offensive; but, I do want to emphasize that I am not as such condemning the influence of ideology on science. Apart from the fact that such a condemnation would be on a par with Canute's lecturing the waves, I believe that the urge to build science in accordance with basic metaphysical beliefs is one of the most fruitful sources of innovative and important science. The great importance of the balance hypothesis attests to this fact. And, whether or not the theory of punctuated equilibria sinks or swims, there is little doubt that it has advanced the cause of paleontology, forcing even the most orthodox of Darwinians to reexamine their premises and to search for new empirical evidence. Everyone has benefited from Gould's Marxist urges. Indeed, even Spencer helped to spread the idea of evolution, although I still wonder how far he aided the cause.

You must realize now that I am *not* now saying that ideology is all. Confirming facts must still be sought. Science is not a subjective mess, where anything goes. What I am saying is that some of the most important forces leading to new science are fundamental beliefs, held by scientists, about the way they feel the world *should* and *must* be. But, once an empirical claim is formulated, whether it be through Baconian induction by simple enumeration of a few cases, or just from the hopes of a committed scientist, the claim must stand or fall by the general criteria of good science.

A final, obvious question. What about the Darwinism I am defending in this essay? Do I pretend that it reflects no ideology? Do I claim that all of its hypotheses are so firmly based, that no sense of values and of wishes can be found behind the claims within its boundaries? Do I think that the extension to human social behavior reveals no commitment to any value system?

No indeed! I believe that Darwinism, especially as it extends into human sociobiology, reflects a strong ideology. Moreover, this is one to be proud of. I suggest that Darwinians today show a strong liberal commitment, of a kind urged by (among others) John Rawls, in his deservedly celebrated *A Theory of Justice*. They do not think we are all identical, but they do think we are of equal worth, as full human beings.

This commitment comes through time and again as Darwinians argue that their models apply to all peoples, black and white, preliterate and industrialized, rich and poor. The argument over and over is that all human beings are joined in being the products of, and still subject to, the same causal models. The Kalahari bushman and the New York business executive are not alien beings. For all their differences, they are brothers under the skin, united by their evolutionary predicament. They love, hate, play, work, fight, help, fear, worship, for the same reasons. They are members of the same species: *Homo sapiens*.

One cannot pretend that hard physical evidence proves this unity. At present, much is based on hope. But, this is nothing to be ashamed of. All great science is constantly stretching beyond its empirical reach. And, if this essay has shown anything, it has shown that Darwinism is more than just a self-contained scientific theory. It touches at chords and beliefs of the most fundamental kind, stirring us in a way that only the greatest of ideas can. Part of this reason today is because it mirrors and in turn illuminates a social philosophy which is dear to the heart of all civilized people. No apology or defense is necessary.

Part V
Darwinism Besieged

Chapter 13
Creationism Expounded

Just a few years ago, with the final sentence of the last chapter, this essay would have been finished. Already, we would be into the bibliography and index. Unfortunately, today, we are not yet done. From outside the scientific community has come a major threat to Darwinian evolutionary theory, and no defence of Darwinism would be complete without some discussion of it. I refer of course to the so-called "Creationists": the modern-day representatives of those people who opposed the *Origin,* simply because it denied the story of creation, as given in the early part of Genesis. Who are these critics of Darwinism? What do they believe? How should we react to their ideas? Let us start with some background.

Creationism: American style

We know full well that, in 1859, when Charles Darwin published the *Origin of Species,* much of the opposition to his theory was religiously inspired. People feared for the special status of man, which they thought was guaranteed by the Bible: after all, it does speak of God creating man in his own image. People feared for the creative design which they saw everywhere in nature: brute law leads only to randomness, or so they thought. Hence, Darwinism was fought and rejected, both by those who yet endorsed some sort of "guided" evolutionism, and by those who continued to subscribe to a world created by miraculous intervention.

However, by 1859, even in Victorian Britain, nearly all intelligent and informed people realized that one could no longer hold to a traditional, Biblically inspired picture of the world: a world created by God in six days (of twenty-four hours each); a world of very, very recent origin (4004 B.C. was the favored date of creation, based on the genealogies of the Bible); and, a world which at some subsequent point had been totally covered and devastated by a monstrous flood. Through the first half of the nineteenth century, scientific discovery after scientific discovery had modified these traditional beliefs (Ruse, 1979a). The geological record and many other facts spoke of a world of great age, told of the successive appearance over countless years of new forms of life, and failed altogether to yield traces of a universal global deluge.

Revealingly, when Philip Gosse tried to combine his belief in science with a literal view of the Bible, suggesting that perhaps fossils had been put into the rocks by God to test our faith, he was treated with ridicule and laughed out of the scientific community. Even totally committed Christians, like Sedgwick, wanted no truck with *that* kind of compromise.

But, of course, one talks here of a certain, rather small segment of society. Those at a distance from the intellectual centre of the world continued to treat the Bible far more literally, and they continued to downplay and to deny the dangerous heresies of science. In the zions of the North and in the chapels of Wales, few voices were raised against even one jot or tittle of Genesis. God created the world in a working week, and that is that. Energies were not to be wasted on Biblical interpretation, but were to be preserved for seeing that the seventh day is kept holy and for fighting such desecrations as Sunday trains.

Nevertheless, for all that their numbers were great, it seems true to say that, in Britain, those who believed in the literal truth of the Bible never really became an organized force. Certainly, they did not become a force which could significantly affect the content of the science which was starting to be introduced into British education. Indeed, those most vigorously promoting the cause of education in general and science education in particular tended to be those most committed to evolutionism, in one form or another. Huxley's place on the London School Board has already been mentioned.

The story in North America was rather different. In the U.S. particularly, believers in the literal truth of the Bible have always been better organized, and very much more determined to see that nothing in the educational curriculum offends their deeply held religious convictions. The United States may be founded on a separation of church and state, but how separate this separation has to be is another matter indeed. After the Civil War, particularly in the South, more than one movement was formed, dedicated to stemming the insidious infiltration of Bible-threatening scientific doctrines into the schools and colleges. One early martyr to the cause of science was the geologist Alexander Winchell, who lost his job at Vanderbilt University for telling his class that humans are descended from pre-Adamite beings (de Camp, 1968, 1969; see the bibliographic essay for further references on the past and present states of Creationism).

But, it was in this century, particularly in the decade after the First World War, that the believers in the literal truth of the Bible scored their most notable triumphs. Emboldened by their success in the drive for Prohibition, conservative Christians (now known as "Fundamentalists," because they subscribe to the Bible-affirming fundamental principles enunciated by the 1895 meeting of the Niagara Bible Conference) turned their attentions to the contents of science classes, particularly those in schools.

As a result of their lobbying efforts, Oklahoma passed a law banning evolutionary textbooks, and in 1925 the Tennessee state legislature went so far as to introduce a bill making it a crime to teach evolutionary ideas. Apparently, few of the state politicians felt much enthusiasm for the bill; but, fearing repercussions, they voted for it, hoping that someone else would kill it. And so the bill became law, even though the state governor assured people that: "Nobody believes that it is going to be an active statute."

It was this Tennessee law that led to one of the most famous trials of this century. Encouraged by the American Civil Liberties Union, a young schoolteacher, John Thomas Scopes, let himself be prosecuted for teaching evolutionary ideas in the Dayton (Tennessee) High School. Almost at once, the case blew up into an event of national proportions, with three-times presidential candidate, and noted fundamentalist, William Jennings Bryan for the prosecution, and devastating jury-pleader, and noted agnostic, Clarence Darrow for the defense. Matters took on an almost carnival air when, having been refused permission to introduce expert scientific witnesses for the defence, Darrow cross-examined Bryan, as an expert witness on the claims of the Bible! (Cole, 1959). (See Figs. 13.1a and 13.1b)

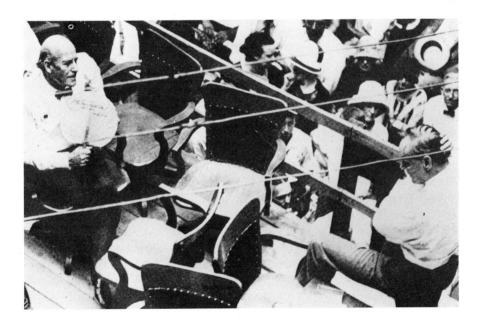

Fig. 13.1a
The climax of the Scopes trial as Darrow (right) cross-examines Bryan (left), before 2000 spectators!

Fig. 13.1b
John T. Scopes is sentenced in Dayton.

The trial ended in the only way that it could, with Scopes being found guilty. After all, he had broken the law! But, a minimal penalty of $100 was levied, and, in fact, the conviction was reversed on appeal, on a technicality. More importantly, the evolutionists won a great moral victory, for Scopes and Darrow showed how dangerous it is to attempt to legislate the nature of science. And, even more importantly, the whole nation laughed at Tennessee, thanks particularly to the reporting of H. L. Mencken, who used his savage pen to good effect, referring to the good citizens of Dayton as "anthropoid rabble" and "gaping primates".

Although, in fact, Tennessee was followed by two other states (Mississippi and Arkansas) in making the teaching of evolution illegal, and although, in fact, the laws remained in effect for forty years (they were declared unconstitutional by the U.S. Supreme Court in 1968), the Scopes' Trial had the effect that the evolutionists hoped. Most states had no desire to be portrayed in the same ridiculing light as Tennessee. Hence, proposed "monkey laws" were

Fig. 13.2
A cartoon from the *Columbus Dispatch* which appeared just after Scopes was found guilty. Labeled "The big worry", it expressed general concern over the threat of the monkey laws. (Used by permission of the *Columbus Dispatch*.)

quietly dismissed or otherwise shelved. Delaware referred its law to the Committee on Fish, Game and Oysters, where it was obviously out of water and thus peacefully expired. (See Fig. 13.3.)

And, at the same time, the steam went out of the fundamentalist drive, caused in no small measure by the personal failings of its leaders. Well known is the sad story of the revivalist and strong anti-evolutionist, Aimee Semple McPherson. Reappearing after a mysterious absence, she claimed to have been kidnapped by those opponents of morality: gamblers, dope pedlars, and evolutionists. Unfortunately for her credibility, it transpired later that she had rather been anticipating heavenly bliss, with one of her assistants.

But, even though evolutionism was not harrassed quite so actively in the succeeding years, one cannot honestly say that it was particularly well served in the schools. Indeed, the success of the Russian Sputnik, in 1957, showed

Fig. 13.3
In 1967 Tennessee's monkey law was finally repealed. Herblock's apt commentary was labeled, "Okay, if you're sure it's all right to eat." (Used by permission of Herblock.)

Americans that science generally was not particularly well served in the schools. In response to this perceived threat to American supremacy, great efforts were made to invigorate American science and technology, and one immediate consequence was a drive to upgrade high-school science education. New, up-to-date textbooks were produced, and their adoption was strongly urged upon those responsible for the teaching of American children. As a matter of course, evolutionary ideas were naturally included in these books, and it seems to have been this fact that triggered new efforts by religious fundamentalists. Once again, they were spurred to fight what they see as religiously and morally offensive doctrines, being purveyed as the truth, to the young people of the land. Hence, the past twenty years have seen a whole new drive against evolutionism and in favor of Creationism, particularly with respect to high school science courses.

Even though the same Biblical motives fuel the drive, the new movement fighting against evolution has moved with the times. In respects, it is very different from the Elmer-Gantry-like circus that one senses of the Creationist movement of the 1920s. Today's opponents of evolutionism take great pains to portray themselves as respectable thinkers: no Bible-thumping, revival tenters, they! Leading the fight is the Institute for Creation Research (ICR), affiliated with the Christian Heritage College (CHC) of San Diego. Its founder and director is Henry M. Morris, PhD, a former hydraulic engineer at Virginia Polytechnic Institute, and its associate director is Duane T. Gish PhD, who has a background in biological science. Although there are no formal ties with the ICR, a sympathetic ally is the Creation Research Society (CRS), a group of creationist scientists, with about 500 full members. Full membership is restricted to those who hold an advanced degree (e.g., MSc or PhD) in a natural science. As a matter of fact, few members are active biologists. Most have a background, like Morris, in some sort of technical science.

Relatedly, today's Creationists have changed their tactics. No longer do they openly press a crude Biblical literalism, insisting that it be taught in the schools. Apart from anything else, they realize that, in the United States, this approach would flounder on the Supreme Court ruling it to be unconstitutional. Instead, they portray themselves as *Scientific* Creationists. That is to say, *they claim that all their beliefs can be backed and justified by facts and methodology of normal empirical science!* That their beliefs happen to coincide precisely with what they find in the Bible, they take as irrelevant to their case; although, obviously, as individuals, they take such coincidence to be proof of God's greatness, in giving us two independent sources of His creative power and actions.

In short, Creationists today put forward their position *as science.* They argue therefore that, constitutionally, their position may properly be taught in publicly financed schools. And, this is their hope. At present, they do not aspire to the removal of evolutionary doctrines from biology courses. What they do argue is that Creationism may and should be taught as an alternative scientific theory of world origins. Furthermore, when they talk of "origins," they include here the origins of all organisms, not excepting man. The Creationist cry, therefore, is for "equal time" — not in religion classes, but in biology classes.

If the Creationists' aim were simply to popularize their ideas and to win support for their aims, then they could congratulate themselves on succeeding mightily. As part of the general trend towards conservative values and attitudes which has swept the United States in recent years, many laypeople have flocked to the Creationist banner. Understandably depressed by what they see as a collapse of moral decency and behavior, in part triggered by the insidious effects of the sciences, people have turned to the comforting beliefs of the Creationists. Here at least, one can find a firm basis for morality. And, that such a move to Creationism causes consternation and dismay among the "experts" is an added attraction. For once, the common people can have their own ideas.

Furthermore, even with those not directly committed to the cause, the Creationists have had great success. Through skillful tactics, they have kept their cause constantly in the public eye: in newspapers, magazines, television, and radio. Moreover, the seeming reasonableness of their position — all they ask is that their case be given a fair hearing — has received a sympathetic response from many quarters. As noted earlier, even Ronald Reagan is on record as agreeing with their request.

Well, it is a theory, it is a scientific theory only, and it has in recent years been challenged in the world of science and is not yet believed in the scientific community to be as infallible as it once was believed. But if it was going to be taught in the schools, then I think that also the biblical theory of creation, which is not a theory but the biblical story of creation, should also be taught. (Speech in the 1980 Presidential Election Campaign.)

Of course, support is one thing, solid achievement is another. To date, the Creationists can count only limited success in actually getting their doctrines formally instilled right into the schools. Their greatest triumph probably occurred in 1969 in California, during the governorship of Ronald Reagan. The then Board of Education included in its guidelines to teachers the demand that Creationism be given equal time, in biology classes, with evolutionism. This ruling has since been overturned, but the Creationists are now fighting the reversal in the courts. Rather cleverly, they are trying to turn the tables on the evolutionists, arguing that belief in evolutionism of any kind is really an act of faith, not of science. Hence, if Creationism is to be excluded from the schools, the same treatment should be accorded to evolutionism and any of its theories! An appeal court has so far agreed with the Creationists as to rule that evolutionism may not be taught as "fact."

Very recently, the Creationists have scored other major coups, these times in Arkansas and Louisiana. The Creationists persuaded the legislatures to pass bills requiring that "Creation-science" be given equal treatment in biology classes with "evolution-science." Having been signed by the Governors of the two States, the bills are now law; although, we have here in these cases reversals of the California situation, in that it is evolutionists who are now taking legal action. They demand that the laws be dismissed, as a violation of the separation of church and state. Significantly, the Arkansas law makes the same charge as that levelled by the California Creationists, claiming that, if anything, it is the teaching of evolution which is unconstitutional! Although evolution is still to be given equal time, it is at fault because "it produces hostility toward many theistic religions and brings preference to technological liberalism, humanism, nontheistic religions and atheism, in that these religious faiths generally include a religious belief in evolution." (For details, see the editorials in *Nature,* 290, p. 75; 291, p. 179; 291, p. 271. As this book goes to press, the American Civil Liberties Union has successfully challenged the constitutionality of the Arkansas law. For details of the result, see *Science,* 215, p. 381. I myself was privileged to stand alongside such evolutionists as Francisco Ayala and Stephen Gould in the attack on Creationism. The reader will be amused to learn that I was cross-examined at length on the manuscript of this book. Obviously, I am saying something threatening.)

As can be imagined, whatever the formal situation may be, either now or in the future, informally the Creationists have had and can anticipate great success. Even though the teaching of evolution may not be actually proscribed, given the controversy, many school boards prefer to keep the teaching of evolutionism to an absolute minimum, if indeed it is allowed at all. Darwinism sends shivers down the back (I will not say "spine") of the average school trustee. Equally significantly, textbook publishers — whose primary concern is, after all, to make money — realize that too prolonged or too favorable a discussion of evolution will not commend their products to conservative members of school boards. Hence, evolution tends to get minimal treatment. Note that this means that, even in areas of the United States where Creationism is not that strongly entrenched, course materials are directly affected by the beliefs of those who take the Bible literally (Nelkin, 1976a, b).

Finally, in this brief survey, let me prick the smugness of those of us who do not live and work in the United States. Already, the influence of Creationism has spread beyond the borders. In Canada, for instance, in the province of British Columbia, at least one school board gives Creationism equal time in biology classes. In parts of Alberta, apparently, one has nothing but Creationism taught! And, teachers in many other provinces are warned to tread very carefully around the subject of evolutionism. But, perhaps the most incredible sign of the success of Creationism has occurred in England, at the Natural History branch of the British Museum, of all places. In a major exhibition, on the "Origin of Species," mounted in 1981 by the Museum to mark its centenary, Creationism was openly portrayed as an alternative to Darwinism. This is the "equal time" doctrine with a vengeance, indeed! Thomas Henry Huxley must be turning in his grave.

"Scientific Creationism"

Obviously, the present-day Creationists are people to be reckoned with, and "Scientific Creationism" is a doctrine which cannot be ignored. What exactly is being said?

Unfortunately for the would-be expositor, the Creationists are Victorian, not only in their beliefs, but in their prolixity. Perhaps the closest they have come to producing an "official" statement of their position is in a volume published in 1974: *Scientific Creationism*. This is a work "prepared by the technical staff and consultants of the Institute for Creation Research," under the general editorship of Henry Morris, director of that institute. It comes in two editions, one with Biblical references for its various claims, and the other, the "Public School Edition."

In the body of this second text, care is taken not to let Biblical beliefs openly intrude. Indeed, the explicitly stated intention is to justify all claims "solely on a scientific basis" without reference to any religious beliefs or dogmas (Morris, 1974, p. iv). Hence, since this seems to be the "purest" form of the Creationists' position, or rather that form which they want introduced in the schools, it is on this latter edition that I shall base my exposition here.

To avoid the charge of distortion as best I can, I shall follow the argument of the text through in the way it is given. Ideally, I would quote copiously to give full effect to the Creationist arguments. Unfortunately, because of copyright restrictions, this is not possible. Therefore, I shall paraphrase as closely as I can, pointing out that if the Creationists feel that nevertheless I do distort their views — although I can honestly say that it is my most earnest endeavor not to distort — they should be prepared to extend to their critics the normal academic courtesies. In fairness and for clarity, it seems best to leave all comment, critical or otherwise, until the next chapter, by which point the full Creationist position will have been presented. For ease of cross-reference, I shall structure my comments on the order given here, and in both exposition and commentary I shall italicize the Creationists' chapter headings.

The first chapter, *Evolution or Creation?*, presents the two, alternative positions: evolutionism (essentially Darwinism) and Creationism. The authors prefer not to think in terms of "theories," because in fact neither evolution nor Creation can form the basis of a true theory. Creation was a one-of-a-kind phenomenon which occurred in the past, and "thus is inaccessible to the scientific method" (p. 5). Evolution is no true theory for many reasons, a major one being that the central mechanism is a tautology. Natural selection simply states that those which survive in the struggle are the fittest, because the fittest are those which survive! As (the Nobel Prize winner) Peter Medawar has observed: "There are philosophical or methodological objections to evolutionary theory. ... It is too difficult to imagine or envisage an evolutionary episode which could not be explained by the formulae of neo-Darwinism" (Morris, 1974, p. 7 quoting Medawar, 1967, p. xi).

However, one can properly talk of "model," meaning a conceptual system that tries to correlate data. Although one can always save a model by adding additional claims to diffuse apparently contradictory phenomena, if one model needs less face-saving than another, then it is to be preferred. Viewed in this light, therefore, we have two models. On the one hand, we have the evolutionist position, where it is claimed that organisms evolved naturally, primarily through a process of natural selection. On the other hand, we have the Creationist position, which supposes that in the fairly recent past, the world was created miraculously by God, that animals, plants, and humans, were all brought into existence at that time, and that that was it as far as new life is concerned. Additionally, there was some sort of catastrophe or catastrophes, which occurred at some time(s) in the history of the globe.

It is argued that these two models lead to a number of predictions which fall into various categories and which apply at various levels. Some of these predictions are of a fairly general nature. For instance the "Evolution model" implies that natural laws are always in a state of flux and changing; on the contrary, the "Creation model" implies that law is unchanging and never alters. Then we have a set of predictions about the inorganic universe. The evolution model predicts that galaxies are constantly changing, that stars evolve from one sort to another, that the earth on which we live is very old, and that rock formations differ from age to age. As before, the Creation model points the other way. Given its premises, it follows that galaxies never change, that stars do not evolve but remain the same, that this earth of ours is probably very young, and that rock formations start and stay the same from beginning to end.

Then, most crucially, we have the different predictions between the two models about the organic world. The evolution model predicts that life evolved (and apparently is evolving) from non-life, that organisms today present a sort of continuum or unbroken spectrum, that the fossil record has lots of specimens bridging or intermediate between one distinct form and another, and that new "kinds" of organism are always coming into being. Additionally, with respect to mechanisms, the evolution model sees mutation as beneficial, and it sees natural selection as a creative force. Finally, in the context of our own species, the evolution model looks for ape-human forms in the fossil record, it regards man as superior only in degree to other animals (*i.e.,* we have no unique features), and it believes civilization to have developed in a slow and gradual fashion.

The Creation model opposes all of these inferences about organisms. Life comes only from other life: a living organism must have a living parent or parents. Organisms today are broken up into distinct kinds, there are many gaps in the fossil record, and no new kinds ever appear. Mutations are harmful and natural selection is, at best, a minor conservative force, eliminating the inadequate. And most pertinently, there are no ape-human intermediates, and there never have been, man is qualitatively different from the brutes, and as long as there has been man, there has always been a fully developed civilization.

We have therefore, two completely different sets of predictions: those given by the evolution model and those given by the Creation model. It is claimed by the authors of the text that, judged purely by *scientific* criteria, we shall see that the Creation model wins. (For a full description of the different supposed predictions of the two models, see Morris, 1974, p. 13.)

With the stage set, we move to a discussion entitled: *Chaos or Cosmos?* Here, a number of rather metaphysical questions are raised, and it is concluded that they all imply great difficulties for evolutionism. Let me pick out three of the most important.

First, there is the fact that the evolutionist is committed to the constantly changing nature of law, even though there is absolutely no empirical evidence for such change. To the best of our knowledge, all of the great laws of science — the law of gravitational attraction, Newton's laws of motion, the laws of thermodynamics, and so forth — go on their ways, without any change or variation whatsoever. Clearly, this poses grave difficulties for the evolutionist, and it would seem that his beliefs are thus countered. Creationism, on the other hand, predicts what seems to occur, namely that laws remain constant (Morris, 1974, p. 18).

Second, there is the question of cause and effect. One cannot get more from effect, than one puts in as cause. Therefore, the cause of human love must be loving. Blind matter cannot be loving. Hence, it cannot be, as supposed by the evolutionist, that blind matter is the cause of human beings. The ultimate cause must be an All-loving Being. "An omnipotent Creator is an adequate First Cause for all observable effects in the universe, whereas evolution is *not* an adequate cause. The universe could not be its own cause" (Morris, 1974, p. 20).

Third, there is the question of purpose. The Creationists point out that the world is purposeful, and that evolution denies such purpose, whereas Creationism affirms it. "The creation model does include, quite explicitly, the concept of purpose. The Creator was purposive, not capricious or indifferent, as He planned and then created the universe" (Morris, 1974, p. 33). A point that should not go unmentioned is that, here, as indeed throughout the whole discussion, frequent reference is made to the writings of non-Creationist scientists to support or otherwise justify the arguments and conclusions of the text.

We come next to the chapter that raises the question of *Uphill or Downhill?* In fact, as before, a number of discussions are subsumed under this general heading. First, we get a much-favored argument of the Creationists, namely that all forms of evolutionism violate the second law of thermodynamics. This law states essentially that physical processes always go from order to randomness — you can scramble an egg, but you cannot unscramble it. (More formally, the law states that entropy always increases, where entropy can be thought of as a measure of the energy which can no longer be used to get things done.) But, evolution supposedly is a process from randomness to order. Hence, the clash. The second law of thermodynamics says that the world is running down. Evolution says that it is not. There is, however, no clash between Creationism and physics. The Creationist agrees that all is downhill, since the beginning of the world.

As the Creationists realize, evolutionists have a standard reply to this objection. They distinguish between "closed systems," where no new usable energy can come in, and "open systems," where new usable energy can come in. The second law obviously applies only to closed systems. But, argue evolutionists, given the influx of usable energy from the sun, the organic world is an open system. Hence evolution is possible. Entropy may be increasing through the universe, taken as a whole, but it does not mean that, in small localized areas, entropy cannot decrease. The world of organic evolution is one such area. The sun shines down on the Earth. This makes the plants grow. Animals live and feed on the plants. And thus life goes forward.

Nevertheless, the Creationists are not convinced. They deny that the second law of thermodynamics could be broken in such a case as evolution. There is simply no way in which any kind of process of growth can or could occur, if one starts with and uses only randomly caused phenomena. All one can possibly get in such a situation is a diffuse heterogeneous mess. In order to get structured functioning, one *must* put in design: a "blueprint" or a pattern or something. Just as one must have the architect's plans before one can put up a building, so one must have the information encoded in the DNA molecule before an organism can be produced (Morris, 1974, pp. 43-44). Evolution denies the existence of such a blueprint for organisms. Hence, it offers no protection against the unfettered randomizing operation of the second law of thermodynamics.

Second, in this chapter, the problem of the origin of life is raised. The very thought of this phenomenon creates a difficulty for the evolutionist, who is "really" committed to the idea that life is constantly being created. Therefore, since life is obviously no longer being created naturally, before the evolutionist can even start to explain the origin of life, ad hoc hypotheses must be introduced, "proving" that life no longer can be created naturally. But then, of course, we still have the difficulty of explaining how life was produced naturally, at some point in the past. In fact, no one is anywhere close to solving this problem. Artificially created amino acids are just simply not genuinely living things (Morris, 1974, p. 49). And, in any case, even if life were produced, it proves nothing. The production of life through careful thought and precise experimentation is hardly analogous to life coming through random, blind law.

Third, we get discussion of variation and selection. Both of these concepts are inadequate for the tasks assigned to them by evolutionists. There is no example of variation leading to truly new characteristics of the kind required by evolutionists, and selection is a purely conservative force. Selection never leads to new kinds of features. It merely eliminates the inadequate, and other kinds of subnormal features and organisms. And obviously, this very limited power of selection is just what one is led to expect from the Creation model, which is thus confirmed (Morris, 1974, p. 54).

Finally, in this chapter, the topic of mutation is raised. The simple fact of the matter is that mutation is totally inadequate for the tasks supposed by the evolutionists. It is quite impossible that a complex, functioning organism could have been built, step by step, out of mutations. Indeed, the words of evolutionists are turned against themselves. Mutations are random (Waddington), very rare (Ayala), and, almost invariably, very harmful to their possessors (Muller and Julian Huxley). They just cannot lead to new kinds of organisms.

"Scientific Creationism" continued

Moving along, we come to the chapter dealing with the question of: *Accident or Plan*? A major discussion here is of the complexity of living organisms, and of the total improbability of such complexity arising instantly, by chance. Suppose we have an organism made of only 100 parts. Each of these parts must link up, in a unique way, with every other part. One can show, mathematically, that there are 10^{158} different possible ways for linkage. Hence, the chance of the organism being formed is only 1 in 10^{158}! This is totally improbable. If one considers all of the molecules in the universe, and all of the instants of time (10^{-9} seconds) since the beginning of the universe, and if one pretends that new combinations are constantly being formed, then at most one could get 10^{105} new combinations. Hence, there is only a 1 in 10^{53} chance of our 100 unit piece of life being formed, which means that in actual fact there is no chance whatsoever of life being formed (Morris, 1974, p. 61). And, a 100 unit piece of life is impossibly simple.

Would it help to suppose that life is formed on a gradual process? Not at all! Pretend that one needed 1500 steps to make primitive life. Pretend, also, that there was a 50:50 chance that random processes would bring about the required step at any stage. Were one to go on successively to the formation of higher and higher living order, every new step would have to be a success and to help the newly forming organism. One could not have or allow any steps which "failed," that is, which took the organism back to a more primitive form or which killed it entirely. Hence, the probability of new life is $(1/2)^{1500}$, or, approximately, one chance in 10^{450}. This is an impossible demand. Even if one took a new step every billionth of a second, there would only be time for 10^{107} steps! Life could not have been formed by chance (Morris, 1974, p. 63).

Next, in this chapter, we have discussion of things like homologies, which phenomena evolutionists take to be evidence of common ancestry. The Creationists make short work of this. Relying on the authority of Ernst Mayr, they point out that classification above the species' level is really all very arbitrary. Hence, homologies between organisms of different groups may indeed be indicative of common ancestry; but, this proves nothing very much really. By evolutionists' own admission, the groups are man made! There is no "real" breaking into separate classes. And, even if there were, this would be an embarrassment for the evolutionist. "If an evolutionary continuum existed, as the evolution model should predict, there would be no gaps, and thus it would be impossible to demark specific categories of life" (Morris, 1974, p. 72). The Creationists treat other biological similarities, like those of embryology and behavior, in the same way.

Following this, the question of vestigial organs and of recapitulation is raised. The "biogenetic law," namely that "Ontogeny recapitulates phylogeny," is presented. It is pointed out that this once popular rule is now discredited by most modern embryologists. Nevertheless, to their surprise the Creationists find that evolutionists — important evolutionists — go on citing the law as evidence for their evolutionary case. This is despite the fact that anyone who knows anything at all about embryos or fossils knows the law to be false (Morris, 1974, p. 77).

Concluding the chapter, we get a fairly extensive discussion of the fossil record. The space given to this topic is in line with Creationist claims elsewhere, that: "The only *solid* evidence in the discussion of origins is the fossil record — anything else is circumstantial evidence and conjecture" (advertisement blurb for *Evolution? The Fossils say Not* by Duane T. Gish). Expectedly, much is made of gaps in the record. Even more expectedly, much is made of what the Creationists believe to be one of the most dreadful gaps of them all, namely that which occurs between the supposed micro-organisms of the pre-Cambrian era, and the very rich and complex organisms of the Cambrian: the gap between virtually nothing and the thriving and abundant trilobites (Morris, 1974, p. 80). Several evolutionists are quoted to show what a problem this is. Similar attention is drawn to other gaps in the record, including that between reptiles and birds. What about *Archaeopteryx*? Well, with respect, because it had feathers, it has to be classed as a bird. Hence, since *Archaeopteryx* is a bird, it cannot be "a reptile-bird transition"! The gap remains. Also noted in this discussion are the many "living fossils," which live today, but which occur only in ancient strata. These should not exist, given evolutionism. Given Creationism, they are expected. All of today's organisms go back to the beginning of time.

To this point, discussion has been more one of criticism (of Darwinian evolutionism) than one of positive affirmation (of Creationism). However, in the next chapter, *Uniformitarianism or Catastrophism?*, much of the positive, Creationist case is laid out. After noting how many geologists today feel unhappy with uniformitarianism (Gould is a leading authority here), we are given a major part of the Creationist thesis. Originally, all of the organisms that we find living today *and* all those organisms that we find represented in the fossil record lived together in the world, as it was created by the Creator during that initial time when everything was produced. Obviously, although organisms all lived together at the same time, this early life was subject to the ecological restraints we find in operation today. Everyone did not live on top of everyone, humans cheek to jowl with trilobites. As today, those organisms suited for water lived in water, and those suited for dry land lived on dry land.

Then, into this picture of harmony there came a monstrous flood. The heavens opened and, if this were not enough, at the same time, water poured forth from subterranean sources. This deluge went on for weeks on end, until the whole earth was submerged. Simultaneously, along with all of these watery calamities, there were earthquakes, volcanic eruptions, landslides, and just about every other possible natural disaster. Clearly, this all had horrendous implications for organisms, particularly for land animals. They ran hither and thither, trying to escape their awful fate; but, inevitably, the forces of nature eventually caught up with them. At long last, unless a few enterprising humans had managed to build super-strong boats to ride out the flood, all organisms (especially all land organisms) were drowned.

Finally, bringing everything to a conclusion, sediments settled down out of the waters, forming the various strata that we find around the whole world today. As a function of various physical and chemical processes and constraints, the layers of presently visible or discoverable rocks were formed. And, at the end, for some reason or reasons, the waters receded and dry land appeared once more. (For details, see Morris, 1974, pp. 117-118.)

But what about the fossil record? Does not the gradual, progressive rise, that we see, support evolution? Not really! First of all, the record is truly not all that progressive. Indeed, many if not most plants and animals living today can be found in the fossil record. Conversely, a huge number of fossil animals and plants have similar living counterparts, and such differences as do exist between past and present are easily and totally explicable in terms of en-

vironmental effects (Morris, 1974, p. 116). Also, Mayan relief sculptures show
that *Archaeopteryx* lived at the same time as man. And, in the cretaceous Glen
Rose formation of central Texas, there are dinosaur and human footprints occurring together. There are even human traces in trilobite beds! (I had hoped
to be able to show the reader photographs which the Creationists use to bolster
their case for contemporaneous human and dinosaur prints. Unfortunately,
the Creationists did not feel that they could let me use their pictures. Let me
therefore draw your attention to (Milne, 1981), where the pictorial evidence is
laid out in full.)

Second, in reply to evolutionist queries about progression, there is the
simple fact that the Creationist expects a broadly progressive fossil record! As
organisms rushed (unsuccessfully) to avoid the flood, they left their remains in
a progressive fashion, because of their different original habitats and abilities.
Thus, for instance, one expects to find mammals and birds higher up in the
fossil record than reptiles and amphibians. Mammals and birds live at higher
elevations than do reptiles and amphibians. Moreover, the former are more
mobile than the latter, and thus would have scrambled to greater heights, in
their desperate albeit futile efforts to avoid the rising flood waters (Morris,
1974, p. 119).

The penultimate chapter, *Old or Young?*, deals with the question of the
age of the earth. It is pointed out that "no one can possibly *know* what happened before there were people to observe and record what happened. Science
means knowledge and the essence of the scientific method is experimental
observation" (Morris, 1974, p. 131, his italics).This means that, at best, we
can really only go, with certainty, back to the beginning of written records,
some 2000 to 3000 years before Christ.

But what about physicochemical methods of dating the age of the earth
and of the fossils? What about so-called "radiometric dating"? The Creationists claim that every one of these methods is highly speculative, probably
leading to quite erroneous results. Essentially, all of the methods work on the
same principle: certain elements "decay" into other elements. Hence, by
measuring the amount of decay that has gone on in a rock sample, knowing
the rate of decay, one can calculate the absolute age of the rock. The Creationists argue that at least three things could go wrong, and probably do go
wrong. First, all sorts of elements could come in and out of the rock, after it
formed. This would obviously render the extant ratios totally meaningless.
Second, one cannot know the initial composition of the rock. Hence, the final
ratios could be distorted, because of initial ratios. Third, who can say that
rates of decay are constant? Processes in nature go at all sorts of different
rates, dependent on intervening factors. Change the factors and the rates
change. In any case, rates are statistical. They are never constants (Morris,
1974, p. 139).

What, then, is the age of the earth? All the evidence points to a very recent
origin. For instance, Dr. Thomas G. Barnes, Professor of Physics at the
University of Texas in El Paso, has shown that the earth's magnetic field
strength is decaying, with a most probable half-life of 1400 years. Immediate-

ly, this gives rise to some interesting implications. Only 1400 years ago the magnetic field was twice what it is today, and going back in such a geometric fashion we very soon get an incredibly strong field. Within 10,000 years we get a putative magnetic field which is at least as powerful as that which one finds on a magnetic star. Obviously, this is totally impossible, for the earth would be destroyed under such a force. "Thus, 10,000 years seems to be an outside limit for the age of the earth, based on the present decay of its magnetic field," (Morris, 1974, pp. 157–158). Interestingly, in this part of the discussion, the authors do not refer solely to external, non-Creationists, as their authorities. Dr. Barnes is, in fact, one of the writers and/or consultants of this text we are discussing.

Finally, in this examination of time-spans, a rather different, Malthusian argument is offered, to show that man is a recent phenomenon. Annual human population growth rate today is of the order of 2 percent. Which model, evolutionism with a human-span of at least a million years, or Creationism, with a human-span of 4000–5000 years, best fits with this figure? In fact, it is easy to show that it is the Creationist model. With an average growth rate of 1/2% (adjusted down to take account of war and disease), we can get today's numbers (3.5×10^9), in about 4000 years.

Conversely, under the burden of the demographic facts just mentioned, the evolution model collapses entirely. Suppose, with the evolutionists, that humans have been around for a million years. This gives us about 25,000 generations. Hence, one has to infer that all of these humans could have produced only 3.5 billion people by today. This is ridiculous! Pretend that population increased at only the above-supposed rate of 1/2%; that is, pretend that there were only 2.5 children per family. Given 25,000 generations, we would expect there to be 10^{2100} people today. This is an absolutely impossible figure. There are, after all, only 10^{130} electrons maximally possible in the entire known universe. Hence, evolutionary hypotheses come crashing down, salvable only through the addition of all sorts of implausible secondary *ad hoc* suppositions. (See Morris, 1974, p. 169, for full details of this argument.)

Finally, we come to the question everyone has been waiting for: *Apes or Men?* Many phenomena (languages, cultures, religions) point to recent human origins; but, of course, the most important information comes from the fossil record. There is absolutely no solid evidence, whatsoever, for Darwinian claims that humans evolved from the apes. Neanderthal man was probably an ordinary man, with arthritis or rickets. *Homo erectus,* also, seems to have been a true man, although hardly a prime specimen. Unfortunately, because of inbreeding, inadequate food, severe environmental forces, and the like, he was second-rate, both in size and in culture (Morris, 1974, p. 174). What about *Australopithecus?* With respect, he was no man at all, but a kind of ape. He had a small brain, was long-armed and short-legged, and probably walked on his knuckles, rather than in an upright fashion, like us. "In other words, *Australopithecus* not only had a brain like an ape, but he also looked like an ape and walked like an ape. He, the same as *Ramapithecus,* is no doubt simply an extinct ape'' (Morris, 1974, p. 173).

Creationism wins; evolutionism loses!

Chapter 14
Creationism Considered

You know where I stand, of course. But, let me be quite categorical. I believe Creationism is wrong: totally, utterly, and absolutely wrong. I would go further. There are degrees of being wrong. The Creationists are at the bottom of the scale. They pull every trick in the book to justify their position. Indeed, at times, they verge right over into the downright dishonest. Scientific Creationism is not just wrong: it is ludicrously implausible. It is a grotesque parody of human thought, and a downright misuse of human intelligence. In short, to the Believer, it is an insult to God.

Obviously, my whole essay is intended to be a refutation of the Creationist position. Virtually all of their claims have already been dealt with, in one way or another. To those of my readers who decided simply to dip into this final part, in order to find out what the Creationist controversy is all about, can I beg that you go back to the beginning and work through?! But, to recap and to give a systematic response, I shall now run briefly through the main Creationist arguments, showing why they have failed to make their case. As noted earlier, I shall follow the Creationists' order of presentation, and, for convenience of reference, I will again introduce each of the chapter headings.

Models, causes, and purposes

We began with the discussion of *Evolution or Creation*? It will be remembered that a crucial distinction, here, was drawn between a "theory" and a "model." It was argued that, judged as theories, neither evolutionism nor Creationism succeed, since neither can be falsified. However, judged as models, we can make predictions from both evolutionism and Creationism, and Creationism succeeds as science, because it needs fewer ad hoc secondary face-saving hypotheses.

As you know, I myself would distinguish between a theory and a model, arguing that a theory in a sense is a family of models. However, in the present context, the distinction is unclear to the point of confusion. For the Creationists, both theories and models apparently contain hypotheses about the world, and this being so, each seems equally open to check or non-check. If natural selection is a tautology in evolution-as-theory, why is it any less a tautology in evolution-as-model? If uniqueness and unrepeatability is a problem in Creation-as-theory, why is it any less a problem in Creation-as-model? Indeed, the Creationists themselves seem to concede the futility of their distinction, because, having introduced the concept of "model" in order to get away from unfalsifiability, they admit at once that the determined defender of a position can always find a face-saving hypothesis! This being the case, a model is no more or less scientific than a theory.

I certainly would not condemn anyone for making a mess of their philosophical claims about science. Philosophy of science confuses most of us, including professional philosophers of science! I am far more concerned about the unfair things said about evolutionary theory. Perhaps we should not really fault the Creationists for raising the hoary chestnut of natural selection as a tautology, since so many people seem to think this objection has validity. But, as we know, it fails, nevertheless. What is really disturbing is the rather dishonest list of "basic predictions" that the evolutionist is supposedly committed to. (Refer back to p. 295.)

No evolutionist, since before Darwin, has wanted to claim that life is "evolving" from nonlife. All argue that, if it happened at all, it happened a long time ago. (Refer back to Chapter 6.) To suggest that evolutionist position forces its supporters to an ongoing continuous creation today is just not true. Equally false is the suggestion that Darwinism commits one to a "continuum of organisms." Darwin, and all of his followers, have always been quite explicit in their claim that splitting and speciation are key parts of the evolutionary process. (See Fig. 2.4.) In the course of the process, one does expect small continua at times, between two groups as they are splitting into separate species, and this is what we do find. Remember Ayala's studies of South American fruitflies. (Refer back to Figs. 5.19 and 5.20.) But generally, the Darwinian expects separate groups, which is just what we do find. And, to pick another supposed prediction from Darwinism, which neo-Darwinian ever simply said that mutations in organisms must be "beneficial"? Time and again, we are taught that, generally, mutations will not be at all helpful to their possessors.

I could go on taking up the supposed implications of the "evolution-model," showing that no Darwinian would ever dream of inferring them. However, my point is made. It is far easier to make a case against evolutionism, when, as the Creationists have done here, they systematically distort the Darwinians' position. Unfortunately the ease of argument is purchased at the cost of worth of conclusion. Given the Creationists' proudly flaunted academic credentials, given the obvious care that is devoted to their cause, as is evidenced by the many, many references, one does start to have serious questions about integrity.

Next, in the Creationist case, comes the chapter: *Chaos or Cosmos?* Remember that here we get (for want of a better term) a number of "metaphysical" arguments. It is claimed that the evolutionist is committed to evolving laws, that the law of cause and effect shows that matter cannot be the cause of such things as human love, and that the purpose in the world proves the existence of a creator.

As far as the question of evolving laws is concerned, once again we find Darwinians saddled with claims they would not hold. Certainly, no believer in organic evolution thereby thinks that all of the laws of nature are subject to constant change. The theory of evolution through natural selection is a scientific theory about the empirical world. It is not a philosophical theory about the nature of ultimate reality. Darwinism presupposes invariant law; it does not imply it. It is, incidentally, a little odd of the Creationists to take such pride in their commitment to uniformity, given that later, in their discussion of methods of dating, part of their case is based on the possibility that various, apparently stable processes may speed up or slow down.

The argument about cause and effect, supposedly proving that the first cause of life must be loving and so forth, is totally fallacious. It is, indeed, on a par with arguments that people with red hair must be hot tempered, because red is the color of fire and fire is hot. It simply is not true that the law (if law it be) of cause and effect implies that the cause of x must be x-like. Does the cause of green colored things have to be green itself? Obviously not! If you mix a bucket of blue paint and a bucket of yellow paint, you get two buckets of green paint. Similarly, the cause of motion is not necessarily moving. A gallon of gasoline will get you moving from A to B; but, it was certainly not moving when you went to the gas station to fill up your car. You put horse manure on your rhubarb to make it tasty and nutritious. Is the horse manure tasty and nutritious? I leave this question to others to answer. Perhaps a loving first cause does exist. Perhaps the chain of life does not end in brute matter. The Creationist argument does not prove it.

One way to try to counter the Creationists' arguments about purpose — that the world seems to show purpose and design because there was a Designer — is to deny that the living world is purpose-like. As a good Darwinian, I will not do this, because I agree with the Creationists that, in respects, the living world is purpose-like. The eye is like a telescope. The heart is like a pump (Ruse, 1981). But, even granting this claim about the "teleological" nature of the organic world, the Creationist conclusion that one must therefore accept an intervening Designer does not follow. For a start, as we saw Darwin himself pointing out, if you are going to emphasize the design-like aspects of the eye, it is only fair to acknowledge the non–design-like aspects of many other features in the organic world: skeletal homologies and male nipples, for instance. (Refer back to Fig. 2.6.) Perhaps God exists, and He created homologies and male nipples. The point is that one has to explain homologies and male nipples, despite God; they do not force one to God.

This all leads to the second argument refuting Creationism, at this point. Darwinian evolutionary theory, based as it is on natural selection, fully acknowledges and *expects* the design-like aspect of the world. It argues that design-like features aid in the struggle for existence! In other words, one can as well say that purpose in nature leads to Darwinism, as that it leads to God. Moreover, Darwinism points also to such nondesign features as homologies. They are a product of common descent. Therefore, by the Creationists' own criterion of scientific excellence — "The only way to decide objectively between [the two models], therefore, is to note which model fits the facts and predictions with the smallest number of these secondary assumptions" — one ought to prefer Darwinism!

Origins, probabilities, homologies, and fossils

We move along to the dilemma: *Uphill or Downhill?* A number of topics were included here: the alleged incompatibility of evolution with the second law of thermodynamics; the impossibility of the natural creation of life (and, its irrelevance, even if one were to create life); the failure of variation and selection to do what Darwinism requires of them; and, the unsuitability of mutations for evolution.

The argument based on thermodynamics has intuitive appeal. Certainly it is one that is received sympathetically by many laypeople. The second law states an "obvious" fact about the world: things tend to go from order to randomness. You start with a nice, neat garden, and the weeds overrun it. You start with a shiny new car, and it rusts and buckles when you run into the garage door. The only way one can reverse this randomness is by thoughtful human intervention. Hence, because evolution and life generally seem obviously to be creating integrated order out of randomness, there must be a Designer.

Of course, as the Creationists note, the evolutionist has an answer: the second law holds only for a closed system. The world is not a closed system: usable energy is always coming in from the sun. Hence, evolution is possible. Is the Creationist able to get around this counterreply? I rather think not! At least, the Creationists do not in fact get around the reply. Remember how they argue that blind or random processes simply cannot lead to order, tending rather to heterogeneous messes. Thus, they feel that there must be some sort of design behind any process which leads to integrated functioning. The information of the DNA molecule demands a creative intelligence, no less than does the plan of the architect. "Some kind of pattern, blueprint, or code must be there to begin with, or no ordered growth can take place" (Morris, 1974, pp. 43–44).

But, with respect, this is no argument! This is simply stating as a premise, the conclusion the Creationists want to infer! The evolutionist claims that, by a natural process, evolution occurs, and that there is no violation of thermodynamical principles. Moreover, he shows why the second law does not prohibit evolution: the second law applies only to closed systems. The second law says nothing about *also* having to have a blueprint, before it does not apply. Perhaps one does need a blueprint for life, and for the evolution of life forms. *The second law of thermodynamics does not say so!* The Creationists have simply added the blueprint requirement themselves, and then they pretend that it comes out of physics. They assume their conclusion, and then they try to fob it off on us, as proven.

Equally fallacious is the Creationist argument about the origin of life. We know full well that work on this problem has far to go. But, present progress surely merits detailed treatment, not a back-of-the-hand dismissal. Take the Creationists' claim that Stanley Miller's synthesis of amino acids proves nothing, since amino acids are not living things. Whoever said they were? Miller himself certainly never did want to claim that amino acids are living things. The point is that their synthesis does seem to be an important stage in the natural production of life, and can rightly be respected as such. Take also the Creationists' flat claim that the amino acids would not have survived — "protection would not have been available on the primitive earth." At the very least, this claim needs justification. Simply stating your position is no argument. (Refer back to Chapter 6, for the evolutionists' positive case.)

Nor is it much of an argument to say that, even were life created, it would prove nothing. Of course, what the evolutionists must do is show that their laboratory conditions, at the various stages, are what we would have expected on earth, at the corresponding stages. But, if they can do this, and evolutionists are certainly aware of the need to do this, then they can properly be said to have achieved their aim of showing how life could have been produced naturally.

Put matters this way. Suppose a detective is trying to reconstruct a crime, in order to pin blame on a suspect. At the scene of the actual crime, there had been a trail of rather distinctive footprints in the soil: instead of the heel digging more deeply than the toe, the reverse had been true. The detective first, therefore, tries to show how this effect might have been caused: running, walking backwards, or whatever. Then, the detective must show that his suspect did in fact behave in this hypothesized way. Splitting up the task in this manner is obviously the right thing for a criminal investigator to do. Why should it be any less right for the evolutionist?

Finally, in this chapter, we have the claims that variation, selection, and mutation cannot do the sorts of things that Darwinian evolutionary theory demands — that selection is conservative, and that variations and mutations never lead to new useful features. Here, the best I can do is refer the reader back to the second section of this essay, where I tried to document some of the massive evidence for the Darwinians' claims. At this point, let me simply say that the Creationists' case flounders on their ignorance of what Darwinians really say.

Most particularly, the Creationists fail through ignorance of the incredibly significant implications of the balance hypothesis. A group of organisms is not sitting around, waiting for a good new mutation to occur as the need arises, which mutation will then be cherished by selection. Rather, all the time, there is massive variation within populations, waiting to be drawn upon, as the need arises. (See Chapter 4 in particular.) Thus selection can create new features, because there is a veritable bank or library of mutations, to draw on. Remember the beautiful confirmation of this fact by the McDonald-Ayala experiments, showing how fruitflies could, as needed, develop alcohol tolerance. (Refer back to Fig. 4.1.) It simply is not fair to portray and criticize Darwinism as supposing and requiring one solitary mutation, followed at length by another. Even if Darwinism is wrong, the Creationists cannot show this by criticizing some other theory.

The chapter, *Accident or Plan?* also covers a number of topics: the statistical improbability of life ever being created; the irrelevance to the Darwinian case of such phenomena as homologies; embryology and recapitulation; and gaps in the fossil record.

The first argument, purportedly showing how even a 100 unit piece of life could never come into being by chance, in fact proves absolutely nothing. Both evolutionists and Creationists can agree that the chances of a 100 unit piece of life, just coming together, are infinitesimally small; but, this was never the claim of the evolutionist. He claims that it happened, bit by bit, with only the successful at each stage allowed to go on by selection. New life appeared gradually, not in just one instant. Nor can the Creationist properly object to this gradual process, supposing that each step must be instantly successful, or we must all go back to zero (rather like a game of snakes and ladders, with no ladders). Having made a step forward, the evolutionist argues that life or proto-life will have many copies, and that therefore, if some one instance now makes a fatal step, all the others are left. In other words, *gains are preserved and consolidated.*

Perhaps, at this point, I can best introduce an analogy, which is very familiar to evolutionists. Consider a monkey, sitting at a typewriter, randomly striking the keys. Prima facie, the production of life by random processes seems about as likely as the monkey's typing out the whole of *Hamlet,* or even the soliliquy, "To be or not to be." It may not be logically impossible; but, as the Creationist argues, it is practically impossible. Suppose, however, that every time the monkey strikes the "right" letter, it records; but, suppose also that "wrong" letters get rubbed out (literally or metaphorically!) And suppose that elimination of the wrong letter is the full consequence of a "mistake": one does not lose what has already been typed. Thus, if, having typed "to be or ...," the monkey types an *n*, it records, but, if the monkey types (say) *x*, it does not record.

The typing of *Hamlet* no longer seems anything like so impossible, even by a "blind law" phenomenon, like a typing monkey. The Darwinian's point is that the evolution of life occurs in this sort of way. Natural selection allows the successes, but "rubs out" the failures. Thus, selection creates complex order, without the need for a designing mind. All of the fancy arguments about a number of improbabilities, having to be swallowed at one gulp, are irrelevant. Selection makes the improbable, actual.

The Creationists' discussion of morphology, embryology, and paleontology, is one of the most revealing parts of their work. It is even more revealing for what the Creationists do not say! Let us start with these omissions. In looking at such questions as homology and embryology, the Creationists are dealing with, what I have characterized as, the "subdisciplines" in the Darwinian synthesis: those areas illuminated by the core of population biology. Where then is organic geographical distribution? We have seen that biogeography is *the* strongest point in the whole Darwinian story: from Darwin on, the Galapagos finches have been the paradigm of evolutionism. *They are nowhere to be found in the Creationist discussion!* Given the time that the Creationists have obviously spent on their task, given the importance of biogeography for the Darwinian, I cannot believe that such an omission was inadvertant.

Other topics favorable to Darwinism are also conspicuous by their absence. For instance, there is no discussion of the way in which Darwinians think that the gradual order of complexity, to be found in organisms today, supports their claims about the temporal ordering of complexity. Additionally, those topics which are discussed get disproportionate treatment. Morphology, a very important topic for all evolutionists, is brushed aside quickly, whereas the fossil record gets very extended treatment.

It is perhaps worth spending a moment or two on the Creationists' treatment of morphology, despite its brevity. It shows very clearly the level at which the Creationists argue. The Creationists begin by acknowledging that evolutionists take morphology seriously as evidence of common ancestry. The arm and hand of man, the wing of bird, the front-leg of horse, all tell of evolution from the same organisms. What can the Creationists do in the face of such devastating proof? They admit the possibility of ancestry, but then go on to say that this does not prove evolution anyway! In the Creationists' opinion, the division of organisms into different categories above the species level (genera, families, orders, etc.) is all entirely arbitrary. Hence, if one points out that organisms from different genera (say) have come from common ancestors, one proves nothing really. This is because the division into genera is totally man-made, and says nothing about the real biological world. One is certainly not proving that genuinely different organisms all evolved from the same ancestors.

Furthermore, the Creationists invoke Ernst Mayr of Harvard in support of their case. A reviewer of Mayr's book, *Principles of Systematic Zoology* (New York: McGraw-Hill, 1969) had the following to say.

According to the author's view, which I think nearly all biologists must share, the species is the only taxonomic category that has at least in more favorable examples a completely objective existence. Higher categories are all more or less a matter of opinion. (This reviewer of Mayr's book was G. W. Richards, *Science,* 167, p. 1477, and is quoted in Morris, 1974, p. 71.)

Hence, argue the Creationists, we can see that morphology proves nothing about evolution, for as even the evolutionists themselves are forced to admit, the divisions into which organisms are supposed to have evolved are

without significance. Moreover, conclude the Creationists, what little morphology does tell us about the past points more towards Creationism than
towards evolutionism. The evolution model implies that there are no gaps between different forms of living organisms. Since there are obviously gaps, the
evolution model fails, whereas the Creation model, which implies such gaps,
succeeds (Morris, 1974, p. 72).

The half-truths and distortions in this whole Creationist argument about
morphology are there for all to see. The evolutionist says that, since there is
isomorphism (homology) between say the arm of man and the front leg of
horse, and since there is no adaptive reason for this, the reason must be descent from common ancestors. Inasmuch as the Creationists answer this point
— and really, of course, they do not address themselves to it — as we have just
seen, they have to admit that, perhaps, homologies are indeed indicative of
common ancestry. But, at the same time they say that this common descent
does not prove evolution, because all higher classes of organisms are basically
arbitrary anyway. I suppose this can only mean that man and the horse are
part of the same genus! And, even this does not really do what the Creationist
wants: he needs man and the horse in the same species, and doing the same
things with their forelimbs. Otherwise his god acted capriciously.

Note, also, how Mayr's position is obviously twisted. Even though Mayr
thinks that there is an arbitrary element to higher taxa, he certainly does not
think that all is totally arbitrary. One may argue (say) about whether to put
Australopithecus afarensis in the same genus as *Homo erectus*. One cannot put
A. afarensis in the same genus as *Drosophila pseudoobscura*. I might add, incidentally, that I find something a little dishonest about all of the references by
the Creationists to eminent evolutionists. The evolutionists' works have been
scanned for every doubt and ambiguity. One would think the greatest cham-
pions of the Creationist cause were Dobzhansky, Mayr, Simpson, and Gould.
If Mayr is such an acceptable authority, why not accept his main claims about
evolution?

Finally, in discussing the preceding argument about morphology, I note
without further comment the repeated claim that evolution implies that there
can be no gaps between organisms. No Darwinian has ever said this — or ever
could. If one travels through time, there are no gaps between earlier and later.
But if one looks across the organic world at any particular instant in time,
there are gaps. (Look back at Darwin's own picture, Fig. 2.4.)

The Creationist discussion of embryology is an interesting case of implying guilt by association. Darwin never accepted the biogenetic law. Today's
Darwinians do not accept the law. Why then introduce it into the discussion at
all? The Creationists claim that for some odd (and no doubt disreputable)
reason evolutionists continue to cite the law as evidence for evolutionism,
despite all the facts of embryology and paleontology which count against it
(Morris, 1974, p. 77). But, the Creationists give no citations to back up their
charge of irrationality/dishonesty. Let me say simply that if the Creationists
have a case to make, then they should document their claim. Otherwise, forget it.

Gaps in the fossil record get pride of place in the Creationist discussion. Happily, the Darwinian is able to show the disinterested judge that science has started to pass the Creationist by. We know full well that there is still a lively discussion in paleontological quarters about the nature of the record; but, no one at all knowledgeable thinks it supports the Creationist. For a start, we have seen that much progress has been made towards the revealing of pre-Cambrian life. We now have far more evidence than of supposed micro-organisms, which (as the Creationists rather imply) might not really be organisms at all. Moreover, in addition to indisputable pre-Cambrian organisms, the order of pre-Cambrian life seems to be what the evolutionist expects. One starts with the most primitive forms, and then works up to full-bodied multicellular organisms. (Refer to Chapter 6.)

The later record has many gaps. It also has many sequences, as expected by the evolutionist. It would be nice to see the Creationist take on the question of the horse, which is one of the best documented cases of evolutionary change. (See Fig. 14.1.) The argument of the Creationist about *Archaeopteryx*,

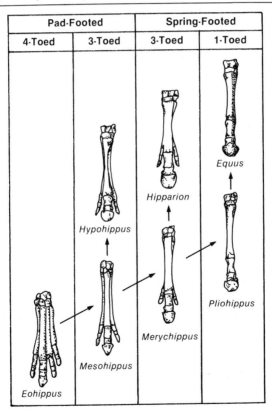

Pad-Footed		Spring-Footed	
4-Toed	3-Toed	3-Toed	1-Toed

Equus

Hipparion

Hypohippus

Pliohippus

Merychippus

Mesohippus

Eohippus

Fig. 14.1
Perhaps the most famous aspect of horse evolution, from the four-toed eohippus (*Hyracotherium*) to the modern one-toed horse (*Equus*). (Adapted by permission from G. G. Simpson, (1951). *Horses,* New York: Oxford University Press.)

namely that it is a bird and therefore no true link, is obviously just a verbal quibble. Moreover, the argument presupposes that the class of birds is a fixed definite thing, which goes against the earlier Creationist claims about the arbitrariness of all classification. Even if one calls *Archaeopteryx* a bird, because of its feathers, this still does not deny its status as a link, given the combination of reptilian features — such a combination not to be found in today's birds. (See Figs. 14.2, 14.3.)

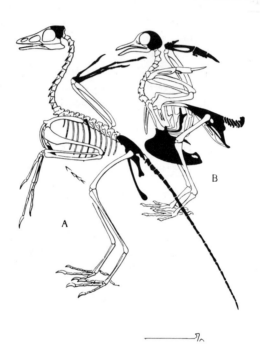

Fig. 14.2
Why do evolutionists make such a fuss over *Archaeopteryx*? They classify it as a bird because it has feathers, but comparison of *Archaeopteryx* (A in this figure), with a modern bird (B, in this figure, a pigeon) and reptiles of its own time (b and c in the succeeding figure) show what an incredible intermediate it really is. Like modern birds, *Archaeopteryx* not only has feathers, but fused clavicles (the furcula, or wishbone) which stabilize the shoulder joint, preventing collapse of the front in flight. Unlike modern birds, but like the reptiles, *Archaeopteryx* has a small brain, long tail, separate hand bones, and non-expanded sternum (used in modern birds to attach the major flight muscles), to name but some features. It is nonsense simply to say that *Archaeopteryx* is a bird, and hence not a true intermediate. (Taken by permission from E. H. Colbert, (1969). *Evolution of Vertebrates,* New York: John Wiley.)

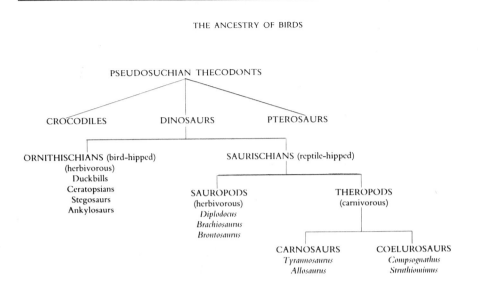

THE ANCESTRY OF BIRDS

Fig. 14.3a

There is some debate today over the true ancestry of *Archaeopteryx*. Some scholars think that *Archaeopteryx* comes from the Pseudosuchian thecodonts. Perhaps down the same line as the crocodiles. Others go back to the position of T. H. Huxley, and think that the birds are the modern-day representatives of the dinosaurs, having evolved through the Coelurosaurs. Neither position gives any comfort to the Creationist. (Taken by permission from A. Feduccia, (1980). *The Age of Birds*, Cambridge, Mass.: Harvard University Press.)

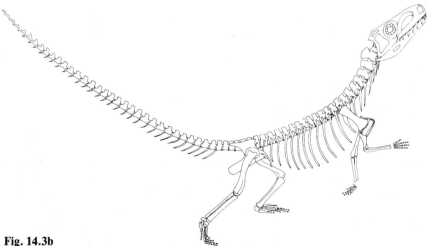

Fig. 14.3b

Euparkeria, an early Triassic pseudosuchian thecodont from South Africa. (Taken by permission from R. F. Ewer, (1965). The anatomy of the thecodont reptile *Euparkeria capensis* Broom. *Phil. Trans. Roy. Soc.*, 176(2), 197-221.)

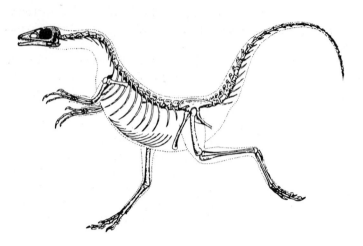

Fig. 14.3c
Heilmann's reconstruction of the skeleton of the coelurosaur *Compsognathus longipes*, from the upper Jurassic Solnhofen limestone. (From G. Heilmann, (1926). *The Origin of Birds.* London: Witherby.)

I confess I fail entirely to see why "living fossils" refute Darwinian evolutionary theory. If one had an evolutionary theory which supposed that life was created at some one point, in the distant past, and then there had been an inevitable, steady progress, up a chain of being, then living fossils would indeed cause trouble. But, Darwinism does not suppose this. If conditions are stable and there are no virtues in change, then so be it. Certainly, living fossils do not prove the Creationist case. If all organisms were created at one point in time, why are living fossils so rare and what is it that distinguishes them, that they left fossil traces and yet still exist?

One final point, before we leave this chapter: philosophers identify a form of invalid argument, which they call the "fallacy of complex question." It is a kind of argument that forces upon one's opponent premises, that he would not necessarily want to accept. Thus, if I ask you: "Have you stopped beating your wife?", whether you answer yes or no, you seem to be committed to the premise that, at one point, you were beating your wife! The Creationists are playing a similar game here. They rush one through the evolutionary spectrum, and then force one to spend masses of time on the fossil record, thereby establishing that this, and this alone, is the key evidence for evolution. But, we know that this is not true. Paleontology gives unique insights into phylogenies; but, for the general story of evolution, especially the story of causes, one must refer to the whole biological world, living and past. Spending undue time with the fossils puts the evolutionist in a false position.

Floods, time, and man

I rather rejoice in the discussion, *Uniformitarianism or Catastrophism?* The Creationists have to speak on their own account, and the silliness of their ideas is made plain for all to see. Thus, for a start, they want to claim that there really is not that much progression in the fossil record, after all. Remember how the suggestion is made that most of today's plants and animals can be found in the fossil record. Relatedly, it is stated that most fossilized organisms can be found living today, if one ignores differences caused by environmental fluctuations (Morris, 1974, p. 116). Of course, this is just not true. It is certainly not true in any sense that would make the Creationist case at all plausible. Do you fear to go out at night because you might bump into *Tyrannosaurus rex*? Do you eat your trilobites raw, or do you prefer them cooked in garlic? Should the hunting season on *Archaeopteryx* be lengthened or shortened? Perhaps the problem was that they were overhunted by the Mayas. Conversely, not even the Creationists have found mammals in the pre-Cambrian. Nor are they very likely to!

But what about the case of human footprints, in the Cretaceous? All one can say is that there is a very fishy, or rather dinosaurish, smell about the whole thing (Milne, 1981). Some of the footprints are twenty-one inches long, and exhibit a seven-foot stride. Helpfully, one Creationist author has noted that Genesis tells us that "there were giants in the Earth, in those days." Some of the footprints are very like dinosaur footprints. One's queries on this point are not allayed, when one learns that some of the Creationist photos are "improved," by the judicious use of sand, to highlight the features the Creationists want their audience to see and note. Some of the footprints have a rear claw, and the "instep" occurs along the outside edge of the foot. In short, this evidence has all the status of the bent spoons, which were so popular with students of the para-normal, a few years back. (See Fig. 14.4.)

Then, having been warned against too sequential a reading of the fossil record, we have the Creationist story of the catastrophic flood, which supposedly led to the progressiveness which we do see in the record. Remember what this all involved. Given their ability, organisms scrambled further and further up the hills, until the rising waters overtook them. "Mammals and birds would be found in general at higher elevations than reptiles and amphibians, both because of their habitat and because of their greater mobility" (Morris, 1974, p. 119).

Let us be quite clear what this all means. The detailed record, from simple to more complex, from general to special, from fish to man, is entirely an artifact of the flood. There was *not one* human being, or horse, or cow, or fox, or deer, or hippopotamus, or tortoise, or monkey, who was so slow, or so stupid, or so crippled, that he/she/it, lagged behind his/her/its fellows, and thus got caught down at the bottom of the hill. *Not one!* Conversely, there was *not one* dinosaur, or trilobite, or mammoth, that was lucky enough, or clever enough, or fast enough, to climb up to the top of the hill, and thus escape the fate of its fellows. *Not one!* And this we are asked to believe as sound science?

Fig. 14.4
Dinosaur footprints in Cretaceous Glen Rose limestone, (Taken by permission from F. J. Pettijohn and P. E. Potter, (1964). *Atlas and Glossary of Primary Sedentary Structures.* New York: Springer-Verlag). I draw your attention to the toe-mark of the print in the lower left-hand section. Viewed back-to-front this looks remarkably like a human footprint. Given the fact that several of the Creationist photographs have other marks around their "footprints" which look very much like the rest of the dinosaur print, an obvious conclusion can be drawn. As noted earlier, regretfully I have been refused permission to reproduce the photographs used by the Creationists.

In the discussion, *Old or Young?,* the Creationists raise questions about the absolute ages of the earth and its inhabitants, arguing for their own limited time span, of less (possibly quite a bit less) than 10,000 years. First, let me challenge strenuously the Creationist claim that the only "true" knowledge is observable knowledge, or written records thereof. The authors of the text point out that our earliest written records go back only to the first Egyptian dynasty, that is to say, to some period within the third and fourth millenia before Christ (2200 to 3500 B.C., to be precise). They argue that genuine scientific knowledge before this period is absolutely impossible, because science depends on observation, and that consequently, without such observation or without written record of such observation, the essence of science is missing.

Hence, the Creationists conclude that no genuine scientific knowledge of early earth history is possible, because there is no *direct* testimony. Any claims about the first stages of the universe in general and of our world in particular "must therefore be indirect, and will be uncertain at best" (Morris, 1974, p. 131).

As I have been at pains to show, earlier in this book, all of this is absolute nonsense. Indirect evidence is certainly not "uncertain at best." Given the right-wing political and social views of the average Creationist, I would like to see the reaction to the suggestion that no one should ever be convicted of murder, certainly not executed, in the absence of direct, eyewitness testimony, because indirect evidence is "uncertain at best." I have made my case earlier, so I will not repeat it. Personally, I distrust a great deal of supposed eyewitness testimony. Do you really believe all those Medieval reports about the Devil and witches, and so forth? Perhaps Dr. Morris does, given his views on the connexion between Satan and evolution.

If the Creationists' arguments about methods of calculating absolute time spans were well taken, then obviously the whole Darwinian edifice would come crashing right down. However, the evolutionist has little to fear at this point, because the Creationists' arguments keep to their usual standards. The Creationists argue that all the physicochemical methods of calculating absolute dates are totally untrustworthy, because the premises assumed by these methods could be false. However, it is one thing to say that the premises could be, or are, false. It is another to prove it. And this, the Creationists do not do.

The Creationists state quite without proof that pertinent elements can, almost at will, move in and out of rocks being studied. No evidence is offered for these claims. No discussion is given of the very detailed studies by geologists of when pertinent materials might or might not be expected to be lost or overrepresented in rocks. Similarly, no proof is offered for the claim that one can never tell the initial composition of rocks, nor is there refutation of the geologists' claim that there are ways of inferring initial compositions. No consideration is given to the technique of comparing rocks of different chemical composition from the same molten substance ("magma"), which jointly point to their common initial conditions. (Refer back to Fig. 2.15.)

And, above all, no proof is offered for the Creationist claim that processes of decay may have speeded up, in the past, thus yielding drastically inflated figures when we study rocks today. Of course, if rates of decay do change, then inflated figures will be obtained. But, it is one thing to suggest that perhaps rates do change; it is another to give a serious proof. Since, apparently, an acceptable mode of scholarly argument is simply to quote authorities sympathetic to one's own position, perhaps I might be permitted to quote from a recent textbook.

The use of radioactive decay to measure the ages of rocks and minerals also implies the assumption that the decay constants have not changed during the past 4.6 billion years. This assumption is justified because radioactive decay is a property of the nucleus which is shielded from outside influences by the electrons that surround it. ... Consequently, there is no reason to doubt that the decay constants of the naturally occurring long-lived radioactive isotopes used for dating are invariant and independent of the physical and chemical conditions to which they may have been subjected since nucleosynthesis (Faure, 1977, p. 48).

Also missing from the Creationists' arguments is mention of the fact that different dating techniques can sometimes be used on the same rocks or minerals: when these yield comparable ages one has (through one's consilience) a far greater degree of confidence in one's results. A striking example of this occurred in the efforts to date Lucy, made even more memorable by the fact that two completely different approaches were used. (See Fig. 14.5.) The Creationists will have to do a little better than quoting refuting passages from their own writings, if they are to be taken seriously at this point.

14.5

Fission-track dating: In order to date Lucy and other specimens of *Australopithecus afarensis* several techniques were used to measure the ages of surrounding rocks, including the potassium-argon method (see Fig. 2.15) and the fission-track method. In this latter method, one examines very small crystals called "zircons" to be found in volcanic rocks. These contain a radioactive form of uranium which decays into lead. However, rather than trying to calculate the extant ratio of uranium to lead (as in the potassium-argon method), one counts the individual number of atoms of uranium that have decayed! Thus, given a measure of the uranium remaining in the zircon crystal, one can calculate the age.

It is possible to detect the decay of a uranium atom, because the process sets off a release of energy, which gets recorded as a slight mark or "track" within the crystal. Each track represents one atom decayed.

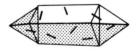

Obviously, if one can cross-compare a thus obtained fission-track date with a potassium-argon date, and they agree, then one has a consilience which much increases one's confidence in the believed date of the rocks being studied. In the case of *A. afarensis*, it was found that the fossils occurred below rock that was dated at 2.8 million years (potassium-argon method) and 2.7 million years (fission-track method). Within experimental limits, this is a close agreement.

Also, as I noted earlier, they would do well to remove the contradictions in their position. If, as the Creationists argue, evolutionists are committed to evolving laws and processes, and the Creationists are not, then the Creationists have no right to suggest that the laws and processes change at this point. Conversely, if the Creationists really do not believe in change, then they might reconsider Dr. Barnes' argument that the earth's magnetic field is decaying exponentially, and that hence Earth cannot be more than 10,000 years old.

Finally, while on the subject of age, let me raise the Creationists' quite incredible argument based on population numbers. They ask "whether the creation model or the evolution model most [sic] easily correlates with the data of population statistics." (Morris, 1974, p. 167). And, as we saw, the answer is: "the creation model!" Putting the matter bluntly, this is total nonsense. In no way does a million-year history for man strain Darwinism "to the breaking point." All of the evidence that we have from the animal and plant worlds shows that population numbers can remain relatively steady, or even decline, despite birthrates of far, far higher levels than is ever dreamt of in the human realm. Natural causes more than control population numbers. Even if the world were as the Creationists suppose, and less than 10,000 years old, if natural causes were not thus effective, we would long have been swamped by houseflies, and herrings, and God knows what else. Therefore, Darwinism is not strained in any way whatsoever, if it is supposed that natural causes might have kept human numbers way below their theoretical maximum.

Of course, one must suppose that natural causes were thus effective, but, outside of the sheltering influences of Western Industrialized Society, there is no reason to think that they would not be. Even today, as in Africa or Asia, we see how such forces as famine, war, and disease, wipe out whole populations. Since there is lots of evidence that civilization is a recent phenomenon, Darwinism is under no pressure at this point.

Given that the Creationists are obviously so impervious to the effects of empirical evidence, I am not sure that there is much point in making detailed reference to it. But, for the benefit of those who think that, in scientific arguments, reference to the facts is of some importance, the following information may be of some interest (Coale, 1974). It is believed that agriculture was introduced around 8000 B.C., and several estimates put the human population at that time at about 8 million. By 1 A.D., the human population had jumped to about 300 million. This is not a figure picked out of thin air, but one based on such things as records left by the Romans and Chinese at that time. The increase represents a yearly growth rate of 360 per million, or .36 per 1000 (or .036 percent per year).

From 1 to 1750 A.D. (at which point modern census-taking started), we have a population jump of about 500 million. This represents an annual growth rate of .56 per 1000. Then the acceleration of growth began. From 1750 to 1800 we go to about a billion people, with a rate of 4.4 per 1000; from 1800 to 1850 to 1.3 billion, with a rate of 5.2 per 1000; from 1850 to 1900 to 1.7 billion, with a rate of 5.4 per 1000; from 1900 to 1950 to 2.5 billion, with a rate of 17.1 per 1000; and (estimated) from 1974 to 2000 to 6.4 billion, with a rate of 19 per 1000. The jump in the rates can be directly correlated with such causes as improved hygiene and medical facilities, and so forth.

Obviously the figures make a total mockery of the Creationists' case. The present growth rate of around 2 percent has only just been edged up to, and for only 200 years have we had anything like the 1/2 percent that the Creationists employ in their calculations. We know (in the Creationists' sense of "know," since it is based on documentary evidence), that, for nearly 2000 years before the eighteenth century, the growth rate was but a tenth of the Creationist estimate. And this, please remember, is *after* humans had achieved the level of civilization to be found in Greece and Rome. Need I say more? In their silly population argument, the Creationists are clutching at straws — lots of them, multiplying at a high rate!

And so finally, we come to the discussion of our own species: *Apes or Men?* Remember, the key argument is that there is no such thing as a "missing link": the most-likely candidate, *Australopithecus,* is no real ape-man in-intermediate. He "not only had a brain like an ape, but he also looked like an ape and walked like an ape" (Morris, 1974, p. 173). What else can one say than that Lucy, and the rest of her fellows in *Australopithecus afarensis,* have brought the Creationist argument crashing down? Perhaps one might more appropriately say that our ancestors have lifted the Creationists clear off the ground, with their free hands, as they walk upright on their hind legs! (See Fig. 14.6.)

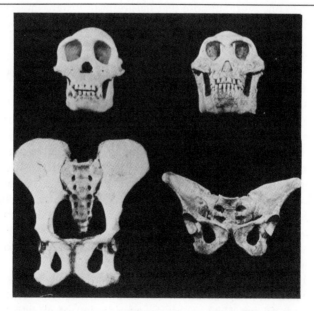

Fig. 14.6

Comparison of a chimpanzee (left) with *Australopithecus afarensis* (right). Above the neck, chimp and *A. afarensis* look very similar, except that *A. afarensis* has human-like teeth. Below the neck, the differences are enormous. *A afarensis* has a human-like pelvis. (Used by permission of Larry Rubins.)

In conclusion, therefore, I argue that the Creationists fail entirely to make their case. Their arguments are rotten, through and through. Further, they twist, misrepresent, and otherwise distort Darwinian evolutionary theory, as they attempt to refute it. Their position is not simply inadequate: it is dishonest.

Equal time?

But, should the Creationists nevertheless be given the chance to make their case? Obviously I feel very strongly that Darwinism is correct. Obviously they feel equally strongly that Creationism is correct. What right have I and fellow evolutionists got to impose our will on the Creationists, insisting that our position be taught as orthodoxy, and that their's not be taught at all? Surely, down this road lies fascism! We all know what happens as soon as one insists that certain ideas be taught as dogma, and when one refuses to let other ideas be taught at all. What has happened now to the high moral ideals I was professing at the end of the last section? Let me try to make my own position clear, and then defend it.

I would not argue that Creationist ideas be banned. Frankly I do not know how one could even set about doing this effectively, and even if one could, I would find such a course of action morally repugnant. In a free society, which I cherish, people should have the right to believe any kind of stupid thing they like. Nor would I want to ban the dissemination of Creationist literature. I am not absolutely against censorship: I think, for instance, that a case can certainly be made for censorship of certain forms of pornography (e.g., that involving children). But, there are degrees, and again I believe that the virtues of a free society include the right of people to convince other people of their ideas, however stupid.

I would not even try to stop Creationists setting up schools, in which they taught their children Creationist ideas. To be honest, I feel worried about any child being taught Creationist ideas as possible truth; but, again, I think one has a question of individual freedom. I find repugnant the idea of the state preventing parents from passing on dearly held beliefs to their children. Western society has many faults, but only a fool or a knave would deny that the freedoms we enjoy are far sweeter than the mindless conformity that the totalitarian regimes of the East force upon their peoples. Freedom means letting other people do what you do not very much like or approve of — because they want to.

However, I draw the line absolutely and completely at the introduction of Creationist ideas into the educational curricula of state-supported schools, except possibly as something to be talked about in current affairs, or as the subject of a comparative religion class. Under no circumstances would I let Creationist ideas into biology classes, or anywhere else where they might be taken by students as possible frameworks of belief. I would not give Creationism equal time. I would not give it any time. Let me give three reasons for my stand. They are obviously directed particularly to the situation in the United States; but, I trust, are sufficiently broad to be generally applicable.

Why Creationism should not be taught: Religion

The first reason is based on *religion*. I take it as axiomatic that, in our society, particular religious beliefs should not be taught, and thereby endorsed, in state-supported schools. In the United States, the situation and justification is quite simple. Such teaching stands in violation of the Constitution. But, a more general case can be made for this stand, based on moral and pedagogical grounds. In a pluralistic society, such as the United States or Canada, people have the right to hold any particular religious belief that they like: and they do. We have Catholics, Anglicans (Episcopelians), Jews, Jehovah's Witnesses, Muslims, Atheists, and many more. Furthermore, people have the right to these beliefs and associated practices, even though others find the beliefs ridiculous or offensive. I find the Jehovah's Witnesses' stand on blood transfusions ridiculous; many feel just as strongly about the Catholic stand on abortion.

Clearly, one important way of preserving this right to freedom of religious belief is to insist that no particular belief be taught, and thereby endorsed, in state-supported schools. Otherwise, teachers, students, and parents, will soon find themselves having to present, or being presented with, ideas as fact, which they do not, and would not, themselves accept. In short, if the state is to allow freedom of religious belief — and this freedom can be justified on just about every moral system one can think of — and if indeed we have a pluralistic society, then the state ought not itself promote any particular belief in its own institutions, including its schools.

But, this means that the Creationist case should not be taught in schools, for, whatever may be said to the contrary, "Scientific Creationism" does move right over into religion. Of course, in a sense, the whole Creationist position is a fraud: all that it is trying to do is to push a literal reading of Genesis, very thinly veiled as science. I really do not see how anyone could get through a class-room course in Scientific Creationism, without mentioning the Bible, ever. How could one talk about the Flood, without mentioning Noah? What does one do, if some bright student asks about the survivors of the Flood? At the very least, the teacher is put in a totally insincere position, telling children all about something, knowing full well that it is the tip of a very large iceberg.

Furthermore, even if Scientific Creationism were totally successful in making its case as science, it would not yield a *scientific* explanation of origins. Rather, at most, it could prove that science shows that there can be *no* scientific explanation of origins. The Creationists believe the world started miraculously. But miracles lie outside of science, which by definition deals only with the natural, the repeatable, that which is governed by law. Hence, Creationism can aspire only to a Pyrrhic victory: that the evidence of nature and the methodology of science show that no natural laws explain the ultimate past. As Whewell used to say: "When we inquire whence [organisms] came into this world, geology is silent. The mystery of creation is not within the range of her legitimate territory; she says nothing, but she points upward" (Whewell, 1840, 3, 588). At least, he was candid.

However, pretend for a moment that the Scientific Creationism ploy is viable. Pretend that one could teach the doctrines given in the textbook, *Scientific Creationism,* without bringing in the Biblical background. Religion still intrudes in a very big way — if not revealed religion, then natural religion. Both the cosmological argument (argument from first cause) and the teleological argument (argument from design) have starring positions in the book.

Remember the discussion about the nature of laws, and remember how the evolutionist supposedly is committed to ever-changing laws. This leads right into a discussion about origins: a discussion which reads just as though it came straight from the pen of Archdeacon Paley, the well-known early nineteenth-century natural theologian. Specifically, the Creationists tell us that even if the evolutionist does not believe in God, he simply must believe in some sort of uncaused First cause, which was responsible for everything around us, and indeed for ourselves. But, more than this, the Creationists argue that this First cause must have all sorts of properties, capable of producing the kind of world of which we are a part. In particular, since space is limitless, the First cause must be infinite. And analogously, given the existence of other phenomena, such as spirituality, morality, and human love, we can and must infer "from the law of cause-and-effect that the First cause of all things must be an infinite, eternal, omnipotent, omnipresent, omniscient, moral, spiritual, volitional, truthful, loving, living Being" (Morris, 1974, p. 20). Conversely, the Creationists point out that brute matter and blind cause have none of these properties.

What more needs to be said? If this is not blatant propaganda for a particular religious position, I do not know what is! What I do know is that talk of "an infinite, eternal, omnipotent, omnipresent, omniscient, moral, spiritual, volitional, truthful, loving, living Being!" is not science. As the Creationists themselves admit; for with a gall which leaves me quite breathless they calmly acknowledge that belief in such a "Creator God" is "not completely a *scientific* decision" (Morris, 1974, p. 19). It is added for good measure that belief in evolution is not completely scientific either!

Remember, also, the discussion further on in the chapter, about purpose. Again, quite explicit reference is made to "an omnipotent Creator," who supposedly was behind both the design and the construction of humans. We are told that only by supposing such a Creator can we circumvent the problems posed by the second law of thermodynamics, and moreover that, given such a Creator, life takes on a real meaning and value. Without the Creator, nothing matters (Morris, 1974, p. 35).

Obviously, this conclusion does not belong in science. It is a religious conclusion, and that is all there is to it. Please note that I am not here denying the validity of the argument for the existence of God from the supposedly purposeful nature of the world, nor even am I denying the validity of the earlier-given causal argument for God's existence and nature. In fact, as I showed earlier, there are major questions about both arguments; but criticism of them is not my present purpose. All I claim, and no further argument is necessary, is that they take one out of science and into religion. What a sham Scientific Creationism really is!

I suspect that one response of the Creationists will be that, even if Scientific Creationism should not be taught, because it veers into religion, then the same is true also of evolutionism in general, and Darwinism in particular, for they too are unsupported testaments of faith. I shall not bother to respond further to a charge like this. If my first and second sections have not persuaded you otherwise, there is little more I can say here. Let me simply conclude this discussion of the religious aspect to the Creationist/evolutionist debate, by drawing your attention to a very great threat I see lurking in the Creationist position.

A favorite gambit of nineteenth-century religious opponents of evolutionism was to argue that one might legitimately consider the Bible as documentary evidence for the past: the Bible is taken, not so much as the inspired word of God, but as reliable eyewitness testimony to past events. The Scientific Creationists seem to be clearing the way to this path. Remember their claims that the only true knowledge of the past comes from human reports. I fear very much that, once this premise is granted, it will prove to be the thin end of a very large wedge. Religion will be brought in even more blatantly.

Why Creationism should not be taught: Morality

My second objection to the teaching of Scientific Creationism is one based on *morality*. In a sense, obviously, this is closely related to my case about religion, but there is some difference. I cannot see that one could ever avoid teaching some moral code in schools, nor would I (nor I suspect, anyone else) want a morality-free curriculum. Children must be taught not to lie, cheat, steal, bully, and a host of other behaviors associated with proper interpersonal conduct. Moreover, children should be taught to behave properly, not simply because it is expedient, but because it is right. If you avoid cheating, only because you fear being caught, then the educational system has failed you.

Why is the teaching of morality permissible, even desirable, whereas the teaching of religion is not? There are three reasons. First, although most religious systems do incorporate a moral code, and although (as we saw for the nineteenth century) many people in justifying their morality do refer to religion, there is in fact no logical connexion between basic morality and religion. The atheist, no less than the sincere believer, can (and frequently does) have a deep sense of morality. The status of morality is, in important respects, akin to the status of mathematics. No God could (or would) want to deny certain central moral tenets, any more than He could (or would) want to deny $2 + 2 = 4$; but, just as $2 + 2 = 4$, not because God wants it but because it is true, so the moral tenets follow because they are true, rather than because God wants them. Of course, if you really believe that God could have made $2 + 2 = 5$, then you will not agree with me on this point; but, I think you purchase your disagreement at too great a price. Could God really have made it moral to rape small children? I say not! Hence, I argue that morality and religion are not the same, and so one can consistently advocate the teaching of morality but not religion, in the schools.

Second, morality can properly be taught in state schools because people of different faiths come together on the basic claims of morality. Catholic, Protestant, Jew, Atheist, Hindu, and others agree that one ought to be kind, one ought not steal and cheat, and so forth. Hence, no tension or violation of rights is involved by expecting teachers to inculcate moral values, or for students to be so exposed. (I realize that one consequence of this argument might be that in a society with a commonly held religion, one could properly teach religion in state schools. I think I would accept this conclusion, subject to some sort of opting out clause.)

Third, morality affects us all. You may think incredibly daft things as part of your religion, but that is your business. If you think it is morally acceptable to steal and cheat, then that becomes my business also. In other words, rights in a free society are preserved by the teaching of morality, not threatened. You may think that what counts here is not the teaching of morality, but the teaching of moral behavior. So long as you do not cheat, that is what counts, whether your actions be because cheating is wrong or because you fear the consequences of being caught. But, with the sociobiologists, let me point out that you will probably be a more effective and consistent non-cheater, if you think cheating is wrong. It is wrong, independent of your opinions, but you will cheat less if you agree. Also, I am sufficiently old fashioned to agree with Plato that only the good man is the happy man.

However, having made these three points about morality and teaching, let me go on to add the very important proviso that I refer only to basic morality. Many religions (sacred and secular) add their own particular twists. All of the previous arguments about religious faith reapply here, with full force. Perhaps the Catholics are right about birth control. In such a society as ours, it is not right that these norms be taught in state-supported schools. Similarly, if the orthodox Jew wants to observe rigid dietary laws, that is his business. The rest of us should not be taught that it is morally desirable to abstain from pork. Nor should the Jehovah's Witnesses' views about blood transfusions be given to our children. And so forth.

The trouble with the Creationist position is that it really does open the way to the teaching of a specific, religiously based morality. The authors of the textbook, in their *Foreword*, are quite explicit about this connection between their religion and their morality. They tell us in no uncertain terms that evolutionism is a morally bad thing and simply ought not be taught in schools.

Evolutionism goes against both Christianity and Judaism, and runs counter "to a healthy society and true science as well" (Morris, 1974, p. iii).

In the light of comments like these, it is obvious that the teaching of Scientific Creationism is simply going to pave the way for the pushing of a morality based on narrow Biblical lines. Remember how blatant the Arkansas bill is on this matter. Homosexuals will be condemned and excoriated as moral degenerates. Women will be confined to perpetual second-rate citizenship. And all nonbelievers will be labeled perfidious infidels. Given religious freedom, I do not see that one can or should prohibit people from believing these things. I do object most strenuously to such "norms" being squeezed into the school curriculum. One certainly cannot pretend that such a Biblically based code is part of a commonly accepted basic morality: people are as split on such questions as the status of women and proper treatment of homosexuals, as they are on such obviously religion-linked problems as abortion.

One final point of defence: The Creationists point out, with reason, that some fairly unpleasant racist doctrines have been pushed in the name of Darwinism. One thinks particularly of claims about the superiority of certain races over others. Surely one ought therefore keep Darwinism out of the schools, since it too squeezes in special "moral" doctrines? Indeed, I myself admitted already to the underlying ideology of present-day Darwinism!

But, in fact, this argument does not follow. It is true that one can saddle Darwinism with some vile racist doctrines, for instance, about the superiority of white, Anglo-Saxon males in the struggle for existence. But, one can do the same for a Biblically based religion! We all know the racist doctrines supposedly based on the misdeeds of Ham, Noah's son; and, indeed, if one wants out-and-out fascism/racism/sexism, the writings of the nineteenth-century Creationists are full of such sentiments. The comments of Hugh Miller on the

status of the Irish are a good place to start.

More pertinently, with respect to the present, we have seen a Darwinism stripped of the offensive nineteenth-century views on race and sex and the like. The ideology has gone from the basic claims about evolution, and about the Darwinian causes operating in the animal and plant world. Even the ideology remaining in the claims about the human world is, I suggest, based on a generally acceptable moral ethic. No sociobiologist argues that blacks are inferior, or whatever.

I add, however, that I am certainly not arguing here that every last scrap of human sociobiology be taught as truth! As you know, full well, I do not think that it is yet established truth. I would certainly want students exposed to the various positions taken on human nature. I would feel very uncomfortable were either a strict environmentalism or a strict hereditarianism taught as gospel. But, my immediate concern here is with the teaching of the basic fact of evolution, together with illustration of some of the proposed natural causes of it. Claims of this kind are value-free.

Why Creationism should not be taught: Knowledge

My third objection to the teaching of Scientific Creationism is, for me, the most important. It centres on what one might, roughly, call the problem of *knowledge*. Human beings have many, many failings. In a century which has seen both Auschwitz and Hiroshima, I need hardly dwell on them. And yet, for all this, there is something noble about humanity. We may be little higher than the apes. We are also little lower than the angels. We strive to live, and thus we produce our technology. But, man does not live by bread alone: he produces art, and literature, and knowledge, *for its own sake.* Perhaps the model of the double helix will lead, through recombinant DNA techniques, to great technological advances. But, the model in itself is a thing of beauty, and an inspiring testament to human achievement. We have a thirst to know, and this raises us above the brutes.

This thirst for knowledge, and the methodologies and results that it has led to, were among our parents' greatest gifts to us. Not just because they led to a greater standard of living — although, this is true, and should be acknowledged and valued. But also because they made us human beings, in the best sense of the word. Hence, among our greatest needs and duties is that of passing on, to our children, the accumulated wisdom of the past, together with our zest and our achievements. We owe this to our children, as our parents owed it to us.

Scientific Creationism stands right against this. It is intellectual Ludditism of the most pernicious kind. It is a betrayal of ourselves as human beings. And, it is therefore for this reason, above all others, that I argue that it should not be part of the material taught in schools.

At this point, there will be an outcry. Surely, I have jumped altogether too quickly from premises to conclusion? I have argued that the quest for knowledge, and the successes, make for one of the great marks of the human spirit. Who would deny this? The search for the truth is cherished by all. Indeed, it has all the status of motherhood. But, having pronounced these noble ideals, it is too fast a move to translate them straight into the practicalities of the school curriculum, and thence to deny the Creationists a place in biology classes.

Indeed, prima facie, a good case can be made for the opposite conclusion. A key element in the hunt for knowledge is that all ideas, however ridiculous, however repellant, must be given their chance to win their spurs. As soon as one begins to insist that the truth must be fitted into certain prescribed molds, as soon as one puts dogma above free inquiry, one is lost. One need go no further than the sad story of Russian biology, in this century, to realize this. State-endorsed Lysenkoism tells all (Joravsky, 1970). But, surely, refusal to give Scientific Creationism equal time is part and parcel of the same repression, and denial of the human spirit? Evolution is being set up as dogma, and Darwin is its god. Far from endorsing the search for knowledge, my adamant stand against Scientific Creationism is a stand against the human spirit.

Whether or not *I* accept or reject Scientific Creationism, my obligation to my children is to let them accept or reject it for themselves.

Not quite so! I endorse freedom of inquiry, and I too believe that ideas must be judged on their own merits, not simply upon their ideological acceptability. Moreover, the very last thing I want to call for is a ban on ideas, any ideas, including Scientific Creationism. With John Stuart Mill, I say: "If all mankind minus one were of one opinion, and only one person were of the contrary opinion, mankind would be no more justified in silencing that one person, than he, if he had the power, would be justified in silencing mankind" (Mill, 1975, p. 188).

But, our concern here is with what we are going to teach our children in state schools, and at this point, a number of factors become pertinent. The most important is that one cannot simply expose children (or older students) to every possible idea that people have held, and then just leave matters at that. This is not possible, *nor should one aspire to make it possible!* An indifferent purveying of wares is not education. One must offer children the best-sifted and most firmly grounded ideas that we have, together with the tools to move inquiry forward. Choice must be made about what the teacher is to present to pupils.

This fact follows both as a matter of practical necessity, and also as a principle of proper teaching. Without careful control of the content of the curriculum, one cannot inform and guide young minds. This is not facism, but good educational theory. One would never simply tell a child that some people think the Earth is round and others have thought it flat, and then leave it to the child to decide its own preference! One would never let a child read any kind of book it wanted, without commenting on the quality. Rather, building on the solid achievements and understandings of the past, one passes them on to the next generation.

Do not misunderstand me. I am not saying that we never make mistakes. Generations of geology students were taught that the continents never move! What I do say is that we must select, and to pretend otherwise is just plain bad philosophy of education. Unless we exercise control over what we present, the next generation will have no criteria by which to evaluate and advance knowledge. But, at the same time, in selecting, we try to give children critical standards, so that perhaps, indeed, they will be drawn back to redo some of the heritage we pass on to them.

Seen in this light, Scientific Creationism fails badly. Creationism generally has had its chance in the arena of free inquiry — a very long chance. It was rejected, because it failed. The reincarnated version of today commits just about every fallacy known to man — and then some. It is not something just to be judged as an alternative view, as perhaps one might feel about punctuated equilibria. It is wrong, viewed by just about every reasonable standard that we have. It makes one mistake after another, and pulls one deception after another. Exposing young minds to it, thinking that it passes for reasonable intellectual activity, reveals irresponsible behavior by the teachers. It is not simply mistaken: it is corrosive. Teaching Scientific Creationism will stunt abilities in all areas, if its standards and methods are taken as acceptable.

All must agree that there has to come a time when we have to cry "finis" to the teaching of certain ideas. After a while they become no longer tenable, and trying to make them so is positively harmful. It is an act of bad faith even to present such ideas as a possible basis of belief. Would you really want your children taught that the Earth is the center of the universe, and that the moon is held in place by a crystal sphere? My claim is that Scientific Creationism has an equal status, and this is reflected in the arguments for it. I am not being personally vindictive or "subjective" in saying this. To pretend that there are no valid general criteria for evaluating good and bad arguments is to promote subjectivity, and to point once again to a failure in educational philosophy. Scientific Creationism is fallacious by every canon of good argumentation. Thus, I say "Keep it out of the schools!"

"Fight on!"

Let me conclude with one last reflection. Obviously, I love and cherish Darwinian evolutionary theory, as one of the great intellectual achievements of all time. But my pleading is not just for Darwinism, or any kind of evolutionism. It is for all human inquiry, particularly all scientific inquiry. If Darwinism is beaten down by the Creationists, who falls next? Remember that the Bible speaks of the sun stopping for Joshua. Both Luther and Calvin took this as textual evidence against Copernicus. Will we have to make room for religion in physics, also? And if religion, why not astrology, and all the other world systems? There is no shortage of believers prepared to fight for their causes. And, as I have noted, if Scientific Creationism is taught as a viable alternative, there cannot fail to be a deadening of the critical faculties. What is known to be fallacious will then be judged valid, and what is seen to be inadequate will be taken as proven. Hence, my fight is not just a fight for one scientific theory. It is a fight for all knowledge.

In a sense, these are dark days. The threat will not vanish, unless we fight. But, the battle can be won. Darwinism has a great past. Let us work to see that it has an even greater future.

Supplementary Reading

The literature on Darwin and Darwinism is absolutely vast. At most, all that I can or want to do is give interested readers a few guides so that they can then go on to explore for themselves. Full references for every work mentioned can be found in the Bibliography.

Darwinism Yesterday

Strangely enough, there is no major work on Charles Darwin himself. Probably the best single introduction is G. de Beer (1963), *Charles Darwin*. A useful supplement to this is by H. E. Gruber (1981), *Darwin on Man*. de Beer gives one the general facts, but Gruber gives a much better sense of the gifted individual, Charles Darwin. If your tastes run in that direction, R. Colp (1977), *To Be an Invalid,* gives a professional opinion on Darwin's maladies. More importantly, one should not miss Darwin's own *Autobiography*: make sure that you read the unexpurgated version published in 1969 by Darwin's granddaughter, Nora Barlow. It contains his views on sensitive subjects like religion, not to mention all sorts of gloriously candid remarks about his contemporaries. Supposedly Darwin was just writing for the benefit of his children; but I am sure that he had one eye on posterity!

The overall Darwinian Revolution has been rather more fully treated by scholars. L. Eiseley (1958), *Darwin's Century* is still the liveliest and most enjoyable trip through the period. G. Himmelfarb (1962), *Darwin and the Darwinian Revolution* is just what one might expect from a good historian: very perceptive about people and the background; totally at sea when it comes to scientific issues. J. C. Greene (1959), *The Death of Adam* gives a careful introduction to the events leading up to Darwin and his work, and M. J. S. Rudwick (1972), *The Meaning of Fossils* is absolutely first class on the history of paleontology. A sensible introduction to Lamarck is E. Mayr (1972), "Lamarck revisited." And, if you liked this book, you will probably enjoy my own work (1979a), *The Darwinian Revolution: Science Red in Tooth and Claw*. Otherwise, not.

For the content of Darwin's theorizing, the one work that you absolutely must tackle is *On the Origin of Species*. It is very readable, no doubt chiefly a function of the fact that Darwin sat down and wrote it quickly, drawing on his knowledge, but without qualifying and referencing all of the ideas to death. Please read the first edition, not the (usually reprinted) sixth edition. You can tell the difference because, in Chapter 4 when Darwin introduces natural selection, in and only in the later edition he also uses Spencer's alternative phrase, "the survival of the fittest": a disasterous qualification which led straight to all of the silly arguments about selection being tautological. Harvard University Press publish a (paperback) facsmile of the first edition, with a useful introduction by E. Mayr. Penguin books also publish a paperback version of the first edition, with an excellent preliminary essay by J. Burrow.

A general survey of Darwin's work can be found in M. T. Ghiselin (1969), *The Triumph of the Darwinian Method*. Ghiselin tends to be somewhat ahistorical, but he is very perceptive and has never yet penned a dull word: he has some scabrously funny asides about his opponents, real and apparent. Also, you might want to look at D. L. Hull (1973), *Darwin and His Critics*, which is a collection of nineteenth-century scientific responses to the *Origin*. Two rather more specialized books which are well worth reading, are P. J. Bowler (1976), *Fossils and Progress*, and J. D. Burchfield (1975), *Lord Kelvin and the Age of the Earth*. And additionally, you should thumb through the pages of the *Journal of the History of Biology*, which includes articles on Darwin in almost every issue. Some of the discussions deal, at length, with very minor points.

Darwinism Today

There are several strong, readable introductions to neo-Darwinian evolutionary theory. The first book I ever read on the subject and I think still one of the very best, especially for the nonbiologist, is J. Maynard Smith (3rd ed., 1975), *The Theory of Evolution*. This should be supplemented by an absolutely fantastic issue of *Scientific American* (September 1978, now published as a book), devoted exclusively to neo-Darwinism. It contains articles by E. Mayr, F. J. Ayala, J. Maynard Smith, R. C. Lewontin, and others. If you want to dig a little more deeply into the subject, a good, recent survey is F. J. Ayala and J. W. Valentine (1979), *Evolving*. It is particularly strong on the genetic factors in evolution, but perhaps a little disappointing in some other areas, particularly ecology. Even more-detailed treatments can be found in T. Dobzhansky et al. (1977), *Evolution* and D. Futuyama (1979), *Evolutionary Biology*. After you have worked through these, you will need little help from me!

For the reader who is interested in the historical development of the synthetic theory, all of the classics of neo-Darwinism (mentioned in the text) still read extremely well. Unfortunately there is as yet no full history of modern evolutionary theory, but W. B. Provine (1971), *The Origins of Theoretical Population Genetics* gives important background, and reports of what must have been an incredibly stimulating conference on the forming of the modern synthesis have been skillfully edited in Mayr and Provine (1980), *The Evolutionary Synthesis*. An excellent history of twentieth century biology in general, is G. Allen (1975), *Life Science in the Twentieth Century*. There are many good books on genetics. A recent, much-praised work is Ayala and Kiger (1980), *Modern Genetics.*

The reader who wants to delve a little more deeply into contemporary theoretical and experimental work in population genetics should not miss R. C. Lewontin (1974), *The Genetic Basis of Evolutionary Change*. In respects, Lewontin's discussion is one-sided — the author's political opinions lead inexorably towards the final chapter — but, without doubt, it is a brilliant addition to evolutionary thought. It is beautifully clear, and wins my prize as one of the top two works in biology in the past decade. Incidentally, the position I have taken in this essay on the nature of models and their role in evolutionary theorizing is one strongly promulgated by Lewontin, and more details on this position can be found in an excellent textbook, R. Giere (1979), *Understanding Scientific Reasoning,* and in a first-class article by J. Beatty (1980), "Optimal-design models and the strategy of model building in evolutionary biology".

E. B. Ford (1971), *Ecological Genetics* is a valuable survey of work by English evolutionists, particularly those who specialize in fast-breeding organisms in nature. D. M. Raup and S. M. Stanley (1978), *Principles of Paleontology* tells you just what the title promises: it is a paradigm of what a textbook should be. G. C. Williams (1966), *Adaptation and Natural Selection* is still far and away the best modern discussion of natural selection. For a vigorous attack on natural selection as a meaningful evolutionary force, one which I think he would now modify, see K. R. Popper (1974), "Darwinism as a metaphysical research programme." Finally, let me recommend everything and anything written by S. J. Gould, whatever he thinks about Darwinism! Especially noteworthy are his (1977a), *Ontogeny and Phylogeny,* and his delightful collections of essays, (1977b), *Ever Since Darwin* and (1980b), *The Panda's Thumb.*

Darwinism Tomorrow

J. Farley (1977), *The Spontaneous Generation Controversy* tells you everything that you are ever likely to want to know about the history of that particular topic, and several of the items mentioned in the last section (most especially the *Scientific American* Darwinism issue) cover contemporary work on the origin and early history of life. See especially, R. E. Dickerson (1978), "Chemical evolution and the origin of life," and J. W. Schopf (1978), "The evolution of the earliest cells."

Recently, a number of eminent scientists have taken to arguing that life did not originate here on Earth, but came from outer space. Typical is F. Hoyle and N. C. Wickramasinghe (1981), *Evolution from Space,* which traces everything back to some unkown, electronic life force: "The Great Silicone Chip in the Sky," to use Beverly Halstead's wicked metaphor. I do not deal with views of this ilk in the text, for they appear to be written in total ignorance of pertinent empirical studies, and to commit all the fallacies of the Creationists, a group I do study later. I take a certain morbid delight in the fact that well-known physicists are no less capable than well-known philosophers of making complete asses of themselves: an evolutionary feat which certainly does have direct observational evidence!

Evolutionary ecology is given a brilliant exposition in J. Roughgarden (1979), *Theory of Population Genetics and Evolutionary Ecology: An Introduction.* The reader is warned, however, that mathematically speaking, the going is rough. But do not be too discouraged. Sophisticated mathematics is beyond the grasp of most biologists, too! I say this factually and not critically, for biologists are meant to be biologists and not mathematicians. Their job is not to build glorious Platonic castles in the sky, but to find out about organic nature. Hence, they take the maths on trust and work with the results, which is a good rule for the rest of us also.

The literature on sociobiology is still growing exponentially, not logistically. At some point, if you are going to take the subject seriously, you must read my other prize-winner for the most important book of the past decade: E. O. Wilson (1975a), *Sociobiology: The New Synthesis.* In a stunning fashion, Wilson surveys theoretical and empirical work on animal behavior, right up through the kingdom, from the lowest form to the highest. As is only too well known, Wilson caps his discussion by turning to our own species, *Homo sapiens.* If you cannot deal calmly with the thought that we might bear traces of our evolutionary origins, then tear out that chapter of your copy of Wilson's book, and read the rest. It is a wonderful journey that he takes us on.

Anything read after Wilson is bound to be a little anticlimactical, but a useful standard introduction to the subject is D. Barash (1977), *Sociobiology and Behavior.* Also you should not miss that delightful romp through metaphor-land, R. Dawkins (1976), *The Selfish Gene.* Personally, I like Dawkins' style just for itself; but do not fail to see the serious purpose beneath his approach. He is determined to show that science does not have to be drenched in Teutonic pseudo-jargon to be important. Anyone who thinks this is a message already heard by all scientists should glance for a moment at any passage by any member of the cladistic school of taxonomy, a group whose penchant for unpronounceable polysyllables is equalled only by their unrelenting hostility towards anyone who does not rigorously toe their party-line: "names and nastiness," to use a memorable characterizing phrase of Gould.

The punctuated equilibria hypothesis is expounded in N. Eldredge and S. J. Gould (1972), "Punctuated equilibria: an alternative to phyletic gradualism"; S. J. Gould and N. Eldredge (1977), "Punctuated equilibria:

the tempo and mode of evolution reconsidered''; and S. M. Stanley (1979), *Macroevolution.* Additionally one might look at S. J. Gould (1980a), "Is a new and general theory of evolution emerging?" The Darwinians strike back in several places, including essays in A. Hallam (1977), *Patterns of Evolution as Illustrated by the Fossil Record.* See especially the article therein, P. D. Gingerich (1977), "Patterns of evolution in the mammalian fossil record". Another reply which is as reasoned as it is brief is J. Maynard Smith (1981), "Did Darwin get it right?" See also L. B. Halstead, (1981), "The natural sciences and Marxism." Additionally, one should look at the journal *Paleobiology,* a lively newcomer to the field of evolutionary studies, with a rather wider scope than its title implies. Unlike some of the staid, already established journals in the field, its authors care about concepts as well as facts.

For discussion of the thesis that the fossil record is substantially governed by random processes, see D. M. Raup (1977), "Probabilistic models in evolutionary paleobiology." A marvelous new book on the evolution of the birds, A. Feduccia (1980), *The Age of Birds,* written for the nonspecialist, shows just why it is that *Archaeopteryx* is such an important and fascinating organism.

If you want to learn a little more about taxonomy, then on the evolutionary front, E. Mayr (1969), *Principles of Systematic Zoology* is a solid guide. For phenetic taxonomy, you should consult P. H. A. Sneath and R. R. Sokal (1973), *Numerical Taxonomy.* Virtually every issue of *Systematic Zoology* for the past ten years has had some article extolling the virtues of cladism. A recent book on the subject, which has even won grudging praise from critics, is N. Eldredge and J. Cracraft (1980), *Phylogenetic Patterns and the Evolutionary Process.*

Darwinism and Humankind

A very short time in the company of human evolutionists totally destroys any illusions one might have had about the ethereal objectivity of science. Put together any two such students of our past, and either they will fall out or they will combine in joint criticism of a third! Even if it were desirable, it would not be possible for me to give you a list of works which are generally accepted as important contributions or introductions to the field. At best, therefore, I can tell you of some works I found useful or interesting.

Starting historically, one really ought to look at Darwin's second greatest work, the *Descent of Man.* To be honest, one can skip large passages devoted to sexual selection; unless, of course, one's interests lie in that direction. Also one might read T. H. Huxley (1863), *Evidence as to Man's Place in Nature,* which is still readily available in various modern reprints. The vigor of Huxley's prose has not been diminished by the passage of time. Secondary material on Darwin and man include Gruber's essay mentioned earlier, and a fascinating discussion in a two-part article by Sandra Herbert (1974 and 1977), "The place of man in the development of Darwin's theory of transmutation."

Also informative is a brief history of nineteenth-century thought about human origins, K. P. Oakley (1964), "The problem of man's antiquity."

Several of the general works on evolutionary theory listed earlier cover recent work on human origins, for instance Dobzhansky et al. (1977), and Ayala and Valentine (1979). A lot more information can be gained from G. L. Isaac and E. R. McCowan (1976), *Human Origins: Louis Leakey and the East African Evidence,* and R. Leakey and R. Lewin (1977), *Origins.* A recent work which I have seen highly praised is J. Reader (1981), *Missing Links.* However, in my opinion nothing can compare to a current best-seller, D. Johanson and M. Edey (1981), *Lucy: The Beginnings of Humankind.* This includes a survey of the history of human fossil discoveries, which is then used as a prolegomenon for the story of Johanson's own discoveries of *Australopithecus afarensis* and of the implications that he and his co-workers have drawn from them.

Professional reaction to this book has tended to be somewhat cold, and one can understand why: Johanson comes across as one of the most big-headed people in a field noted for hominids with large crania; he is certainly not beyond telling you in no uncertain terms whom he likes and whom he dislikes; and he is very much more forthcoming about the sex-lives of others than about his own. But, if you can live with all of this, if indeed you think that a sense of the scientists as real people is a plus rather than a minus, then when you read *Lucy* you are in for a great treat. You will be caught up in the thrill of vital discoveries, and because everything is so beautifully explained, you will understand step by step the matters at issue. The authors never condescend to their readers, asking that things be taken on trust: the problems of walking, the importance of teeth, the ways and difficulties of dating rocks, the tasks of classification, all of these and many more topics are made crystal clear. I think *Lucy* is science writing for the nonexpert at its very best.

The best overall introduction to human sociobiology is probably E. O. Wilson (1978), *On Human Nature.* But a book you should not miss is P. van den Berghe (1979), *Human Family Systems: An Evolutionary View.* Always insightful, always witty, van den Berghe challenges assumption after assumption of his fellow anthropologists. A somewhat more specialized book, which will undoubtedly offend if you are an ardent feminist, is D. Symons (1979), *The Evolution of Human Sexuality.* Any work which was described by one social scientist as "the moral equivalent of fast food ... not artlessly neutral [but] skillfully impoverished" must be saying something interesting.

For the opposition, I recommend a sprightly tract by the anthropologist M. Sahlins (1976), *The Use and Abuse of Biology,* and a collection of essays put out by The Ann Arbor Science for the People Editorial Collective (1977), *Biology as a Social Weapon.* The key essay in the latter is by the Sociobiology Study Group, "Sociobiology — a new biological determinism."

Let me also mention two balanced collections of essays. A. Caplan (1978), *The Sociobiology Debate* contains writings from the past as well as the present, and G. W. Barlow and J. Silverberg (1980), *Sociobiology: Beyond Nature/Nurture?* contains a valuable series of reports from an AAAS meeting, one made even more memorable by the fact that critics poured a jug of cold water all over E. O. Wilson's head. Fortunately, in their presentations, the opposing sides really tried to grapple with issues rather than simply resorting to rhetoric.

Perhaps, the best single introduction to evolutionary ethics is A. G. N. Flew (1967), *Evolutionary Ethics*. Would that a few other authors could say as much as Flew, in so few words. A fair, although I think ultimately unsuccessful, attempt to make a case for evolutionary ethics can be found in C. H. Waddington (1960), *The Ethical Animal*. Also in this context, one should look at the already cited works by E. O. Wilson.

There is, as yet, no really good, balanced study of the ideology of science. There are a number of collections of articles dealing with the question from a left-wing perspective. I cannot accept all of their conclusions; but the Marxists have certainly shown the issue to be real and important. Let me recommend, R. Arditti, P. Brennan, and S. Carrak (1980), *Science and Liberation*. For a different perspective, you might look at my (1981), *Is Science Sexist?* although I cannot pretend that I deal very adequately with the whole question of values in science.

Darwinism Besieged

I have not found a really good historical treatment of the Creationist movement, although this of course does not mean that one does not exist! There are, however, several books on the Scopes trial. Two recent works are L. S. de Camp (1968), *The Great Monkey Trial* which is long, and M. L. Settle (1972), *The Scopes Trial*, which has nice pictures. A wonderful play (in thinly veiled fictional form) was made about the trial: *Inherit the Wind*. The movie version, starring Spencer Tracy (as Darrow), Frederick March (as Bryan), and Gene Kelley (as Mencken), appears occasionally on the late show, and is well worth staying up for. Some of the facts behind the recent Creationist revival can be gleaned from J. Moore (1976), "Creationism in California," and D. Nelkin (1976), "Science or Scripture: the politics of 'equal time'."

Obviously, if you want to discover for yourself what the Creationists themselves are saying, you should read the textbook I discuss at length in the text: H. M. Morris (1974), *Scientific Creationism*. There are many other works by the Creationists devoted to similar themes. One such book which I have often heard mentioned with praise is J. C. Whitcomb and H. M. Morris (1961), *The Genesis Flood*. Within its pages, you will find useful discussions of such questions as to how large the Ark would need to be, in order to carry all of the animals it would need to carry. Other works include R. E. Kofahl and K. L. Segraves (1975), *The Creation Explanation*; J. N. Moore and H. S. Slusher (1970), *Biology: A Search for Order in Complexity*; and G. E. Parker (1980), *Creation: The Facts of Life*. For blatantly dishonest use of sources, I have never encountered anything like Parker's treatment of R. C. Lewontin's article on "Adaptation" (from the *Scientific American* issue on Darwinism, mentioned earlier).

Finally, let me mention the *American Biology Teacher,* which valiantly fights the good fight against the Creationists. A recent, feisty contribution to the cause, which it published, is D. H. Milne (1981), "How to debate with Creationists — and 'win'."

Looking back through this bibliographic survey, I am appalled at how many good books and articles I have failed to mention. My excuse for not adding more is that there is only one thing worse than too little information, and that is too much information. With what I have given you here, together with my other references, you will have quite enough to grapple with Darwinism yourself. I hope you have as much fun as I have had!

Bibliography

Abbott, I., L. K. Abbott, and P. R. Grant (1977). Comparative ecology of Galapagos Ground Finches (*Geospiza* Gould): evaluation of the importance of floristic diversity and interspecific competition. *Ecol. Monogr.*, 47, 151-184.

Adams, M. S., and J. V. Neel (1967). Children of incest. *Pediatrics*, 40, 55-62.

Alexander, R. D. (1971). The search for an evolutionary philosophy of man. *Proceedings of the Royal Society of Victoria*, 84(1), 99-120.

Alexander, R. D. (1974). The evolution of social behavior. *Ann. Rev. Ecology and Systematics*, 5, 325-384.

Alexander, R. D. (1979). *Darwinism and Human Affairs*. (Seattle: University of Washington Press).

Alexander, R. D., and P. W. Sherman (1977). Local mate competition and parental investment patterns in the social insects. *Science*, 196, 494-500.

Allen, E. et al. (1977). Sociobiology: a new biological determinism. In Sociobiology Study Group of Boston (ed) *Biology as a Social Weapon*. (Minneapolis: Burgess).

Allen, G. (1975). *Life Science in the Twentieth Century*. (New York: Wiley).

Alvarez, L. W. et al. (1980). Extraterrestrial cause for the Cretaceous-Tertiary extinction. *Science*, 208, 1095-1108.

Arditti, R., P. Brennan, and S. Carrak (1980). *Science and Liberation*. (Montreal: Black Rose Books).

Ardrey, R. (1961). *African Genesis*. (New York: Atheneum).

Ayala, F. J., and J. Kiger (1980). *Modern Genetics*. (Reading, Mass.: Addison-Wesley).

Ayala, F. J., and M. L. Tracey (1974). Genetic differentiation within and between species of the *Drosophila Willistoni* group. *Proc. Nat. Acad. Sci. USA*, 71, 999-1003.

Ayala, F. J., M. L. Tracey, L. G. Barr, J. F. McDonald, and S. Perez-Salas (1974a). Genetic variation in natural populations of five Drosophila species and the hypothesis of the selective neutrality of protein polymorphisms. *Genetics*, 77, 343-384.

Ayala, F. J., M. L. Tracey, D. Hedgecock, and R. C. Richmond (1974b). Genetic differentiation during the speciation process in *Drosophila*. *Evolution*, 28, 576-592.

Ayala, F. J., M. L. Tracey, L. G. Barr, and J. G. Ehrenfeld (1974c). Genetic and reproductive differentiation of *Drosophila equinoxialis caribbensis*. *Evolution*, 28, 24-41.

Ayala, F. J., and J. W. Valentine (1979). *Evolving: The Theory and Processes of Organic Evolution*. (Menlo Park, Calif.: Benjamin, Cummings).

Barash, D. P. (1977). *Sociobiology and Behavior*. (New York: Elsevier).

Barlow, G. W., and J. Silverberg (1980). *Sociobiology: Beyond Nature/Nurture?* (Boulder, Col.: Westview).

Beatty, J. (1980). Optimal-design models and the strategy of model building in evolutionary biology. *Phil. Sci.*, 47, 532–561.

Best, R. V. (1961). Intraspecific variation in *Encrinurus ornatus. J. Paleont.*, 35, 1029–1040.

Bethell, T. (1976). Darwin's mistake. *Harpers Magazine*, 252, 70–75.

Bieber, I., H. J. Dain, P. R. Dince, M. G. Drellich, H. G. Grand, R. H. Gundlach, M. W. Kremer, A. H. Rifkin, C. B. Wilbur, and T. B. Bieber (1962). *Homosexuality: A Psychoanalytic Study of Male Homosexuals.* (New York: Basic Books).

Block, N., and G. Dworkin (1974). I.Q., heritability and inequality. *Philosophy and Public Affairs*, 3, 331–409, 4, 40–99.

Boag, P. T. and P. R. Grant (1981). Intense natural selection in a population of Darwin's Finches (Geospizinae) in the Galápagos. *Science*, 214, 82–85.

Bonnell, M. L., and R. K. Selander (1974). Elephant seals: genetic variation and near extinction. *Science*, 184, 908–909.

Bouchard, T. J., and M. McGue (1981). Familial studies of intelligence: a review. *Science*, 212, 1055–1058.

Bowler, P. J. (1976). *Fossils and Progress.* (New York: Science History Publications).

Bowler, P. J. (1979). Theodor Eimer and orthogenesis: Evolution by "definitely directed variation". *J. Hist. Med.*, 1979, 34: 40–73.

Bowman, R. I. (1961). *Morphological Differentiation and Adaptation in the Galapagos Finches.* University of California Publications in Zoology, LVIII.

Burchfield, J. D. (1975). *Lord Kelvin and the Age of the Earth.* (New York: Science History Publications).

Cain, A. J. (1979). Reply to Gould and Lewontin. *Proc. Roy. Soc. Series B*, 205, 599–604.

Cain, A. J., and P. M. Sheppard (1952). The effects of natural selection on body colour in the land snail *Cepaea nemoralis. Heredity*, 6, 217.

Cain, A. J., and P. M. Sheppard (1954). Natural selection in Cepaea, *Genetics*, 39, 89–116.

Campbell, B. (1972). *Sexual Selection and the Descent of Man.* (Chicago: Aldine).

Caplan, A. ed. (1978). *The Sociobiology Debate.* (New York: Harper and Row).

Carson, H. L. (1973). Reorganization of the gene pool during speciation. In "Genetic Structure of Populations," N. E. Morton, ed, *Pop. Gen. Monog.* III (Hawaii: University Press of Hawaii), 274–280.

Carson, H. L. (1975). The genetics of speciation at the diploid level. *Amer. Nat.*, 109, 83–92.

Carson, H. L., D. E. Hardy, H. T. Spieth, and W. S. Stone (1970). The evolutionary biology of the Hawaiian Drosophildae. In M. K. Hecht and W. C. Steere eds., *Essays in Evolution and Genetics in Honor of Th. Dobzhansky.* (New York: Appleton-Century-Crofts), 437–543.

Chagnon, N. (1980). Kin-selection theory, kinship, marriage and fitness among the Yanomamö Indians. In G. W. Barlow and J. Silverberg eds., *Sociobiology: Beyond Nature/Nurture?* (Boulder: Westview), 545–572.

Chargaff, E. (1976). On the dangers of genetic meddling. *Science*, 192, 938–940.

Cherfas, J. and J. Gribbin (1981). The molecular making of mankind. *New Scientist*, 91, 518–521.

Coale, A. J. (1974). The history of the human population. *Scientific American.* September, 231, 40–51.

Cole, F. C. (1959). A witness at the Scopes trial. *Scientific American*, 200, 121.

Coleman, W. (1964). *Georges Cuvier Zoologist. A Study in the History of Evolution Theory.* (Cambridge, Mass.: Harvard University Press).

Colp, R. (1977). *To Be an Invalid.* (Chicago: University of Chicago Press).

Cracraft, J. (1978). Science, philosophy, and systematics. *Syst. Zool.*, 27, 213–215.

Darwin, C. (1839). *Journal of Researches into the Geology and Natural History of the Various Countries Visited by H.M.S. Beagle, etc.* (London: Colburn).

Darwin, C. (1851a). *A Monograph of the Sub-class Cirripedia, with Figures of all the Species. The Lepadidae; or Pedunculated Cirripedes.* (London: Ray Society).

Darwin, C. (1851b). *A Monograph of the Fossil Lepadidae; Or, Pedunculated Cirripedes of Great Britain.* (London: Palaeontographical Society).

Darwin, C. (1854a). *A Monograph of the Sub-class Cirripedia, with Figures of all the Species. The Balanidae (or Sessile Cirripedes); The Verrucidae, &c.* (London: Ray Society).

Darwin, C. (1854b). *A Monograph of the Fossil Balanidae and Verrucidae of Great Britain.* (London: Palaeontographical Society).

Darwin, C. (1859). *On the Origin of Species by Means of Natural Selection.* (London: Murray).

Darwin, C. (1868). *The Variation of Animals and Plants under Domestication.* (London: Murray).

Darwin, C. (1871). *Descent of Man, and Selection in Relation to Sex.* (London: Murray).

Darwin, C. (1960). Darwin's notebooks on transmutation of species. Part 1 (Notebook 'B') ed. G. de Beer. *Bull. Brit. Mus. (Nat. Hist.) Hist. Ser.,* 2, 27–73.

Darwin, C. (1969). *Autobiography,* ed. N. Barlow. (New York: Norton).

Darwin, C., and A. R. Wallace (1958). *Evolution by Natural Selection.* (Cambridge: Cambridge University Press).

Darwin, E. (1803). *The Temple of Nature.* (London).

Darwin, F. (1887). *The Life and Letters of Charles Darwin, Including an Autobiographical Chapter.* (London: Murray).

Dawkins, R. (1976). *The Selfish Gene.* (Oxford: Oxford University Press).

de Beer, G. (1963). *Charles Darwin: Evolution by Natural Selection.* (London: Nelson).

de Camp, L. S. (1968). *The Great Monkey Trial.* (New York: Doubleday).

de Camp, L. S. (1969). The end of the monkey war. *Scientific American,* February, 220.

de Wet, J. M. J., J. R. Harlan, H. T. Stalker, and A. V. Randrianasolo (1978). The origin of tripsacoid maize (*Zea mays* L.). *Evolution,* 32, 233–244.

Dickerson, R. E. (1978). Chemical evolution and the origin of life. *Scientific American,* September, 70–86.

Dobzhansky, T. (1937). *Genetics and the Origin of Species.* (New York: Columbia University Press).

Dobzhansky, T. (1951). *Genetics and the Origin of Species,* 3rd ed. (New York: Columbia University Press).

Dobzhansky, T. (1962). *Mankind Evolving.* (New Haven: Yale University Press).

Dobzhansky, T. (1970). *Genetics of the Evolutionary Process.* (New York: Columbia University Press).

Dobzhansky, T., F. J. Ayala, G. L. Stebbins, and J. W. Valentine (1977). *Evolution.* (San Francisco: W. H. Freeman).

Dobzhansky, T., and O. Pavlovsky (1957). An experimental study of interaction between genetic drift and natural selection. *Evolution,* 11, 311–319.

Dörner, G. (1976). *Hormones and Brain Differentiation.* (Amsterdam: Elsevier).

Eiseley, L. (1958). *Darwin's Century.* (New York: Doubleday).

Eldredge, N., and J. Cracraft (1980). *Phylogenetic Patterns and the Evolutionary Process.* (New York: Columbia University Press).

Eldredge, N., and S. J. Gould (1972). Punctuated equilibria: an alternative to phyletic gradualism. In T. J. M. Schopf ed. *Models in Paleobiology.* (San Francisco: Freeman, Cooper).

Farley, J. (1977). *The Spontaneous Generation Controversy: From Descartes to Oparin.* (Baltimore: Johns Hopkins University Press).

Faure, G. (1977). *Principles of Isotope Geology.* (New York: Wiley).

Feduccia, A. (1980). *The Age of Birds.* (Cambridge, Mass.: Harvard University Press).

Flew, A. G. N. (1967). *Evolutionary Ethics.* (London: Macmillan).

Ford, E. B. (1971). *Ecological Genetics,* 3rd ed. (London: Methuen).

Futuyama, D. (1979). *Evolutionary Biology.* (Sunderland, Mass.: Sinauer).

Geison, G. L. (1969). Darwin and heredity: the evolution of his hypothesis of pangenesis. *Bull. Hist. Med.,* 24, 375–4ll.

Ghiselin, M. T. (1969). *The Triumph of the Darwinian Method.* (Berkeley: University of California Press).

Giere, R. (1979). *Understanding Scientific Reasoning.* (New York: Holt, Rinehart and Winston).

Gingerich, P. D. (1976). Paleontology and phylogeny: patterns of evolution at the species level in early tertiary mammals. *Amer. Jour. Sci.,* 276, 1–288.

Gingerich, P. D. (1977). Patterns of evolution in the mammalian fossil record. In A. Hallam ed. *Patterns of Evolution, As Illustrated by the Fossil Record.* (Amsterdam: Elsevier), 469-500.

Goldschmidt, R. B. (1940). *The Material Basis of Evolution.* (New Haven: Yale University Press).

Goldschmidt, R. B. (1952). Evolution as viewed by one geneticist. *American Scientist,* 40, 84–135.

Gould, S. J. (1973). Positive allometry of antlers in the "Irish Elk," *Megaloceros giganteus. Nature,* 244, 375–376.

Gould, S. J. (1977a). *Ontogeny and Phylogeny.* (Cambridge, Mass.: Harvard University Press).

Gould, S. J. (1977b). *Ever Since Darwin.* (New York: Norton).

Gould, S. J. (1980a). Is a new and general theory of evolution emerging? *Paleobiology,* 6, 119–130.

Gould, S. J. (1980b). *The Panda's Thumb.* (New York: Norton).

Gould, S. J. (1980c). The Piltdown conspiracy. *Natural History,* 89, 8–29.

Gould, S. J., and N. Eldredge (1977). Punctuated equilibria: the tempo and mode of evolution reconsidered. *Paleobiology,* 3, 115–151.

Gould, S. J., and R. C. Lewontin (1979). The spandrels of San Marco and the panglossian paradigm: a critique of the adaptationist programme. *Proc. Roy. Soc., Series B,* 205, 581–598.

Goy, R. W., and C. H. Phoenix (1972). The effects of testosterone propionate administered before birth on the development of behavior in genetic female rhesus monkeys. In C. Sawyer and R. Gorski (eds) *Steroid Hormones and Brain Function.* (Berkeley: University of California Press).

Grant, P. R., and I. Abbott (1980). Interspecific competition, island biogeography and null hypothesis. *Evolution,* 34, 332–341.

Green, R. (1974). *Sexual Identity Conflict in Children and Adults.* (New York: Basic Books).

Greene, J. C. (1959). *The Death of Adam.* (Ames: Iowa University Press).

Gribbin, J. and J. Cherfas (1981). Descent of man — or ascent of ape? *New Scientist,* 91, 592–595.

Gruber, H. E. (1981). *Darwin on Man,* 2nd ed. (Chicago: University of Chicago Press).

Gruber, H. E., and P. H. Barrett (1974). *Darwin on Man.* (New York: Dutton).

Hallam, A. (1977). *Patterns of Evolution as Illustrated by the Fossil Record.* (Amsterdam: Elsevier).

Halstead, L. B. (1981). The natural sciences and Marxism. In R. Duncan and C. Wilson (eds.) *Marx Refuted.* (Oxford: Pergamon).

Hamilton, W. D. (1964a). The genetical evolution of social behaviour. I. *J. Theor. Biol.,* 7, 1–16.

Hamilton, W. D. (1964b). The genetical evolution of social behaviour. II. *J. Theor. Biol.,* 7, 17–32.

Harris, M. (1971). *Culture, Man, and Nature: An Introduction to General Anthropology.* (New York: Crowell).

Hempel, C. (1966). *Philosophy of Natural Science.* (Englewood Cliffs, N.J.: Prentice-Hall).

Herbert, S. (1974). The place of man in the development of Darwin's theory of transmutation. Part 1. To July 1837. *J. Hist. Bio.,* 7, 217–258.

Herbert, S. (1977). The place of man in the development of Darwin's theory of transmutation. Part 2. *J. Hist. Biol.,* 1977, 10: 155–227.

Herschel, J. F. W. (1831). *Preliminary Discourse on the Study of Natural Philosophy.* (London: Longman, Rees, Orme, Brown, and Green).

Himmelfarb, G. (1962). *Darwin and the Darwinian Revolution.* (New York: Anchor).

Hoyle, F., and N. C. Wickramasinghe (1981). *Evolution from Space.* (London: Dent).

Hudson, W. D. (1970). *Modern Moral Philosophy.* (London: Macmillan).

Hull, D. L. (1972). Reduction in genetics — biology or philosophy? *Phil. Sci.,* 39, 491–499.

Hull, D. L. (1973). *Darwin and His Critics.* (Cambridge, Mass.: Harvard University Press).

Hull, D. L. (1976). Informal aspects of theory reduction. In A. C. Michalos et al. eds, *PSA 1974.* (Dordrecht: Reidel).

Hume, D. (1740). *Treatise of Human Nature.* (London).

Huxley, J. (1942). *Evolution: The Modern Synthesis.* (London: Allen and Unwin).

Huxley, L. (1900). *Life and Letters of Thomas Henry Huxley.* (London: Murray).

Huxley, T. H. (1861). On the zoological relations of man with the lower animals. *Nat. Hist. Rev.,* 67–84. (*Scientific Memoirs,* 2, 471–492).

Huxley, T. H. (1863). *Evidence as to Man's Place in Nature.* (London: Williams and Norgate).

Huxley, T. H. (1869). Anniversary address of the president. *Quart. J. Geol. Soc. Lond.,* 25, xxviii–liii. (*Scientific Memoirs,* 3, 397–426; Essays, 8, 308–342).

Huxley, T. H. (1901). *Evolution and Ethics, and Other Essays.* (London: Macmillan).

Isaac, G. L., and E. R. McCowan (1976). *Human Origins: Louis Leakey and the East African Evidence.* (Menlo Park, Calif.: Benjamin).

Jenkin, F. (1867). The Origin of Species. *North Brit. Review,* 42, 149–171.

Johanson, D., and M. Edey (1981). *Lucy: The Beginnings of Humankind.* (New York: Simon and Schuster).

Jolly, C. J. (1970). The seed-eaters. *Man,* 5, 5–26.

Jones, J. S. (1981). Models of speciation — The evidence from *Drosophila. Nature,* 289, 743–744.

Jones, J. S., B. H. Leith, and P. Rawlings (1977). Polymorphism in *Cepaea:* A problem with too many solutions? *Ann. Rev. Ecol. Syst.,* 8, 109–143.

Joravsky, D. (1970). *The Lysenko Affair.* (Cambridge, Mass.: Harvard University Press).

Kaback, M. et al. (1974). Approaches to the control and prevention of Tay-Sacks disease. In A. Steinberg and A. G. Bearn (eds.) *Progress in Medical Genetics,* X. (New York: Grune and Stratton).

Kant, I. (1929). *Critique of Pure Reason,* trans. N. Kemp-Smith. (London: Macmillan).

Kant, I. (1949). *Critique of Practical Reason,* trans. L. W. Beck. (Chicago: Chicago University Press).

Kellogg, D. E. (1975). The role of phyletic change in the evolution of *Pseudocubus vema* (Radiolaria). *Paleobiology,* 1, 359–370.

Kerr, R. A. (1980). Origin of life: new ingredients suggested. *Science,* 210, 42–43.

Kessler, S. (1969). The genetics of *Drosophila* mating behavior. II. The genetic architecture of mating speed in *Drosophila pseudoobscura. Genetics,* 64, 421–433.

Kettlewell, H. B. D. (1955). Selection experiments on industrial melanism in the *lepidoptera. Heredity,* 9, 323–342.

Kettlewell, H. B. D. (1973). *The Evolution of Melanism.* (Oxford: Clarendon).

Kilias, G., S. N. Alahiotis, and M. Pelecanos (1980). A multifactorial genetic investigation of speciation theory using *Drosophila melanogaster. Evolution,* 34, 730–737).

Kimura, M., and T. Ohta (1971). *Theoretical Aspects of Population Genetics.* (Princeton: Princeton University Press).

King, J. L., and T. H. Jukes (1969). Non-Darwinian evolution. *Science,* 164, 788–798.

King, M. C., and A. C. Wilson (1975). Evolution at two levels: molecular similarities and biological differences between humans and chimpanzees. *Science,* 188, 107–116.

Knight, G. R., A. Robertson, and C. H. Waddington (1956). Selection for sexual isolation within a species. *Evolution,* 10, 14–22.

Kofahl, R. E. and K. L. Segraves (1975). *The Creation Explanation: A Scientific Alternative to Evolution.* (Wheaton, Ill.: Harold Shaw).

Koopman, K. F. (1950). Natural selection for reproductive isolation between *Drosophila pseudoobscura* and *Drosophila persimilis. Evolution,* 4, 135–148.

Körner, S. (1955). *Kant.* (Harmondsworth: Penguin).

Körner, S. (1960). On philosophical arguments in physics. In E. H. Madden ed. *The Structure of Scientific Thought.* (London: Routledge and Kegan Paul).

Kuhn, T. (1970). *The Structure of Scientific Revolutions,* 2nd ed. (Chicago: University of Chicago Press).

Lack, D. (1947). *Darwin's Finches: An Essay on the General Biological Theory of Evolution.* (Cambridge: Cambridge University Press).

Lande, R. (1980). Review of Stanley's *Macroevolution. Paleobiology,* 6, 233–238.

Leakey, R., and R. Lewin (1977). *Origins.* (New York: Dutton).

Lewontin, R. C. (1974). *The Genetic Basis of Evolutionary Change.* (New York: Columbia University Press).

Lewontin, R. C. (1980). Theoretical population genetics in the evolutionary synthesis. In E. Mayr and W. Provine eds. *The Evolutionary Synthesis.* (Cambridge, Mass.: Harvard University Press), pp. 58–68.

Livingstone, F. B. (1971). Malaria and human polymorphisms. *Annual Review of Genetics,* 5, 33–64.

Lotka, A. J. (1945). Population analysis as a chapter in the mathematical theory of evolution. In *Essays on Growth and Form.* (New York: Oxford University Press).

Lovejoy, C. O. (1981). The origin of man. *Science,* 211, 341–350.

Lumsden, C. J., and E. O. Wilson (1981). *Genes, Mind, and Culture: The Coevolutionary Process.* (Cambridge, Mass.: Harvard University Press).

Lyell, C. (1830–1833). *Principles of Geology.* (London: Murray).

Malthus, T. R. (1826). *An Essay on the Principle of Population,* 6th ed. (London).

Manser, A. R. (1965). The concept of evolution. *Philosophy,* 40, 18–34.

Maynard Smith, J. (1962). *The Theory of Evolution.* (Harmondsworth: Penguin).

Maynard Smith, J. (1972). Game theory and the evolution of fighting. In *On Evolution.* (Edinburgh: Edinburgh University Press).

Maynard Smith, J. (1974). *Models in Ecology.* (Cambridge: Cambridge University Press).

Maynard Smith, J. (1975). *The Theory of Evolution,* 3rd ed. (Harmondsworth: Penguin).

Maynard Smith, J. (1976). Evolution and the theory of games. *Amer. Sci.,* 64, 41–45.

Maynard Smith, J. (1981). Did Darwin get it right? *London Review of Books,* 3(11), 10–11.

Mayr, E. (1942). *Systematics and the Origin of Species.* (New York: Columbia University Press).

Mayr, E. (1963). *Animal Species and Evolution.* (Cambridge, Mass.: Belknap).

Mayr, E. (1969). *Principles of Systematic Zoology.* (New York: McGraw-Hill).

Mayr, E. (1972). Lamarck revisited. *J. Hist. Bio.,* 5, 55–94.

Mayr, E. et al. (1978). *Evolution* (San Francisco: W. H. Freeman).

Mayr, E., and W. B. Provine eds. (1980). *The Evolutionary Synthesis.* (Cambridge, Mass.: Harvard University Press).

McDonald, J. F., G. K. Chambers, J. David, and F. J. Ayala (1977). Adaptive response due to changes in gene regulation: a study with *Drosophila. Proc. Nat. Acad. Sciences, U.S.A.,* 74, 4562–4566.

Medawar, P. (1967). P. S. Moorhead and M. M. Kaplan (eds). *Mathematical Challenges to the Neo-Darwinism Interpretation of Evolution.* (Philadelphia: Wistar Institute Press).

Meteyard, E. (1871). *A Group of Englishmen 1795–1815.* (London: Longmans, Green).

Mill, J. S. (1975). *On Liberty,* ed. D. Spitz. (New York: Norton). First published 1859.

Miller, H. (1847). *Footprints of the Creator; Or the Asterolepis of Stromness.* (Edinburgh: Constable).

Milne, D. H. (1981). How to debate with Creationists — and "win." *American Biology Teacher,* 43, 235–245.

Mivart, S. J. (1871). *Genesis of Species,* 2nd ed. (London: Macmillan).

Money, J., and A. A. Ehrhardt (1972). *Man and Woman: Boy and Girl: The Differentiation and Dimorphism of Gender Identity from Conception to Maturity.* (Baltimore: Johns Hopkins University Press).

Moore, G. E. (1903). *Principia Ethica.* (Cambridge: Cambridge University Press).

Moore, J. A. (1976). Creationism in California. In G. Holton and W. A. Blanpied eds., *Science and Its Public: The Changing Relationship.* (Dordrecht: Reidel), 191–207.

Moore, J. N. and H. S. Slusher (1970). *Biology: A Search for Order in Complexity.* (Grand Rapids, Mich.: Zonderran).

Morris, H. M. ed. (1974). *Scientific Creationism.* (San Diego: Creation-Life).

Munsinger, H. (1975a). Children's resemblance to their biological and adopting parents in two ethnic groups. *Behav. Genet.,* 5, 239–254.

Munsinger, H. (1975b). The adopted child's IQ: A critical review. *Psychol. Bull.,* 82, 623–659.

Nagel, E. (1961). *The Structure of Science.* (London: Routledge and Kegan Paul).

Nelkin, D. (1976a). Science or Scripture: the politics of "equal time." In G. Holton and W. A. Blanpied eds., *Science and Its Public: The Changing Relationship.* (Dordrecht: Reidel), 209–227.

Nelkin, D. (1976b). The science-textbook controversies. *Scientific American.* April, 234(4), 33–39.

Nelson, G. (1978). Classification and prediction: a reply to Kitts. *Syst. Zool.,* 27, 216–217.

Oakley, K. P. (1964). "The problem of man's antiquity," *Bull. Brit. Mus. (Nat. History), Geological Series*, 9, no. 5.

O'Brien, C. F. (1970). Eozoon Canadense: The dawn animal of Canada, *Isis*, 61, 206–223.

Olby, R. C. (1966). *Origins of Mendelism*. (New York: Schocken).

Oster, G., and Wilson, E. O. (1978). *Caste and Ecology in the Social Insects*. (Princeton, N.J.: Princeton University Press).

Owen, R. (1858). On the characters, principles of division, and primary groups of the class Mammalia, *J. Linn. Soc. (Zool.)*, 2, 1–37.

Ozawa, T. (1975). Evolution of *Lepidolina multiseptata* (Permian Foraminifer) in East Asia. *Mem. Faculty of Science, Kyushu University*, 23, 117–164.

Parker, G. E. (1980). *Creation: The Facts of Life*. (San Diego: C. L. P. Publishers).

Paterniani, E. (1969). Selection for reproductive isolation between two populations of maize, *Zea mays* L. *Evolution*, 23, 534–547.

Patterson, C. (1978). Verifiability in systematics. *Syst. Zool.*, 27, 218–221.

Peters, R. H. (1976). Tautology in evolution and ecology. *American Naturalist*, 110, 1–12.

Platnick, N., and E. Gaffney (1978). Evolutionary biology: a Popperian perspective. *Syst. Zool.*, 27, 137–141.

Popper, K. R. (1959). *The Logic of Scientific Discovery*. (London: Hutchinson).

Popper, K. R. (1962). *Conjectures and Refutations*. (New York: Basic Books).

Popper, K. R. (1972). *Objective Knowledge: An Evolutionary Approach*. (Oxford: Oxford University Press).

Popper, K. R. (1974). Darwinism as a metaphysical research programme. In P. A. Schilpp ed., *The Philosophy of Karl Popper*. (LaSalle, Ill.: Open Court).

Popper, K. R. (1978). Natural selection and the emergence of mind. *Diale ctica*, 32, 339–355.

Popper, K. R. (1980). Letter to the editor. *New Scientist*, 87, 611.

Powell, J. R. (1978). The founder-flush speciation theory: an experimental approach. *Evolution*, 32, 465–474.

Prakash, S. (1972). Origin of reproductive isolation in the absence of apparent genic differentiation in a geographic isolate of *Drosophila pseudoobscura*. *Genetics*, 72, 143–155.

Provine, W. B. (1971). *The Origins of Theoretical Population Genetics*. (Chicago: Chicago University Press).

Quinton, A. (1966). Ethics and the theory of evolution. In *Biology and Personality*, ed. I. T. Ramsey. (Oxford: Blackwell).

Race, R. R., and R. Sanger (1954). *Blood Groups in Man*, 2nd ed. (Oxford: Blackwell).

Raup, D. M. (1977). Probabilistic models in evolutionary paleobiology. *American Scientist*, 65, 50–57.

Raup, D. M., and S. M. Stanley (1971). *Principles of Paleontology*. (San Francisco: Freeman).

Raup, D. M., and S. M. Stanley (1978). *Principles of Paleontology*, 2nd ed. (San Francisco: Freeman).

Rawls, J. (1971). *A Theory of Justice*. (Cambridge, Mass.: Belknap).

Reader, J. (1981). *Missing Links: The Hunt for Earliest Man*. (New York: Little, Brown).

Rensch, B. (1947). *Neuere Probleme der Abstammungslehre*. (Stuttgart: Enke).

Ridley, M. (1981). Who doubts evolution? *New Scientist*, 90, 830–832.

Robertson, M. (1981). Lamarck re-visited; The debate goes on. *New Scientist*, 90, 230–231.

Roughgarden, J. (1979). *Theory of Population Genetics and Evolutionary Ecology: An Introduction*. (New York: Macmillan).

Rudwick, M. J. S. (1972). *The Meaning of Fossils*. (London: Macdonald).

Ruse, M. (1979a). *The Darwinian Revolution: Science Red in Tooth and Claw*. (Chicago: University of Chicago Press).

Ruse, M. (1979b). *Sociobiology: Sense or Nonsense?* (Dordrecht: Reidel).

Ruse, M. (1980). Charles Darwin and group selection. *Annals of Science*, 37, 615–630.

Ruse, M. (1981). *Is Science Sexist? And Other Problems in the Biomedical Sciences*. (Dordrecht: Reidel).

Sahlins, M. D. (1976). *The Use and Abuse of Biology*. (Ann Arbor: University of Michigan Press).

Sahlins, M. D., and E. Service (1960). *Evolution and Culture*. (Ann Arbor: University of Michigan Press).

Scharloo, W. (1971). Reproductive isolation by disruptive selection. Did it occur? *Amer. Natur.*, 105, 83–86.

Schopf, J. W. (1978). The evolution of the earliest cells. *Scientific American,* September, 110–138.

Science for the People Collective (1977). *Biology as a Social Weapon.* (Minneapolis: Burgess).

Settle, M. L. (1972). *The Scopes Trial.* (New York: Franklin Watts).

Shepher, J. (1979). *Incest, The Biosocial View.* (Cambridge, Mass.: Harvard University Press).

Sheppard, P. M. (1951). Fluctuations in the selective value of certain phenotypes in the polymorphic land snail *Cepaea nemoralis. Heredity,* 5, 125.

Simpson, G. G. (1944). *Tempo and Mode in Evolution.* (New York: Columbia University Press).

Simpson, G. G. (1953). *The Major Features of Evolution.* (New York: Columbia University Press).

Smith, R. (1972). Alfred Russel Wallace: philosophy of nature and man. *Brit. J. Hist. Sci.,* 6, 177–199.

Sneath, P. H. A., and R. R. Sokal (1973). *Numerical Taxonomy.* (San Francisco: W. H. Freeman).

Solbrig, O. (1971). The population biology of dandelions. *Amer. Scientist,* 59, 686–694.

Spencer, H. (1852). A theory of population, deduced from the general law of animal fertility. *Westminster Review,* n.s.1, 468–501.

Spencer, H. (1857). Progress: Its law and cause. *Westminster Review.* In *Essays,* 1, 1–60.

Spencer, H. (1864). *Principles of Biology.* (London: Williams and Norgate).

Stanley, S. M. (1979). *Macroevolution: Pattern and Process.* (San Francisco: W. H. Freeman).

Stebbins, G. L. (1950). *Variation and Evolution in Plants.* (New York: Columbia University Press).

Stebbins, G. L., and F. J. Ayala (1981). Is a new evolutionary synthesis necessary? *Science,* 213, 967–971.

Steele, E. J. (1979). *Somatic Selection and Adaptive Evolution.* (Toronto: Williams and Wallace).

Stidd, B. M. (1980). The neotenous origin of the pollen organ of the gymnosperm *Cycadeoidea* and the implications for the origin of higher taxa. *Paleobiology,* 6, 161–167.

Strong, D. R., et al. (1979). Tests of community-wide character displacement against null hypotheses. *Evolution,* 33, 897–913.

Sulloway, Frank J. (1979). *Freud, Biologist of the Mind: Beyond the Psychoanalytic Legend.* (New York: Basic Books).

Symons, D. (1979). *The Evolution of Human Sexuality.* (New York: Oxford University Press).

Taylor, P. W. (1978). *Problems of Moral Philosophy.* (Belmont, Calif.: Wadsworth).

Templeton, A. R. (1977). Analysis of head shape differences between two interfertile species of Hawaiian *Drosophila. Evolution,* 31, 630–641.

Thoday, J. M., and J. B. Gibson (1962). Isolation by disruptive selection. *Nature,* 193, 1164–1166.

Thomson, W. (1862). On the age of the sun's heat. *Macmillan's Mag.,* 5, 288–293.

Trivers, R. L. (1971). The evolution of reciprocal altruism. *Quart. Rev. Bio.,* 46, 35–57.

Trivers, R. L. (1974). Parent-offspring conflict. *Am. Zoo.,* 14, 249–264.

Trivers, R. L. (1976). "Foreword" to R. Dawkins, *The Selfish Gene.* (Oxford: Oxford University Press), v–vii.

Trivers, R. L., and H. Hare (1976). Haplodiploidy and the evolution of social insects. *Science,* 191, 249–263.

Tudge, C. (1981). Lamarck lives — In the immune system. *New Scientist,* 9, 483–485.

Val, F. C. (1977). Genetic analysis of the morphological differences between two interfertile species of Hawaiian *Drosophila. Evolution,* 31, 611–629.

van den Berghe, P. L. (1979). *Human Family Systems: An Evolutionary View.* (New York: Elsevier).

Waddington, C. H. (1960). *The Ethical Animal.* (London: Allen and Unwin).

Wade, M. J. (1978). A critical review of the models of group selection. *Q. Rev. Bio.,* 53, 101–114.

Wallace, A. R. (1870a). "The measurement of geological time," *Nature,* 1, 499–501; 452–455.

Wallace, A. R. (1870b). The limits of natural selection as applied to man, in *Contributions to the Theory of Natural Selection.* (London: Macmillan).

Wallace, B. (1954). Genetic divergence of isolated populations of *Drosophila melanogaster. Proc. Nat. Acad. Sci. U.S.,* 36, 654–657.

Watson, J. D., and F. H. C. Crick (1953). Molecular structure of nucleic acids. *Nature,* 171, 737.

Westermarck, E. (1891). *The History of Human Marriage.* (London: Macmillan).

Whewell, W. (1837). *The History of the Inductive Sciences.* (London: Parker).

Whewell, W. (1840). *The Philosophy of the Inductive Sciences.* (London: Parker).

Whitcomb, J. C., and H. M. Morris (1961). *The Genesis Flood.* (Nutley, N.J.: Presbyterian and Reformed Publishing Co.).

White, M. J. D. (1978). *Modes of Speciation.* (San Francisco: Freeman).

Wiley, E. O. (1975). Karl R. Popper, systematics, and classification: A reply to Walter Bock and other evolutionary taxonomists. *Systematic Zoology,* 24, 233–243.

Williams, G. C. (1966). *Adaptation and Natural Selection.* (Princeton, N.J.: Princeton University Press).

Wilson, E. O. (1975a). *Sociobiology: The New Synthesis.* (Cambridge, Mass.: Belknap).

Wilson, E. O. (1975b). Human decency is animal. *The New York Times Magazine,* 12, October, 38–50.

Wilson, E. O. (1978). *On Human Nature.* (Cambridge, Mass.: Harvard University Press).

Wilson, E. O., and W. H. Bossert (1971). *A Primer of Population Biology.* (Stamford, Conn.: Sinauer).

Wright, S. (1931). Evolution in Mendelian populations. *Genetics,* 16, 97–159.

Wynne-Edwards, V. C. (1962). *Animal Dispersion in Relation to Social Behaviour.* (Edinburgh: Oliver and Boyd).

Name Index

349

Subject Index

Acquired characteristics. *See* Lamarckism.
Adaptation, 27, 88, 92, 96, 200, 213-215, 223-224, 270, 272, 277
Aegyptopithecus, 244
Age of Earth, 11, 13, 37, 55-56, 59-60, 165, 167, 171, 286, 300-302, 316-320
Aggression, 195-198
Allele, 66
Altruism, 190, 203-206, 235-236, 272
Amino acid, 72-73, 160, 236-237, 297, 307
Analogy, 47-50, 192-193, 258-259, 261, 308
Archaeopteryx, 208, 220, 299-300, 311-314
Aristotelianism, 4
Artificial selection. *See* Selection.
Australopithecus, 302
    afarensis, 241-242, 244-246, 318, 320
    africanus, 240-242
    boisei, 240-241
    robustus, 240-242
Axiom, 44, 51

Balance/classical controversy, 86-87, 108-112
Barnacles, 29
Bathybius haeckelii, 158-159
Bauplan, 214, 218, 220
Behavior. *See* Sociobiology.
Betta splendens, 198
Bible, 4-5, 8-9, 13, 26-27, 157, 230, 265-266, 285-286, 291-292, 322-326
Biogeography. *See* Geographical distribution.
Bipedalism, 242, 245-246
Biston betularia, 101-103

Camarhynchus, (see also Darwin's finches)
    pallidus, 119
    parvalus, 119
    psittacula, 119
Cambridge, 16, 21, 24, 48
Canada, 293
Catastrophism, 13-14, 22, 24, 207-208, 230, 299

Cause, 45-50, 53, 70, 115, 211, 245, 248, 252, 295-296, 305, 314, 323
Cell, 65, 169
    diploid, 67
    haploid, 67
    somatic, 66, 145
Cepaea nemoralis, 97-100
Chagas' disease, 19
Chance, 95 (*see also* Genetic drift)
Chemical evolution, 160-164
Chimpanzee. *See Pan troglodytes.*
Chromosome, 66, 237
Clade, 216-217
Cladism, 212
Classification, 40, 298 (*see also* Cladism)
Collyria calcitrator, 199
Consilience of inductions, 46, 53-57, 131
Cope's rule, 125-127, 213
Cousins, 261-263
Creationism, 285-329
Creation Research Society, 291
Creator, 296, 323
Cyanobacteria, 169-170
Cytology, 65

Darwinian fitness, 80, 135
Darwinism. *Passim*
Darwin's finches (Geospizinae), 24, 115-124, 224
Descent of Man, 234-236
Design, 8, 12, 27, 42, 51-52, 54, 59, 234, 285, 296-298, 305, 323
Dimetrodon, 134, 138-139
Dinosaurs, 126, 139, 172-173, 300, 313-315
DNA, 71-73, 145, 160, 162, 296, 306
Dodo, 12, 37, 137
Domestic bliss strategy, 200
Dominance, 66
Drift. *See* Genetic drift.
Drosophila, 92, 122
    equinoxial, 146-147

353

Tay-Sachs disease, 90
Teaching. *See* Schools.
Testability, 131-142, 259-260, 294-295
Testing, 254-264
Theory, 58, 136-137, 149, 155, 176-177, 179-180, 275-276, 294, 303-304 (*See also* Model)
Tierra del Fuega, 28-29, 254
Tortoise, 24-25
Trilobites, 127-130, 300

Uniformitarianism, 10-12, 24, 230, 266, 269, 299

Variation, 27, 35, 51, 56-57, 112, 127, 146, 297, 307
Vera causa. See Cause.
Voyage of the Beagle, 17-18

Xenophobia, 252, 255, 264

Yanomamö, 259

Zea mays, 220-222
Zygote, 66-67

70 11

Processed by **ERI** **Data Communication**
Typesetting and Production — **ERI Phototypesetting**
Type is set in 10 pt. English Times.